T0316421

On Commerce and Usury (1524)

Von Kauffshand=
lung vnd wu=
cher.

Martinus Luther.

Vuittemberg.

1524.

On Commerce and Usury (1524)

Martin Luther

Edited with Introduction and Notes by
Philipp Robinson Rössner

ANTHEM PRESS

Anthem Press
An imprint of Wimbledon Publishing Company
www. anthempress. com

This edition first published in UK and USA 2015
by ANTHEM PRESS
75–76 Blackfriars Road, London SE1 8HA, UK
or PO Box 9779, London SW19 7ZG, UK
and
244 Madison Ave #116, New York, NY 10016, USA

British Library Cataloguing-in-Publication Data
A catalogue record for this book is available from the British Library.

Library of Congress Cataloging-in-Publication Data
Luther, Martin, 1483-1546.
On commerce and usury (1524) : Martin Luther / edited with Introduction and Notes by
Philipp Robinson Rössner.
pages cm
Includes bibliographical references and index.
ISBN 978-1-78308-385-5 (hard back)
1. Luther, Martin, 1483-1546. 2. Commerce. 3. Usury. 4. Economics. I. Rössner,
Philipp Robinson, editor. II. Luther, Martin, 1483-1546. III. Title.
BR334. 3. L88 2015
261. 8'5–dc23
2015015238

ISBN-13: 978 1 78308 385 5 (Hbk)
ISBN-10: 1 78308 385 9 (Hbk)

Cover Image: Martin Luther (1546), after Lucas Cranach, presumably Lucas Cranach the
Younger. © Stadtmuseum Erfurt "Haus zum Stockfisch" 2014

This title is also available as an ebook.

CONTENTS

ACKNOWLEDGEMENTS

It was Erik Reinert who suggested that I should produce a commented new translation of Luther's *On Commerce and Usury/ Von Kauffshandlung und Wucher* (1524) – for which I am immensely grateful because I believe I have learnt a lot more about Luther from this exercise than I had before, when I had studied the monetary economics of the early Reformation in Germany. Contrary to most mainstream accounts in history, theology, church history and economics, I have taken the freedom to interpret Luther as someone who contributed to *modern* economics and political economy. This is something which most mainstream accounts would probably reject, but as will be shown in the book, there are quite enough cognitive distortions in modern economic theory – which has also considerably influenced historians' interpretations – to suggest that some overhaul of the modern or neoclassical paradigm would be in order. This book can be only a very modest contribution to the debate, but from a somewhat unexpected vantage point, and the viewpoint of a historian.

Surely the volume will contain a few mistakes; these will have to be booked to the author's account. The following people have contributed a fair share towards its improvement. I should like to thank above all Erik Reinert and his wife Fernanda, as well as my colleague Chris Close at St John's University (USA) who all read the entire manuscript and provided most generous comments and feedback. Erik proved absolutely inspirational along the way; his knowledge of history and ancient (or heterodox) economic theory is unsurpassed. I am also grateful to Prasannan Parthasarathi and Francesco Boldizzoni, as well as two anonymous referees who read the manuscript and pointed towards areas of improvement. My colleagues and friends – too numerous to list – at Manchester and Leipzig commented upon several aspects to be found within this work. Special thanks are also due to the editorial staff of Anthem, in particular Brian Stone, as well as my research assistants Stefan Lehm and Juana Schubert, who produced an index, procured and processed book orders and bibliographical tasks and took care of the copyright issues relating to the pictures and images reproduced in the book.

I should like to thank the following people and institutions for granting permission to use images under copyright: Peter Schmelzle (Wimpfen) for the altarpiece of Wimpfen town church (chapter 1), Dieter Knoblauch at Annaberg-Buchholz for the Annaberg altarpiece images (chapter 2), the Sächsische Landesbibliothek/Staats- und Universitätsbibliothek Dresden (SLUB) for the Saiger hearth (chapter 2), as well as the Stadtmuseum Erfurt 'Haus zum Stockfisch' for the 1546 Luther image by (or after) Cranach (title page) and, finally, the Bayerische Staatsbibliothek for the frontispiece of the 1524 edition of *Kauffshandlung und Wucher*.

And at last, my special acknowledgements and love go to my family, Britta, Ailidh and Marit.

Leipzig, December 2014

Philipp Robinson Rössner

Chapter 1

APPROACHING LUTHER

Noch vor dreissig Jahren erfuhr es keinen Widerspruch, als Johann Baptist Say den Werth einer Geschichte der politischen Oekonomie mit den Worten läugnete: 'Sie ist weiter nichts, als die Darstellung der mehr oder minder gelungenen, zu verschiedenen Zeiten und an verschiedenen Orten wiederholten Versuche, die Wahrheiten, woraus sie besteht, zu sammeln und festzustellen. Was würde es uns helfen, abgeschmackte Meinungen und mit Recht verrufene Lehren zusammen zu tragen? Dieselben zu Tage zu fördern, wäre ebenso unnütz als langweilig'. Dieser Ausspruch war die einfache Folge der damaligen Ansicht von der absoluten Wahrheit der neueren national-ökonomischen Theorie, welche man, losgerissen von allem geschichtlichen Boden, von allen Bedingungen des Raums, der Zeit und der Nationalität, als eine rein aus den Principien des Verstandes gefolgerte Summe von Wahrheiten betrachtete, deren Verständniss allen früheren Geschlechtern verschlossen, die aber einmal aufgestellt und entwickelt, für alle Zeiten und Völker wahr und in sich geschlossen sein sollten.

Die Reformation des 16. Jahrhunderts musste vorhergehen, ehe im 18. und 19ten die Dampfmaschine erfunden werden und die National-Oekonomie als selbstständige Wissenschaft erfasst werden konnte. Nicht nur für Kant und Hegel, auch für Adam Smith und die grossen Geister im Gebiete der technischen Erfindungen bildet – so paradox es klingen mag – die nothwendige Voraussetzung die deutsche Reformation.

[As recently as 30 years ago, no one would have objected when John Baptist Say denied a history of political economy its relevance by saying that it was 'nothing more than a compilation with mixed success of past attempts during various times and locations at finding and collecting the eternal economic truths. What help would it be to collect old vulgar and tasteless opinions and theories that had rightly been refuted? Tracing them would be as useless as it would be boring'. This uttering was the expression of a simple consequence of the prevailing idea that current economic theory would have universal currency as an inherent truth, detached from its historical context and conditions of space, time and nationality; a sum of truths and laws derived purely from principles of reason, from which our ancestors had been precluded but which – once they had been discovered and fully developed – would attain universal truth for all times and peoples as a closed theory.

The sixteenth-century Reformation had to precede the steam engine of the eighteenth and nineteenth century and the development of economics as a separate science. In fact, the German Reformation is the intellectual and necessary predecessor not only for Hegel and Kant but – paradoxically as it may sound – for Adam Smith and all the great inventive geniuses of the mechanical age also.]

– Gustav (von) Schmoller, 'Zur Geschichte der national-ökonomischen Ansichten in Deutschland während der Reformations-Periode', *Zeitschrift für Gesamte Staatswissenschaft*, 16 (1860), 461–716 (461 and 716).

I see us free, therefore, to return to some of the most sure and certain principles of religion and traditional virtue – that avarice is a vice, that the exaction of usury is a misdemeanour [...] We shall once more value ends before means and prefer the good to the useful.

John Maynard Keynes, *Economic Possibilities for our Grandchildren*, 371–72

Do Markets Need Rules? The Idea and Plan of the Book

A recent blockbuster (2012) on markets and morality found that 'in recent decades, markets and market thinking have reached into spheres of life traditionally governed by non-market norms. More and more we are putting a price on noneconomic goods'.[1] Almost exactly five hundred years ago, things were not so different. Luther's teaching on indulgences publicized by the 95 Theses in 1517 developed into a religious programme that subsequently attained its own inner life generating some long-lasting dynamics, not only in the religious but also in the cultural, social and economic landscape of Europe in the five hundred years to come. In many ways and shapes, Luther's religious critique, as well as his more economic writings – such as the present *Sermon on Commerce and Usury*, evolved around the very same question, that is the invasion of markets and economistic reasoning into realms where they didn't really belong (the prime example of this is his critique of indulgence sales, on which his Reformation of 1517 was based). In fact, Luther did produce some major insights into matters of economic theory and policy also – something that is not usually acknowledged; these will be the focus of volume. The charges frequently levied against Luther mainly by modern scholars – that he didn't really acknowledge the working mechanisms of an increasingly 'modern' economy or that his theoretical grasp of economics and economic behaviour wasn't quite up to scratch – miss the point, as will be argued in subsequent sections and chapters. It is certain forms of behaviour that Luther identified as fallacious and wrong from an ethical stance; this stance is virtually timeless.[2] So the 'Luther question' in economics does not have anything to do with the somewhat problematic quest for progress in the economic sciences (very popular nowadays still); it is rather up to the *view point* or *perspective* we choose when framing actions and decisions and building our models. Luther developed nothing more or less than the

---

1. Michael J. Sandel, *What Money Can't Buy. The Moral Limits of Markets* (New York: Farrar, Straus and Giroux, 2012), 48.
2. Thomas Piketty, *Capital in the Twenty-first Century* (Cambridge, MA: The Belknap Press of Harvard University Press, 2014).

important insight that it was necessary to bring back ethical stances and value judgements into economics. Or, to use Keynes' dictum above, he would have realized that 'certain principles of religion and traditional virtue – that avarice is a vice, that the exaction of usury is a misdemeanour' are important in terms of guarding our everyday choices and actions – even within the seemingly sterile and value-free realm of economics.

Arguably, with the presently discussed *Sermon on Commerce and Usury* (1524), Luther not only produced one of the finest pamphlets ever written on *business ethics* (for this he is well known) but also made a significant contribution to *economics* and *political economy*. This is not usually acknowledged, let alone appreciated. It has been, after all, a modern fiction in academic discourse and teaching to separate 'economics' from 'business ethics' – one discipline usually claimed by economists, the other (chiefly) by academic theologians. The following pages will hopefully make clearer why this has led to dire consequences both in our experiences of economic reality and the framework guarding economic decisions and in economic theory and political economy as a general backdrop against which individual economic decision-making processes have evolved during the past five hundred years or so. Luther's sketch dealt with the individual in the contested field of society, economics and culture. Here, Luther engaged with a problem that has captivated mankind from the earliest times of its existence: the phenomenon of the *market* and its peculiar and uneasy mutual and bilateral interactions with the sphere of religion. On top of that, and quite incidentally, with his stance on *indulgences* Luther also prefigured an important theoretical insight that would loom large in later political economy writings of the pre-classical age between the 1650s and 1800s: a deep aversion towards *hoarding*, that is reducing money's velocity in economic circulation by leaving it either unspent or invested in non-productive purposes.

The argument will proceed as follows. A general introduction of the issue (chapter 1) is followed by an economic and cultural context of Luther's life and times (chapter 2), as well as a discussion of his economic ideas within a wider frame of theory and discourses on political economy (chapter 3). A detailed discussion of his stance on hoarding money will be provided in chapter 4, as this is a new field, adding a new note to his writings on economics and theology which previous research has overlooked. A detailed comment of the actual *Sermon on Commerce and Usury* follows (chapter 5), before the analytical part ends with a brief conclusion in the light of the modern world and its problems (chapter 6). The second part consists of a much revised and updated English version of the original (1524) *Von Kauffshandlung und Wucher* which will be translated here – contrary to older suggestions which have come up with the somewhat clumsy and quite inexpressive '(On) Trading and Usury' – in its more proper meaning: On *Commerce* and *Usury*.

Reasons and causes for this exercise are manifold. At all times and places in recorded history, some people seem to have come up with ideas that would classify as either weird or ingenious, depending upon one's own perspective, as well as the forces of history, tradition and personal socialization within the ties that bind, such as family, kith and kin, confession and religion. In the Middle Ages, court cases were waged against animals – less so as show trials: it seems as though people sometimes genuinely *believed* in the virtue of accusing and dressing the animal properly as a culprit and formally placing it before a court judge and jury.[3] Witches were burnt until the eighteenth century following rationales the ultimate essence of which seems now to be lost on us, although we can speculate about proximate motivations, causes and reasons, such as religious fears, the desire for scapegoats or opportunities to get rid of someone that was hated. But as late as the 1720s, the last show trials against child witches were staged in the German lands[4], and scientific treatises about the nature and existence of Angels were published. At the same time, the cultural process known as 'Enlightenment' had taken hold, based on the idea that superstition had been replaced by scientific observation in the ultimate Faustian goal of understanding what held the world together in its innermost nature. The idea took hold that man had finally brought nature under control.[5] The Newtonian revolution was framed primarily within a natural science approach, witnessing the rise of modern engineering, physical science, chemistry and biology, and it also had important spill-overs and multilateral feedback processes into the realm of philosophy and modern social sciences. Around the same time, the idea of *natural order* emerged. It did so especially in the writings of some French and Scottish philosophers such as Francois Quesnay, the Marquis de Condorcet, Adam Smith and David Hume, who emphasized the notion that a natural order mechanism existed not only in nature and biology but also in the sphere of economics (the suggestion of economics as a separate sphere detached from other realms of human agency co-emerged with this idea also). This mechanism was bound to settle demand and supply spontaneously to the benefit of everybody without the need for outside intervention. In other words, this order should be left uninhibited by mankind.[6] We have come to know this paradigm by the metaphor of the invisible hand which its imputed inventor, Scottish moral philosopher A. Smith, used exactly once in his famous text on the *Inquiry into the Nature and Causes of the Wealth of Nations*, 1776. Chances are that later theorists of the 'free market' did over-interpret Smith here and read axiomatic and insights into the text which Smith would have never underwritten himself. This does not matter so much as in fact Smith's text provided the foundation stone for the mainstream theory in the social and economic sciences in the centuries to come – regardless how unwittingly or unintentional. And he provided – and still provides – the stepping stone for subsequent theoretical contributions to the debate, be that affirmative (which we may label 'neoclassical') or critical deconstructive (which we may call 'heterodox' economics).

This random list of cultural beliefs may certainly be extended at will. But for the present context it is especially the latter, the idea of *free markets*, which has proven peculiarly superstitious – in the same way as it has been very susceptive. As a discursive figure, it co-emerged with Europe's transformation into an industrial economy over the past three

---

3. For example, Peter Dinzelbacher, *Das fremde Mittelalter. Gottesurteil und Tierprozess* (Essen: Magnus, 2006).

4. Rainer Beck, *Mäuselmacher oder die Imagination des Bösen. Ein Hexenprozess 1715–1723* (Munich: C. H. Beck, 2011).

5. The literature on the so-called Enlightenment is endless, both in English and in other languages. Dorinda Outram, *The Enlightenment*, 3rd ed. (Cambridge: Cambridge University Press, 2013), is not bad.

6. Bernard Harcourt, *The Illusion of Free Markets: Punishment and the Myth of Natural Order* (Cambridge, MA: Harvard University Press, 2011).

centuries. But strangely, no one has ever managed to prove the existence of free markets empirically. First of all, no market in history has ever or anywhere been completely free, if we define 'free' as 'fully de-regularized'. The mere concept is oxymoronic. Because if a market is entirely free, that is without any regulation, there will be freedom for *some* people to exploit market asymmetries such as usury, rent seeking, arbitrage, speculation to their benefit and the detriment of *others*. Which can only mean that the market is still essentially un-free. If, on the other hand, freedom is understood as *personal and economic freedom of the individual* – in the sense of harmonized capabilities, improved distributions of chances of participation, as well as a general absence of asymmetry and usurious behaviour – then the market requires tight rules. But then again it literally cannot be free. Markets and freedom are mutually exclusive.

This can be illustrated using some historical evidence. In the eighteenth century, for instance, two competing notions of market behaviour and two distinct strands of political economy had developed, or rather diverged from what seems to have been, deep back in time, a shared consensus. The one notion, marked by the natural order idea of the French économistes leading up to the Physiocrats and Adam Smith, had it that free uncoordinated market cleared spontaneously to the benefit of all.[7] The other notion was an idea we may call, borrowing a term coined by Eichengreen for post-1945 European economic development, 'coordinated capitalism'.[8] This was the market theory entertained by the continental economists we have come to know by the name of cameralists. Upon first sight, the *market order* which the cameralist authors had in mind, from the days of Johann Joachim Becher (1635–1682) and Veit Ludwig von Seckendorff (1626–1692) until high cameralists such as Johann Heinrich Gottlob von Justi (1717–1771), was very similar to our modern notion of the free market. But it was so mainly in terms of the empirical result or visual figuration; the epistemology and techniques of *achieving* this economic freedom in the market were radically different (and that has not been usually or particularly well understood by social scientists until late). The cameralists defined 'free' essentially in the same way as the Anglo-Saxon tradition would in the wake of A. Smith, D. Hume and D. Ricardo, in fact, as everyone of us presumably would – as, say, free of exploitation possibilities and rent seeking.[9] This translates as 'free of market distortions' such as monopoly, ruinous competition, speculation, arbitrage and other forms of usurious exchange, or what Martin Luther in the 1520s and Cyriakus Spangenberg in the 1590s called *vngleiche hendel* (asymmetrical exchange).[10] But the means

---

7. Ibid.
8. Barry J. Eichengreen, *The European Economy since 1945: Coordinated Capitalism and Beyond* (Princeton, NJ: Princeton University Press, 2007).
9. See Birger P. Priddat, 'Kameralismus als paradoxe Konzeption der gleichzeitigen Stärkung von Markt und Staat. Komplexe Theorielagen im deutschen 18. Jahrhundert', *Berichte zur Wissenschaftsgeschichte* 31 (2008): 249–63. On cameralism from the viewpoint of history of discourse, see Keith Tribe, *Strategies of Economic Order. German Economic Discourse, 1750–1950* (Cambridge: Cambridge University Press, 1995), chap. 1 (esp. 5–7).
10. 'Tractat M. Cyriaci Spangenberg vom rechten Brauch und Mißbrauch der Muentze', in M. Tilemann[us], *Muentz Spiegel* [...] (Frankfurt-on-the-Main, 1592), 240.

to *achieve* freedom were different; in the latter view – the coordinated capitalism model of the continental cameralists and their predecessors, or the medieval authors that have come to be known as *scholastic* theorists – free markets needed control and supervision if they were to function properly and to the benefit of everybody.[11] This notion subsequently got lost in the Anglo-Saxon liberal and classical and later on neoclassical tradition in the wake of the French and Scottish Enlightenment after c. 1750, where it was held that markets achieved Pareto-optimality spontaneously, meaning an optimum distribution of market outcomes and transactions, *when left without regulation and interference*. That this could not possibly work in reality would have been obvious to many a continental thinker from the 1400s until later on. Within the Anglo-Saxon scientific tradition, however, which also influenced the epistemological design of modern economics and much of modern social theory across the rest of the world, it attained a certain fetish-like position that does not match particularly well with empirical reality – the explanation of which lies outside the scope of this book.[12]

On the other hand, as we speak, many people are still fundamentally convinced that free markets as understood by the liberal or neoclassical paradigm in the wake of the French and Scottish enlightenment discourse are a *real* phenomenon and that they matter for historical progress (assuming that there is such a thing in history as progress; a questionable proposition in itself).[13] Moreover, many would maintain that free markets as understood by this specific paradigm do carry *real* significance for our lives, choices and beliefs as well as economic development at large, and, on top of this, that free markets are a desirable thing in itself, that is a *goal* on its own that needs no further explanation or theoretical substantiation. Mainstream micro- and macroeconomics still start with markets as the fundamental *explanans*, an idea which has spilled over, during the 1960s and 1970s in particular, into other realms of social science analysis, as though the (free) market could serve as a catch-all panacea explaining away just about every facet of human behaviour, action and interaction.[14] The debate reached a climax of absurdity when scholars began to explain even love, faith and religious belief within the framework of 'rational choice theory' (thankfully the field has moved on). Yet the idea that markets may be an *explanandum* (something that does not *provide* but rather *requires* explanation) has hardly occurred to economists. It is a field still left, by and large, to sociologists,

---

11. A good introduction to cameralist market theory is to be found in Priddat, 'Kameralismus als paradoxe Konzeption'. Excellent is the chapter of Bertram Schefold, 'Glückseligkeit und Wirtschaftspolitik: Zu Justis "Grundsätze der Policey-Wissenschaft"', in *id.* ed., *Vademecum zu einem Klassiker des Kameralismus: Johann Heinrich Gottlob von Justi, Grundsätze der Policey-Wissenschaft* (Düsseldorf: Verlag Wirtschaft und Finanzen, 1993), 5–44, and Heinz Rieter, 'Justis Theorie der Wirtschaftspolitik', in Schefold, ed., *Vademecum*, 45–80 (esp. 51–54 and 69–70).
12. Harcourt, *Illusion of Free Markets*, serves as a good starting point.
13. For example, David S. Landes, *The Wealth and Poverty of Nations. Why Some Are So Rich and Others So Poor* (New York: W. W. Norton, 1998), or Eric L. Jones, *The European Miracle: Environments, Economies and Geopolitics in the History of Europe and Asia*, 3rd ed. (Cambridge: Cambridge University Press, 2003).
14. A good read, in an almost heart-warming manner, is Paul Seabright, *The Company of Strangers: A Natural History of Economic Life* (Princeton, NJ: Princeton University Press, 2004).

ethnologists and anthropologists, in the wake of fundamental studies by Mauss, Polanyi, Geertz or Godelier (and some of these studies will arrive at a viewpoint on markets, which is fundamentally different from mainstream economics).[15] Moreover, the free market idea is highly charged up without really lending itself to a cool, objective and value-free judgement. Policies recommended since the 1980s to Third World countries by the World Bank and the International Monetary Fund in return for development aid come to mind which have given rise to much popular dissent. In post-1979 Thatcherist Britain, the free market doctrine served as an important ideological blueprint of an intended complete reconfiguration: not only of the economy but also of an imputed morally corrupt British *society* at large. Whenever the late Baroness spoke about the market, the subject matter attained a quasi-religious dimension, and some modern scholars, such as Fergusson, have been as religious in their belief in markets as the Baroness.[16] This is not to say that religion is in any way bad (quite to the contrary), but it does not have much to do with empirical reality (which is one commonly accepted characteristic of religion). Even the most ardent free market advocates would probably admit that proof of its existence is hard to come by, especially in those historical periods in which it is usually assumed to have been crucial for economic development, such as England's eighteenth- and nineteenth-century industrialization.[17] And nobody would – presumably – object to

---

15. See, for example, Karl Polanyi, *The Great Transformation* (Boston, MA: Beacon Press, 1944); Clifford Geertz, 'The Bazaar Economy: Information and Search in Peasant Marketing', *American Economic Review* 68 (1978), 28–32; or Maurice Godelier, *The Enigma of the Gift* (Chicago, IL: University of Chicago Press, 1999). On modern research on markets in economic sociology and anthropology, see Stuart Plattner, ed., *Economic Anthropology* (Stanford, CA: Stanford University Press, 1989), or Richard Swedberg, *Principles of Economic Sociology* (Princeton, NJ: Princeton University Press, 2003); Chris M. Hann and Keith Hart, *Economic Anthropology: History, Ethnography, Critique* (Cambridge: Polity, 2011); Fred L. Block and Margaret R. Somers, *The Power of Market Fundamentalism: Karl Polanyi's Critique* (Cambridge, MA: Harvard University Press, 2014); and the survey article by G. M. Feinman and C. P. Garraty, 'Preindustrial Markets and Marketing: Archaeological Perspectives', *Annual Review of Anthropology* 39 (2010), 167–91.
16. Eric J. Evans, *Thatcher and Thatcherism*, 2nd ed. (London: Routledge, 2004).
17. Lars Magnusson, *Nation, State and the Industrial Revolution: The Visible Hand* (London: Routledge, 2009). For a diverging viewpoint, see, for example, J. V. C. Nye, *War, Wine, and Taxes: The Political Economy of Anglo-French Trade, 1689–1900* (Princeton, NJ: Princeton University Press, 2007), or Joel Mokyr, *The Enlightened Economy: An Economic History of Britain, 1700–1850* (New Haven, CT: Yale University Press, 2009) who argues that the free market was one of the essentials of British economic development on the eve and in the wake of industrialization. In Nye's view – which is not backed up by much empirical evidence – Britain achieved economic supremacy *despite*, rather than *because of*, protectionist legislation during the eighteenth and nineteenth century; a point derived from Adam Smith's dictum (*Wealth of Nations*), which is not shared by everyone (and most certainly it was not by German economist Friedrich List); see, for example, Prasannan Parthasarathi, *Why Europe Grew Rich and Asia Did Not. Global Economic Divergence, 1600–1850* (Cambridge: Cambridge University Press, 2011); Ha-Joon Chang, *Kicking Away the Ladder: Development Strategy in Historical Perspective* (London: Anthem, 2003). Julian Hoppit, 'Bounties, the Economy and the State in Britain, 1689–1800,' in Perry Gauci, ed., *Regulating the British Economy, 1660–1850* (Farnham, VT: Ashgate, 2011), 139–60, or *id.*, 'The Nation, the State, and the First Industrial Revolution', *The Journal of British Studies* 50, no. 2 (2011), 307–31 adds context for the British case. In a wider context, see Erik Reinert, *How Rich Countries Got*

the idea that all markets do need a certain safety net or web of regulations and that this is more than just a question of ethics, but rather an issue of good market performance.[18] So it is not easy to disentangle the unconditional belief in free markets – as portrayed in many a textbook on micro- and macroeconomics up to more popular works such as influential journalist Thomas Friedman's *The World is Flat* (2005)[19] – from older forms of superstition which most of us would nowadays perhaps identify as either childish or irrational, such as witchcraft, magic, supernatural powers, sorcery, etc. But there is a certain bias in our modern reading of recorded history related to market behaviour which may be corrected by a re-reading and fresh contextualization of an ancient text, such as Martin Luther's *Sermon on Commerce and Usury*.

Free Markets and Capitalism in History

Before we proceed with the analysis, we must stop and realize that the modern free-market idea has a pedigree that dates back much further than the cleverest and most ardent recent critics of it will usually admit.[20] It did not emerge during the eighteenth century, when Mandeville published his rather infamous *The Fable of The Bees: or, Private Vices, Public Benefits* (1705), or Smith his *Inquiry into the Nature and Causes of the Wealth of Nations* (1776). Smith and Mandeville's basic ideas can be found in Augsburg notary Conrad Peutinger's[21] reports on the German Imperial Diets of the 1520s, or Leonhard Fronsperger's *Von dem Lob deß Eigen Nutzen* (*On the Virtues of Self-Interest*, Frankfurt-on-the-Main, 1564). Actually they emerged during the times of Martin Luther, which is another reason for rediscovering the monk from Wittenberg and his writings on economics. And

---

Rich… And Why Poor Countries Stay Poor (London: Constable 2007), or Peer Vries, 'Governing Growth: A Comparative Analysis of the Role of the State in the Rise of the West', *Journal of World History*, 13 (2002), 67–193. The debate is far from settled. Obviously, there is much irrational belief on either side of the argument. But that is alright, as Nietzsche has reminded us long time ago: science cannot be completely value free, unless it is either meaningless or unscientific.

18. On the modern business ethics of this question, see, for example, Peter H. Sedgwick, *The Market Economy and Christian Ethics* (Cambridge: Cambridge University Press, 1999), chap. 1; Albert O. Hirschman, *Entwicklung, Markt und Moral – Abweichende Betrachtungen* (Munich: Hanser, 1989); Kurt W. Rothschild, *Ethik und Wirtschaftstheorie* (Tübingen: J. C. B. Mohr, 1992), 32–37; Amartya Sen, *Development as Freedom* (New York: Knopf, 1999). A useful compendium to the emergence of the 'invisible hand' idea since the eighteenth century is Lisa Herzog and Axel Hometh, eds, *Der Wert des Marktes: Ein ökonomisch-philosophischer Diskurs vom 18. Jahrhundert bis zur Gegenwart* (Berlin: Suhrkamp, 2013).

19. Thomas L. Friedman, *The World is Flat: A Brief History of the Twenty-First Century* (New York: Farrar, Straus and Giroux, 2005).

20. Harcourt, *Illusion of Free Markets*, dates the emergence of it to the mid-eighteenth century. Most historians and economists will probably identify Mandeville's *Fable of the Bees* as its earliest expression. But the idea as such is much older than Mandeville.

21. Clemens Bauer, 'Conrad Peutingers Gutachten zur Monopolfrage', *Archiv für Reformationsgeschichte* 45 (1954), 1–43, 145–96; *id.*, 'Conrad Peutinger und der Durchbruch des neuen ökonomischen Denkens an der Wende zur Neuzeit', in Hermann Rinn, ed., *Augusta 955–1955* (Munich: Rinn, 1955), 219–28.

it is likely that they circulated widely amongst certain groups or members of society in the early modern period. In a similar way to Mandeville and Smith, Fronsperger and Peutinger argued – out of different motivations – that taming the individual's utility maximizing interests was societally less optimal than leaving them free to unfold, that is in a way that everyone was put in the position to fend for themselves in the strife to fulfil their individual goals and desires. During the eighteenth century, however, the idea experienced its final breakthrough.[22] It co-emerged, if not entirely synchronously, with the modern market economy, which can be found either in the sixteenth- and seventeenth-century Netherlands (as some have said[23]) or in the post-1688 English economy on the eve of the first industrial revolution (as others have said).[24] Timelines and continuities are hard to pin down, however. The trajectories towards the 'modern' economy and 'capitalist' society were broken and idiosyncratic, varying from country to country. True, no one could seriously doubt that over the three centuries or so of what historians have called the Early Modern Period (1500–1800 AD) public debates on the role of markets changed, if gradually, towards a more positive appraisal of what was identified as free markets. Whilst the perfectly free, that is completely deregulated market for the above-mentioned reasons is as rare a species as the Yeti – everyone knows it, yet no one has been able to spot it[25] – most of us probably are in broad agreement about its powerful nature as a metaphor and guideline in political and economic discourse. Whilst there is nothing wrong with the idea as such – as a hypothetical model – we ought to acknowledge that the very notion of 'freedom' in market behaviour as portrayed in the modern discourse is somewhat counterfactual, counterintuitive and inherently oxymoronic.

Very often the idea of free markets has been linked to the evolution of *capitalism*.[26] Neither of the two, however – capitalism on the one hand and free markets on the other hand – can be found in the historical record in its pure shape; not even remotely so, or in more recent times, in a sense that we can exactly pin down their emergence, rise or biographical dates. Our daily lives, and many markets of today which we would consider as free or archetypically capitalist – such as the New York Stock Exchange or the Chicago

22. Harcourt, *Illusion of Free Markets*, chaps 1–5.
23. Jan de Vries and Ad van der Woude, *The First Modern Economy: Success, Failure, and Perseverance of the Dutch Economy, 1500–1815* (Cambridge: Cambridge University Press, 1997); critical towards the former: J. Luiten van Zanden, 'The "Revolt of the Early Modernists" and the "First Modern Economy": An Assessment', *Economic History Review*, Second Series, 55, no. 4 (2002), 619–41; more recently Marten R. Prak, *The Dutch Republic in the Seventeenth Century: The Golden Age* (Cambridge: Cambridge University Press, 2005).
24. Daron Acemoglu and James A. Robinson, *Why Nations Fail: The Origins of Power, Prosperity, and Poverty* (New York: Crown, 2012).
25. Even relatively market-friendly societies such as Britain between 1840 and 1914 or Britain and the US after 1979/1980 in the Thatcher–Reagan ascendancy have kept the state within the game in certain sectors and branches of social and economic life.
26. Joyce O. Appleby, *The Relentless Revolution: A History of Capitalism* (New York: W. W. Norton, 2010); Jürgen Kocka, *Geschichte des Kapitalismus* (Munich: C. H. Beck, 2013), and, of course, Fernand Braudel, *Civilisation matérielle, économie et capitalisme (XVe–XVIIIe siècles)*, Eng. trans. S. Reynolds, *Civilization and Capitalism, 15th–18th century*, 3 vols (New York: Harper & Row, 1982–84).

Wheat Exchange – are so tightly regulated and shot-through with regulations that the Soviet *Politbüro* would have been proud of it.[27] Just try to run with impunity a diesel car without the ecological upgrade to the EUR3 norm by means of a soot particle filter in the emerging 'green lungs' of Germany's inner cities (called *Umweltzone* in Germany). Or contemplate building an extension to your house; try to fell a tree on your private property, try applying for a current account at a local bank: you'll face a dense web of legislation, forms to fill in and laws to comply with. Modern society is anything but free. Much better, if you belong to the protected species of European farmers – an endangered species which according to Ricardian trade theory (much favoured in international economics) shouldn't really exist. European farmers have, for the best part of a century now, benefited from a consequent by-passing of the market, effected by state and European legislation known as the CAP (Common Agrarian Policy) which has safeguarded sales of milk, grain and meat at prices that are grotesquely above the world market-clearing level (at the intersection of demand and supply curve) and which could be stabilized only above market-clearing levels by strict government interference in the market and intervention support, thus keeping alive an industry which – according to the textbook paradigm– ought to have vanished from the world market a long time ago. This is not to say that regulation is bad. Quite the contrary. It is needed for markets to work properly and to allow a degree of freedom and welfare that everybody can subscribe to. But much of modern political discourse has been two-faced, preaching water (free markets) whilst drinking wine (keeping up dense levels of market regulation). At least we should be honest to ourselves.

On the other hand, we find what we may call 'capitalistic behaviour' (a term that does not lend itself to consensual definition; most would agree that it covered profit orientation and increasingly rationalistic business behaviour; others would insist on the existence of more modern forms of business organisation and labour/production relationships) very early; some would argue since the earliest written records were produced several thousand years ago, but this notion is controversial. Others have pinpointed the commercial revolution in Italy's trading cities during the thirteenth century or the beginnings of European overseas expansion and the creation of economic empires since the late fifteenth century as a reference point for capitalism's breakthrough. *Capitalism* and the *free market* are above all mythical concepts, charged up with political meaning, social codes and cultural syntax; they usually give away more about each scholar's individual standpoint than capitalism itself as a historic moment.[28] As a form

---

27. Harcourt, *Illusion of Free Markets.* In a similar fashion: Alessandro Stanziani, *Rules of Exchange. French Capitalism in Comparative Perspective, Eighteenth to Early Twentieth Centuries* (Cambridge: Cambridge University Press, 2012).

28. A good overview still is Anthony Giddens, *Capitalism and Modern Social Theory. An Analysis of the Writings of Marx, Durkheim and Max Weber* (Cambridge: Cambridge University Press, 1971), 1–64; 119–248. Alongside Marx and Weber, big names such as Schumpeter, Braudel, Wallerstein, Arrighi and Werner Sombart's theory about luxury trade and the development of capitalism come to mind; good overviews may be found in Kocka, *Geschichte*, and DuPlessis, *Transitions to Capitalism*, esp. chap. 1.

of behaviour – if defined broadly as profit-maximizing private entrepreneurship using markets and monetary relationships as the predominant form of resource allocation and economic interaction – capitalism did not change its shape or direction very much over the centuries. This is important because earlier scholarship has stressed that Luther's age would have witnessed the 'rise of capitalism'. The rise of early capitalism and the *early bourgeois revolution (Frühbürgerliche Revolution)* were seen, especially by Marxist historians, as the decisive elements of socio-economic change that would help *explain away* Luther and other social and religious reform movements.[29] But as the discussion in subsequent chapters will show, this notion is at variance with most of the recent evidence; capitalism neither emerged in Germany around Luther's time (it had been there long before) nor did it change much of its shape at that time.

Rather than pinpointing hypothetical frameworks of capitalism's emergence, we should perhaps better look for its evolutionary mutations and changes in drive, verve and scope, that is those changes in rhythm which made contemporaries aware of its potential dangers, placing the topic at the pole position of the debates and public discourses they waged. Such a time was the early sixteenth century indeed – Martin Luther's age. Many would argue that around 2000 AD financial capitalism as we know it had reached another climax. At such times, which have been recurring without being subject to any meaningfully examinable pattern of controlled emergence or evolution – times and periods to be measured in fluid terms or decades rather than single years with overlapping streams and currents of structures and events – capitalism may have become more characteristic. It may have turned into *more* of a driving force than usual, as well as becoming *more* representative a configuration of the social, economic and productive landscape than before, gradually turning from an *explanandum* (medieval social theory was adamant about governing market behaviour within a referential framework provided by Christian faith) into an *explanans* (e.g. 'only free markets can cause the best outcome for everyone'). This should warn us against an understanding of history as something that moved in either cycles or, even worse, linear fashion, or something that could ever attain the characteristics of being determined, lending itself to 'ex-post prediction' (deductivism; cliometrics). What matters instead are the contingencies, parallels and similarities of historical trends and developments, both over time and cross-sectionally, and which we may study so as to get deeper insights about capitalist dynamics and human behaviour in their respective idiosyncratic location points in time and space. And here again, a re-reading of Luther can be enlightening. In the German lands, capitalism had developed centuries long before 1500. It can be traced in the written record in the Upper German financial metropolis of Augsburg, a wealthy free imperial city proverbial for her high financiers, since the thirteenth century – and surely much earlier than that. Economic behaviour and social life took place within a constant tension field of 'unrestrained profit maximizing' on the one hand and the desire to secure one's *gerechte Nahrung* on the other

---

29. An excellent overview and insight into this in many ways interesting paradigm can still be found in Adolf Laube, Max Steinmetz and Günter Vogler, *Illustrierte Geschichte der deutschen frühbürgerlichen Revolution* (Berlin [East]: Dietz, 1974).

hand, meaning an honest and fair if not equitable outcome for everyone under the parameters of mediaeval scholastic social theory.[30] The configurations of this tension field did not change that much over the centuries; perhaps Müller-Armack dictum that capitalism is thousands of years old was a bit overdrawn, but the essential point remains.[31] Sketching an argument of historical dynamics that is, implicitly or explicitly, based on capitalism's *evolution*, that is its emergence in sequences or steps, or even *progress*, probably does more violence to history than contributing to an improved understanding of the phenomenon as such. Rather we may entertain assumptions of irregular recurrences and contingencies. And here a re-reading of Luther may help towards a more nuanced understanding of capitalism as a matter of *style*.

What's Your Style? Or Setting the Goals

German economics has had a long tradition of thinking about economic development as something that evolves not through *stages* (of, say, growth à la Rostow) but rather across *spectrums* of empirical behaviour coupled with certain cultural beliefs which have come to be known as economic *styles* (*Wirtschaftsstil*).[32] This is important for the present task. With the works by Adam Smith, David Hume and the nineteenth-century English classical economists, a view took hold more firmly and broadly as a consensus that competition would be *generally* good for economic health and *general* development. The less restraint there was on behavioural choice, the more chances there were for individual betterment and overall growth. The cake grew because it was in everybody's interest to eat more. The automatism of a Smithian invisible hand and 'cooperation with no one in charge'[33] are still held by many to automatically steer society into the bliss of optimal resource allocation. Sometimes, even nature is evoked as a protagonist, and evolutionary theory is quoted to actually suggest that these mechanisms

---

30. Rolf Kiessling, 'Im Spannungsfeld von Markt und Recht', in Christoph Becker and Hans-Georg Hermann, eds, Ökonomie und Recht – historische Entwicklungen in Bayern (Münster: LIT Verlag, 2009), 73–98. See also Wolfgang Stromer von Reichenbach, *Oberdeutsche Hochfinanz 1350–1450* (Wiesbaden: Franz Steiner, 1970); id. ed., *Venedig und die Weltwirtschaft um 1200* (Stuttgart: Thorbecke, 1999); Rolf Kiessling, *Die Stadt und ihr Land. Umlandpolitik, Bürgerbesitz und Wirtschaftsgefüge in Ostschwaben vom 14. bis ins 16. Jahrhundert* (Cologne: Böhlau 1989), and most recently for a survey on market regulation in the middle ages, Eberhard Isenmann, *Die deutsche Stadt im Mittelalter 1150–1550* (Cologne: Böhlau, 2012), 978–95.

31. Alfred Müller-Armack, *Religion und Wirtschaft. Geistesgeschichtliche Hintergründe unserer europäischen Lebensform*, 3rd ed. (Berne: Haupt, 1981), 56.

32. It should be noted that Müller-Armack's model of what he and others called 'economic style', i.e. the existence of a 'homogenous set of expressions and beliefs manifested in many areas of human action and interaction' unified by a shared set of perceptions regarding the material environment and human purposes of interaction within this environment, which would characterize a historical period in the same way as *Rococo*, *Baroque* or *Renaissance* would classify as artistic style labels manifested in building and painting, is likewise treacherous when contrasted with modern empirical and theoretical development in the historical sciences. Because how do we define 'unity in expression' in a meaningful way? Original: 'Stil ist so die in den verschiedensten Lebensgebieten einer Zeit sichtbare Einheit des Ausdrucks und der Haltung.' Ibid., 57.

33. Seabright, *Company of Strangers*.

represent basic human traits (presumably inherited from our imputed ape-like predecessors?) that lend themselves to be studied using the toolkit of evolutionary biology.[34] If everyone is left to pursue what they do best, then cooperation (division of labour) will set in as an automatism (but what about war?). This will automatically create a better outcome for everyone. This postulate, intellectually challenging in positive as well as negative ways (it cannot be empirically proven; it says nothing about ethics and it suggests, perhaps even worse, that we are basically still apes after all, thus giving away more of the authors' individual outlook on the world than any economic insights of significant epistemological value), co-emerged in turn with the idea of the economy as a separate realm of human behaviour and interaction. This realm followed what German critics later called *Eigengesetzlichkeiten*: principles which could be analysed and understood – and ultimately *predicted* – using specifically calibrated theory and methodology, as though there existed laws and working mechanisms in economics.[35] Again, this is a very peculiar epistemological notion that has developed rather lately in modern economic thought. It has been derived from a rather idealistic, if not naïve, belief that nature has set some sort of individual guiding principle or *movens* behind the great mechanical working mechanism of the economy (and it became mathematized in the economic sciences after c. 1880). But what if this is simply wrong? What if the economy, contrary to the physical and other natural sciences, does not work like a *mechanism* but rather like an *organism*? What if it evolves and mutates following neither law nor algorithm; sometimes erratically, but always idiosyncratically, that is ultimately unpredictably?

For exactly these reasons dictated by a healthy dose of scepticism towards a pure deterministic approach, some writers did argue, even in the more market-friendly twentieth century, for a coexistence of such market mechanisms with super-ordinate goals that were to be determined, that is set, *outside* the parameters of the system itself. These could be particular ethical, political and social goals framed, for instance, within what some scholars defined as the economic style (*Wirtschaftsstil*) of German post-war *Soziale Marktwirtschaft* (an economic style that integrated Christian social norms and values and ethical judgement with more liberal or market-friendly ideas). More radical voices since the days of market-friendly or liberal thinkers such as Friedrich von Hayek, Milton Friedman or Gary S. Becker, however, took a different turn. Their style (as hip-hoppers would say) set the market allocation principle on top of the possible choices of theories explaining and predicting human behaviour, preferences and economic allocation processes.[36] The famous Ricardian model of comparative advantage – predicting in its essence that two nations trading with each other will specialize in the production of the commodity in which they enjoy a comparative advantage, one peculiarly significant manifestation of the so-called classical economics, can still be found in many a recent textbook on international economics. Its simple mathematical qualities make it appear inherently true. But just what truth is, is not usually explained. And while the Ricardian

---

34. Ibid., chap. 1 and *passim*.
35. For example, Peter Koslowski, *Prinzipien der ethischen Ökonomie* (Tübingen: J. C. B. Mohr, 1988), new imprint 1994, 139s. A useful overview also is Bruno Ingrao, 'Free Market', in Richard Arena and Christian Longhi, eds, *Markets and Organization* (Berlin: Springer, 1998), 61–94.
36. See, for example, Rothschild, *Ethik und Wirtschaftstheorie, passim*.

model may be quite useful in terms of explaining exchange patterns amongst partners that are equal (or near equal) regarding productivity and stage of development, it does not take much expertise in theory, but simple visual evidence of modern developing countries specializing in raw material exports, coupled with a good dose of common sense, to realize that the comparative advantage argument, developed synchronously with the invisible hand mythology during the Scottish Enlightenment philosophical discourse around 1750 is, in many regards, simply wrong.

About five hundred years ago, this insight would have sounded utterly trivial. No one would have seriously *doubted* that markets *did* need rules, that the state *should* intervene in the economic process and that unrestrained competitive markets were *unsuitable* to raise general welfare. And no one would have believed in the existence of any economic laws of significance. Dr Conrad Peutinger (1465–1547) used the idea of such laws during the monopoly debates of the 1520s as a discursive figure in his zeal of legitimizing the continuation of big corporations; he was financed, in a sense, by a lobby headed by Augsburg high financiers such as Jakob and Anton Fugger, who would have stood to lose if the monopoly debates would have been finally settled to their disadvantage (but they weren't eventually: the Emperor owed these companies too much money to afford a formal criminal conviction of monopoly charges on the Imperial Diets). Also, with Luther's violent polemic against the excesses of capitalism, Fugger and Welser and other prominent entrepreneurs of their age would have felt on the defensive; their very right to exist in the light of the larger common good was questioned, they felt, when the case against monopoly practices was brought before the same Imperial Diets that dealt with the Luther case in the 1520s (more on which in subsequent chapters). So we need to remember, if put somewhat pointedly – but what good is a story that is not sharpened by exaggeration? – that the free-market-invisible-hand argument was first developed by someone who was *paid* for formulating it; someone who was actually *hired* for defending it against a tide that had turned against it and a public discourse on monopoly and un-Christian-like business practices that had assumed increasingly vicious characteristics. That certain economic models or propositions may be borne out of specific interest constellations of their author(s) does not belittle their theoretical quality and stringency a priori. After all, most economic models are based on certain sets of cultural belief as well as, however implicitly, vested interests that stand behind their authors; one must not forget that David Ricardo was a broker before he turned to writing professionally about political economy. But Dr Peutinger and the Fugger merchants (and, ironically, Emperor Charles V also) were, during the early 1520s, representing the minority voice in the discourse on 'good vs. bad' economics. This will be drawn out in more detail in chapters 2 and 5. But they won the upper hand, eventually. This was part and characteristic of the socio-political dynamics of the day. And it was one of the several reasons that caused Luther to write his 1524 *Sermon on Commerce and Usury*.

The obvious question arises: were our ancestors wrong – and are our models better? Or do we simply ask the wrong questions nowadays?[37] The present book cannot offer an ultimate answer. Partly this is because the issue is open to value judgement, partly

---

37. Recent contributions to the debate – from different approaches and viewpoints – include Tomáš Sedláček, *Economics of Good and Evil. The Quest for Economic Meaning from Gilgamesh to Wall*

because the focus will be on one particular author and pamphlet, that is Martin Luther's *Von Kauffshandlung und Wucher*, published in Wittenberg in 1524. There were more and perhaps even more refined economic models around. Others developed the questions Luther only touched on in more detail and perhaps with more analytical rigour than the churchman from Wittenberg. But what the present interpretation *can* do is to pave the way towards a better understanding, both of the economic configurations *we* live in and of those prevalent in the early 1500s, as well as our moral questions regarding the market in general terms – because these questions are timeless. They do not change with variations in the level of wealth, productivity and technology. They are as valid today, in a world that is fully industrialized even managing the switchover to post-industrial post-modernism, as they were 500 years ago when technology was more primitive, society was profoundly agrarian and levels of disposable wealth, income and living standards were a tiny fraction of what they are today in the north-west of Europe. It may also contribute to the somewhat simple if not trivial insight that modern economics as a social science has a pedigree that dates far back before Adam Smith and that – in fact – Smithian and Ricardian economics represent a detour, a *Sonderweg* taken over the past two-and-a-half centuries or so, from a mode of economic thinking we may call 'continental European economics' that was simply different.

Purgatory, Indulgences and Salvation: Luther as an Economist

The present book therefore studies Luther's theology from an economic viewpoint, examining his contribution to European economic thought. This may seem alien to most historians and theologians of our age, since economics – curiously – is usually left out from Luther studies, in the same way as Luther is usually left out from research in both economics and 'straight' economic history. Having said this the obvious questions remain (1) whether we can learn something from Luther the economist, (2) if so, what and, by turning the question on its head, (3) whether economics as a science can or should be free of ends (*telos*) and ultimate value judgement – because this is, alongside the big question about markets, one of the other big questions raised by Luther's text. Can we – must we – separate economics from ethics? Some have argued, if implicitly, that we can; and the approach used to be rather popular until very recently. But the subsequent chapters will show why this view is, in all likelihood, mistaken.[38]

Street (Oxford: Oxford University Press, 2011); Robert Skidelsky and Edward Skidelsky, *How Much is Enough? Money and the Good Life* (London: Allan Lane, 2012).

38. Examples, if random, include Gary S. Becker, *The Economic Approach to Human Behavior* (Chicago, IL: University of Chicago Press, 1976); Robert B. Ekelund, Jr., Robert F. Hebert and Robert D. Tollison, 'An Economic Model of the Medieval Church: Usury as a Form of Rent Seeking', *Journal of Law, Economics, & Organization* 5 (1989), 307–31, or Alberto Cassone and Carla Marchese, 'The Economics of Religious Indulgences', *Journal of Institutional and Theoretical Economics (JITE) / Zeitschrift für die gesamte Staatswissenschaft* 155, no. 3 (Sept. 1999), 429–42. It is interesting that such an article as the latter one would appear within the same journal that published Schmoller's monograph-length article 'Zur Geschichte der national-ökonomischen Ansichten in Deutschland während der Reformations-Periode' in 1860.

Arguably the sermon *Von Kauffshandlung und Wucher* was Luther's most famous pamphlet delivered on economic matters; economics, however, never was the focus of Luther's oeuvre. Rather, as is well-known, Luther's forthcoming as a theologian in and before 1517 evolved around the problem of *indulgences*. These were, as it seems, a religious or soteriological problem. The idea ran as follows. People commit sins, habitually; they do so on a daily basis. The spiritual life cycle of Christians at the time evolved around the focal points of an ellipsis or cycle which went from sin → confession → absolution → penitence → sin, from which the cycle started anew, as even the most pious Christian was bound to sin almost continuously. It was the human condition.[39] A rueful and repentant sinner had to perform acts of penitence – worldly acts, that is; the sin as such could not be forgiven through worldly acts. These were called 'good works'. They were things such as pilgrimages, visits to particularly earmarked churches, prayers, communion and ritual confession. Whilst the act of forgiveness was neither in the hand of man nor in the hand of the church, the latter could give you a discount on the *good works* to perform for *worldly* acts of penitence, if you paid a notional fee. This was called 'indulgence'. The Church had, over the centuries, accumulated what was called a treasure of mercy (*Gnadenschatz*) through the good deeds of her martyrs and saints. This treasure could be administered to the faithful in return for the *indulgence fee*, which, as people believed, reduced the actual amount of worldly repentance. Overall, if used in combination with good works this would reduce the amount of time spent in purgatory – the antecedent or twilight zone before Hell; the crucial difference being that you could get out of Purgatory, whilst spells in Hell were final (figure 1.1).

As the image below depicts quite nicely, Purgatory was a place where you were burnt, but surely not as badly as in Hell. This twilight zone had been, in the pointed interpretation by eminent French medievalist Le Goff, 'invented' in the twelfth and thirteenth century in order to deal with problems of usury (lending upon interest) and the emerging financial economy. Purgatory and indulgences may, therefore, have represented a coping strategy addressed at alleviating the consciousness of societies that, during the twelfth and thirteenth-century commercial revolution, had turned more and more capitalistic.[40]

Originally, however – and this is very important– indulgences were neither the main form of nor could they be substituted for the actual act of penance. Indulgences have continued in Catholic faith and church practice until today; but what was barred in the sixteenth century in the wake of Luther's Reformation was their *sale*, based on the idea that indulgences (and penitence) were something *marketable, measurable* and defrayable. In fact, by the early 1500s the sale of indulgences had become increasingly popular. Basically, the church had, over the high and late Middle Ages, discovered them as a powerful cash machine. Two perversions – in the view of Luther and many reformers who came before and after him – had entered the mechanism. First, you could buy indulgences for the future. This notion seems to have been developed by the popes and

---

39. I am following Euan Cameron, *The European Reformation*, 2nd ed. (Oxford: Oxford University Press, 2012), chap. 6.
40. Jacques Le Goff, *The Birth of Purgatory* (Chicago, IL: University of Chicago Press, 1984).

Figure 1.1 Depiction of Purgatory (Altarpiece, Wimpfen Town Church, 1519; Photo © Peter Schmelzle, Wimpfen, Germany).

had taken hold by the 1470s. It worked, if the analogy may be allowed, in a way similar to topping up your mobile phone on a pre-paid card. You could buy a future indulgence – so that achieving forgiveness for your future sins was not a matter of 'if' but rather 'when'. This would keep variable the actual date and time of your confession. Second, since the 1470s indulgences could also be purchased for the deceased, meaning you may as well get Granny out of purgatory in case she hadn't been able or careful enough to save enough money to do it herself during her lifetime.

That this couldn't possibly be the original purpose and intent of indulgences was nothing new to contemporaries in Luther's days. Indulgence critique had a long history leading back to the most venerable medieval heretics. Indulgences, or rather their abuse and misuse, had been subject to criticism, notably by the Germans and the French, at the great Council of Constance (1414–18) connected to the trial of Bohemian 'heretic' (we may say early Reformer) Jan Hus (c. 1369–1415).[41] Hus' heterodox visions of religion had developed with condemning standard church practice in the German village of Wilsnack in the Archdiocese of Magdeburg in the 1380s, where the relics and miracles performed by local saints were used as a source of veneration and thus income for the local church that was in possession of the said relics and miracles. Wilsnack was by no means a special case; the late medieval or Catholic church had turned into Europe's largest and most successful financial corporation. It generated ample profits and revenue across the board,

---

41. Phillip H. Stump, *The Reforms of the Council of Constance (1414–1418)* (Leiden: Brill, 1994), 67–72.

not least from marketing the cult around saints' relics. Considerable chunks of cash were moved around year after year. Miracles and indulgences were only part of the game, but surely important enough to incense much criticism.[42] Jan Hus was one of three members appointed by a Bohemian church commission to examine and report back to his native lands in Bohemia about the practice of pilgrimage to Wilsnack which had developed soon after the 1383 miracle. It had drawn, amongst others, an increasing stream of pilgrims and devotees from the Bohemian realms.[43] Hus reported back to Prague 'that the reported blood at Wilsnack did not effect miracles'.[44] In fact, he had in many ways a similar approach to Luther as a theologian (*sola fide* principle; statement that the pope could err; immediate position of the individual to God; no superior position of the church in the landscape of faith, belief and salvation; and translation of the Bible into the Czech vernacular); strikingly he also attacked the practice of indulgences, but only inasmuch as they were dealt out in an inflationary manner.[45] In 1412 Prague streets saw processions in which chests 'intended for indulgence money were smeared with mud; at the cathedral the treasure chest received a pronouncement addressed sardonically to the disciples of the evil demon Asmodeus, Belial and Mammon'. [46] In the words of an authority, in Hus' view 'indulgences were more about economics than salvation'. [47] A lot of money, gold and silver flew from Bohemia to Rome in return for simony, church sinecures, benefices, indulgences and other payments; many contemporaries considered the Church to be morally corrupt and remote-controlled, not only by Rome but also by the cash nexus in more general terms.[48] The later Reformers of Luther's age picked up on the very same topics. Jan Hus was finally summoned to the Council of Constance, where his teachings were identified as heretical. He was burned at the stake on 6 July 1415. Since the time around 1410, as well as the first two decades of the sixteenth century were marked by economic and monetary contraction,[49] we may wonder, perhaps, whether calls for abolishing the worst excesses of spending money on aspects that were purely soteriological in nature (such as the marketing of indulgences) or voices calling for a

---

42. Cameron, *European Reformation*, 2nd ed., 30–35.

43. Thomas A. Fudge, *Jan Hus, Religious Reform and Social Revolution in Bohemia* (London: Tauris, 2010), 27–28.

44. Ibid., 28.

45. Ibid., 11, 13–15, 36–37, 41, 61 109, 234 on indulgences in Hus' belief, and chap. 3 on Hus' theology in general.

46. Malcolm Lambert, *Medieval Heresy. Popular Movements from the Gregorian Reform to the Reformation*, 2nd ed. (Oxford: Blackwell, 1992), 304.

47. Thomas A. Fudge, *The Trials of Jan Hus. Medieval Heresy and Criminal Procedure* (Oxford: Oxford University Press, 2013), 156 (for the quote); 155–159 on the connections between money and indulgences.

48. Josef Macek, *Die hussitische revolutionäre Bewegung* (Berlin [East]: Deutscher Verlag der Wissenschaften, 1958), 8–11.

49. Philipp Robinson Rössner, *Deflation – Devaluation – Rebellion. Geld im Zeitalter der Reformation* (Stuttgart: Franz Steiner, 2012); John Day, 'The Great Bullion Famine of the Fifteenth Century', *Past & Present*, LXXIX (1978), 3–54; *id.*, 'The Question of Monetary Contraction in Late Medieval Europe', in Jørgen Steen Jensen, ed., *Coinage and Monetary Circulation in the Baltic Area, c. 1350–c. 1500* (Copenhagen: Nordisk Numismatisk Unions Medlemsblad, Nationalmuseet, 1982), 12–29.

streamlining of church practice according to more ancient and just ways resounded peculiarly popularly with the people at time of financial crisis, monetary contraction and deflation. Some of these parallels will return in the macroeconomic framework of Germany in the early 1500s in chapter 2.

By 1500, when Luther was in his twenties, the supply of indulgences had grossly inflated the market. In the words of an authority on that matter, 'By 1500 "full confessionals" were offered: these allowed the purchaser to choose a confessor, who could give absolution once in life and on the point of death even for sins normally reserved for the pope to forgive; could grant a plenary indulgence at any time when there was a risk of death; and could administer the Eucharist whenever it was requested.'[50] The practice had progressively diverted public attention away from the moral issue of repentance, replacing the Christian imperative to repent with a simple financial mechanism instead. At least this was the superficial yet also ultimately powerful common interpretation. The idea was that not only could you pay a certain sum to get out of, or at least reduce, the time spent in purgatory but also the 'time' (the chronological concept of time applied here surely was a virtual one and quite different from ours) spent in purgatory varied proportionally with the sum of money spent on indulgences. This notion had a peculiarly uneasy undertone. Because if you pushed it further, the implication was that principally the spell in purgatory varied with personal income or individual wealth. We must be careful here, as earlier research has established the existence of a 'social discount' system: richer people paid multiples of the standard rate for an indulgence.[51] But calling this system in any way democratic as some scholars have would mean taking things too far.[52] Because in principle – all possible social discounts apart – the richer you were, the higher the sum of years that could potentially be cancelled from your purgatory bill.

Scholars and writers more sympathetic towards the Old Catholic church practices have sometimes called – and defended – this transformation of indulgence practice condemned by Luther a sort of 'insurance policy'. For a comparatively small sum of money, you could considerably lift your conscience. In an age of fear and anxiety, which the later Middle Ages moving towards the magical date 1500 certainly were; in such an age which as yet knew neither mind-enhancing chemical drugs nor antidepressants, indulgences would have been a very nice little helper. Because burn you would, be that in purgatory or hell – that was for sure. Luckily the printing press had been invented recently, in the 1450s, so that the indulgence campaigns attained the characteristics of big advertising sprees. The proverbial flyer ad with which indulgence collectors promoted the product in Saxony went: *Sobald das Geld im Kasten klingt, die Seele in den Himmel springt* ('When the coin in the chest rings, the soul forth to heaven springs'). This saying had, by the 1470s, attained the status of a proverb.[53] Or, somewhat related, *Kupfernes Geld, hölzerne Seelmess* ('copper money, wooden requiem'), as another proverb had it; denoting

50. Cameron, *European Reformation*, 2nd ed., 87.
51. Helga Schnabel-Schüle, *Die Reformation 1495–1555* (Stuttgart: Reclam, 2006), 62. The term was coined by Bernd Moeller.
52. Others have even likened the practice of buying indulgences to a form of insurance policy. See also Thomas Kaufmann, *Geschichte der Reformation* (Frankfurt: Verlag der Weltreligionen, 2009), 83.
53. Ulinka Rublack, *Reformation Europe* (Cambridge: Cambridge University Press, 2005), 12–13.

not only the low purchasing power of small change coins (pennies and *hellers* consisted mostly of copper or other base metal) but also the imputed perversion of a soteriological scenario where money had entered the syntax of religious practice and the equation as a crucial variable determining the individual's position before God. Pushed even further, why should you even bother to do good works if you may as well *pay* for absolution? When Luther discovered about the *Ablasszettel* (indulgence note) promotion by Johann Tetzel around 1515, the saying even went that whatever you did – 'whoring, adultery, usury, and all other sorts of wrongdoing' – it didn't matter. You could buy yourself out of it. Neither did it matter *when* you committed these sins, when you had committed them or when you would commit them in the future (see above), as long as you bought an indulgence of sufficient value.[54] Although this notion certainly did not correspond to the *actual* and *original* model of indulgences developed by the Catholic Church – nor was it usually understood this way by most academic theologians – public discourse and religious *practice* around 1500 had in many ways come to see things that way.

Towards the end of the fifteenth century, indulgence practices had been going through an Indian summer. Contrary to older accounts, there would have been no general crisis of the late medieval church in sight, against which Luther took arms.[55] He was in a sense fighting the mainstream. In terms of numbers, new church foundations, massive streams of pilgrimages, the veneration of martyrs and relics had reached a peak around 1500. We should note, though, that in business cycles terminology, a crisis is by definition marked or triggered by a climax or climacteric of an ongoing event that comes before it – that is a 'high point' or vertex of a cyclical upswing. So there is nothing wrong in principle with employing the notion of crisis still when talking about indulgences and the raise of Luther the heterodox reformer.[56] If all recent accounts on the pre-history of the Reformation are accurate, by the early 1500s popular piety and church practice had reached the basic conditions necessary for a crisis to unfold. In 1514 and 1516, when the pope issued a 'General Indulgence' in order to finance the wars against the Turks, as well as the construction of St Peter's Church in Rome, indulgences had turned into one of Europe's strongest financial businesses. The Fugger Company,[57] one of the biggest financial corporations of the age, headed by Jakob Fugger, and after his death in 1525, Anton Fugger (his nephew), acted as bankers for the Curia, in the same way as they did for the emperor. They were the main agents remitting indulgence money collected in the German lands to Rome. Such payments came to the tune of several hundreds of thousands of florins or gulden per year – at conservative estimates.[58] The general

---

54. An excellent account still remains Heinz Schilling, *Aufbruch und Krise. Deutschland 1517–1648* (Berlin: Siedler Taschenbuch, 1988), 96–99.

55. Cameron, *The European Reformation*, 2nd ed., chaps 1, 2.

56. Rössner, *Deflation – Devaluation – Rebellion*, chap. 2 is devoted entirely to explaining why the 1500/1530 period was a time of (economic) crisis.

57. Most recently Mark Häberlein, *The Fuggers of Augsburg: Pursuing Wealth and Honor in Renaissance Germany* (Charlottesville, VA: University of Virginia Press, 2012) with references to further literature.

58. There existed a bewildering number of currencies that circulated in the German realms with different types of florins or guldens, *groschen, batzen, kreuzer*, pennies and *heller* coins. Good

indulgence collector for the German lands, Cardinal Albrecht of Brandenburg (1490–1545) allegedly used half of the sums collected in Germany to repay his debts to the Fuggers, because in a not unusual manner he had accumulated a number of high-ranking church positions as Archbishop of Magdeburg, Halberstadt and Mainz which made him elector and one of the most powerful rulers in sixteenth-century Germany. For this he had to pay dearly: in cash. Thus the circle became closed. Only half of the indulgence money under Albrecht actually went to Rome. The other half went into the coffers of some of the richest and biggest private business corporations of the age who worked with that money and quite profitably so, as the debates on monopoly practices and big business on the Imperial Diets of the early 1520s show. Jakob and Anton Fugger shuffled millions of florins across Europe within weeks, if we can believe their own testimony; the indulgence campaign headed by Albrecht would have represented a minor branch of their financial business in the early 1500s and 1510s. But surely they reaped nice benefits out of the indulgence deal. Contemporaries may be forgiven for believing that the cash nexus determined what you were worth before God. But they had witnessed one of the ugliest examples of how salvation, a sanctuary, personal, inner-most and strictly non-economic good that should never be alienated, *had* become commercialized and *had* been tainted by the financial market. Indulgences, as practised around 1500, represented the perversion of an originally much more innocent idea, which had put the task of repentance at the centre of the exercise, and the monetary donation accompanying the indulgence only as a secondary or top-up requirement, underlining – but never replacing it for – one's good intentions to repent. The situation had become so utterly shameful that a then 33-year-old monk from a remote and stinking mud-hole – as some would

surveys include Michael North, *Das Geld und seine Geschichte. Vom Mittelalter bis zur Gegenwart* (Munich: Beck, 1994); *id.*, *Kleine Geschichte des Geldes. Vom Mittelalter bis heute* (Munich: Beck, 2009); Bernd Sprenger, *Das Geld der Deutschen. Geldgeschichte Deutschlands von den Anfängen bis zur Gegenwart*, 3rd ed. (Paderborn: Schöningh, 2002), Herbert Rittmann, *Deutsche Geldgeschichte 1484–1914* (Munich: Battenberg, 1975), Arthur Suhle, *Deutsche Münz- und Geldgeschichte von den Anfängen bis zum 15. Jahrhundert*, 8th ed. (Berlin: Deutscher Verlag der Wissenschaften, 1964); Hans-Jürgen Gerhard, 'Miszelle: Neuere deutsche Forschungen zur Geld- und Währungsgeschichte der Frühen Neuzeit. Fragen – Ansätze – Erkenntnisse', *Vierteljahrschrift für Sozial- und Wirtschaftsgeschichte*, LXXXIII (1996), 216–30; *id.*, 'Ein schöner Garten ohne Zaun. Die währungspolitische Situation des Deutschen Reiches um 1600', *Vierteljahrschrift für Sozial- und Wirtschaftsgeschichte*, LXXXI (1994), 156–77; *id.*, 'Ursachen und Folgen der Wandlungen im Währungssystem des Deutschen Reiches 1500–1625. Eine Studie zu den Hintergründen der sogenannten Preisrevolution', in Eckart Schremmer, ed., *Geld und Währung vom 16. Jahrhundert bis zur Gegenwart* (Stuttgart: Franz Steiner, 1993), 69–84. Older numismatic works include Ferdinand Friedensburg, *Münzkunde und Geldgeschichte der Einzelstaaten des Mittelalters und der Neueren Zeit* (Munich: R. Oldenbourg, 1926); A. Luschin v. Ebengreuth, *Allgemeine Münzkunde und Geldgeschichte des Mittelalters und der Neueren Zeit*, 2nd ed. (Munich: R. Oldenbourg, 1926), as well as Friedrich Freiherr von Schrötter, 'Das Münzwesen des Deutschen Reichs von 1500 bis 1566', *Jahrbuch für Gesetzgebung, Verwaltung und Volkswirtschaft*, XXXV (1911) and XXXVI (1912), repr. in Friedrich von Schrötter, *Aufsätze zur deutschen Münz- und Geldgeschichte des 16. bis 19. Jahrhunderts (1902–1938)*, ed. Bernd Kluge (Leipzig: Reprintverlag Leipzig im Zentralantiquariat, 1991), 3–76.

say[59] – the country town of Wittenberg in the heart of Germany stood up in 1517 and formulated an alternative explanation of Scripture.

Initially what Luther simply wanted to do was to attack the current indulgence practice on scholarly grounds. Nothing less and nothing more. In a letter accompanying the 95 Theses he sent to the cardinal in 1517, Luther stressed what he saw as a perversion of the Christian practice, people actually believed that the payment of indulgence would absolve you from sin (not true) and that this would happen the very moment your coin fell into the indulgence man's chest (not true, either).[60] Luther also criticized the somewhat misgiven notion that indulgences would whitewash or reduce the time spent in purgatory for just about any sin – not true again. Instead, Luther offered his own re-interpretation of Scripture – which he never intended to use as a cause for overthrowing the current Catholic faith. Sinfulness as a state of affairs could never be resolved or lifted by either deeds or payments of money. It was something that was in God's hands alone. From this sprang two implications that would become important in Luther's later career: the *sola fide* and *simul iustus et peccator* principle (more on which below) – and the disentanglement of church practice, repentance and acts of piety from the *cash nexus*. Cash had no business in religion.

Luther's re-formulation of Christian dogma, which has come to us as the Reformed faith in all its manifold idiosyncratic shapes and versions had many precedents and side-strands, both pre- and post-1517, so diversified in fact that historians are nowadays increasingly sceptical about its uniqueness or coherence.[61] Be that as it may, Luther's Reformation was the first that proved to have lasting success, so we need not be too anxious about deconstructing just about every received wisdom accumulated on the historiography of the German Reformation over the past two centuries or so since, at the time of historians such as Leopold von Ranke (1795–1886), historians began to study the problem academically. The Church had defeated many heretics before Luther. But Luther was the first who would get away with impunity. Others followed, almost simultaneously, such as Calvin or Zwingli at Zurich and Geneva, or John Knox in Scotland, or the more radical German preachers such as Thomas Müntzer at Mühlhausen. Although we don't have to invoke grand narratives à la Max Weber or Tawney[62] about the Reformation and the imputed rise of modern capitalism, there can be no doubt that without the events unfolding in Wittenberg in 1517 the mental, social, economic and cultural landscape and history of Europe, if not the world, would have looked very different. You could say that Luther took the fun out of life, because committing sin would become so much more difficult if it could not be pre-emptively cancelled out by an indulgence. It would make your life much more earnest, more inward-looking and harsher, as the more radical expressions of Calvinist piety and asceticism in religion, ritual as well as social and daily life seem to show. And after all, what Luther's Reformation did away with was all the

---

59. Rublack, *Reformation Europe*, blurb.
60. I am following Peter Blickle, *Die Reformation im Reich*, 3rd ed. (Stuttgart: Ulmer, 2000), 46–63.
61. See, for example, the pointed overview in Peter Marshall, *The Reformation: A Very Short Introduction* (Oxford: Oxford University Press, 2009), of which I perused the German edition.
62. R. H. Tawney, *Religion and the Rise of Capitalism: A Historical Study* (New York: Harcourt, Brace and Co., 1926).

practical, immediate, visual, sensual, *haptic* stance of pietism and popular religion. Relics, hosts, images – all these things disappeared in the wake of Lutheran church reform. A whole 'event culture' (T. Kaufmann) that had surrounded medieval Catholicism simply vanished in thin air.[63] But there was some sense to it, even economically, as subsequent sections will highlight in more detail.

As a Reformer and historical figure, Luther needs no further introduction. Useful recent Luther biographies exist in German[64] (less so in English). A host of excellent surveys on the German and European Reformations have appeared recently both in English and in German[65]; this stream of books is likely to swell in the upcoming quincentenary of the 95 Theses 'nailed' to the castle church door at Wittenberg on October 31st, 1517. Nailing one's theses at that time simply marked the official act of publication, but only as the grand narrative has it. Reality may have looked different, as Luther would have rather sent his 95 Theses as a letter to Cardinal Albrecht of Brandenburg on October 31st, 1517.[66] The 95 Theses turned into a public affair almost by chance. But as an *economist*, Luther has rarely been studied; the mere thought may seem alienating. The present volume attempts to show why this is mistaken.

Recent histories on the German Reformation have by and large rather shied away from economic topics whatsoever, even though it is unclear whether this has happened out of ignorance (the worst-case scenario), lack of interest (bad, but moderately more excusable) or simply misunderstanding. Only the last would be excusable, because misunderstandings can be cured by corrections. And yet, in the words of nineteenth-century economist and economic historian Gustav (von) Schmoller, Luther's big pamphlet of 1524 *On Commerce and Usury* may be regarded as 'the most interesting text on economics that has survived from the Reformation period'.[67] Schmoller of course represented, alongside Leipzig economist Georg Friedrich Wilhelm Roscher, the towering figure of the German historical school in economics.[68] There was, at the same time, an equivalent 'school' in

---

63. Kaufmann, *Geschichte der Reformation*, 29; 74–75.

64. Martin Brecht, *Martin Luther*, 3 vols, 3rd ed. (Stuttgart: Calwer Verlag, 1990); Heiko A. Oberman, *Luther: Mensch zwischen Gott und Teufel* (Berlin: Severin und Siedler, 1981); Volker Leppin, *Martin Luther* (Darmstadt: Wissenschaftliche Buchgesellschaft, 2006); most recently, Heinz Schilling, *Martin Luther. Rebell in einer Zeit des Umbruchs* (Munich: Beck, 2012).

65. Diarmait Macculloch, *The Reformation* (New York: Penguin, 2005); Cameron, *European Reformation*; Marshall, *The Reformation*; Rublack, *Reformation Europe*; Kaufmann, *Geschichte der Reformation*; Volker Leppin, *Die Reformation* (Darmstadt: Wissenschaftliche Buchgesellschaft, 2013); Harm Klueting, *Das konfessionelle Zeitalter Europa zwischen Mittelalter und Moderne. Kirchengeschichte und allgemeine Geschichte* (Darmstadt: Wissenschaftliche Buchgesellschaft, 2007), to name but some of the more important recent works.

66. Today the practice is resembled in the common act of online submission; to a supervisor, a learned journal or a publisher; the difference being that nowadays the anonymous referees have taken over the role of the Catholic inquisitors.

67. Original: 'mit Ausnahme der Schrift Luthers Über den Wucher, das interessanteste, was uns in nationalökonomischer Beziehung aus der Reformationsperiode erhalten ist.' Schmoller, 'Zur Geschichte der national-ökonomischen Ansichten', 492.

68. An excellent analytical introduction to the historical school in economics as part of the *Alteuropäische Gegenpol* is to be found in the joint work by historian Burkhardt and economist Priddat: Johannes Burkhardt and Birger P. Priddat, eds, *Geschichte der Ökonomie* (Frankfurt:

history, led by venerable men such as Leopold von Ranke (1795–1886), Johann Gustav Droysen (1808–1884), Heinrich von Sybel (1817–1895) or Heinrich von Treitschke (1834–1896), who laid the foundations, amongst many other things, of the technique of historical objectivism and critical source interpretation (*Hermeneutik, Historische Methode*), parts of which have stayed with us, informing historical scholarship to-date.[69] As the historical school in economics, their approach was strictly inductive – up to a point where an extreme, and from the modern viewpoint untenable, position emerged: to 'tell about things in the past as they had really been', as Ranke would occasionally frame his methodological approach of historical positivism.[70] As historical deconstructivism and the cultural and many other 'turns' in the historical sciences since the 1970s have reminded us, such a Rankenian position seems naïve from a modern vantage point: we cannot *know* what happened. But we can try to reconstruct 'most likely' scenarios and get a better understanding of the past actors and their motivations by studying what these actors have left us in written and non-written sources, material (documents; artefacts, such as coins) as well as immaterial (customs, institutions, fairy tales and myths).

All their mishaps apart, the two German historical schools (in history as well as economics) have left us with at least three lessons that are of almost timeless importance: first, *idiosyncrasy* matters. We cannot understand events, structures or forms of human (inter)action and agency without considering their peculiar location in time, space and society. In other words, context matters. Second, this insight should prevent us from using *deductive* or – more extremely – *predictive* models for describing phenomena that are by definition *contingent*, that is which cannot possibly lend themselves to any sort of determinism or, worse, prediction. The Anglo-Saxon epistemology in economics has rested upon the latter very much (see above); it has reigned more or less supreme in the economics discipline for the following two centuries, with some exceptions. Scottish economic thought for instance is sometimes said to have remained more empirical-inductive,[71] but we must, of course, remember always that the foundations of the

---

Deutscher Klassiker Verlag, 2009), 645–72 (in the following, whenever 'Frankfurt' is given as place of publication, reference will be to Frankfurt-on-the-Main). An account of this school's survival in twentieth-century economics is provided in Bertram Schefold, 'Der Nachklang der historischen Schule in Deutschland zwischen dem Ende des zweiten Weltkriegs und dem Anfang der sechziger Jahre', in Karl Acham, Knut Wolfgang Nörr and Bertram Schefold, eds, *Erkenntnisgewinne, Erkenntnisverluste. Kontinuitäten und Diskontinuitäten in den Wirtschafts-, Rechts- und Sozialwissenschaften zwischen den 20er und 50er Jahren* (Stuttgart: Franz Steiner, 1998), 31–70.

69. A good recent anthology and introduction can be found in Fritz Stern and Jürgen Osterhammel, eds, *Moderne Historiker. Klassische Texte von Voltaire bis zur Gegenwart* (Munich: Beck, 2011), which is a revised update of Fritz Stern, ed., *The Varieties of History. From Voltaire to the Present* (New York: Meridian, 1956). On Ranke, see Osterhammel and Stern, eds, *Moderne Historiker*, 91–102. A useful recent survey is Stefan Jordan, *Theorien und Methoden der Geschichtswissenschaft. Orientierung Geschichte* (Paderborn: Schöningh, 2009), 39–61.

70. For example, Rudolf Vierhaus, 'Rankes Begriff der historischen Objektivität,' in Reinhart Koselleck, Wolfgang J. Mommsen and Jörn Rüsen, eds, *Objektivität und Parteilichkeit in der Geschichtswissenschaft* (Munich: Deutscher Taschenbuchverlag, 1977), 63–76.

71. See, for example, A. L. Macfie, 'The Scottish Tradition in Economic Thought', *Scottish Journal of Political Economy* (June, 1955), repr. in Douglas Mair, ed., *The Scottish Contribution to Modern Economic Thought* (Aberdeen: Aberdeen University Press, 1990), 1–18.

modern deductive paradigm were, if unintentionally, actually laid by Scotsmen, above all A. Smith in his *Wealth of Nations*. Third, economics should be ethical, that is based on *perspective*. Ethical goals and strategies cannot be derived from a standpoint outside the system of economic analysis; values, goals and aims are a constitutional part of the system and must be explicitly formulated so as to make the models work. No system can be ultimately value-free, that is fully objective.[72] Nor can – and this would be even worse – value judgements, such as friendship and love and ethical stances in general, be derived from an economic standpoint à la G. Becker and rational choice theory.

The 'German' tradition or historical school, representing the cornerstones of what has been called *der Altökonomische Gegenpol*[73] or the 'Other Canon'[74] in more recent years, was well aware of this. But it got subsequently lost as a paradigm in modern economics. This is one of the likely reasons why writers such as Luther were, after the 1860s, when Schmoller and Roscher produced their grand accounts on the history of political economy, not usually studied under an economist's epistemology. There appeared two commented German editions of the present pamphlet after 1945, one joint effort by historian Burkhardt and economist Priddat (1990) directed at a general historical readership[75]; the other one in the Vademecum series on pre-classical economic ideas edited by H. C. Recktenwald (1987) addressing primarily economists and scholars working on political economy.[76] In the nineteenth century, it was Schmoller and the Leipzig economist Roscher (1817–1894) who provided detailed analyses not only of Luther's oeuvre but also of 'Reformation' (i.e. sixteenth-century) economics in general.[77] Twentieth-century renderings of Luther's text in English, based on Charles M. Jacobs' 1931 translation in vol. 4 of the 'Old' or Holman Philadelphia edition of Luther's works[78] begun in 1915 and carried through to the University of Philadelphia multi-volume series of the 1960s,[79] have made the sermon *Von Kauffshandlung und Wucher* available for non-German speaking audiences. However, these editions were part of historical–theological projects and studies; the accompanying comments and notes were written by the general editors of the series and for an audience who had neither detailed knowledge nor much interest in placing Luther's ideas into a

---

72. See, for example, Peter Koslowski, ed., *The Theory of Ethical Economy in the Historical School: Wilhelm Roscher, Lorenz von Stein, Gustav Schmoller, Wilhelm Dilthey and Contemporary Theory* (Berlin: Springer, 1995).
73. Burkhardt and Priddat, eds, *Geschichte der Ökonomie*, 649.
74. For example, Reinert, *How Rich Countries Got Rich*, 1–100, and fig. 3 on p. 33, as well as *id.* and Arno Daastøl, 'The Other Canon: The History of Renaissance Economics. Its Role as an Immaterial and Production-based Canon in the History of Economic Thought and in the History of Economic Policy', in Erik S. Reinert, ed., *Globalization, Economic Development and Inequality: An Alternative Perspective* (Cheltenham: Edward Elgar, 2004), 21–70.
75. Burkhardt and Priddat, eds, *Geschichte der Ökonomie*.
76. Helmut Hesse and Gerhard Müller, eds, Über *Luthers 'Von Kauffshandlung und Wucher'. Vademecum zu einem frühen Klassiker der Weltliteratur* (Frankfurt: Verlag Wirtschaft und Finanzen, 1987).
77. Schmoller, 'Zur Geschichte der national-ökonomischen Ansichten', 558–67 (on usury and interest); 586–88 (on surety and credit), and *passim*.
78. *Works of Martin Luther*, vol. 4 (Philadelphia, PA: A. J. Holman/Castle Press, 1931).
79. Here: *Luther's Works, Vol. 45: Christian in Society II*, ed. Walther I. Brandt, gen. ed. Helmut T. Lehmann (Philadelphia, PA: University of Philadelphia Press, 1962).

general *economic* context. The mainstream in modern economics has largely forgotten about the German historical school, as well as earlier predecessors, such as Martin Luther (1483–1546), frequently even denying the pre-classical authors their pedigree in the family tree of economics and political economy as academic disciplines. This is a very peculiar aspect of how modern social science has evolved. Economics has often enough been labelled the 'queen' of sciences, dominating society and public discourse with its judgmental nature on markets, efficiency and productivity and its axiomatic assumptions which were often clouded into the protecting veal of asserted objectivity, purported exactness, mathematical expression and its corresponding complexity. By this the discipline of neoclassical economics has managed to attain a degree of mythical aloofness notwithstanding the fact that, based on the turnout rate of correct predictions of future scenarios (which has been depressingly low), it has, by and large, remained a fictional science which would find a more appropriate place perhaps in the company of equally creative arts, such as novel writing or cultural studies.

That does not mean that a science whose predictions are wrong is necessarily unscientific in any way or per se, as an important historian of economic thought has reminded us: 'In this respect it may perhaps be useful to recall that a system of concepts (which is the result of a specific process of abstraction, and which is utilized for simplified representation of a real world whose most essential characteristics are taken to have been captured) can be verified neither through direct comparison with the real world, nor by checking whether forecasts drawn from it actually come about.'[80] Science does not have to be fact-based. Ultimately, we should, following a Popperian epistemological rationale, constantly look out for the black swan – within an empirical world that knows only *white* ones. In other words we may rationalize, theorize and speculate about things that do not exist, or possible realities that are unknown to us due to a lack of *perspective*, observation or experience. Modern economics has done a pretty good job on this task. But since economics is more of an art than a science, and usually conceived as a toolkit directed at *practical* resource allocation in the light of multiple *real* budget and *real-world* behavioural constraints, economists should perhaps try at least every so often to approximate and come nearer to what we call reality (an admittedly treacherous concept), so as to help improve the resources available to everyone *here* and there and in the future (and leave speculation to philosophers and theoretical physicists, perhaps?). Therefore, it is obligatory to acknowledge that alternative views and theories *were* available in the past; alternatives which were not necessarily better or worse, but which simply reflected *differing*, if competing, viewpoints.[81] Luther's economics is a prime example of these alternatives. Therefore, it may be a timely occasion to engage in some Foucauldian archaeology of knowledge and dig out the wisdom that has been locked into the German language, once – but no longer – a lingua franca of the economics profession.

---

80. Alessandro Roncaglia, *The Wealth of Ideas. A History of Economic Thought* (Cambridge: Cambridge University Press, [2005] 2009), 17.
81. Ibid., chap. 1, drawing on theories developed by Kuhn and Lanakos. Roncaglia makes the useful distinction between a 'cumulative' and 'competitive' view in the history of economic reasoning.

We must start with the question: who was Luther, then? On this question, historians, theologians and social scientists have waged endless debates. Luther quickly turned into a celebrity from 1517 onwards. In his later days, when firmly established as a public figure at Wittenberg in the 1530s and early 1540s and habitually delivering his 'Table Talk', he had regular visitors from England and other foreign nations.[82] Not all of them were firm in the German tongue. Luther used this as a welcome occasion to digress and develop at length what his condensed views on the Christian in the world and other matters of salvation were. It has been suggested that anality would have been a fixation point in his life, as would his stoutness as a physical-praxeological trait[83], and that Luther could be studied using the methodological tools of psychoanalysis.[84] 'Masculine Luther' may well have suffered from general anxiety disorder as well as an over-dose of testosterone. But it remains yet to be established to what extent, say, a slimmer and more feminine, or less fearful and less clinically depressed character would have come to radically different conclusions about economy, society and theology. His repeated experiences of doubt and anxiety throughout various periods of his life, including his years as 'old Luther' in the 1530s and 1540s, are something which many adults share at least once or twice during their lifetime. To label such conditions either peculiar or decisive for the unfolding of events means, to an extent, over-stretching the historical evidence, as well as Luther the *human*. Whilst not wrong in any way, it does not lead to particularly new or fundamentally challenging insights. His sayings on women, particularly in his *Table Talk*[85] easily classify as misogynous, to say the least. But to read something such as a particular 'masculinity'[86] out of this would mean that this would have been either special or peculiar. In fact, it wasn't; Luther probably was an ordinary young man of his age who acted as could be expected, unfortunately, from an ordinary young man these days: masculine, in the praxeological sense of actively acting out a *role* that was expected from him as a 'strong' individual; the more so as he had to fight his position and stance as a reformer continuously throughout his later career as religious reformer at Wittenberg. Impulsive he was, too; very incoherent in his position at times; and definitely anti-Semitic and anti-Islamic, making him the perfect goal for the politically correct exercise of post-modern clobbering: for those sins of the twentieth century (racial anti-Semitism, totalitarian reasoning and general xenophobia) which he could not have possibly either foreseen or intended to commit himself. Luther never minced his words and he used

---

82. For example, *D. Martin Luther's Tischreden oder Colloquia*, ed. Johann Georg Walch (Halle, 1743), XIV, 14 (782).
83. Lyndal Roper, 'Martin Luther's Body: The "Stout Doctor" and His Biographers', *American Historical Review* (April, 2010), 351–84 (esp. 383s).
84. Erik H. Erikson, *Young Man Luther: A Study in Psychoanalysis and History* (London: Faber & Faber, 1958).
85. A good study in sixteenth-century misogyny is provided in the (later) collection of *Table Talk* anent marriage, for example, *Martin Luther's Tischreden V. Vom Ehestande* (Leipzig: Bibliographisches Institut, 1903), *passim*.
86. For example, Susan Karant-Nunn, '"Fast wäre mir ein weibliches Gemüt verblieben": Martin Luthers Männlichkeit,' in Hans Medick and Peter Schmidt, eds, *Luther zwischen den Kulturen* (Göttingen: Vandenhoeck & Ruprecht, 2004), 49–65.

violent and drastic language throughout, frequently verging on the uncouth.[87] There are also passages in his *Table Talk* in which he praises the virtue of the forefathers, who led a primitive agrarian life: 'As Doctor Martinus picked up a very juicy turnip, he went on, saying "Our Dear fathers must have been truly healthy people, living and feeding off the fruits and roots which the soil yielded, receiving all the food and drink they needed from those gifts the earth gave them. I believe Adam would much rather have liked fruit and vegetables than a partridge; these would have tasted him much better than roasted and boiled meats."'[88] But would this really make him a vegetarian in the modern sense?

Much rather Luther, with the present example, but also most other examples to be considered in more detail in the following passages, constructed an idealized version of a true Christian society. This was, above all, a blueprint, of which the underlying material or economic basis was a sort of idealized society in which, ironically, productivity levels and performance were the least things one should care about. Is this not something we can learn from Luther for today? After we have lived through an age of unlimited growth possibilities, roughly between 1945 and 1973, with continuing but lessening growth rates until the 2000s: is there anything that we can pick up from Luther's text, in a world where total factor productivity (TFP) increases have stopped? And chances of future economic growth seem more pessimistic than ever? Luther's model of agrarian society was tied to his overarching model of Christian society. And it was above all – and this is what many scholars interpreting Luther literally have failed to appreciate – a *model* (a theological one), but certainly not his *vision of reality*. If the latter was the case, this would indeed have made him a very naïve and ignorant man haunted by cognitive distortion. Thus, whilst recent historical research has found it more fashionable to interpret the history of the early Reformation and its actors in the light of how they clothed themselves,[89] how they acted out their bodies and masculinity and many more aspects,[90] the present work takes the freedom to adopt a likewise original approach by interpreting Luther as an economist. The previous aspects are also important for an economic interpretation of Luther's oeuvre; they have usually been missed by scholars engaged in the somewhat simplistic game of Luther-bashing for which Doctor Martinus represented an easy prey, especially when completely misunderstood. Many historians and social scientists have implied that Luther's economics and sociology were backward and primitive and that contemporary alternative models such as Augsburg merchant son and notary Dr Conrad Peutinger's, who in 1530 is said to have sketched a proto-Mandevillian and proto-Smithian view of the modern, functionally differentiated market economy ruled by self-interest as a virtue rather than vice (see above), would have been more clever or refined because their ideas were more akin to the modern paradigm in the social sciences (see below). Such interpretations, however, rest on a fundamental simultaneous misunderstanding

---

87. Especially in his pamphlets and replies when addressing his religious adversaries.
88. My own translation, based on *Tischreden I*, Meyers Volksbücher (Leipzig: Bibliographisches Institut, 1906), 50s.
89. For example, Ulinka Rublack, 'Grapho-Relics: Lutheranism and the Materialization of the Word', *Past & Present* 5 (2010), 144–66; *id.*, 'Matter in the Material Renaissance', *Past & Present*, May 2013, 41–84.
90. Roper, 'Martin Luther's Body'.

of Luther's general *theology*, as well as his *economics*. Subsequent sections will highlight in detail why the primitivism charge is fallacious. At present we must stress that care should be taken with value judgements, or interpreting too much of either post-modern theory (which has often enough evolved around feelings, sentiment, habit and the praxeological aspects of human behaviour and interaction), or worse, received wisdom from modern neoclassical economics on what is good and what is bad theory into texts that date from a half-millennium earlier, when both means and ends of economic reasoning were different from our modern ones. Everything Luther might have thought, meant and felt, that is *Luther's* reality, is irretrievably lost on us. And it would have been lost on his contemporaries, in the same way as we can grasp Gregory Mankiw's economics from Gregory Mankiw's textbook on economics, but what we cannot grasp exactly is how Gregory Mankiw thinks about economics, because that is something that will remain within the confines of Gregory Mankiw's admittedly extremely clever brain. Language is a hopelessly limited transmitter of emotion, meaning and feeling. But Luther had something to say which we may listen to and accordingly appreciate more carefully by trying to step back and unto the same level from which he operated. This means *approaching* the man on his own terms, as well as the idiosyncratic coordinates of time, space and society. This should be done using a sensible mix of source-based evidence, coupled with some historical and economic theory where appropriate, avoiding the usual theoretical overdose implicit in many a modern cultural, historical as well as economic study, but above all, a solid degree of common sense.

The present study thus takes the freedom to interpret Luther as an economist, without either suggesting that he *was* an economist (which would be quite frankly stupid) or insisting that an economist's interpretation would necessarily be the best, the most apt or the only feasible reference framework of interpreting that man (although admittedly tempting, this would clearly be hubris).

Plus ça change? Change and Progress in History and Political Economy

One last time we must address the concept of *change*. Even the most recent and clearly the best scholarly Luther biography still has it that Luther was someone who was wrestling with changes brought on by times that were 'new' – the mainstream view.[91] Earlier master narratives on the crossroads of economic theory, history and religion in the wake of Weber, Tawney or Alfred Müller-Armack had it as a matter of fact that the sixteenth-century was an era of *change* in what could be called 'economic style' (*Wirtschaftsstil*), that is economic outlook and perception (see above). This was the classic and yet evasive field of interaction between culture and economics as two poles of an ellipsis, divergent and yet symbiotically cooperative sources of historical dynamics manifested in the numerous discourses and metaphysical sketches and new configurations; Luther and the Reformation would have occupied centre stage within this process, as the reading

---

91. Schilling, *Martin Luther – Rebell in einer Zeit des Umbruchs.*

goes.[92] Whilst the notion of *economic style* had been developed as an explicit alternative to a more primitive and tautological notion of historical process as progressing sequences of economic stages, implying linear-mechanistic development (or synchronous asymmetries) of societies' wealth and *rafinesse* from (or between) developed and primitive, even alternative concepts as economic style (*Wirtschaftsstil*) have their problems, as they are as fundamentally based upon the epistemological concept of historical change as the older models which they were intended to repel. But as we have already seen earlier on, 'change' and 'new' are concepts which fall uneasily on the ears of many modern historians, to say the least. There are always changes somewhere; change is so basic a fact of human life and experience that it is almost not worth speaking about it. Chances are, if you are a professional historian on the lookout for change in historical times, that you'll find it, and quite easily so, anywhere you look for it. And if not – just look for it long enough and it will come to you eventually. But in order to understand Luther's contribution to European history and economic thought, it is important to understand *which* changes there were and *which* changes can be seen to have been relevant in terms of shaping *Luther's* experiences. And these were most certainly not the ones usually depicted in the traditional literature which saw the big combustion-like emergence of early capitalism in and around 1500 as the main blueprint against which Luther the Reformer operated. The virtues and pitfalls of this interpretation will be sketched in more detail in chapter 2. Many of the traditional accounts have sketched an imbalanced picture of the changes around 1500. Some of them seem plainly wrong, for example, when reiterating the somewhat shorthanded old hat that the time around 1470–1530 was a time of economic expansion (which it wasn't, at least not in terms of per capita GDP, the most commonly used definition of economic growth) and economic change (some structural change there was, but only partly, and mostly regionally limited).[93] Apart from the fact that population and general economic activity increased after the 1470s in Germany, as well as over most other parts of Europe, there was no real advance in per capita wealth and per capita resources in the German lands. Nor was there any marked or peculiarly visible transition to capitalism around 1500 that would explain Luther's verve in his writings directed at economic matters. Much of the 'early capitalism' myth of the twentieth century was based on Marxist historiography on the lookout for the earliest traces of a communist revolution (the so-called 'early bourgeois revolution', which was often modelled as a logical forerunner of the political revolutions in 1917).[94] What *does* come across, however, from the written record of the age, was a *change in focus* on capitalist practice as reflected, for instance, in the public debates and economic discourse of the day, of which Luther was an important part.

Then, of course, one must acknowledge, at least in passing, lest our Luther picture does get unduly biased, that Luther was neither the first nor the only, nor the last of

---

92. Müller-Armack, *Religion und Wirtschaft*, esp. 29–34.
93. See chapter 2 for a more detailed discussion.
94. An overview can be found in Matthias Middell, 'Marxistische Geschichtswissenschaft', in Joachim Eibach and Günther Lottes, eds, *Kompass der Geschichtswissenschaft. Ein Handbuch* (Göttingen: Vandenhoeck & Ruprecht, 2002), 69–82.

the 'Reformers'. Just think of Jan Hus in Bohemia in the early 1400s, who has been briefly discussed above; the medieval Cathars or other sixteenth-century 'big men' like Calvin, Zwingli, or John Knox. And within a larger global context, it perhaps does not matter so much that Luther stood up in 1517. As we speak, there are about 1.2 billion of practising Catholics in the world, representing more than one-half of total Christians, the other half of which are made up by adherents to the Reformed, the Orthodox and the Anglican and 'free' churches. Less than one-fifth are 'Reformed' or Protestant Christians, that is people we may identify as Lutheran in a wide sense. Not to speak of the other big faiths of the world, headed by Atheism, currently the biggest religion in the western world, at least according to the official censuses, followed by Islam, Judaism, Hinduism, or Buddhist Shintoism (which some say is not a religion). But whilst all such caveats are certainly in order, it cannot be doubted that for German history, as well as European history at large, the Reformation 1517 provided a critical juncture. And this must be borne in mind also when studying Luther's economics.

Adding Value: Bringing Ethics Back into Economic Analysis

Of course, Luther was no economist. But neither was Adam Smith. The latter was a moral philosopher. But whilst Smith is often hailed, especially in the Anglo-Saxon academic tradition, as the Godfather of modern economics, the idea that Luther would have made a similar contribution to European knowledge in economics obviously must seem strange, as is borne out by a very apparent lacuna in the literature on pre-Smithian economists. Only less than a handful of scholars, most of them either long-dead German or modern 'heterodox' economists,[95] would acknowledge that Luther wrote a handful of economic texts containing important insights that made a valuable contribution to the evolution of modern economic thought. Pribram, in his classical history of economic thought, was overall dismissive; he devoted exactly half a page to Luther, treating him, interestingly, within a chapter on *cameralist* economics, which he found, quite unsurprisingly, to have made no contribution of significance to modern economic thought.[96] Schumpeter, who wrote the most famous history of economics in the twentieth century, did not discuss Luther at all but conveyed great admiration for the scholastic authors and expressed some admiration of cameralist author Johann Heinrich Gottlob von Justi.[97] Blaug, who is said to have had similar aspirations as Pribram and Schumpeter as a historian of economic thought in the twentieth century, was either silent or dismissive on pre-classical

---

95. Schmoller and Roscher were amongst the major economists to study Luther. Odd Inge Langholm, 'Martin Luther's Doctrine on Trade and Price in Its Literary Context', *History of Political Economy* 41, no. 1 (2009), 89–107, is a good recent contribution. See also Helge Peukert, 'Martin Luther: A Modern Economist', in Jürgen G. Backhaus, ed., *The Reformation as a Precondition for Capitalism* (Münster: LIT Verlag, 2010), 13–63.

96. I have used the German edition: Karl Pribram, *Geschichte des ökonomischen Denkens*, vol. I (Frankfurt: Suhrkamp, 1994), 181.

97. Joseph A. Schumpeter, *History of Economic Analysis* (New York: Oxford University Press, 1954), 170–74.

theory, even though he, luckily, acknowledged that economic reasoning before Adam Smith had existed.[98]

Current undergraduate textbooks on the history of economic thought are usually even worse in their omissions of pre-classical authors, although that is probably due to the fact that they are directed at a non-specialist audience who will never have to deal with *historical* problems during their professional careers as businessmen and economists. Usually they will commence with Adam Smith or the physiocrats, or, if they discuss the mercantilist and cameralist authors at all, they will suggest, at least implicitly, that these did not matter for the history of the discipline, because their framework was either not theoretical (but a definition of what classifies as theoretical is usually missing) or their theory was not good enough, incoherent or incomplete. Only less than a handful will discuss scholastic authors and other contributions to pre-classical theory such as Platonic and Aristotelian economics in depth.[99] Many professional economists working on the

---

98. By editing compendiums of some scholarly articles that had appeared on pre-classical economics. See Mark Blaug, ed., *St. Thomas Aquinas (1225–1274)* and his three volumes on the mercantilist authors in *Pioneers in Economics* 6–8 (Aldershot, VT: E. Elgar, 1991).

99. As can be immediately grasped from a random browse of campus libraries. Agnar Sandmo, *Economics Evolving. A History of Economic Thought* (Princeton, NJ: Princeton University Press, 2011), has 467 pages on the evolution of economics, but only 17 on economics before Adam Smith, and 3 in total on the scholastic authors and the mercantilists (17–20); so we may assume that there cannot have been much of an evolution here? If there was one, it surely must have been akin to a spontaneous combustion, a Big Bang. The book also reiterates an age-old and by and large incorrect stance that mercantilism was no theory but an ideology and that it was centred on the ruler's needs and rent-seeking desires of some members of society. Recent research especially on cameralist economics has refuted this thesis convincingly – see previous footnotes. Roger Backhouse, *A History of Modern Economic Analysis* (London: Basil Blackwell, 1985), starts with Adam Smith; Horst Claus Recktenwald, *Geschichte der Politischen* Ökonomie. *Eine Einführung in Lebensbildern* (Stuttgart: Kröner, 1971), commences with Quesnay; Peter Rosner, *Die Entwicklung des* ökonomischen *Denkens. Ein Lernprozess* (Berlin: Duncker & Humblot, 2012) reiterates that mercantilist political economy was no theory but just a formulation of *Partikularinteressen* (69) and presents the somewhat astonishing finding (in the light of recent advances in the field) that the mercantilists had no concept of the economy as a whole ('Analysen der gesamten Wirtschaft gibt es hingegen nicht', 69) assuming moreover that there was progress in economic theory. The title of the book gives it away: a *Lernprozess*. And if progress existed, surely mercantilist and most other pre-classical thought was 'less good' than more modern theories. Another major undergraduate textbook in German, Fritz Söllner, *Geschichte des* ökonomischen *Denkens* (Berlin: Springer, 1999) has a few pages on the cameralists and mercantilists (10–18, i.e. 8 out of a total of 328), suggesting the cameralists created 'no theoretical insights' ('Wenngleich die Kameralisten keine grundlegenden theoretischen Erkenntnisse hervorgebracht haben…', 18). The book by Heinz D. Kurz is as short as the author by name: *Geschichte des ökonomischen Denkens* (Munich: Beck, 2013), as are the passages therein on mercantilism (4 out of 124 pages). It argues that the mercantilists never achieved systematic or coherent theoretical reasoning (19), but that is again quite at variance with recent research on the history of political economy. A more balanced account on mercantilism and cameralism as systematic and theoretical disciplines can be found in Gerhard Kolb, *Geschichte der Volkswirtschaftslehre. Dogmenhistorische Positionen des ökonomischen Denkens*, 2nd ed. (Munich: Vahlen, 2004), 15–36, and in Bernd Ziegler, *Geschichte des ökonomischen Denkens. Paradigmenwechsel in der Volkswirtschaftslehre*, 2nd ed. (Munich: Oldenbourg, 2008), 45–51. Toni Pierenkemper, *Geschichte*

history of political economy are nowadays well aware of the rich legacy of pre-Smithian economic thought; however, due to the shorthanded nature of most textbooks, this means that a significant chunk of young professionals working in business will never be given the opportunity to discover that alternatives existed, even rival theories, an 'Other Canon' so to speak, and that some of the key axiomatic taught in modern undergraduate economics curricula is either fictional, sometimes wrong or generally unsuitable to model current economic phenomena. As mentioned before, nineteenth-century economists were somewhat more attentive and mostly German, which is partly understandable if one traces the different development paths of the continental economies, as well as their history of ideas, which were different from the Anglo-Saxon path towards the industrial economy.[100] Roscher devoted a whole section to Luther's *Kauffshandlung* in his *Geschichte der National-Oekonomik in Deutschland* (1874),[101] as did Schmoller in his book-length article on economic ideas during the Reformation in the *Zeitschrift für die gesamte Staatswissenschaft* (1860), one of the still-existing and most venerable journals in the economic sciences, but nowadays aptly renamed *Journal of Institutional and Theoretical Economics*.[102] Even Marxist political economy had a place reserved for Luther, earmarking him as the 'first bourgeois economist', simultaneously acknowledging Luther's fundamentally anti-capitalist and apparent backward-orientated attitude.[103] This view classified him, somewhat pejoratively, as *petit bourgeois*, which in Marxist theory was even worse than straight bourgeois (the true capitalist will stand for and act according to his class position; the petit bourgeois is awkward in his behaviour as his economic position is more akin to the working class, whilst in his aspiration and praxeology he usually tries to mimic the bourgeois). Burkhardt and Priddat, in the recent commented edition of pre-classical German economic texts (2000),[104] represent one shining exception. They begin their edition with an eighteenth-century version (in modernized German) of Luther's *Kaufshandlung* by J. Walch, excluding

---

des modernen ökonomischen Denkens. Große Ökonomen und ihre Ideen (Göttingen: Vandenhoeck & Ruprecht, 2012), is also very wise and critical towards the idea of progress in the economic sciences, but after the excellent introduction and a brief treatment of pre-classical economics gives up the discussion of pre-Smithian economics completely, because, as the author says, the material environment (industrialization) changed so decisively around 1800 so as to give way for a completely changed epistemology in the economic sciences. Again this is somewhat at variance with recent studies in the history of political economy. Pierenkemper suggests that texts and theories must be placed in their idiosyncratic context and evaluated using appropriate benchmarks. And that is a very valuable insight. Many works still treat the mercantilists within the same chapter or section as the physiocrats, as in Karl-Heinz Schmidt, 'Merkantilismus, Kameralismus, Physiokratie', in Otmar Issing, ed., *Geschichte der Nationalökonomie*, 4th ed. (Munich: Vahlen, 2002), 37–66 which does violence to both physiocracy and mercantilist epistemology.

100. Reinert, *How Rich Countries Got Rich*.

101. Wilhelm Roscher, *Geschichte der Nationaloekonomik in Deutschland* (Munich, 1874).

102. Gustav (von) Schmoller, 'Zur Geschichte der national-ökonomischen Ansichten in Deutschland während der Reformations-Periode', *Zeitschrift für Gesamte Staatswissenschaft*, 16 (1860), 461–716.

103. Günter Fabiunke, *Martin Luther als Nationalökonom* (Berlin/East: Akademie Verlag, 1963), 153–57 and introduction.

104. Burkhardt and Priddat, eds, *Geschichte der Ökonomie*.

the *Sermon on Usury*, delivered in 1520, as well as the 1524 addition or part III of the pamphlet which are all presented in this volume (see below). Apart from these works cited, Luther's views on economics are featured chiefly in scholarly monographs on business ethics, a discipline which has, until recently, been dominated by a theological, rather than economic, perspective.[105]

This long lacuna of scholarly attention is more significant as in Luther's time some important economic ideas began to form. Apart from the concept of national income or GDP in terms of measurable units or variables, they seem to have comprised most key elements of the modern economic sciences. Just consider the pamphlets on monetary theory written by authors such as Prussian cathedral canon Nikolaus Koppernigk (*Copernicus*, 1473–1543), Saxon metallurgist Georg Pawer or Bauer (better known by his Latinized name *Agricola* 1494–1555), Tübingen academic theologian Gabriel Biel (c.1415–1495) or the Spanish theologians of the Salamanca school. In 1530–31 an anonymous Saxon pamphlet identified flexible exchange rates by means of currency debasement as a way of stimulating export-led growth – a neo-mercantilist and twentieth-century argument which most straight scholastic and contemporary mercantilists of the seventeenth and eighteenth century would have rather abhorred.[106] Ideas about economic policy emerged in the early sixteenth century that went beyond mere social control and supervision of the common good, including proto-mercantilist strategies of reconfiguring the productive landscape, for instance, by a strategic design of import and export duties and other measures addressed at what would later be called import substitution and infant industry protection, as in Giovanni Boteros *Della ragione di stato*, 1589.[107] More flexible attitudes towards the taking of interest developed. The idea of capital as a productive factor emerged.[108] First traces of what we may call development economics and proto-mercantilism can be found in the present text written by Luther in 1524 also (see analysis in chapter 5). In many ways the economic understanding of

---

105. For example, Hans-Jürgen Prien, *Luthers Wirtschaftsethik* (Göttingen: Vandenhoeck & Ruprecht, 1992). Helpful but also slightly muddled works on Luther's ethics include Ricardo Rieth, *'Habsucht' bei Martin Luther: ökonomisches und theologisches Denken, Tradition und soziale Wirklichkeit in der Reformation* (Weimar: Böhlau, 1996), Philipp Koch, *Gerechtes Wirtschaften: das Problem der Gerechtigkeit in der Wirtschaft im Lichte lutherischer Ethik* (Göttingen: V & R unipress, 2012), and Andreas Pawlas, *Die lutherische Berufs- und Wirtschaftsethik: Eine Einführung* (Neukirchen: Neukirchner Verlag, 2000).

106. Philipp Robinson Rössner, 'Mercantilism as an Effective Resource Management Strategy: Money in the German Empire, c. 1500–1800', in Moritz Isenmann, ed., *Merkantilismus. Wiederaufnahme einer Debatte* (Stuttgart: Franz Steiner, 2014), 39–64. See also Bertram Schefold, 'Wirtschaft und Geld im Zeitalter der Reformation', in *id.*, ed., *Vademecum zu drei klassischen Schriften frühneuzeitlicher Münzpolitik* (Düsseldorf: Verlag Wirtschaft und Finanzen, 2000), 5–58; also Roscher, *Geschichte der Nationaloekonomik*, 102–6; Hans-Joachim Stadermann, *Der Streit um gutes Geld in Vergangenheit und Gegenwart. Enthaltend drei Flugschriften über den Münzstreit der sächsischen Albertiner und Ernestiner um 1530 nach der Ausgabe von Walther Lotz* (1893) (Tübingen, Mohr Siebeck: 1999).

107. Schefold, 'Wirtschaft und Geld im Zeitalter der Reformation'; Reinert, *How Rich Countries Got Rich*.

108. Francesco Boldizzoni, *Means and Ends: The Idea of Capital in the West, 1500–1970* (Basingstoke: Palgrave Macmillan, 2008), chap. 1.

the sixteenth century still remained vested in medieval scholastic economics, which was a science embedded within a moral-religious understanding of the world informed by the Christian faith. But some of the contributions now attained a different shape, representing a departure from medieval economic theory which had been more concerned with retaining static equilibrium, evolving towards a concept which had an eye for economic expansion and dynamism. Luther was part of this scholarly tradition. But in many ways, he formulated his own stance and very distinct view. He cannot, therefore, be classified as a straight scholastic author, partly because he denied to be that himself (he had a very pejorative view on scholastic theology), partly because a lot of high and later medieval scholasticism was axiomatically more abstract, even deductive, than Luther's theory. He would have called the scholastic authors 'sophists'. But then it would surely be hyperbolic to say that late medieval scholasticism was more sophisticated as an economic and social theory than Luther's ideas on business ethics and economics, because that would represent a misunderstanding of Luther's goals and intentions (see below). Luther was after something else. His economics was much more direct, much more *impulsive* as an economist than the late medieval schoolmen, who appear from their writings to have developed quite a rationalistic and abstract notion of the economy within their general and still soteriologically framed concepts of price formation and the taking of interest. They actually seem to have been quite laissez faire and market friendly if modern terms are allowed.[109] But they had been – in Luther's view – corrupted by the market. His debate with Catholic churchman Johannes Eck in 1514 about the legitimacy of a general interest rate ceiling in the order of 5 per cent p.a. is characteristic of that. The scholastic authors had taken ways and means of bending Scripture to fit it with changing conditions on the financial markets. They had adjusted the interpretation of Scripture to changing economic conditions. Luther wouldn't have that.

Luther's works then, assembled in the *Weimarer Ausgabe* (WA), begun in 1883 and completed in 2009, comprise 127 volumes with a total page count running up to 80,000 pages and accordingly a word count of several hundred million words; much of it comments and editorial notes. Those works Luther wrote specifically on economic matters, on the other hand, comprise two sermons on usury (the 'little' one in 1519 and the 'great' one in 1520 which was added to the 1524 pamphlet on merchants and commerce, thus 'Commerce and Usury' 1524), his *Sermon on Commerce and Usury* (1524) – the work under consideration – and his late admonition to the Saxon pastors to preach against usury (*Vermahnung an die Pfarrherren, wider den Wucher zu predigen*, 1540). But he discussed economic questions in many other works, such as his 1520 address 'To the Christian Nobility of the German Nation' (*An den Christlichen Adel Deutscher Nation*) or in his writings directed at the rebellious peasants in 1525. Only the above-mentioned works were *specifically* concerned with economic questions, especially usury and the taking of interest. They comprise barely about two hundred pages in modern typesetting (in the

---

109. Raymond de Roover, 'Scholastic Economics: Survival and Lasting Influence from the Sixteenth Century to Adam Smith', *The Quarterly Journal of Economics*, LXIX (1955), 161–90 is still useful.

Weimarer Ausgabe) including comments. In other words, they seem negligible, compared to what Luther had to say as a theologian.

In Luther's times, however, no one would have differentiated between theologian and economist. Separating the two would have seemed strange if not perverse. Economic activity was embedded in theology. The successful businessman constantly had one foot in purgatory if not hell almost by default, especially whenever his speculative tricks and operations went over the top. Medieval businessmen such as the merchant from Prato Francesco Datini actually included special accounts devoted towards spiritual salvation within their business ledgers; when closing their books the overall balance would also feature payments made to God and the Angels. And by definition, following canon or church law, this going-over-the-top happened practically every day, if you were a successful and vigorous entrepreneur driven by the need to succeed (if not, you were neither vigorous nor successful, nor a real businessman). And since, in a similar way as today, economics and business invariably involved legal disputes and law courts, a lot of sixteenth-century economic knowledge was also formulated by lawyers in spontaneous statements, rulings and expert opinions, mostly on the fulfilment of contracts, often evolving around changing monetary values of the currencies specified within a specific contract, which was an important problem within the larger framework of institutions stabilizing expectations and safeguarding property rights in commerce and economy; the usury problem was part of it.[110] Luther himself had been on his way towards a higher degree in law before everything changed in 1505. But strikingly all major texts on economics in the late Middle Ages, to which we may for convenience count the sixteenth century (in the German lands there was no early modern in the way of life until late in the century) came out of theologians' hands. Only in 1727, the first university chairs in economics ever to be established in Europe or the wider world were founded in Germany, in cameralist science, by the somewhat psychopathic father of Frederick the Great, soldier-king Frederick William I of Prussia (1688–1740), at the enlightened University of Halle near Leipzig and Frankfurt-on-the-Oder.[111]

Thus in the Middle Ages and the early modern period, it was above all theologians who framed the economic ideas that built Europe. These were churchmen such as Thomas Aquinas (1225–1274), Bernardino di Siena (1380–1444), German scholastic Gabriel Biel or the mid-sixteenth-century theologians at Salamanca, amongst whom Luis Ortiz or Martín de Azpilcueta (1492–1586) are the most famous. They blended a rich legacy of ancient Greek, Christian, Judaist and Islamic economic thought into a late bloom of medieval social, general economic and monetary theory.[112] Some historians, including Raymond de Roover

---

110. Thomas J. Sargent and François R. Velde, *Big Problem of Small Change* (Princeton, N.J.: Princeton University Press, 2002).

111. Anton Schindling, *Bildung und Wissenschaft in der frühen Neuzeit, 1650–1800* (Munich: Oldenbourg, 1994), 41.

112. Marjorie Grice-Hutchinson, *The School of Salamanca. Readings in Spanish Monetary Theory 1544–1605* (Oxford: Clarendon Press, 1952), esp. 40–59 and texts 79–120; Ead, 'Martin de Azpilcuetas "Comentario resolutorio de Cambios"', in Bertram Schefold, ed., *Vademecum zu zwei Klassikern des Spanischen Wirtschaftsdenkens* (Düsseldorf: Verlag Wirtschaft und Finanzen, 1998), 49–72; Marjorie Grice-Hutchinson, *Early Economic Thought in Spain 1170–1740* (London: Allen & Unwin, 1978), esp. 91–107. Ead, 'Contributions of the School of Salamanca to

and Marjorie Grice-Hutchinson, even called the Salamanca theologians the founders of modern economic theory.[113] Some institutions, events, structures and conjunctures helped in the process. Sixteenth-century economics was taught and researched as an integral part of a theological curriculum. It was so for a reason. Not only did it correspond to the mercantile desire of the age to legitimize and whitewash all sorts of financial and commercial activity, such as currency arbitrage (including coin usury, *Münzwucher*, and transactions on bills of exchange) and the taking of interest. The sixteenth century was also a century of economic and financial expansion. It saw the onset of the so-called globalization. The Spanish doctors accordingly had to come to terms with a somewhat altered commercial and economic landscape, especially in the wake of Spain's imperial expansion in the Americas and the resulting gigantic inflows (and quick outflows) of silver into and out of the Spanish realms. Likewise, the analytical separation of human spheres of agency, interaction and matters of governance into the realms of theology, economics, politics, sociology, etc. is a modern fiction, mostly a child of the European enlightenment and its peculiar understanding of academic science and knowledge management. This paradigm broke with an older one that entertained different strategies of knowledge management and curricula of academic science. To what extent this loss of precarious knowledge in the course of the enlightenment was a uniformly or a net positive thing on balance is still a matter of debate.[114] But more importantly to an academic in the thirteenth, fourteenth, fifteenth and sixteenth centuries, economic questions were ultimately morally embedded and soteriologically framed. They always related in one way or another to the bigger question of the individual's position before God. What you did you should not do purely for pleasure or self-interest; striving for profit for profit's sake or following efficiency rationales of maximizing benefit and minimizing input (the modern principles of economic analysis). Rather it should be in accordance with the ethical principles as laid out in Scripture. This is something modern economics and business administration have shed in their epistemology; there is little ethics in economics (but a lot of economics in ethics, as a long-popular stance in the social sciences had it following the recently deceased Gary S. Becker[115]). We entertain the concept of economics as a thing that is separated from its idiosyncratic conditions of time, space and morals. We also, sometimes, believe that morals are something which economics not only cannot but also should not deal with. It is, of course, left to the reader to decide which side to take. But Luther's oeuvre will suggest that a modern economic determinism is dangerously shorthanded. Here we find some aspects where the modern economic sciences may actually learn something from Luther.

Monetary Theory as a Result of the Discovery of the New World', in ead, *Economic Thought in Spain. Selected Essays*, ed. Laurence S. Moss and Christopher K. Ryan (Aldershot: E. Elgar, 1993) 1–22, and her essay on 'The Concept of the School of Salamanca: Its Origins and Development', ibid., 23–29 on the position of the Salamanca economists as a distinct 'school'.

113. Moss and Ryan, eds, *Selected Essays*, editors' introduction, xxiii, referring to a personal letter by Grice-Hutchinson. Roover, 'Scholastic Economics'.

114. Martin Mulsow, *Prekäres Wissen: Eine andere Ideengeschichte der Frühen Neuzeit* (Berlin: Suhrkamp, 2012).

115. Gary S. Becker, *The Economic Approach to Human Behavior* (Chicago, IL: University of Chicago Press, 1976).

Chapter 2

CONTEXTUALIZING LUTHER: THE POWERS OF TIME AND SPACE

The Powers of Space

Two things must be noted when locating Luther in the idiosyncratic coordinates of his times and space. First, he was an agrarian man. He spent the majority of his career as a reformer in Wittenberg. Wittenberg was located in the north-west of Saxony, in the *Kurkreis* or electoral Saxony – there were two Saxon territories, one ruled by the duke and the other by the elector – that is the part of the Saxon lands which had by far the largest share of grain sales in total Saxon government revenue at the time (if we may interpret revenue accounts as reflective of this area's stage of development and structure of economic activity).[1] The area produced regular grain supplies that were used in provisioning those parts of Saxony further to the south-west, in the Erzgebirge Mountains, where employment and production were geared towards non-agrarian activities, mainly mining. Here, in the Erzgebirge Mountains and its offshoots, native grain production had for a long term proved unable to keep up with the surging demand for foodstuffs. This was due to the structural changes in this area which saw increasing numbers of people emerge outside the agrarian sector. At Luther's times day after day whole caravans of carts loaded with grain would ply Saxon roads southward from the northern areas, passing through Grimma near Leipzig[2] and other staging posts where the Saxon rulers levied the *Geleit* payment, a convoy duty, leaving us with an ample record of quantitative sources documenting the frequency and intensity of domestic transport patterns.[3] Thus, the areas in need were relieved from those areas with a grain surplus. In 1525 circa 3,500 carts with teams of up to 14,000 horses and oxen carrying a total of perhaps 8,000 tons of grain passed through the Saxon *Geleit* or toll of Borna to the south of Leipzig, bound for the Erzgebirge Mountains. At conservative estimates, assuming an average per capita consumption of 200 kilograms of grain per annum, these grain supplies may

1. Figures from 1580 in Uwe Schirmer, 'Teil F 3.4. Ertragsstrukturen der kursächsischen Ämter 1580 (Map)', in: Landesvermessungsamt Sachsen, ed., *Atlas zur Geschichte und Landeskunde von Sachsen* (Dresden, 2006). These figures are, of course, tentative, due to the nature of statistical capture in sixteenth-century government documents.
2. Uwe Schirmer, *Das Amt Grimma 1485–1548. Demographische, wirtschaftliche und soziale Verhältnisse in einem kursächsischen Amt am Ende des Mittelalters und zu Beginn der Neuzeit* (Beucha: Sax Verlag, 1996).
3. Manfred Straube, 'Zum überregionalen und regionalen Warenverkehr im thüringisch-sächsischen Raum, vornehmlich in der ersten Hälfte des 16. Jahrhunderts', unpublished Diss. Phil. B (=*Habilitationsschrift*), 4 vols (Leipzig, 1981).

have nourished about 40,000 non-peasants, that is people following an occupation in the mines and related branches outside agriculture.[4] These figures need to be set in context. Within a world that was still profoundly agrarian, with the share of people living on and off the land at anywhere between 80 and 90 per cent, depending upon the respective region within the German lands, the mining regions were exceptional, inasmuch as they were significantly more urbanized and industrial than any other region and district in contemporary Germany. Its 40,000 people would have been about four-and-a-half times the population of large mining towns such as St Annaberg in the Saxon Erzgebirge Mountains or about seven times the population of Leipzig. Around 1500 St Annaberg was Saxony's largest city (at about 9,000 inhabitants), followed by Leipzig which by that time had already acquired a reputation as one of the larger supra-regional markets and fair cities of Germany. Most towns in the central German lands ranged from about 2,000 to 3,000 inhabitants (such as the residential country town of Mansfeld, where Luther grew up). Moreover the early 1500s were a time of depression in the Saxon mining region, as recent data on silver mining assembled by the late John Munro demonstrate and which will receive more detailed consideration below. So the grain trade figures of 1525 – which was also the main year of the German Peasants' War (1524–26) – likely reflect a low or dip in overall trading conditions. During the boom years of the Saxon silver-mining cycle in the 1470s and 1480s and then again during the 1530s, the amounts of grain and other goods intended to supply the Saxon mining regions with the essentials of daily life surely would have been higher. It is clear that such figures are above all impressionistic. Yet they serve to provide us with the rough dimensions. A significant share of the central German working population had become dis-imbedded from the surrounding countryside and agrarian economy and had to be catered for using regular supplies from outside their regional economic system. This pattern of division of labour and structural–economic change, triggered by the silver-mining boom of the 1470s and 1480s, must have left an imprint not only on the regions under consideration here, which by means of trade became connected and integrated into the emerging global economy of the day, but also on young Martin Luther. The needs, causes and effects of trade as a means of clearing markets, equalizing demand and supply and achieving general connectivity would have been quite obvious to many around 1500.

Strikingly, Luther also knew the other side of the coin: the area where the grain of the *Kurkreis* actually went to. This would have been a more urban industrial world, which is equally important for locating him in time and space. He spent his early years – and protracted periods later on – within a *mining region*. Recent research has identified mining

---

4. Manfred   Straube,   'Nahrungsmittelbedarf,   Nahrungsmittelproduktion   und Nahrungsmittelhandel im Thüringisch-Sächsischen Raum zu Beginn des 16. Jahrhunderts', in Herwig Ebner *et al.*, eds, *Festschrift Othmar Pickl zum 60. Geburtstag* (Graz: Leykam, 1987), 579–88 (582). *Id.*, 'Notwendigkeiten, Umfang und Herkunft von Nahrungsmittellieferungen in das sächsische Erzgebirge zu Beginn des 16. Jahrhunderts', in Ekkehard Westermann, ed., *Bergbaureviere als Verbrauchszentren im vorindustriellen Europa. Fallstudien zu Beschaffung und Verbrauch von Lebensmitteln sowie Roh- und Hilfsstoffen (13–18. Jahrhundert)* (Stuttgart: Franz Steiner, 1997), 203–21 (203–4; 208–9). The figure for grain consumption has been taken from Eberhard Isenmann, *Die Deutsche Stadt im Mittelalter 1150–1550* (Cologne: Böhlau, 2014), 979.

regions as a very peculiar if not entirely unusual type of economic, social and cultural configuration, with all their idiosyncratic socio-cultural and economic dynamics[5] that will be teased out in more detail in the sections that follow. The central European mining region comprised of the Erzgebirge Mountains around the Vogtland area, reaching further south into Thuringia, where not only the silver and copper mines but also more importantly the large industrial production complexes usually known as the *Saigerhütten* were located. *Saiger* huts or cupellation plants were larger factory-like complexes where argentiferous copper slate mined from the regional shafts of the area was chemically separated into its components of pure copper and silver. At Luther's time around 50 per cent of the total silver supply in Europe came from this region, that is Saxony–Thuringia, if we further include the Harz Mountains to the west. The remainder of the German and central European silver came from Tyrolean mines, some minor ventures in the Vosges Mountains, as well as Bohemian *Joachimsthal* (today Jàchymov) and some locations in Upper Hungary.[6] These regions were the world's chief source of the white metal; the South American mines had not been tapped to full potential yet. All eyes were on this focal region within the heartlands of the Holy Roman Empire. As silver was a valuable economic resource as well as the main monetary input for European currency circulation, the central European mining region of Saxony–Thuringia stood in the focus of the international economy and the emerging global trades and payments. This contrast – agrarian vs. industrial – must have left a deep imprint on Luther's mind. He would also have been struck by the consequences of early globalization which manifested itself in many branches and areas of daily life. Many of his writings, sermons and pamphlets convey, if in passing, an underlying tension between agrarian life and a more traditional informal economy of obligation, on the one hand, and raw industrial and financial capitalism, if we may use the word, on the other hand.

Young Luder and the Question of Economic Underdevelopment

Luder was his proper surname; only after 1512 did he begin to refer to himself as *Eleutherios* or 'Luther' using the Greek term for 'The Liberated One'. We will use *Luther* throughout for matters of simplifying things. He was born in 1483 in the small town of Eisleben in the County of Mansfeld, located within the present-day German federal state of Saxony-Anhalt. Later on he would stylize himself as someone who was born of peasant stock and origin; simple folk so to speak.[7] In the light of recent historical and archaeological research into his parents' house at Mansfeld which has enabled us to reconstruct the material patterns of

---

5. An excellent conceptual and empirical analysis is Angelika Westermann, *Die vorderösterreichischen Montanregionen in der Frühen Neuzeit* (Stuttgart: Franz Steiner, 2009), esp. chap. 1.
6. Ekkehard Westermann, 'Zur Silber- und Kupferproduktion Mitteleuropas vom 15. bis zum frühen 17. Jahrhundert', *Der Anschnitt* 5–6 (1986), 187–211. A recent synopsis and critical re-evaluation of existing output data can be found in John Munro, 'The Monetary Origins of the "Price Revolution"', in Dennis O. Flynn, Arturo Giráldez and Richard von Glahn, eds, *Global Connections and Monetary History, 1470–1800* (Aldershot: Ashgate, 2003), 1–34.
7. For example, Heinz Schilling, *Aufbruch und Krise: Deutschland, 1517–1648*, pbk ed. (Berlin: Siedler, 1988), 90.

consumption and living in the Luder household,[8] we must acknowledge that his was less than half the truth. His parents had been quite well-off apparently, and not strictly speaking of peasant stock – any more, that is. In fact, Luther was born into a family that had experienced the phenomenon of social mobility. Shortly before his birth in 1483, his family had relocated from the village of Möhra near Eisenach in Thuringia. His father Hans Luder was a mining entrepreneur in the Mansfeld mining district, who had risen from quite modest ranks. But he died leaving some wealth of more than 2,500 Rhenish florins. This sum certainly reflected no phenomenal level of wealth; however, neither did it exactly correspond to the economic capabilities of the *usual* or average peasant or full-time farmer household of the time.[9]

Young Martin received a solid primary and secondary education at a small municipal Latin school in Mansfeld, a small town and capital of the County of the same name, between 1490 and 1497. To him, as many others, these days were an age of fear and doubt, partly because of a general millenarian fear towards 'y1.5k'. Round dates such as 1500 AD always carried a thorough portion of fearful anticipation. What would come: the end of times? The Anti-Christ? 'A right and proper Hell and Purgatory our school was,' Luther recalled, 'where we would be tortured without really learning anything, for all the hitting, shivering, fear and lament.'[10] His schooling years and early adulthood coincided with the end of the post-1470 mining boom in central Europe, which will be discussed below. He moved on to Magdeburg in 1496 or 1497, to become one of the *Brethren of the Common Life*. In 1501 he was admitted to the University of Erfurt, by then a city that formally belonged to the Archbishopric of Mainz, but which effectively was under the control of the Saxon dukes. At Erfurt he studied for a liberal arts degree, including grammar, rhetoric, dialectics, arithmetic, music and astronomy. After finishing his MA in 1505 he continued, following his father's wishes, to study law. But in this very same summer, in July 1505 upon his way back to Erfurt from his parents' house in Mansfeld, he was (as he told) nearly missed by lightning. This happened near Stotternheim, a village located just a few kilometres outside Erfurt. As Luther would later say, this experience made him completely change his mind. He became a monk and member of the Augustinian Friars. After moving into cloister at Erfurt 1505, he studied the writings of the later scholastic churchmen such as Gabriel Biel or William of Occam, in whose works economic problems were discussed within a theological framework of interpretation. In 1508 he was seconded to Wittenberg to take up studies for a degree in theology, which he finished in 1512 with a doctorate in divinity. He would remain in permanent residence in Wittenberg until the end of his days. In 1510–11 he travelled to Rome. There he received first-hand evidence of the luxurious lifestyle led by the popes financed by what he would later condemn as a perversion of the faith through the practice of indulgences.

---

8.   Harald Meller/Landesamt für Denkmalpflege und Archäologie Sachsen-Anhalt, eds, *Fundsache Luther. Archäologen auf den Spuren des Reformators* (Stuttgart: Theiss, 2008).

9.   Martin Brecht, *Martin Luther, Vol. 1. Sein Weg zur Reformation: 1483–1521* (Stuttgart: Calwer Verlag, 1994), chap. 1. See literature referred in chap. 1 for introductory works and other biographical accounts.

10. 'Eine Hölle und Fegefeuer war unsere Schule, darinnen wir gemartert wurden und doch nichts denn eitel nichts gelernt haben durch so viel Stäupen, Zittern, Angst und Jammer', quoted after Günter Fabiunke, *Martin Luther als Nationalökonom* (Berlin: Akademie Verlag, 1963), 27.

Luther was accordingly born into an area which at that time was bustling with commercial and industrial activity. This was somewhat unusual, given that overall, the German-speaking lands remained profoundly agricultural, with a share of population living in big cities (above 10,000 inhabitants) below 5 per cent until late (table 2.1).

Table 2.1 Share of Population Living in Big Cities (>10, 000 Inhabitants), in Percentage of Total Population.

	1500	1600	1700	1800
The Netherlands	18	30	33	29
North/Central Italy	16	14	13	14
Southern Italy, Isles	13	19	16	21
Spain	11	15	10	15
Portugal	5	11	10	8
France	5	6	9	9
Poland	5	7	4	4
'Germany' (Holy Roman Empire)	4	4	5	6
England	2	6	13	22
Scandinavia	1	2	4	5

Source: Jan de Vries, *European Urbanization, 1500–1800* (Cambridge, MA: Harvard University Press, 1984).

In the longer run, throughout the sixteenth, seventeenth and eighteenth centuries, the German lands became progressively less developed than the Atlantic fringe and the Italian south which had been the richest and economically most advanced region of Europe in the Middle Ages, as measured by the urbanization degree and relative real wages (table 2.2).

Table 2.2 Real Wages in Europe (England, 1500 = 100).

	1500–49	1650–99	1700–49	1750–1799	1800–1849
London	100	96	110	99	98
Amsterdam	97	98	107	98	79
Antwerp	98	88	92	88	82
Paris	62	60	56	51	65
South Europe	71	52	61	42	30
Central and East Europe	74	66	58	55	48

Source: Data assembled in Jan de Vries, *The Industrious Revolution: Consumer Behavior and the Household Economy, 1650 to the Present* (Cambridge: Cambridge University Press, 2008), 83 (table. 3.2), derived from studies by Allen and Das Gupta.

Towards the latter half of the sixteenth century, the Atlantic fringe around the big Dutch and English commercial *metropoleis* of Bruges, Antwerp, Amsterdam[11] and finally London commenced on the big process of economic catch-up and overtaking of the south of Europe,

---

11. Most recently, Oscar Gelderblom, *Cities of Commerce: The Institutional Foundations of International Trade in the Low Countries, 1250–1650* (Princeton, NJ: Princeton University Press, 2013).

a process which has been called the 'Rise of the Atlantic Economy' and development of the 'First Modern Economy'.[12] Capital markets in the north-west were more developed and deeper than capital markets towards central Europe; Nuremberg and Augsburg, perhaps, apart. Luther's vitriolic polemic against usury in the present pamphlet *Von Kauffshandlung und Wucher* (1524) reflects, partly at least, a man to whom the more refined financial market techniques practised at places like Rome where the papacy was in the midst of some of the largest financial market speculations of the time, Antwerp or Bruges were known, but who constantly refused to come to terms with them, let alone admitting them into full currency. At places he even expressively referred to situations of underdevelopment, for instance, in the passage in the present sermon regarding imports and the English cloth trade (see chapter 4 and translation, paragraph [5]). Ninety per cent of the German population was, on average, vested and embedded in the agrarian sector. Social problems in the feudal rural economy were virulent, culminating in the great German Peasants' War of 1524–26.[13] Debates on monopoly, a concept which in these times covered a wide range of commercial malpractices, abounded. They were carried up to the Imperial Diets of the 1520s, where matters of monetary regulation and integration were discussed alongside the *Causa Lutheri* or *Luthersache* – the unfolding of the German Reformation.

In the long run, Germany fell behind and became one of the relative losers in the race for economic greatness, while England and the Netherlands were forging ahead with notable and sometimes fundamental shifts in urbanization, which most historians and economists would correlate with shifts in aggregate wealth and economic development commonly measured in terms of per capita GDP. The German Empire during the sixteenth and seventeenth century fell into underdevelopment, as many a cameralist textbook and pamphlet of the post-1650 never ceased to stress.[14] This picture is supported by comparative real wage data for select cities across Europe (table 2.2). It needs to be seen with some caution, as the method of deflating nominal wages by the silver content

---

12. The story was fully developed in vol. 3 of Fernand Braudel, *Civilization and Capitalism* (New York: Harper & Collins, 1982–1984), chaps 2 and 3, but it has been retold in many different shapes and models and from different methodological viewpoints ever since, i.e. Daron Acemoglu, Simon Johnson and James A. Robinson, 'The Rise of Europe: Atlantic Trade, Institutional Change, and Economic Growth', *American Economic Review* 95, no. 3 (2005), 546–79; Daron Acemoglu and James A. Robinson, *Why Nations Fail: The Origins of Power, Prosperity, and Poverty* (New York: Crown, 2012); or Jan de Vries and Ad van der Woude, *The First Modern Economy: Success, Failure, and Perseverance of the Dutch Economy, 1500–1815* (Cambridge: Cambridge University Press, 1997), to name but a few of the more prominent examples.

13. The best account still is Peter Blickle, *Die Revolution von 1525*, 4th ed. (Munich: Oldenbourg, 2004), and a brief précis in *id.*, *Der Bauernkrieg: Die Revolution des Gemeinen Mannes*, 4th ed. (Munich: Beck, 2012). A broader chronological frame is sketched in *id.*, *Unruhen in der ständischen Gesellschaft 1300–1800*, 2nd ed. (Munich: Oldenbourg, 2010). Non-German speaking audiences may appreciate the introduction and selection of translated sources in Michael G. Baylor, *The German Reformation and the Peasants' War. A Brief History with Documents* (Boston, MA: Bedford/St Martin's, 2012).

14. Erik S. Reinert, *How Rich Countries Got Rich… And Why Poor Countries Stay Poor* (London: Constable 2007), esp. chap. 3.

of the regional currencies is a dubious one[15]; in fact, most exercises of deriving economic data calibrated according to modern accounting techniques, for periods and locations that did not work according to these modern economic mechanisms, are almost bound to fail. But the figures probably give a reliable overall impression of relative economic development in early modern Europe. Large parts of central Europe, including cities within the Empire, were significantly behind the north-western/Atlantic fringe as early as 1500. And the difference would widen as the early modern period progressed.

Thus, Luther grew up and spent most of his life within a world region that was considerably less well off than the emerging north and the richer south (mainly the Italian coastal cities), a region that, however, was in constant interaction with the wealthier and industrially and financially more developed parts of the world. Being a mining district this was still a very peculiar area within the productive landscape. Some of Luther's viewpoints on commercial life and business, especially interest rates, may in a sense reflect a sort of backwardness dissonance as found in the works of Albert O. Hirschman or in Latin American theories of periphery capitalism, if a modern analogy is allowed. Whilst Luther was constantly complaining about financial markets, which should in his view be controlled more rigorously, capital markets at Bruges or Amsterdam at the same time were much less restricted and more developed[16]; the turnover on these markets was considerably larger. The more powerful urban economies to the north-west, particularly Antwerp, also had the freest financial markets of the day, borne out by the decisively lower average market interest rates across the entire spectrum of financial market products.[17] But certainly relative underdevelopment represented by far not the only or even the chief *explanandum* of Luther's peculiar and very idiosyncratic economic writings.

Within Germany there were different economic regions and landscapes:[18] with the Hanseatic area, focused on the Baltic trades; the Rhineland, which represented the big north–south axis between northern Europe and Italy, France and the Levant; and central Germany, focused around the Saxon lands and the central European mining

15. Philipp Robinson Rössner, *Deflation – Devaluation – Revolution. Geld im Zeitalter der Reformation* (Stuttgart: Franz Steiner, 2012), esp. chap. 3; *id.*, 'Monetary Instability, Lack of Integration and the Curse of a Commodity Money Standard. The German Lands, c. 1400–1900 A.D.', *Capital and Credit Markets* 47, no. 2 (2014), 297–340. Francesco Boldizzoni, *The Poverty of Clio. Resurrecting Economic History* (Princeton, NJ: Princeton University Press, 2011), 81–82, has stray remarks on this.

16. Gelderblom, *Cities of Commerce*; Ian Blanchard, *The International Economy in the 'Age of the Discoveries', 1470–1570. Antwerp and the English Merchants' World*, ed. P. Rössner (Stuttgart: Franz Steiner, 2009).

17. Jan Luiten van Zanden, 'Die mittelalterlichen Ursprünge des "europäischen Wunders", in J. Robinson and K. Wiegandt, eds, *Die Ursprünge der modernen Welt. Geschichte im wissenschaftlichen Vergleich* (Frankfurt-on-the-Main: Fischer, 2008), 475–516; C. Jaco Zuijderduijn, *Medieval Capital Markets: Markets for renten, State Formation and Private Investment in Holland* (1300–1550) (Leiden: Brill, 2009).

18. Michael North, 'Das Reich als Wirtschaftsraum', in Heinz Schilling, ed., *Heiliges Römisches Reich Deutscher Nation 962 bis 1806 – Altes Reich und neue Staaten, 1495 bis 1806. Essays* (Dresden, 2006), 159–70; Tom Scott, 'Economic Landscapes', in Bob Scribner, ed., *Germany. A New Social and Economic History 1450–1630* (London: Arnold, 1996), 1–32.

district. These regions were topped in commercial wealth by the area known mainly to modern scholars as 'Upper Germany' (*Oberdeutschland*) around the big commercial and financial *metropoleis* of Nuremberg and Augsburg, around which much of the sixteenth-century finance and trade evolved. In terms of urbanization and relative wealth levels, the central German lands around Saxony and Mansfeld were certainly less well-off than the commercialized south. But parts of the region, especially the Saxon Erzgebirge and the Mansfeld copper-mining district near the Harz Mountains, from the 1470s onwards witnessed a process of rapid structural change. Within a brief run of years – we can trace the pattern using output on silver mining within the region which featured an upward cycle between the mid-1470s and the 1490s – they were transformed from backward agrarian mountainous regions into a high-powered urban industrial area bustling with all sorts of economic activity, where mining and smelting, as well as related industrial occupations including services significantly increased their share in output and employment. This structural–occupational change was decisive in terms of the outlook and mentalities of those concerned by and witnessing these developments; it certainly left a powerful impact on Luther.

The Forces of Time: Economic Crisis in Germany, ca. 1490–1525

Before moving on with the spatial context, a very brief note of the economic conjuncture must be given to clarify some of the possible impacts on Luther's thinking. The sixteenth century is generally held to be a century of economic expansion. Population and prices increased, doubling and tripling at some places (depending, of course, upon the nature and quality and location of data observations), yielding the proverbial age of the 'Price Revolution', an inflation that spread outwards from its epicentre in Spain.[19] Notable differentials in terms of wealth and development existed across Europe (tables 2.1 and 2.2 above). They set apart the north-west of Europe from the still wealthier south (Italy), and an even poorer manorial economy east of the Elbe.[20] These peculiarities of development need not concern us here; what is important is that over the sixteenth century and literally everywhere across Europe prices for foodstuffs rose faster than those for manufactured goods and wages. The sixteenth century was, therefore, for many regions and people, a century of net *decrease of wealth*, marked by a decline in per capita income and living

---

19. The classical story by Earl J. Hamilton, *American Treasure and the Price Revolution in Spain, 1501–1650* (New York: Octagon, 1934), has now been superseded. Scholars have endlessly debated whether a monetarist or 'neo-Malthusian' approach resting on the real sector of the economy would the best way to describe the patterns of economic and price level changes. The usual compromise model – 'both were somewhat at work' – is arguably the most credible one as we will simply never know for certain. Good recent surveys on general problems and methodology can be found in Munro, 'Monetary Origins'; or *id.*, 'Price Revolution', in Steven N. Durlauf and Lawrence E. Blume, eds, *The New Palgrave Dictionary of Economics*, 2nd ed., vol. 6 (Basingstoke: Palgrave Macmillan, 2008), 631–34; and N. J. Mayhew, 'Prices in England, 1170–1750', *Past & Present* 219, no. 1 (2013), 3–39. Rössner, *Deflation – Devaluation – Rebellion*, chap. 2.
20. Tom Scott, 'The Economy', in Euan Cameron, ed., *The Short Oxford History of Europe: The Sixteenth Century* (Oxford: Oxford University Press, 2006), 18–57; Robert S. DuPlessis, *Transitions to Capitalism in Early Modern Europe* (Cambridge: Cambridge University Press, 1997), 47–140.

standards. Of course, we must be careful when trying to assess or quantify pre-industrial economies using methods and techniques developed for modern, fully industrialized ones. Our modern terminology and epistemology of crisis, deflation, depression, etc. is based on integrated and functionally differentiated modern economies, in which the majority of transactions are carried out using markets. This syntax uses monetary value signs, such as prices expressed in terms of a specific currency, which, if multiplied by real amounts of goods, may be aggregated yielding a monetary expression of what we would call gross domestic product. Within the historical context of the time around 1500, such modern metaphors and concepts are ill-suited. Neither was economic activity statistically recorded nor was there much of an integrated 'German economy', let alone a state that went by that name. Contemporaries had no modern conceptual framework of assessing and accounting for national income. Moreover, the late medieval and early modern economies of continental Europe were not always or even primarily organized around the market as the clearing agent for economic transactions. Reciprocal (*economy of obligation*) and redistributive (*feudal or manorial economy*) exchange mechanisms were likewise important.[21] But one should also be careful with *über*-culturalizing early modern society. There are clear indications that the market as a clearing agent *had* made significant inroads into economy and society in Luther's time, so significant, in fact, that Luther and many other contemporaries never tired to complain about it. With all caveats we may say that the non-subsistence or market sector of the German economy – however big this share was compared to the non-market/reciprocal/redistributive sector – went into a deep crisis during the first two-and-a-half decades of the sixteenth century, as the combination of some macroeconomic data assembled for the period would suggest (table 2.3).

Recent calculations reproduced in table 2.3 demonstrate that during the first three decades of the sixteenth century, both the overall price level in (south and central) Germany and the real wages *decreased simultaneously* (see also chapter 4). Thus, the decline in bread and grain prices – the drivers of price level changes – was not connected with a rise in well-being, as an all-to-quick assessment following a neo-Malthusian model may suggest, which interprets grain or bread prices as the main determinant of general welfare; with rising prices leading to mass impoverishment and falling prices to an improvement in the economic situation of those who worked for a (monetary) wage in order to make a living. This assumption would be wrong. As population levels *increased* more or less continuously since the 1470s, this period has sometimes also been misinterpreted as a *general* economic expansion, implicitly assuming positive rates of economic growth (i.e. per capita income growth). This interpretation is likewise fallacious. Total economic activity certainly increased in Germany over the sixteenth century, as the number of Germans (and Europeans) grew. Per capita resources, however, that is the average slice of the cake available to each individual (or 'per capita GDP'), *decreased* or at least stagnated around a rather humble baseline, a precarious level of subsistence, certainly during the

---

21. Witold Kula, *An Economic Theory of the Feudal System: Towards a Model of the Polish Economy 1500–1800* (London: N. L. B., 1976), Martha C. Howell, *Commerce before Capitalism in Europe, 1300–1600* (Cambridge: Cambridge University Press, 2010), and more recently Boldizzoni, *Poverty of Clio*.

Table 2.3 Germany in Times of Depression, 1500–1550 (Index 1500 = 100)

	1	2	3	4	5	6
	Price Level (Six South German cities)	Real Wages (Local CPIs)	Coin Hoards	Silver Content South German Penny Currencies	Rye Prices, Germany, Deflated by Silver Content of Circulating Local Penny Currencies (Augsburg, Nuremberg, Frankfurt, Munich and Würzburg)	Silver Output, Tyrol and Saxony
1500	100	100	100	100	100	100
1505	95	105		100		91
1510	57	100	65	93	35	87
1515	80	86		93		77
1520	78	82	73	93		68
1525	72	77		86	43	65
1530	186	82	66	83		81
1535	102	86		82		121
1540	191	82	69	78		85
1545	172	77		76		68
1550	179	73	66	77		

Sources:

Column 1: Own calculations, based on data in Moritz J. Elsas, *Umriss einer Geschichte der Preise und Löhne in Deutschland vom ausgehenden Mittelalter bis zum Beginn des neunzehnten Jahrhunderts*, 3 vols (Leiden: A. W. Sijthoff), 1936–49, augmented by new price data traced by Nils Decken (2011) for Leipzig prior to 1563 in an unpublished MA dissertation.

Column 2: U. Pfister, J. Riedel and M. Uebele, 'Real Wages and the Origins of Modern Economic Growth in Germany, 16th to 19th Centuries', *Working Papers* 0017, European Historical Economics Society (EHES); U. Pfister, 'Consumer Prices and Wages in Germany, 1500–1850', *CQE Working Papers* 1510, Center for Quantitative Economics (CQE), University of Münster (2010); *id.*, M. Uebele and H. Albers, 'The Great Moderation of Grain Price Volatility: Market Integration vs. Climatic Change, Germany, Seventeenth to Nineteenth Centuries' (http://www. wiwi. uni-muenster. de/wisoge/md/ personen/uebele/PfisterUebeleAlbers_Strasbourg_2011_Mi_1400. pdf)

Column 3: See below.

Column 4: Allen-Unger Global Commodity Prices database online: http://www. history. ubc. ca/ faculty/unger/ECPdb/about. html

Column 5: As in col. 1, combined with col. 4.

Column 6: Munro 2003, Appendix.

first three decades of the sixteenth century. Around mid-century a full craftsman's yearly wage would not have sufficed any more to nourish an imputed standard-sized family of five comprising a worker or craftsman, his wife and three hypothetical children. This is what the synopsis of data presented in table 2.3, as well as older research on prices, wages and living standards in the sixteenth century, would suggest.[22] The Peasants' War of 1524–25 which came after a long period of deflation was, after all, a struggle fought over declining per capita resources – economic, as well as social and political. So Luther's time was a time of gradually increasing impoverishment – regardless the fact that there were branches and sectors of the economy as well as individuals that flourished. Above all these were the Upper German trading companies and large firms headed by the Augsburg Fugger, Welser and Höchstetter dynasties, which in the wake of the spice trade and the discovery of the Cape Route made profits that appeared grotesque within a world that saw stagnant incomes and falling grain prices. In a world dominated by peasants and farmers, grain prices meant declining sales revenue and average profits for those dependent upon grain sales for a living. This was an age of increasing inequality; especially the profit rate on investments outside agriculture, for instance, in commerce, finance and trade increased whilst real wages and profit rates in agriculture and farming declined or remained stable.[23] That such a divergence may have caused social imbalances, giving rise to protest is not surprising; the age around 1500 saw a significantly increased number of popular uprisings that were concerned with a call for redistribution of productive resources and a more equalized distribution of shares in national income or rewards to those factors that contributed to it: wages (labour), profits (capital) and rent (land).[24] The gravamina or complaints issued during the Peasants' War of 1524–1526 and its predecessors referred to similar problems.

---

22. For the German lands, Ulf Dirlmeier, *Untersuchungen zu Einkommensverhältnissen und Lebenshaltungskosten in oberdeutschen Städten des Spätmittelalters* (Mitte 14. bis Anfang 16. Jh.) (Heidelberg: Winter, 1978) is still useful, as well as the older research by Wilhelm Abel, *Agrarkrisen und Agrarkonjunktur in Mitteleuropa vom 13. bis zum 19. Jahrhundert*, 3rd ed. (Berlin, 1935; repr. Hamburg: Parey, 1978); *id.*, 'Zur Entwicklung des Sozialprodukts in Deutschland im 16. Jahrhundert', *Jahrbücher für Nationalökonomie und Statistik* 173 (1961), 448–89; *id.*, *Massenarmut und Hungerkrisen im vorindustriellen Deutschland* (Göttingen: Vandenhoeck, 1971); *id.*, *Agricultural Fluctuations in Europe from the Thirteenth to the Twentieth Centuries* (London: Methuen, 1980), which of course has been updated and revised by subsequent scholars. The baseline of Abel's findings, i.e. that there was no advance in per capita income during the sixteenth century, has been confirmed by new research, see Ulrich Pfister, 'Die Frühe Neuzeit als wirtschaftshistorische Epoche. Fluktuationen relativer Preise 1450–1850', in Helmut Neuhaus, ed., *Die Frühe Neuzeit als Epoche* (Munich: Oldenbourg, 2009), 409–34, and more recently, Ulrich Pfister, 'German Economic Growth, 1500–1850, Contribution to the XVth World Economic History Congress, Utrecht, August 3–7 (2009).' A recent survey on methodology is to be found in Hans-Jürgen Gerhard and Alexander Engel, *Preisgeschichte der vorindustriellen Zeit. Ein Kompendium auf Basis ausgewählter Hamburger Materialien* (Stuttgart: Franz Steiner, 2006), and Hans-Jürgen Gerhard, 'Preise als wirtschaftshistorische Indikatoren. Wilhelm Abels preishistorische Untersuchungen aus heutiger Sicht', in Markus A. Denzel, ed., *Wirtschaft – Politik – Geschichte. Beiträge zum Gedenkkolloquium anläßlich des 100. Geburtstages von Wilhelm Abel am 16. Oktober 2004 in Leipzig* (Stuttgart: Franz Steiner, 2004), 37–58. For Europe, a useful survey is Paolo Malanima, *Pre-modern European Economy: One Thousand Years (10th–19th Centuries)* (Leiden: Brill, 2009).

23. Rössner, *Deflation – Devaluation – Rebellion*, chap. 2 (esp. 127, fig. 2).

24. This sounds similar to the situation detected for the later twentieth century by Thomas Piketty, *Capital in the Twenty-first Century* (Cambridge, MA: The Belknap Press of Harvard University Press, 2014).

It is also important to note that in most of the available data series for European cities during the sixteenth century the actual *increase* in grain prices characteristic of the 'Price Revolution'-long cycle cannot be found prior to the 1530s. This makes both the classification of the period ('long' sixteenth century) and the exact dating of the so-called 'Price Revolution', which many traditional accounts suggested to have commenced in the 1470s, or around 1500[25], open to re-consideration. Yes, there had been an increase in the price level and population since the 1470s across the German regions. But no, this did not lead into an increase in general well-being in Luther's age and times. In fact, this trend was reversed in most locations for which price data survives after the 1490s. The three decades or so between ca. 1500 and 1525–30 were a period of *deflation* and economic crisis – and a growing 'scissors' between some of the bigger incomes received from capital (profits, rent) and rewards to labour (wages). At that time most available economic index figures, from coin debasement rates to urban municipal expenditure, from tithe records documenting grain production, prices, wages and living standards, as well as business failure, point downwards. Real wages and per capita incomes contracted. More detail on this crisis will be given in chapter 4; a full discussion of the problem has been presented elsewhere.[26] These were the formative years for Luther as a theologian.

Silicon Valley, or the Rise and Decline of the Central European Mining Region (ca. 1470–1540)

At that time the mountainous regions of central Europe provided Europe's main sources of silver. The precious metal was mined in the Austrian Alps, mainly at the Falkenstein in Schwaz near Innsbruck in Tyrol, in the Saxon and Bohemian parts of the Erzgebirge Mountains, as well as in Hungary/Slovakia near Kremnitz and in the Harz Mountains.[27] Some silver was mined in the Harz Mountains around the old imperial residential city of Goslar. Output in the Saxon Erzgebirge had been through a boom period, marked by a significant increase in silver production levels as given in contemporary tax records, between ca. 1470 and 1477. The boom in Tyrol, where the silver was predominantly mined in the shafts around the Falkenstein Mountain, lasted from about 1470 to 1485. After 1517 the deposits of Bohemian mines near Joachimsthal (present-day Jàchymov in the Czech Republic) were tapped yielding, for a brief period, prodigious amounts of silver. They gave their name to a new silver coin which quickly attained proverbial reputation as a hard currency. This was the *thaler* or dollar (*Joachimsthaler*). It was minted as a full equivalent to the now increasingly moribund gold florin or gulden (Rhenish florin, abbreviated in contemporary usage as Rh. fl. or fl. Rh.). Later on it attained many shapes, such as the German *Reichsthaler* or *Rix dollar* (also a Danish coin and currency denomination), or the Spanish real (or *peso de ocho*). It continues to live on in the contemporary Brazilian real (R$).

25. Scott, 'The Economy'.
26. Rössner, *Deflation – Devaluation – Rebellion*, chap. 2.
27. Blanchard, *International Economy*, chap. 4, and works referred to in this chapter in note 6.

In Tyrol, Thuringia-Mansfeld and the Saxon Erzgebirge, minor towns and hamlets such as Schwaz, Schneeberg and St Annaberg in the Saxon Erzgebirge Mountains since the 1470s witnessed a demographic expansion that saw their populations literally explode. Sometimes population shot up from a mere handful into the tens of thousands of people, where no settlement had existed a few years ago.[28] A rapidly growing share of non-agrarian producers needed to be fed. As seen above, this necessitated imports of foodstuffs on a grand scale, which brought these areas into larger contexts of inter-regional division of labour, integration and structural change.[29] The Thuringian *Saiger huts* were erected, large factory-like plants, where the argentiferous copper mined in the Mansfeld copper-mining district was separated into its components of pure copper (*Garkupfer*) and silver, using lead, consuming prodigious amounts of capital for smelting ovens and silver hearths, infrastructure and environmental resources. This was one of the most complex and capital-intensive production processes one could possibly think of these days. The first production stage involved the mixing of *Schwarzkupfer* or black copper with lead using low *Saigerherde* (Saiger hearths), where the argentiferous copper was 'heated slowly until just about the melting point of the lead. At this point in the operation the greater part of the silver contained in the copper was taken up by the lead combining with any of the precious metal already contained therein' (Blanchard). In the *Treibofen* the argentiferous lead was then separated into its basic components of silver and lead using the cupellation process. A chain of further production processes involving several chemical and smelting processes with temperatures of 1100° Celsius and more followed with a host of by-products and wastage, until, finally, the two key outputs – pure silver and pure copper (*Garkupfer*) had been obtained. They were sold by the Saiger consortia on the world market, travelling as far as Africa and India (see present chapter, below).

The *Saigerprozess* is a classic example of a *joint production process* where the sale profits of the secondary or by-product (in the case of the Saiger process initially: pure *copper*) determines the relative cost structure and profitability levels of the main product (here: *silver*). Within such a complex business situations may arise in which the market turns, making the by-product the more profitable good for sale, which will completely reshuffle the cost-efficiency structure of the entire industry. This situation happened in the Thuringian Saiger industry towards the later 1530s and 1540s, when the incoming silver from the Central and South American mines lowered the world market price for silver, thus increasing the relative costs of producing silver within the *Saiger* process. This was one reason for the notable restructuring and concentration exercises within the Thuringian Saiger industry and the calls for cartelization and nationalization in the 1540s, which Luther became intimately involved in as an expert referee for the Counts

---

28. See discussion in Rössner, *Deflation – Devaluation – Rebellion*, chap. 2. For a conceptual framework of mining regions as social and cultural regions, see A. Westermann, *Die vorderösterreichischen Montanregionen*. For the Erzgebirge the following recent collection of essays is indicative: Martina Schattkowsky, ed., *Das Erzgebirge im 16. Jahrhundert: Gestaltwandel einer Kulturlandschaft im Reformationszeitalter* (Leipzig: Leipziger Universitätsverlag, 2013).
29. See the analysis of the mountainous regions of Europe in the fifteenth and sixteenth century in Sidney Pollard, *Marginal Europe: The Contribution of Marginal Lands since the Middle Ages* (Oxford: Clarendon Press; New York: Oxford University Press, 1997).

of Mansfeld towards the later 1530s. He witnessed the forced restructuration of the most highly capital-intensive industry of his life and times in the face of changing constellations on the world market. As silver declined in price this would potentially make the Saiger industry in Mansfeld–Thuringia cost-inefficient and obsolete; the ailing industry had to be gradually re-shifted to copper which now became, and would remain until the end of the early modern period, the main output.[30]

The complex entanglements of these production processes – both in the silver mining (*Erzgebirge*) and in the silver smelting industries (*Mansfeld–Thuringia*) are obvious. Large imports of lead were necessary to keep the Saiger huts running. The processing of one cwt[31] of argentiferous copper required about 0.5 cwt of lead. Environmental pollution was an issue, as witnessed by landscape features and place names such as *Giftbach* ('poisonous river'), which have survived from the period. They give away a somewhat gruesome impression of the damage done to the environment, especially by the prodigious amounts of chemical waste, such as burned lead or arsenic residuals. The Erzgebirge Mountains, where silver was hewn out of the mountains and, accordingly, the processes were not nearly as complex as further down south-west in the Thuringian Saiger industry, still looked equally estranging to many a contemporary. They were ridden with mine shafts. The methods of mining were still relatively primitive, in a sense that they had not significantly changed since the High Middle Ages. The hills bustled with men and women who were not tied to the soil any more by occupation, family and tradition as opposed to the remaining 90 per cent of the central German population who remained profoundly agrarian. By the sheer wealth they took out of the mountains and the demand for foodstuffs they could not produce themselves, these people increased the level of grain prices, the main item of food consumption. They thereby stimulated the integration of this region, in the same way as the Thuringian industry further south, into wider networks of trade spanning across Europe. Oxen and grain came from far corners of Saxony and Thuringia; sometimes as far away as Hungary–Slovakia. The silver found its way to Cologne, Frankfurt-on-the-Main and Antwerp, to Venice, Lisbon and ultimately around the West and East Coast of Africa into the Indian Ocean and farther on into the Chinese Sea. As much as 70–80 per cent of yearly production levels in the central European mining areas may have flown out and into the international and developing global trade circuits.[32] The famous *Annaberg Bergaltar*, the altarpiece of the church of St Anne in Annaberg/Saxony (1521) is a beautiful graphic depiction of the 'Silicon-Valley'-like feeling during this economic and social transformation of this region (figure 2.1).

Accordingly, the population in these areas increased considerably; in fact, much faster than the general population in the German lands. Such a boom in silver production would have been reflected in a fall in the silver price level, which would have caused overall prices of many goods, including grain, to rise (as silver was the main input used for the production of currency/money). It may also, by ways of monetary expansion, have

30. Ekkehard Westermann, *Das Eislebener Garkupfer und seine Bedeutung für den europäischen Kupfermarkt, 1460–1560* (Cologne: Böhlau, 1971).

31. Hundredweight or German *Zentner*.

32. Rössner, *Deflation – Devaluation – Rebellion*, 251–310.

Figure 2.1 Annaberg Bergaltar (mantlepiece/altar of St Anne Church in Annaberg/ Saxony), 1521. (*Source*: © Dieter Knoblauch/Erzgebirgsbuchhandlung Knoblauch, Annaberg-Buchholz.)

translated into an economic boom or stimulus. Indeed, the time between the mid-1470s and the mid-1490s was a time of inflation. The Leipzig trade fairs also grew prodigiously. Alongside the Naumburg Fairs located close-by, they turned into central Europe's major financial and goods market of the period.[33] The area around Leipzig and Wittenberg, where Luther grew up and spent most of his lifetime, was highly commercialized, with a significant share of the population working outside agriculture and a high degree of interaction with the wider world, integrated gradually into emerging global logistics and financial markets, marked by the global flows of silver.

Research by the late John Munro, based on work by the late Ekkehard Westermann and others, has provided us with reliable estimates of silver output in the central European mines (table 2.4).

33. Uwe Schirmer, 'Der Finanzplatz Leipzig vom Ende des 12. bis zur Mitte des 17. Jahrhunderts. Geldwesen – Waren- und Zahlungsverkehr – Rentengeschäfte', in Markus A. Denzel, ed., *Der Finanzplatz Leipzig* (Frankfurt, forthcoming). Uwe Schirmer provided me with a pre-publication copy of this chapter.

Table 2.4 Silver Output, Central European Mines.

Silver Outputs from the Major South German–Central European Mines 1471–1550, in kg of Fine Metal in 5 and 10-year Means

YEARS 5 Yr Mean / *10 Yr Mean*	SAXONY Est. Total	THURINGIA Est. Total	BOHEMIA Joachimsthal	BOHEMIA Kutna Hora Kasperska Hora	SLOVAKIA Fugger-Thurzo kg	HUNGARY Nagybanya Körmocbanya	TYROL Schwaz	TOTAL Estimated
1471–75	4,361			4,500			4,113	**12,973**
1476–80	10,317			4,250			7,350	**21,921**
1471–80	*7,339*			*4,375*			*5,733*	*17,447*
1481–85	3,743			4,000		1,800	9,746	**19,289**
1486–90	2,770			3,750		3,523	12,751	**22,794**
1481–90	*3,257*			*3,875*		*2,662*	*11,248*	*21,042*
1491–95	3,757			3,500	1,957	3,523	12,423	**25,160**
1496–00	4,642			3,250	1,957	3,796	12,095	**25,739**
1491–00	*4,200*			*3,375*	*1,957*	*3,659*	*12,253*	*25,450*
1501–05	8,979			3,000	2,870	4,069	11,766	**30,685**
1506–10	7,416	4,626		2,750	3,991	4,342	11,438	**34,563**
1501–10	*8,198*	*2,313*		*2,875*	*3,430*	*4,205*	*11,602*	*32,624*

Period								
1511–15	6,925	5,713		2,500	3,632	4,614	11,110	**34,495**
1516–20	5,189	6,079	3,970	2,25	1,983	4,887	10,782	**35,140**
1511–20	*6,057*	*5,896*	*1,985*	*2,375*	*2,808*	*4,751*	*10,946*	***34,818***
1521–25	3,701	6,301	9,703	2,000	2,486	5,160	10,453	**39,806**
1526–30	3,425	7,889	13,795	2,000	2,269	5,433	10,125	**44,937**
1521–30	*3,563*	*7,095*	*11,749*	*2,000*	*2,378*	*5,297*	*10,289*	***42,371***
1531–35	6,663	6,301	16,555	2,000	2,269	5,433	10,125	**49,346**
1536–40	14,973	5,734	13,248	3,947	2,244	5,433	10,125	**55,704**
1531–40	*10,818*	*6,017*	*14,901*	*2,974*	*2,256*	*5,433*	*10,125*	***52,525***
1541–45	7,739	6,144	10,937	3,997	2,142	5,433	9,963	**46,355**
1546–50	4,131	6,576	10,937	700	2,142	5,433	9,963	**39,883**
1541–50	*5,935*	*6,360*	*10,9367*	*2,349*	*2,142*	*5,433*	*9,963*	***43,119***

Source: J. Munro, 'Monetary Origins', and his archived (legacy) website at the University of Toronto: http://www.economics.utoronto.ca/wwwfiles/archives/munro5.

Two things must – in the light of this table and the above remarks – be appreciated at once.

(1) *Luther grew up in an environment where, around 1500, at least one-half, if not more, of Europe's silver, and thus the main contribution of Europe's monetary stock, originated* (the American mines were as yet unimportant).[34] It was in these areas, modern-day Thuringia, that is Ernestine Saxony, rather than Albertine Saxony in the north-west (the Albertine Duke Georg 'the Bearded' was stout Catholic), that the Reformation spread particularly quickly and, in the words of an expert, decisively. Many idiosyncratic variants if not heterodox versions of the Reformed faith took hold here, for instance Müntzer's movement in Mühlhausen, or Karlstadt in Orlamünde.[35] Perhaps, the landscape was made for discursive diversity, mavericks and competition of ideas that were unorthodox, to say the least. In the Mansfeld mining and smelting district, the peak of the mining activities was witnessed during the sixteenth century. Between 1200 and 1700 on average 410 tons of copper came out of the mountains (from which 2.04 tons of silver were yielded). Subsequent periods yielded much less per year.[36] Only from the 1550s onwards, the position of the German mines would be taken over by the South American mines at Potosí, which were under Spain's control. This silver, after the 1530s, supplemented by the quantities released from the dissolution of the monasteries and the stripping of the church altars of ritual silver equipment in the Reformed territories, contributed to the monetary and economic expansion known as the 'Price Revolution' 1520–1620.[37]

(2) *But Luther also grew up at a time when overall, measured across all German mining regions, silver stocks – that is the amounts that stayed in the country and regions where they had been mined – declined.* This may be illustrated by a brief recourse to silver output and export data. As such, output data on silver mining are pretty meaningless unless the basic trade flows are known, that is the balance of inflows and outflows. These in turn were very much dependent upon the question of property rights, ownerships and claims to the silver that came out of the mountains. Claims and stakes were frequently muddled, contested, depending upon complex webs of finance, capital formation, ownership and organization of mining which differed from region to region. The Regal seigniorage rights to silver as a natural resource lay in the hands of the native princes, dukes and other worldly authorities on whose territory the silver mines were located.[38] The worldly rulers often sold their prerogative or preemptive purchasing rights in return for loans and state finance to wealthy merchant consortia who took the mining processes into their own hands. In areas where mining was free, such as in the Erzgebirge Mountains, anyone could descend into

---

34. See also the synopsis in Rössner, *Deflation – Devaluation – Rebellion*, chap. 2.
35. Uwe Schirmer, 'Vor- und Frühreformation in thüringischen Städten. Eine Zusammenfassung', in Joachim Emig, Volker Leppin and Uwe Schirmer, eds, *Vor- und Frühreformation in Thüringischen Städten (1470–1525/30)* (Cologne: Böhlau, 2013), 437–60 (448).
36. Calculated from data presented in R. Slotta and S. Müller, 'Zum Bergbau auf Kupferschiefer im Mansfelder Land', in R. Knape, ed., *Martin Luther und der Bergbau im Mansfelder Land* (Lutherstadt Eisleben: Stiftung Luthergedenkstätten in Sachsen-Anhalt, 2000), 9–27 (25).
37. See above.
38. A. Westermann, *Die vorderösterreichischen Montanregionen*, esp. chap. 1.

the mountains and dig – in return for the seigniorage fee or silver tithe (*Silberzehnt*) to be paid to the Saxon Duke and Elector who administered the mines, as well as currency matters, in unison. As its name suggests, the silver tithe usually, but not necessarily, amounted to somewhere around 10 per cent of silver output.[39] In the Tyrolean Alps, the situation was different. After the 1490s Emperor Maximilian, in his position as Archduke of Austria (Hereditary Lands in the Empire) constantly sold his preferential claims to Tyrolean silver in return for credit, loans and state finance to the Fugger merchants and other wealthy merchant-bankers at the rich imperial city of Augsburg; his successor Charles V did the same. These silver stocks never entered the German realms of circulation in substantial quantities. They were exported to Venice, Antwerp, Lisbon and the Levant instead and ultimately flew into the African and Asian realms.

Whilst this is not the place for an extended discussion,[40] suffice it to say that there were some mining regions that catered for the emerging global silver trades, whilst others provided the main source of domestic currency circulation. The Saxon Erzgebirge mines tended towards the latter. They went through circles of expansion between the mid-1470s and mid-1480s, and again between ca. 1530 and 1540. In-between there was a long slump and lacuna that was only partly compensated for by the additional output yielded by the Thuringian *Saiger* huts (for which output data is available only after 1505). The Thuringian Saiger industry, however, produced – if all the circumstantial evidence on finance, production and business administration we have from the period is correct – entirely for export to areas located outside Germany.[41] The Falkenstein mines at Tyrol peaked in the 1480s and sustained a flat production curve ever thereafter. We know that after the 1490s virtually all newly mined silver in Tyrol was in the hands of the larger merchant consortia of the Upper German trading cities, and that virtually all newly mined silver in the Austrian mines was exported and went into circulation outside the German lands, often Africa and Asia.[42] Disregarding the Bohemian, Slovakian and Hungarian mines, therefore, the Saxon Erzgebirge mountains would, at the time of Luther, have provided Germany's chief source of new – meaning increment to existing stocks of – silver. And as silver was also the base monetary metal, the Saxon output would have been the main, even sole, source for silver coin output and currency reproduction in the German realms. If we now take a closer look at Saxon silver output figures between 1470 and 1550 (table 2.4), we realize that there was a slump in output roughly between the 1490s and the 1530s. Whilst especially the mines around St Annaberg had fuelled the first cyclical increase in the Erzgebirge mines during the 1470s and 1480s, it was the

39. Karl Hahn, 'Die ältesten Schneeberger Zehntrechnungen', *Neues Archiv für Sächsische Geschichte und Altertumskunde* 53 (1932), 35–50. The most recent and comprehensive discussion of the Erzgebirge silver-mining industry and its relation to state finance, including data on output and tithes (*Silberzehnt*), can be found in Uwe Schirmer, *Kursächsische Staatsfinanzen (1456–1656). Strukturen – Verfassung – Funktionseliten* (Stuttgart: Franz Steiner in Kommission, 2006).
40. Rössner, *Deflation – Devaluation – Rebellion*, chap. 2.
41. Ibid.
42. Ibid., 304–6; table on p. 306.

mines around Marienberg which drove the upward cycle in the Saxon mining realm after 1540s. In-between these two dates, before the 1520s, however, due to the enormous exports of silver from central Europe, per capita resources of silver in the central German regions stagnated or declined, as most of the yearly production was exported.[43] Declining per capita silver output would also have led to a slower *monetary* growth, as silver was the main monetary material. Vis-à-vis a generally expanding population, this may well – in fact it is likely to – have triggered deflationary tendencies in the general price level. This in turn may have been one possible trigger for a general or macroeconomic depression. This notion will be important for chapter 4 and Luther's contribution to economics, especially the problem of hoarding as a form of 'crisis economics' (chapter 4). Implicitly or explicitly from the late 1490s onwards, Luther would have become aware of – or rather would have lived through a time characterized by – a gradually declining per capita monetary stock. At least some of his early writings around 1517 reflect this situation of deflationary depression marked or triggered by a reduction in available amounts of silver per capita of the population.

At the time of Luther, mine shafts in the Mansfield copper-mining district were located about 15 metres from one another, worked by teams of 4 to 10 men per shift.[44] The Saiger huts were bigger and more daunting. From the modern view, the whole mining and silver smelting was neither big business nor factory-like; but in the eyes of the contemporaries, it certainly was strange, big and daunting in many ways, both visually physically and mentally. This is borne out in the rich public discourse on big business, monopoly and the intricate connections between financial markets and the stakes in the mining business. Towards the end of the fifteenth century and until the 1520s, the Fugger and Welser merchant companies of Augsburg, as well as a host of other firms of mainly Augsburg origin, controlled the entire output of the Tyrolean silver mines at the Falkenstein Mountain. The emperors (Maximilian, r. 1508–19 and Charles V, r. 1519–58) had signed over their preferential or monopoly claims as Archdukes of Austria to the mine output at a favourite price of five florins, rather than slightly more than eight florins per silver mark (ca. 250 grams of pure silver) – which was the market price – to the big Augsburg companies. In return for the yearly silver output that was then written over for years to the Augsburgers, Emperor Maximilian alone received several million gulden or Rhenish florins as loans, averaging more than 100,000 Rh. fl. per year. The interest rate payable was usually 25 per cent per annum, reflecting a high risk premium on loans to the emperor who was always more likely to default than any other creditor and who yet was in possession of the main sources of European silver. Who was to profit from these investments? One may be inclined to think it was the emperor, as large sums apparently were never repaid, especially in the later period as the Habsburg rulers were particularly likely, in fact, known to default habitually.[45] But actually it was

---

43. See above, and a detailed examination of the most recent literature in ibid., chap. 2.
44. Slotta and Müller, 'Zum Bergbau auf Kupferschiefer im Mansfelder Land'.
45. For the later period, see Mauricio Drelichman and Hans-Joachim Voth, *Lending to the Borrower from Hell: Debt, Taxes, and Default in the Age of Philip II* (Princeton, NJ: Princeton University Press, 2014).

the big Augsburg and Nuremberg merchant firms such as Fugger and Welser, the 'last medieval super-companies', who profited most, as these loans established a direct claim or preferential drawing right on Europe's most productive silver resources. And silver they needed for their emerging global trade in spices from India and other imports from Asia, which Luther mentions early on, in the third paragraph of his *Von Kauffshandlung und Wucher* (see below). Big business, high finance and the emerging proto-modern state went hand in hand, long before the fiscal–military state and both the fiscal and the military 'revolutions' had run their course. And the wealthy Augsburg and Nuremberg merchant dynasties also had many claims in the central German mining region.[46]

Apart from output, which grew considerably in all major European copper and silver-mining districts since the 1470s; first in Saxony, then Tyrol, then Mansfeld, then Joachimsthal and, in the early 1540s, the Saxon Erzgebirge again (at that time at Marienberg), the age and times also witnessed processes of considerable business *concentration*. This is also important for Luther's contextualization in time and space. Around 1525, more than 3,000 hands were employed in the mining of copper slate in the Mansfeld district. This was about the size of medium-sized towns in the County of Mansfeld, such as Eisleben, where Luther grew up, or Mansfeld City, from which the county took its name and where the counts were involved themselves as the largest stake- and shareholders in the copper mines and smelting works in the 1530s.[47] The factual number of employees would have been much higher. The smelting works or *Hüttenfeuer* near-by where the raw silver-bearing copper was yielded from the slate likewise used up considerable amounts of capital and equipment. The master smelters or *Hüttenmeister* usually organized and financed the mining and smelting processes in combination, so that there was a high degree of vertical integration in the industry. The raw copper was to be weighed and taxed at the Eisleben copper weigh (*Eislebener Waage*), from which we know the production lists for the tenth/tithe or *Kupferzehnt* to which the Mansfeld Counts were entitled and which provide a basis for estimating total silver output as given in table 2.4. From Eisleben the copper would be handed over to the factors and agents of the large corporations running the *Saiger* huts near the Thuringian Forest, of which more in the following paragraphs. These corporations had provided generous loans to the smelter masters, as well as the Counts of Mansfeld, resulting in a dense network of mutual obligations. In 1536 the running of the smelting operations was put into the hands of the Counts of Mansfeld themselves, a process which effectively amounted to a nationalization of the industry. This is one of the more interesting aspects of the industrial development of the area, and Luther can be shown to have played a part in this.

Between 1508 and 1536, the number of *Hüttenmeister* (master-smelters) running one or more smelting works or 'Feuer' (literally 'hut fire', *Hüttenfeuer*) in the Mansfeld industrial district halved, whilst the number of 'fires' or smelting works remained unchanged. This

---

46. Richard Dietrich, *Untersuchungen zum Frühkapitalismus im mitteldeutschen Erzbergbau und Metallhandel* (Hildesheim: Olms 1991).
47. Ekkehard Westermann, 'Der wirtschaftliche Konzentrationsprozeß im Mansfelder Revier und seine Auswirkungen auf Martin Luther, seine Verwandte und Freunde', in Knape, ed., *Martin Luther und der Bergbau*, 63–92 (70).

resulted in an increase in the concentration and vertical integration in the industry, as the average number of *Feuer* (smelting works) per master more than doubled from 2.14 in 1508 to 4.43 in 1536.[48] Some of the larger entrepreneurs such as Dr Philipp Drachstedt, counsellor (*Rat*) to Count Hoyer of Mansfeld, owned eight *Feuer*. During the 1530s, the Counts of Mansfeld became directly involved in the mining and smelting of copper by means of acquiring an increasing number of smelting works (see above). This was partly borne out of their desire to get a better control over silver supplies, which could be got only if one controlled the first stage of the production process, i.e. the smelting of the raw copper. This would also have helped in supplying silver to the mint (*Münzstätte*) at Mansfeld on a regular basis to be minted into coins of Mansfeld denomination, following the Saxon currency standard.[49] After 1536, Count Albrecht of Mansfeld-Vorderort (the counts were divided into three lines or dynasties) became principal shareholder of the large Leutenberg Saiger Consortium (*Leutenberger Saigerhütte*), whilst at the same time emerging as one of the chief entrepreneurs in the mining and smelting of raw copper. Thus, he united all three stages of production in his hands: the mining and smelting of raw copper, as well as the separation of copper into its component parts, silver and pure copper (*Garkupfer*).[50] Luther repeatedly intervened and commented on these matters in writing letters and expert reports for the counts in 1540–42 and 1545 close before his death.[51]

But the crowning step in the sequence of production processes was marked by the *Saiger* (or liquation) process. As has been seen above, this was really a big business. It was globalized. It required prodigious amounts of external finance which native entrepreneurs from the Mansfeld and Saxon districts would be unable to provide. It required rapacious amounts of imported lead. The Saiger process quickly became remote-controlled by Augsburg and some Nuremberg merchant financiers. These were the very same merchants who during the 1520s became proverbial in the public discourse on commercial malpractice and monopoly practices violating the common good – in the midst of which Luther's 1524 pamphlet *On Commerce and Usury* appeared. It was a powerful restatement of the Christian viewpoint in the face of big business that had gotten out of control. Originally much of the Saiger trade had been located around Nuremberg, at that time one of Europe's biggest financial and metal markets.[52] After 1461, some of the bigger *Saigerhütten* around Nuremberg had to be closed, mainly for reasons of environmental pollution and excessive use of natural resources such as timber and charcoal which had become near-depleted in this area. In 1461 two Nuremberg financiers, Burkhardt and Martin Semler, erected a Saiger hut in Schleusingen in the County of Henneberg, about 80 kilometres to the south-west of Mansfeld. More ventures followed in 1462 in Gräfenthal and Hohenkirchen, in 1464 at Steinach, in 1471 at Arnstadt, in 1472 at Schwarza, in 1479 at Eisfeld, in 1486 at Ludwigstadt and in

---

48. Ibid., 64–65.
49. Westermann, *Garkupfer*, 137–38.
50. Ibid., 211–12.
51. Westermann, 'Der wirtschaftliche Konzentrationsprozeß', 63.
52. Westermann, *Garkupfer*, 95–96.

Figure 2.2 *Saigerherd* (Saiger hearth), contemporary depiction after G. Agricola, *De re metallica libri XII*, Basle 1556. (*Source*: © Sächsische Landesbibliothek/Staats- und Universitätsbibliothek Dresden, SLUB).

1488 at Hasenthal.[53] The Saiger industry spread like mushrooms. New huts were erected during the first decade of the sixteenth century at Stolberg and Wernigerode, in the County of Stolberg. In the words of an authority on these processes, between ca. 1505 and 1512 the Thuringian Saiger huts for the 'first time proffered a significant challenge to that of Saxony' (Blanchard), i.e. those mines located in the Erzgebirge Mountains which were under shared control of the Ernestine and Albertine lines of the Dukes and Electors of Saxony.

This mining and metallurgical boom in Saxony and Thuringia has to be seen in the light of two factors. On the one hand, the resources further south around Nuremberg had become exhausted. On the other hand, the two decades between ca. 1460 and 1480 have become known as Europe's age of bullion famine (there were several such famines in the fourteenth and fifteenth centuries). This was a time when both silver output in the major mining districts, as well as silver supply in many parts of southern and central Europe, had been at an all-time low. This situation increased silver's price on the market, the metal as well as the money and financial market. And as most of the circulating coins

---

53. Ibid., 96.

contained some silver, silver's purchasing power in terms of goods increased. This led into a deflation or fall in the general price level, which transformed large parts of the European productive landscape. Some of the larger commercial cities and some of the larger enterprises of the day underwent a period of protracted economic depression between the 1440s and the 1460s. Productive factors, such as labour and capital were frequently un- or underemployed. During such times, as silver's price was significantly enhanced and South American supplies were not yet at hand to alleviate this shortage, such cost- and resource-intensive production processes as the *Saiger* process became more and more profitable. In fact, the Saiger process could not have been implemented as a cost-efficient production process in the absence of monetary contraction and a high silver price. It was a high-powered and very complex and capital-intensive technique that paid off only at a high price for silver (and when the general price level in the economy was low). At a time of general depression and silver scarcity, the *Saiger* process turned into a profitable business, especially since the European population was on the increase after 1470, demanding more cash for transactions. The global production logic becomes especially obvious from the fact that the Saiger huts flourished only until the 1540s. After the 1540s, most of the *Saiger* works were given up, as the influx of cheaper American silver made the Saiger process gradually obsolete. As mentioned above, the concentration processes and cartel-forming initiatives, as well as the 'nationalization' of the Mansfeld Saiger huts in the 1530s and 1540s, are a visual expression of these shifts both in technology and in global demand for and supply of silver.[54]

Cartelization, Globalization and Its Discontents

It is quite significant that amongst the founding members of some of the more important Saiger works in Thuringia, such as the Hohenkirchen, Gräfenthal and Schleusingen Saiger huts, were mint masters, i.e. professional entrepreneurs striking coins or producing currency. Naturally such men were experts on mining, metallurgy and financial markets.[55] The connections with the Upper German high financiers of Nuremberg and Augsburg are also quite obvious and marked. Those financiers had an intimate knowledge of Italian and Flemish-Dutch metal markets. Their networks of trade and correspondents reached far into oriental and Asian realms. Around 1500–1505, huge quantities of copper and silver yielded in the Eisleben mining and smelting district were sold regularly by big merchants and *Saigerhändler* (literally, Saiger traders) such as Christoph Fürer on the markets of Antwerp, Lisbon and Venice. From Lisbon the copper and silver went straight into the African trades of the Portuguese in the wake of Vasco da Gama's return

---

54. Ibid., *passim*. This work, which replaced earlier studies by Walter Mück, *Der Mansfelder Kupferschieferbergbau in seiner rechtsgeschichtlichen Entwicklung*, Vol. 2: *Urkundenbuch des Mansfelder Bergbaus* (Eisleben: self-published, 1910), Walter Möllenberg, *Die Eroberung des Weltmarkts durch das mansfeldische Kupfer* (Gotha: F. A. Perthes, 1911) and Walter Möllenberg, *Das Mansfelder Bergrecht und seine Geschichte* (Wernigerode: Harzverein für Geschichte u. Altertumskunde, 1914), is still fundamentally important.

55. Westermann, *Garkupfer*, 96–97.

from India and the opening of the Cape Route trade in 1498–99.[56] As mentioned above, Luther discussed these trades in the opening passages of his present *Sermon on Commerce and Usury*.

Luther, who turned 20 in 1503 and later on had an intimate correspondence with some of the larger entrepreneurs in the Mansfeld mining districts, including the Counts of Mansfeld, thus enjoyed, during the age of his adolescence, a first-hand glimpse of what economic change and rough globalization meant. As seen above, the big copper mines and Saiger huts in the Thuringian Forest were more or less de-contextualized or dis-embedded to borrow a term from modern sociology; detached they were chiefly from their immediate economic landscape that was by and large agrarian by culture and economic outlook. Financed by foreign capital, mainly from Augsburg and Nuremberg, the products and profits yielded within the area immediately left the region, to be integrated into an increasingly globalized system of financial and goods' flows. After 1490, a process of concentration set in, as ventures became larger and capitalization increased. Supplies of argentiferous copper came from as far away as Slovakia.[57] Prodigious supplies of lead were imported from Poland and shipped via Danzig/Gdańsk through the Sound to Lübeck and Hamburg.

Even larger quantities came from England. Simultaneously to the mining/smelting boom of the 1470s and 1480s, output in the English lead mines around Derbyshire and Yorkshire had increased, stabilizing at a level of ca. 300 tons per annum. These quantities were exported through the port of Hull to the Brabant Fairs in Flanders, from whence they were redistributed via Cologne and Frankfurt-on-the-Main, the latter being an important international fair city, before they reached their final destination in the central European mining and smelting districts of Thuringia–Saxony. English output and exports were stimulated by a concomitant rise in the price level on the large German markets, leading to a doubling of average output and export figures to ca. 600 tons per year in the English industry between the mid-1490s and 1506.[58] Lead provided valuable ballast for the cargoes of wool and woollen cloths, England's major export industry in those days which Luther also commented upon in the present *Sermon on Commerce and Usury*. The intrinsic link of the English lead industry and the Thuringian copper smelting and Saiger industry is documented by the near parallel development in English lead exports and Thuringian copper production. In the words of one expert: 'in "normal" trade conditions during the years 1512–1519 a diminutive 15 per cent increase in Thüringian [*sic*] copper production resulted in a corresponding 15 per cent increase in English lead exports.' No wonder, then, that some of the larger stakeholders in the process, such as Augsburg doyen Anton Fugger, became one of the largest financiers of the English Tudor Crown towards the 1540s.[59] The Fuggers also habitually blackmailed

---

56. See above.
57. Ian Blanchard, *International Lead Production and Trade in the 'Age of the Saigerprozess'* (Stuttgart: Franz Steiner, 1995), chap. 2.
58. Ibid.
59. Most recently with an overview on the older literature Mark Häberlein, *The Fuggers of Augsburg: Pursuing Wealth and Honor in Renaissance Germany* (Charlottesville: University of Virginia Press, 2012).

the Saxon Duke and Elector, whenever the latter stated their intent to increase convoy duties and road tolls, 'the Fugger' – Jakob or Anton at Augsburg – would write a letter to the Saxon rulers, openly threatening to re-route the lead caravans that were bound for the Thuringian Saiger huts through foreign territories. The dukes and electors usually abided. They could not possibly afford the loss of such a veritable source of income drawn from the impressive supply network of the Thuringian Saiger industry and its cart loads and wagons that numbered into the hundreds, if not thousands, each year.

Literally, all those big names and family firms which would become proverbial for the capitalist monopoly and rent-seeking entrepreneur, such as Fugger, Welser, Holzschuher, Höchstetter and many more,[60] can be demonstrated to have had direct stakes in at least one Saiger hut or *Saigerhütte*, meaning one of the large Saiger consortia and partnerships which ran the Saiger huts as production plants. These *Saigerhandelsgesellschaften* usually financed the smelting works by providing the smelting masters (*Hüttenmeister*) with operating capital by means of huge cash loans on *Mittfasten* (Laetare Sunday; end of March), Peter and Paul (end of June), St Michael (end of September) and upon New Year. They provided the money usually via the large Leipzig and Naumburg trade fairs, which coincided with these four cut-off dates. These dates represented reference dates for a whole sort of other monetary transactions among society and economy, as significant amounts of money would have been in circulation during the weeks and days on each side of the payment date. In the 1520s, the sums advanced by the Saiger consortia to the smelters running the *Hüttenfeuer* in the Mansfeld district ranged between 160,000 and 240,000 florins per year.[61] The *Saigerhandelsgesellschaften* obtained the liquid funds from the Nuremberg and Augsburg merchants who had sold their produce at the large Leipzig and Naumburg trade fairs, located about 40 kilometres to the south-west of Leipzig (the fair at Naumburg effectively was the fourth yearly 'Leipzig trade fair', three fairs of which were located *in situ* at the Leipzig fairgrounds). Those monetary proceeds which had remained unspent by the merchants could be employed in the nearby copper-smelting district. In return for the cash provided to the Saiger consortia, the merchants drew bills of exchange, which obliged the *Saigerhändler* to pay back these funds at a later date, usually at Frankfurt, Antwerp, Nuremberg or Augsburg. The merchants would have obtained the liquid funds necessary for honouring the bills by their silver sales at Nuremberg.[62] Thus, they had become integrated into the emerging international system of cashless payment.[63] A truly global cycle of silver had been set in motion.

Therefore, as an expert on this topic once pointedly formulated, the smelting works (*Hüttenfeuer*) in the Mansfeld district were not part of the mines; it was the other way around. Prodigious amounts of raw copper slate were necessary to run the smelting works.

---

60. See, for example, Dietrich, 'Untersuchungen'.

61. Westermann, 'Der wirtschaftliche Konzentrationsprozeß', 68.

62. Westermann, *Garkupfer*, 161s. Also *id.* 'Silberproduktion und -handel. Mittel- und oberdeutsche Verflechtungen im 15/16. Jahrhundert', *Neues Archiv für Sächsische Geschichte*, 68 (1997–1998), 47–65.

63. Markus A. Denzel, *Handbook of World Exchange Rates, 1590–1914* (Farnham: Ashgate, 2010); *id.*, *Das System des bargeldlosen Zahlungsverkehrs europäischer Prägung vom Mittelalter bis 1914* (Stuttgart: Franz Steiner, 2008).

The Saiger huts' hunger for the raw argentiferous copper was proverbial. Merchants incorporated in the *Saigerhandelsgesellschaften* repeatedly tried to form cartels and syndicates and thus influence the market price for copper and silver. This was especially the case in the early 1520s, when many of the larger merchant companies such as the Fugger firm headed by Jakob Fugger the Elder complained about flat sales and dire prospects for their copper.[64] It would become more important in the wake of the 1540s and the rise of the South American silver industry around Potosí.

In fact, the 1520s were an age that cried out for cartels, syndicates and other forms of limitations to ruinous 'perfect competition'.[65] Competition amongst Saiger huts even drove up production levels, to be interrupted only temporarily during the Peasants' War 1524–26, and until the 1528 crisis, when supply far outstripped demand leading to a price and profit slash and to a slump in the industry.[66] Some of the bigger firms and consortia went bankrupt. One result was the limitation of copper production per *Feuer* in the Mansfeld mining districts to 300 cwt of raw copper in 1535. Effectively this represented a cartel agreement.[67] A syndicate was formed in 1533–40 in cooperation with the Counts of Mansfeld as main actors, and sales quotas were fixed for years to come.[68] Under this syndicate agreement, it was stipulated that at least a third of the silver smelted in the Mansfeld district had to be sold to the Counts of Mansfeld and delivered to the Eisleben mint, there to be minted into local money, mostly groats (*Mansfelder Groschen*) as well as Mansfeld florins (*Mansfelder Taler*). These currencies and denominations were necessary to pay workers in the smelting works who were usually remunerated in groats; the average weekly salary for a miner (*Hauer*) in the Mansfeld mining districts ranged around nine groats. The Counts of Mansfeld had thus turned into some of the most powerful and richest entrepreneurs of their age. Hardly anywhere does the amalgamation and symbiotic relationship between the state and big enterprise come across more clearly these days than in the central European mining region.

But since the 1530s ailing market performance stood at the heart of the economic reorganization measures intended to keep alive what would have been the region's flagship business and without doubt one of the biggest employers outside agriculture. And again, Luther was in the midst of these changes, closely involved as someone whose father had been a miner-entrepreneur himself and whose personal opinion weighed heavily in the balance – not primarily as a theologian but rather as someone who had been out to train for a law degree; someone, moreover, who knew the mining business as well as the region and its people quite well; someone who as the 'big man' Reformer of his Wittenberg days in the 1530s and 1540s had amassed an impressive publicity and reputation, including a network of followers and powerful men.

---

64. Westermann, *Garkupfer*, 160–62.
65. *Id.*, 'Der wirtschaftliche Konzentrationsprozeß', 71s.
66. Blanchard, *International Economy*, chap. 4.
67. Westermann, 'Der wirtschaftliche Konzentrationsprozeß', 72.
68. Ibid., 73.

Luther: Struggling with the Market Economy?

So if there were changes against which Luther, his oeuvre and his achievement may be usefully contoured, these changes were idiosyncratic; they related to the very time–space-specific dynamics to be found within the central European mining region of Saxony–Thuringia. And here we finally come to the heart of the problem with which much of the remainder of the present introduction as well as Luther's text will be concerned: credit and financial markets. Large parts of Luther's present *Sermon on Commerce and Usury* (1524) evolved around financial market malpractices. Luther makes abundantly clear that the developments he condemned so vigorously would have happened, or increased in intensity, quite *recently*. Here the matter becomes problematic indeed. If there had been, for instance, a recent surge in mortgage-based financial market transactions (for which we have no corroborating or falsifying evidence whatsoever), this could mean that a deeper and more secure financial market had just emerged in Saxony during the days he wrote his early economic treatises (1519–24). This would be because the number and volume of such financial market transactions is most likely to increase if property rights are stable, or more stabilized than before, reducing credit default and other risks. Capital markets may become deeper if more funds are available for investment.

There is another twist to the story, however, which is equally plausible. If we take Luther's remarks as hints to a recent increase in interest rates, it may as well have related to a *contraction in credit supply* vis-à-vis a more vigorous level of demand. Also increased rates of interest may have reflected an increased risk of default; reflecting a deterioration of people's creditworthiness or bad credit rating. The market data, especially on prices and output, as assembled in table 2.3, during the 1510s and 1520s generally suggests that a contraction in liquid funds would be the more plausible scenario; it simply ties in much better with the notion of a deflation and depression around 1500–25 than older accounts which have placed Luther against the framework of inflation and (imputed) economic expansion.[69] This depression could have made interest rates climb up, a growing number of people and businessmen applying for loans, but not necessarily so because of an improved commercial outlook. The ten years or so of inflation (1525–35/40), which contemporaries such as Sebastian Frank and others complained about[70] and which can be corroborated by the available grain price data from this region,[71] did not set in before 1525, i.e. prior to the end of the German Peasants' War 1524–26. The period leading up to the Peasants' War was a period of depression, marked by low grain prices, which would also have depressed profit opportunities of commercial farmers and anyone

69. For example, Hans-Jürgen Prien, *Luthers Wirtschaftsethik* (Göttingen: Vandenhoeck, 1992).
70. For example, Gustav (von) Schmoller, 'Zur Geschichte der national-ökonomischen Ansichten in Deutschland während der Reformations-Periode', *Zeitschrift für Gesamte Staatswissenschaft* 16 (1860), 461–716.
71. This data has been extracted by Nils Decken in an MA thesis produced at the Universität Leipzig in 2011–2012 under my supervision. Data reproduced in Philipp Robinson Rössner, 'Bad Money, Evil Coins? Coin Debasement and Devaluation as Instruments of Monetary Policy on the Eve of the "Price Revolution"', in *id.*, ed., *Cities – Coins – Commerce. Essays in Honour of Ian Blanchard on the Occasion of his Seventieth Birthday* (Stuttgart: Franz Steiner, 2012), 89–120 (97; fig. 1).

dealing in foodstuffs and related goods.[72] We don't know for certain, but if Luther's remarks on an increasing *Auswuchern* (burdening with usury) due to the *Zinsskauf*, rising interest rates and a rising problem of *Überschuldung* (over-indebtedness) were all based on accurate observation of a coherent and homogeneous set of market data, it would most likely have reflected a shortfall of credit supply over demand – an economic depression rather than anything else.

Be that as it may, financial markets had made an inroad into the region, presumably since the legalization of mortgage transactions by the Imperial Decree from 1500 at the very latest; all these issues will be given detailed consideration in the analytical summary of Luther's 1524 pamphlet in chapter 5. They would have gone hand in hand with an increase in the number and level of professional expertise and institutions, such as lawyers, bailiffs and other means, individuals and institutions providing for the enforcement of contracts.[73] Luther, in fact, frequently lamented about lawyers and those following a jurisprudence profession, as though there had been a recent increase in commercial litigation. Contemporaries obviously struggled to come to terms with this rise of the financial market sector. Luther's *Von Kauffshandlung und Wucher* is a powerful manifest of this. In other regions, such as Holland, urban credit and annuity (mortgage) markets had evolved into relative depth and security a long time ago, marked by persistently low interest rates which had gone down from above 10 per cent per annum in the 1300s and early 1400s to a level below 5 per cent by the time Luther was writing.[74] Life rents (in Dutch *lijfrenten*) were deemed not to be usurious. They had been made legal in the German lands from the fifteenth century but somewhat later than in the Dutch cities, which reflects different stages of development and different concepts of political economy. Life rents and annuities were a popular and much sought-after investment. According to a recent study, the volume of *Renten* transactions on the Leipzig municipal capital markets increased from 1,500 florins to above 5,000 florins p.a. between 1479 and 1500. This ties in with a spurt in silver output levels between the mid-1470s and the 1490s (table 2.4) which would have flooded the central German financial and other markets with liquid funds.[75]

Delayed or deferred payment, consumer credit, payments made upon bills of exchange and loans upon interest – the financial market represented a cornerstone of economic and commercial life in the industrial hotspots within the area where Luther grew up, and

72. Walter Bauernfeind, *Materielle Grundstrukturen im Spätmittelalter und der Frühen Neuzeit. Preisentwicklung und Agrarkonjunktur am Nürnberger Getreidemarkt von 1339 bis 1670* (Nuremberg: Schriftenreihe des Stadtarchivs, 1993), is one of the few works mentioning this detail. See discussion of the problem in Rössner, *Deflation – Devaluation – Rebellion*, chap. 2.

73. Zuijderduijn, *Medieval Capital Markets*, 10.

74. John H. Munro, 'The Medieval Origins of the Financial Revolution: Usury, Rentes, and Negotiability', *The International History Review* 25, no. 3 (Sep., 2003), 505–62. See also graphs in van Zanden, 'Die mittelalterlichen Ursprünge des "europäischen Wunders"'.

75. I have used data from an unpublished source: Alexandra Raack [Holzhey], 'Die Geldgeschäfte des Leipziger Rats im Spiegel seiner Jahreshauptrechnungen im Spätmittelalter', unpubl. MA thesis, Universität Leipzig 2002.

where he spent the majority of his life. This was an economy, not of obligation only,[76] but in many ways one that was founded upon credit. And the credit economy, if it was to function smoothly, obviously required the payment of interest – at the time that is. It must be noted that the taking of interest is neither a necessary thing per se, or *conditio sine qua non* for financial markets to work. Nor would it be eternal law that credit must always be borrowed and lent at interest. In September 2014, the European Central Bank lowered its base rate to 0.05 per cent with negative interest (minus 0.20 per cent) charged to the commercial banking sector for money deposited with the Central Bank overnight. At Luther's time, credit and financial markets obviously settled at rates that were above the late Medieval scholastic maximum rate of 5 per cent, reflecting partly at least an increasing scarcity on the financial and credit market.

Globalization was an issue, too. The discovery of the Cape Route and the subsequent foundation of a string of Portuguese forts alongside the Indian Ocean shores (usually called the Portuguese 'Empire') was financed using German silver which had poured out of the mines at the Falkenstein in Tyrol, the Saxon Erzgebirge or the capital-intensive production processes in the Mansfeld copper-mining and -smelting district described above (*Saiger* huts). Heated debates about big companies were waged during the 1520s on the Imperial Diets at Augsburg and Nuremberg. Luther's vigorous condemnation of big business, laid out within the present volume on *Kauffshandlung und Wucher*, is a vivid expression of many a voice in the public discourse of the day regarding the big Augsburg and Nuremberg firms. During the Peasants' War, the rebellious peasants threatened to pillage and burn down the Saiger huts at Hohenkirchen and Arnstadt, as Jakob Fugger the Elder complained in a letter to the Count Albrecht of Mansfeld in 1525.[77] The peasants were perfectly aware of the intricate webs of finance which the Upper German high financiers had spun not only across the German lands, connecting the remote mining region with the financial hot houses of their day, but also across an emerging global economy. The fact that many of the social conflicts in the Mansfeld mining region evolved around the payment of wages in bad coin – with the miners petitioning habitually for an increased share of their wage bill paid in 'good', i.e. more reliable and stable coin or *gute Groschen* – is a vivid expression of the changes in the global logistics and financial networks of the day. The big companies running the mines and smelting works were accused – often explicitly, as the peasant complaints from the Joachimsthal mines in 1525 bear out – of exporting more silver than good for the local economy to be kept running at a healthy base. As a result, the domestic currencies which remained in the region and with which the miners were paid, were usually debased.[78] This led to considerable

---

76. Craig Muldrew, *The Economy of Obligation: The Culture of Credit and Social Relations in Early Modern England* (New York: St Martin's Press, 1998).

77. Walther Peter Fuchs, ed., *Akten zur Geschichte des Bauernkriegs in Mitteldeutschland*, vol. 2 (Leipzig: Teubner, 1942), document no. 1293 (182): The peasants were *willens […], die saigerhutten zu Hochkyrchen, Arnstatt und unser nui erpaute hutten zu plundern und in grund zu zerreissen.*

78. Eckart Schremmer and Jochen Streb, 'Revolution oder Evolution? Der Übergang von den feudalen Münzgeldsystemen zu den Papiergeldsystemen des 20. Jahrhunderts', *Vierteljahrschrift für Sozial- und Wirtschaftsgeschichte* 86 (1999), 457–76; Rössner 'Monetary Instability, Lack of Integration and the Curse of a Commodity Money Standard'.

fluctuation and variance of the purchasing power of the miners' wage bills. They could lead to transactions – manipulative coin use – that were identified as usurious.[79] Here domestic monetary policy, social issues and international webs of finance intermingled in processes which contemporaries perceived to be remote-controlled by a handful of influential merchant companies from Augsburg and Nuremberg.

This depression in silver-mining output between ca. 1500 and 1530 – which was only partly compensated for by the much smaller production levels of the Thuringian Saiger huts –roughly covered the adult lifespan of our monk from Wittenberg. Martin Luther accordingly witnessed, around 1500, the collapse of what had once been a flourishing, if not grotesquely overheated, industrial boom in the Saxon–Thuringian mining region. Only during the 1540s, towards Luther's death, began the mines around Marienberg to yield again, leading into a second upwards cycle or boom period in the Saxon silver-mining district.[80] But the debates about cartelization and syndicates, as well as the nationalization of the Mansfeld copper smelting plants in the 1530s were an indicative sign of an industry with *problems* in output. They are not characteristic of an economic boom or an economy that is doing well. The Luder family stood in the midst of all these changes. Luther's father had been a mining entrepreneur, as had his brother Jakob and three of his brothers-in-law who were all smelter masters in the Mansfeld mining and smelting district.[81] Luther had a good command of the geological and technical lingo employed in copper and silver mining, which is evident in many places of his written works, even in his translations of the Old Testament and other biblical passages, in which he, apparently, frequently used metaphors derived from mining technology.[82] Luther repeatedly went to Mansfeld to intervene in the restructuring of the mining business during the crucial stage of transition in the 1520s and 1530s. In the mid-1530s, he became directly involved in the process of nationalization of the smelting companies in the Mansfeld mining district. Even though we know that he abhorred the practice of financial market speculation, as borne out not least by the present edition of *Von Kauffshandlung und Wucher*, we also know that he must have possessed at least one stock or share certificate (*Kux*) in a Saxon silver mine himself![83] Counsellors of the Counts of Mansfeld were regular visitors in the Luther household, as were smelting masters such as Wilhelm Rinck, who visited Luther in 1529 personally and whose sons studied under Melanchthon in Wittenberg.[84] In 1518 he met with Count Albrecht of Mansfeld somewhere near Gräfenthal, where a large Saiger hut was located; the Count was part of a legal case involving payment and financing of the Stolberg *Saiger* hut, in which the above-mentioned Dr Philipp Drachstedt and a

79. Rössner, *Deflation – Devaluation – Rebellion*, chap. 4.
80. Munro, 'Monetary Origins', tables.
81. Westermann, 'Der wirtschaftliche Konzentrationsprozeß', 81.
82. Ulrich Wenner, '"Fundgrubner, Berckhauer und Schlacktreiber" – Montanwortschatz bei Martin Luther', in Knape, ed., *Martin Luther und der Bergbau im Mansfelder Land*, 205–17.
83. Which is more surprising as he often condemned shares and stocks as 'play money', see Martin Treu, ed., *Martin Luther und das Geld.Aus Luthers Schriften, Briefen und Tischreden* (Wittenberg: Stiftung Luthergedenkstätten in Sachsen-Anhalt, 2000), 86.
84. Westermann, 'Der wirtschaftliche Konzentrationsprozeß', 75.

man named Tyle (Till) Rinke had owned stakes.[85] Luther moreover was in close contact with some delegates who had participated in the Imperial Diets of 1522 and 1523, the Municipal Diet (*Städtetag*) 1523 and the Imperial Diet of Nuremberg 1524 where the monopoly debates had been waged. He corresponded with the founding members of the Leutenberg *Saiger* hut consortium 1523–1524 – one of the largest of its age – where building works commenced in May 1524.[86]

To what extent these experiences and talks, of which we have no further details, would have influenced Luther's little and great sermons on usury (1519–20) or his later works such as *Von Kauffshandlung und Wucher* (1524), is, of course, open to speculation. Nevertheless, with his experience in law, business and administration, as well as his intimate personal knowledge of the structural transformation processes in the Mansfeld mining business, it would be strange to assume that Luther was either ignorant in economics or that his writings were left uninfluenced by the economic matters of his days. Quite to the contrary, Luther was on top of the economic issues of his days. The Peasants' War broke out in the southern German Landgraviate of Stühlingen in April 1524, shortly before the *Sermon on Commerce and Usury* was delivered (in September 1524 the first printed copies of *Von Kauffshandlung und Wucher* were out in print). Meanwhile, events had gone head over heels, with the social revolt of 1524–25 unfolding as the 'greatest stir in German history', as some historians have said, or the *German Revolution* of 1525 (P. Blickle). One could say many things about Luther, good or bad – but certainly not that he was not an expert, not that he did not have a good grasp of the economic questions of his days. His timing was actually quite good. With his big sermon on commerce and usury of 1524 he was right on top of things. He had touched the right chord.

---

85. Ibid., 75.
86. Ibid., 77.

Chapter 3

LUTHER: IMPULSIVE ECONOMICS

This chapter may be kept brief; it is only intended as a general survey of Luther's economic thought. Its main aim is to correct an earlier notion that Luther was either ignorant or disinterested in economic questions or that accordingly his economics was rather primitive. Neither of these charges is accurate. The key points of Luther's economics and business ethics can be grasped from the monographs and articles by Roscher,[1] Schmoller[2], Barge[3], Fabiunke[4], Strohm[5], Scott[6], Pawlas[7] and more recently the present author[8]; as well as the monographs focused on particular aspects of Luther's economics, such as Prien's volume on business ethics,[9] Rieth's volume on the concept of avarice in Luther's theology[10] or Koch's more recent dissertation on business ethics from the Middle Ages to the modern period.[11] They all have some minor as well as (in some cases) major weaknesses, and not always have they advanced the field considerably or significantly. The interpretation to be found in the following lines will, accordingly, differ in places. By sketching out the cornerstones of Luther's economic ideas, this will provide us with the context for the analytical summary of his *Von Kauffshandlung und Wucher* in (chapter 5).

1. Wilhelm Roscher, *Geschichte der National-Oekonomik in Deutschland* (Munich: Oldenbourg, 1874).
2. Gustav (von) Schmoller, 'Zur Geschichte der national-ökonomischen Ansichten in Deutschland während der Reformations-Periode', *Zeitschrift für Gesamte Staatswissenschaft*, 16 (1860), 461–716.
3. Hermann Barge, *Luther und der Frühkapitalismus* (Gütersloh: C. Bertelsmann, 1951).
4. Günter Fabiunke, *Martin Luther als Nationalökonom* (Berlin: Akademie Verlag, 1963).
5. Theodor Strohm, 'Luthers Wirtschafts- und Sozialethik', in Helmar Junghans, ed., *Leben und Werk Martin Luthers von 1526 bis 1546*, vol. 1 (Berlin: Evangelische Verlagsanstalt, 1983), 205–23.
6. Tom Scott, 'The Reformation and Modern Political Economy: Luther and Gaismair Compared', in Thomas A. Brady, ed., *Die deutsche Reformation zwischen Spätmittelalter und Früher Neuzeit* (Munich: Oldenbourg, 2001), 173–202, updated reprint in *id.*, *The Early Reformation in Germany: Between Secular Impact and Radical Vision* (Farnham: Ashgate, 2013).
7. Andreas Pawlas, *Die lutherische Berufs- und Wirtschaftsethik. Eine Einführung* (Neukirchen : Neukirchner Verlag, 2000).
8. Philipp Robinson Rössner, *Deflation – Devaluation – Rebellion. Geld im Zeitalter der Reformation* (Stuttgart: Franz Steiner, 2012), 204–35.
9. Hans-Jürgen Prien, *Luthers Wirtschaftsethik* (Göttingen: Vandenhoeck, 1992).
10. Ricardo Rieth, *Die 'Habsucht' bei Martin Luther. Ökonomisches und theologisches Denken, Tradition und soziale Wirklichkeit im Zeitalter der Reformation* (Weimar: Böhlau, 1996).
11. Philipp Koch, *Gerechtes Wirtschaften: Das Problem der Gerechtigkeit in der Wirtschaft im Lichte lutherischer Ethik* (Göttingen: V & R Unipress, 2012).

Myths

As suggested in the introduction (chapter 1), there are many myths – let us call them over-simplified meta-narratives – about Luther and his times. Let us here consider only those relevant for the present purpose. An older tradition, based not only on Schmoller and Roscher but also on some twentieth-century Marxist historians and their concept of an Early Bourgeois Revolution[12], had it that at Luther's time early modern capitalism came to the fore and that Luther's economics, as well as the early mercantilist authors, with whom he shared some convictions (see chapter 5), would classify as the 'first economic doctrine of the Bourgeoisie'.[13] This is, of course, wrong. Capitalist practices, such as profit-making for profit's sake, had existed for ages. The thirteenth-century Italian giant family firms and 'medieval super-companies' of the Medici, Bardi and Perruzzi and thirteenth-century financial institutions in Siena and Genoa had provided the blueprint and algorithms for modern banking; setting the scene for the sixteenth-century Augsburg Fugger, Welser, Höchstetter and many others of the 'last medieval super-companies'. Germany's feudal world around 1500 was no less (nor more) feudal, or all of a sudden turning more capitalistic, than the world in, say, 1300 or 1600, 1700 or 1800 AD. A large share of output was appropriated by feudal lords within a redistributive framework of exchange (called, by modern scholars, variously the *manorial system, serfdom* or *villeinage* in its different social, institutional and legal shapes and forms and regional variations[14]); the lords took these things away from the peasants because they could do so. They had done so in 1400, and would still do so in 1600 or 1800. Only towards the end of the eighteenth century and more so during the early nineteenth century were decisive social and institutional reforms implemented which led to a gradual liberalization of production and exchange in the German agrarian economies. The share of population living in big towns and cities did not change much in the German lands, either during the 'long sixteenth century' (1470–1620) or the early modern period as such; it continued to hover around 5 per cent, ca. 1400–1800 (table 2.1 in chapter 2). It would be difficult to argue that there would have been a radical shift towards capitalism or new patterns of business and society, as earlier historians on each side of the Iron Curtain loved to suggest.[15] Only the *inroads* external finance had made into the productive landscape of Saxony and central Germany had intensified since the 1470s, as the previous chapter has shown; they were considerably influenced by the central European mining boom, ca. 1470–90. We may speculate that the mining boom temporarily increased the amount of liquid funds and credit paper available in the central German lands, thus stimulating the credit economy and increasing financial market turnover in the period leading up to the millenarian date of 1500. The turn from boom (1470–1500) to bust (1500–25/40)

12. Adolf Laube, Max Steinmetz and Günter Vogler, *Illustrierte Geschichte der deutschen frühbürgerlichen Revolution* (Berlin [East]: Dietz, 1974).

13. Internationales Autorenkollektiv, eds, *Geschichte der ökonomischen Lehrmeinungen* (Berlin, 1965), 37. This is a translation of an original in Russian by N. Karateyev *et al.*, Moscow 1963.

14. Friedrich Lütge, *Geschichte der deutschen Agrarverfassung vom frühen Mittelalter bis zum 19. Jahrhundert* (Stuttgart: Ulmer, 1963) is still the most erudite and differentiated account.

15. See note 12 above.

would have been significant in terms of altering the basic macro-economic framework in central Germany. But it is important to note that financial markets and commercial malpractice, the two cornerstones around which Luther's 1524 pamphlet evolves, were nothing new. In fact, the pamphlet appears virtually timeless in this regard.

The preceding remarks should also caution us against branding Luther's economics as primitive or unrefined, as many scholars did have it especially in the second half of the twentieth century (during the neo-liberal turn). This charge usually goes together with the notion that Luther never treated economic issues in a systematic way: he was no analytical person, so to speak.[16] The 1962 introduction to the translation of *Von Kauffshandlung und Wucher* in the American edition of Luther's works formulates quite accurately what had been *communis opinio* amongst theologians, historians and most certainly also economists (and which has remained, in many ways, common currency until today):

> Although by no means the most important of Luther's writings, this treatise is of considerable significance for understanding his ethics, and of great interest to the economic historian inasmuch as it includes keen observations on the business practices of the early sixteenth century. Luther's frame of reference was of course that of the Middle Ages. He held to the long scholastic tradition which, following Aristotle, taught that money does not produce money. He agreed with the canonists, who for years had taught that usury is something evil. In common with the vast majority of his learned contemporaries, he knew very little about economic laws. Of the far-reaching economic revolution which was gradually transforming Germany from a nation of peasant agriculturalists into a society with at least the beginnings of a capitalist economy, he had no conception whatsoever.[17]

Eminent German historian Johannes Burkhardt has, in his seminal contribution on *Wirtschaft* to the eight-volume strong *Historische Grundbegriffe* encyclopedia – a flagship project in the historical sciences begun in the 1970s and initiated by Reinhart Koselleck and the idea that historical development can be traced studying the history of ideas – maintained that Luther's economic thinking was 'backward-orientated' (*rückwärtsgewandt*) and based on a corporatist-etatist view rooted in a naturalist economy (*ständisch-naturalwirtschaftliche Moral*).[18] Even the most recent and best biography reiterates this stance.[19] In the light of more recent research in economic history, the statement ought to be modified, and considerably so. It is simply not true that Luther knew only little

16. For example, Ricardo Rieth, 'Luthers Antworten auf wirtschaftliche und soziale Herausforderungen seiner Zeit', in Helmar Junghans, ed., *Luthers Ethik: Christliches Leben in ecclesia, oeconomia, politica = Luther's Ethics in the Realms of Church, Household, Politics. Referate und Berichte des Elften Internationalen Kongresses für Lutherforschung, Canoas/RS 21–27 July 2007* (Göttingen: Vandenhoeck&Ruprecht, 2010), 137–58 (139), reiterating what may be called the mainstream.

17. *Luther's Works, 45: The Christian in Society*, II, ed. W. I. Brandt (1962), 233.

18. Johannes Burkhardt, 'Wirtschaft, IV–VII', in Otto Brunner, Werner Conze and Reinhart Koselleck, eds, *Geschichtliche Grundbegriffe. Historisches Lexikon zur politisch-sozialen Sprache in Deutschland*, vol. 7 (Stuttgart: Klett-Cotta, 1992), 550–94 (561).

19. Heinz Schilling, *Martin Luther: Rebell in einer Zeit des Umbruchs* (Munich: Beck, 2012).

about the functioning mechanisms of the economy. Nor were – or are – there any laws of significance in economics (see chapter 1). The postulate of such laws has been an important discursive figuration in recent economic theory (recent: meaning of the last two hundred years); it represents an epistemological peculiarity in its own right which will not be further analysed here.[20] It has led, accordingly and quite excusably, historians to adopt an unwittingly shifted and biased focus. If we interpret the economy to work according to laws, it is most often the laws invoked by twentieth-century neoclassical general equilibrium theory. And of course, Luther's economic thought – as in fact all contributions to economic thought prior to Adam Smith (see chapter 1) – is bound to appear either primitive, unrefined or plain 'wrong' economics when seen within this very peculiar paradigm and its characteristic epistemological parameters. Instead we ought to approach Luther on his own and idiosyncratic conditions, in order to see which specific conditions of economic life his work was actually aimed at and how it was intended to solve the existing problems of its day.

There was, as has been shown in chapters 1 and 2, no 'far-reaching economic revolution' in Luther's days, either, that would deserve the name. Rather there was, as we have seen in chapter 2, *some* considerable structural transformation in *some* regions of Germany towards a more industrial or non-agrarian pattern, as witnessed in Luther's immediate environment, the central European mining region. What Luther *did* see, however, was an apparent structural mismatch between the *financial* economy and the *real* economy, an insight which has lasted in the German economics tradition left and right – from Marx to Schumpeter – but which has subsequently been lost in the neoclassical paradigm. This was the distinction between *creative* and *destructive* capital (in the words of Hilferding) or wealth creation vs. wealth extraction (Lazonick) – a dichotomy and stance which became much abused in anti-Semitic discourses on 'schaffendes' (creative) as opposed to 'raffendes' (rapacious) capital in writings and speeches from Sombart to Hitler and Goebbels.[21] We should employ a more neutral distinction and differentiate between *productive* and *financial* capital.[22]

And lastly, the claim that Luther would have had no conception of those dynamics that were observable in his days is also plain incorrect. It has been repelled by the evidence presented in chapter 2. Surely, the sermon *Von Kauffshandlung und Wucher* was a pamphlet, above all a polemic addressed at a wider non-academic audience. It was written as an impulse, a dramatic accuse of contemporary malpractices that had culminated in the 1520s. It was written according to this purpose, using the emotionally ferocious language and style of a good polemic – not a textbook. In his 1525 letter to the City Council of Danzig, when Luther was asked to comment on similar matters as

---

20. A good recent critique of the neoclassical paradigm can be found in Bernard Harcourt, *The Illusion of Free Markets: Punishment and the Myth of Natural Order* (Cambridge, MA: Harvard University Press, 2011).

21. Rudolf Hilferding, *Das Finanzkapital: Eine Studie über die jüngste Entwicklung des Kapitalismus* (Vienna: Brandt, 1910).

22. Erik S. Reinert and Arno Mong Daastøl, 'Production Capitalism vs. Financial Capitalism – Symbiosis and Parasitism. An Evolutionary Perspective and Bibliography', *Technology & Governance Working Papers* No. 36 (2011), esp. 3–4.

in the *Sermon on Commerce and Usury* (mainly the taking of interest) but in more practical, ad-hoc terms, both his language and his practical suggestions are much more relaxed and neutral, calmer and pragmatic. To take the *Sermon on Commerce and Usury* literally word by word would mean to grossly misunderstand and misinterpret Luther's *model*. Modern undergraduate textbooks on micro- and macro-economics are full of hypothetical, speculative and at times totally fantastic models about how markets work. But no sensible and prudent student, let alone university lecturer, would ever take them literally, for example, by assuming that preferences and demand schedules form according to mathematically exact and quantifiable indifference curves that approach linear-sloping budget constraints within a world that only knows two goods, A and B, and around which allocation decisions have to be formed (this model is frequently used in explaining utility-maximization schedules). So we should give Luther some credit; we should be clear that much of what Luther said was framed in terms of a very peculiar and highly abstract *model* he had in mind – a model informed by his theology as well as his economics.

With his background in the mining business and his university studies prior to his decision to become a cleric (see chapter 2), Luther had good and well-founded insider knowledge of administration, business and the working mechanisms of the economy of his time. He would have seen no need to sketch or analyse these 'working mechanisms' in the shape of an abstract model – he must have known them perfectly well and could not possibly have much interest in *describing* them. What he wanted was to *change* things towards a more just, a more equitable, a fair society – a Christian economy – by *analysing* what was wrong. And just what such an equitable and fair economy looked like certainly wasn't to be learnt from the economy as it existed these days. Quite to the contrary. So there was little need for a man like Luther to write a textbook on positive economics or to discover the working mechanisms of the contemporary economy, or any other sort of eternal economic laws. So most of the modern charges levied (see above) are simply due to skewed contextualization of Luther's economic thought in the light of modern social science paradigms.

Thus, Luther's work ought perhaps better be interpreted and measured against the benchmarks derived from his new interpretation of Scripture which he had developed around 1517. Here his views simply were different from the mainstream; they were *bound* to lead to a different image of the economy also – and a viewpoint that was quite something else than late medieval scholasticism (which had also been a sort of theologically framed economics, but more relaxed towards profit-orientated entrepreneurship and financial capitalism than Luther would ever be). In many ways, Luther took things much further back than the medieval schoolmen, especially the theologians of the mid-sixteenth-century school of Salamanca, who had developed an increasingly market-friendly dogma, and in many ways even quite a theoretically abstract understanding of markets and price formation. Luther's theory on the other hand was prescriptive rather than analytical; more visual-intuitive (*anschaulich*[23]) than theoretical,

---

23. See Bertram Schefold, 'Edgar Salin and his Concept of "Anschauliche Theorie" ("Intuitive Theory") during the Interwar Period', *Annals of the Society for the History of Economic Thought* 46 (2004), 1–16.

something which proved to have an afterlife in the German tradition of economics into the nineteenth and twentieth centuries.[24]

Luther's Economic Theory: Out-of-This-Worldliness and the Seventh Commandment

Everything Luther said was based on his fundamental idea of the Christian individual justified before God. If there was one fundamental principle that stood at the centre of Luther's soteriology, it was that everything you do should be to the good of your fellow Christians. In his 'Treatise on Christian Liberty' (*Von der Freiheit eines Christenmenschen*, 1520), Luther said:

> Man, however, needs none of these things for his righteousness and salvation. Therefore he should be guided in all his works by this thought and contemplate this one thing alone, that he may serve and benefit others in all that he does, considering nothing except the need and the advantage of his neighbour. Accordingly the Apostle commands us to work with our hands so that we may give to the needy, although he might have said that we should work to support ourselves. He says, however, 'that he may be able to give to those in need' [Eph. 4:28]. This is what makes caring for the body a Christian work, that through its health and comfort we may be able to work, to acquire, and lay by funds with which to aid those who are in need, that in this way the strong member may serve the weaker, and we may be sons of God, each eating for and working for the other, bearing one another's burdens and so fulfilling the law of Christ [Gal. 6:2]. This is a truly Christian life. Is not such a soul most obedient to God in all things by this faith? What commandment is there that such obedience has not completely fulfilled? What more complete fulfilment is there than obedience in all things? This obedience, however, is not rendered by works, but by faith alone.[25]

We need to understand this as a fundamental axiomatic principle around which Luther's thinking about other matters evolved. In this way, Reformation economics, as aptly suggested by Schmoller, was a theory diametrically opposed to classical and neoclassical or Smithian economics which usually stressed self-interest as a prime *movens* and optimal allocative factor within the economic system. But where Smith, and before him many others, such as Conrad Peutinger in 1530, Leonhard Fronsperger in his *Von dem Lob deß Eigen Nutzen* (Frankfurt, 1564), or Bernard de Mandeville in the famous *Fable of the Bees* (1714), had stylized self-interest as the prime mover for the economy, Luther and other Reformation economists abhorred it. This does not mean they did not know it as an economic concept. But to the Reformers, unrestrained self-interest simply was the root of society's destruction.[26]

This view was derived from the Bible. Naturally, everything Luther had to say on money, economics and society had to be based on Scripture. As he pointed out in his

---

24. Johannes Burkhardt and Birger P. Priddat, eds, *Geschichte der Ökonomie* (Frankfurt: Deutscher Klassiker Verlag, 2009), is masterful.
25. *Luther's Works, Vol. 31*, ed. Harold J. Grimm, *Career of the Reformer* (Philadelphia: Fortress, 1957).
26. Schmoller, 'Zur Geschichte der national-ökonomischen Ansichten', 465–67 and *passim*.

Sermon on the Abuse of Church Service in 1521, what counted was not how the saints and holy men had lived their lives, but rather what Scripture said about how we should lead our lives. One should not enquire about what had happened in the past but direct all due care and all attention towards how things should happen in the future. Even the saints had been sinners in many ways and to some degree, but Scripture in its pure nature would never err. Whoever put their full faith and life in accordance with Scripture would not be able to err.[27] This mixture of the *logos* idea of pure faith according to a pure interpretation of Scripture teamed up with the characteristic trait in Luther's theory about the *un-worldliness* of true Christian life.

Characteristic of this 'economics of good and evil' (Sedlacek) was a certain *Weltfremdheit*, which we may perhaps translate as 'alien-ness in this world'. The world as it stood contained a lot of inherent evils. These could not be remedied but by strict adherence to the faith and the sayings of Scripture. Chances were, however, that this was a far cry, as most people in Luther's days were acting quite profane with little heed paid to the principles of the holy writings. In Luther's theology the realms of faith and the realms of state – or the world – remained two fundamentally distinct things. They needed to be kept separate in order for Christian society to work. Luther's 'two kingdoms' or 'two governments' or 'swords', the one spiritual, the other temporal, merged or rather touched upon each other not only in many matters of day-to-day politics, such as the Peasants' War or economics, but also more generally, in usury and the problem of *avarice*. For Luther being a true Christian meant to behave according to, and consequentially to believe in, categories that had not much to do with those categories that governed the material world. In a sermon delivered in February 1521, he said that 'as Christians we must have the Devil and the entire world as enemies' (*Wir christen muessen den Tewffel und die weldt zcw feindt haben und von ir vorfolget werden, wie Christus selber gesagtt hatt* (WA IX, 589, Sermon on 17 February 1521). Nothing could circumscribe this theory of *Weltfremdheit* more accurately. But the practical economic consequences derived from this axiomatic were quite considerable.

As much as this *Weltfremdheit*, as a general yet model-like psychological, anthropological and spiritual disposition, was the most fundamental principle of the true Christian faith, Luther also recognized that it was constantly being violated in reality. In the world he was living in, things were unlikely to change within the near future. In this way Luther's theory becomes both hands-on and abstract at the same time. Everything he said and wrote about the place of the Christian in society usually involved the sketch of an idealized world, that is a *model*. He was very aware of the fact that the current world more often than not violated the basic framework of this model; however, he had a clear understanding and strong view of how the model *should* work. We may note that this methodological approach corresponds quite closely to the modern scientific paradigm

---

27. The original reads *Ich habe gesagt, man fragt nicht, wie die heyligen gelebet und geschrieben haben, ßondern, wie die schrifft antzeygt, das wyr leben sollen. Die frag ist nicht von dem, das geschehen ist, ßondern davon, wie es geschehen soll. Die heyligen haben in yren schreyben yrren und in yhrem leben sundigen kuennen: die schrifft kan nit yrren, und wer yhr glewbt, der kan nicht sundigen yn seynem leben (Vom Mißbrauch der Messe, 1521, WA 8, 424).*

in the social sciences, especially the neoclassical notion of pure – meaning abstract and time–space-indifferent – theory and accordingly designed models (the chief difference being that Luther never set out to formulate his ideas using the modern economic language of mathematics).

One powerful derivation of Luther's axiomatic *Weltfremdheit* was that whatever you did in material terms, for example, regardless how much gold and silver monstrances, chalices, ceremonial cloth and other luxury items you spent on church ritual or by donating it to monasteries, churches and cloisters – where these items frequently ended up in the dead hand, on the altar, liturgical equipment etc. – it would make you none the better before God. What mattered was your inner life. It was 'saddening for God and mankind alike to witness how we have come to measure our Christian nature and goodwill against outer appearance and external things' Luther wrote in 1525.[28] At a time when a lot of money was spent on religious donations and indulgences, that is on 'economically unproductive' purposes (see chapter 5), this was a powerful, if not radical, message. The monetary implications of this axiomatic will be studied in chapter 4.

In this way Luther had taken quite a remarkable detour from mainstream scholastic economics.[29] A distinct axiomatic if not economic theory had evolved in the High Middle Ages under the framework of scholastic theory which informed, and to an extent determined, actions and transactions in the real economy, in the same way as the latter influenced and fed back into the realm of theological doctrine.[30] Scholastic economics was chiefly concerned with justifying prevailing economic practices in the light of a generally rather sceptical view on business and commerce as expressed in the writings of Scripture when interpreted literally. Some of the later scholastic authors had accordingly turned quite nit-picky and quirky in their obvious desire to legitimize certain types of business practice and commercial behaviour which the original holy writings had clearly condemned as sinful. Luther called these lines of argumentation sophistry. Scholastic economics centred on distributional justice, geometric mean and moderation in consumption, expenditure and general individual socio-economic aspiration; enrichment for enrichment's sake was therefore abhorred. Everybody should have a fair living within the world of the Creator. This did not equal a general postulate of economic *equality*. Quite to the contrary, feudal society was marked by an extreme

---

28. In the original: *Es ist vordrießlich fur gott und fur den menschen, das wyr unßer Christlich weßen an dem eußerlichen ding ansahen und lassen das recht ynnerlich anstehen.* In *Von beider Gestalt des Sakraments zu nehmen*, 1525 (WA 10.II, 36).

29. See the relevant sections in Odd Inge Langholm, *The Legacy of Scholasticism in Economic Thought. Antecedents of Choice and Power* (Cambridge: Cambridge University Press, 1998); *id., Economics in the Medieval Schools: Wealth, Exchange, Value, Money and Usury According to the Paris Theological Tradition 1200–1350* (Leiden: Brill, 1992); Joseph A. Schumpeter, *History of Economic Analysis* (New York: Oxford University Press, 1954); Karl Pribram, *Geschichte des ökonomischen Denkens*, vol. 1 (Frankfurt: Suhrkamp, 1994); and Raymond de Roover, 'Scholastic Economics: Survival and Lasting Influence from the Sixteenth Century to Adam Smith', *The Quarterly Journal of Economics* 69 (1955). The following paragraphs are partly based on Philipp Robinson Rössner, 'Money, Banking, Economy', in Albrecht Classen, ed., *Medieval Culture: A Compendium of Critical Topics* (Berlin and New York: De Gruyter, forthcoming, 2015).

30. This wise observation was made by Schumpeter in his *History of Economic Analysis*.

degree of inequality between social or feudal classes. But it meant that incomes and chances should be distributed *proportionally* to everyone's position within and contribution to society. Accordingly, the scholastic theorists entertained a general idea of balance, equilibrium, moderation, mean and limit.[31] Charity toward weaker members of society was imperative. There was a functional relation between rich (*dives*) and poor (*pauper*) within a larger sociological and soteriological model of salvation.

From the fourteenth century onwards, however, the discourse had gradually become transformed. The schoolmen had turned increasingly market friendly, or – as we would nowadays say – *laissez-faire*. Poverty became increasingly identified as problematic. Attitudes toward beggars hardened. The marketplace and idea of individual competition had taken its inroad into society and its discourses about economic exchange,[32] presumably as a consequence of the thirteenth-century commercial revolution (Lopez).[33] Apart from usury and the taking of interest, scholastic economics now evolved around the market as an agent clearing demand and supply and framing interpersonal exchange. Some of the medieval scholars' viewpoints were indeed quite modern.[34] Bernardino di Siena (1380–1444) or Martin de Azpílcueta (1492–1586) had no problem with markets that were by and large free, implying that within a perfectly symmetrical exchange scenario between buyer and seller (no usury, information or power asymmetry involved) the free market price actually was close to best outcome, the just price and optimal allocation of resources. As an authority notes, 'in the medieval context, it makes more sense to interpret the market estimate of the just price [...] as a means to combat the exploitation of individual economic need.'[35] Modern legislation would take no issue with this; our modern usury definitions relating to economic transactions as framed in civil law are similar, and usury (today defined as the deliberate exploitation of asymmetrical distribution of capabilities and personal weaknesses of the individual in the market place) is still defined as an incriminatory behaviour, if not criminal offence. San Bernardino di Siena even developed a very clear and abstract set of basic economic principles such as the different sources of value of things. He made the point that *value* – and accordingly a particular good's market price – could be derived from three sources, first its 'utility' (*virtuositas*), second, its relative 'scarcity' (*raritas*) and finally, this good's 'pleasurability' (*complacibilitas*). This is not radically different from what undergraduate textbooks in micro- and macro-economics tell us about price formation.

So the late medieval schoolmen had thus developed a quite refined model of market exchange, where 'just' prices increasingly turned into just prices, to use Bin Wong's

---

31. Diana Wood, *Medieval Economic Thought* (Cambridge: Cambridge University Press, 2002).
32. Ibid.
33. Robert S. Lopez, *The Commercial Revolution of the Middle Ages, 950–1350* (Cambridge: Cambridge University Press, 1995).
34. De Roover, 'Scholastic Economics'; Tomás Sedláček, *The Economics of Good and Evil* (Oxford: Oxford University Press, 2011).
35. Langholm, *Legacy of Scholasticism*, 87–87. Also *id.*, 'Monopoly and Market Irregularities in Medieval Thought', *Journal of the History of Economic Thought* 28 (2006), 395–411.

pointed formulation,[36] accepting at least in its rough sketches the idea of price formation within a competitive market. What differed from a more modern axiomatic, still, even in the case of the Salamanca schoolmen of the mid-sixteenth century, was that their economic theory was still embedded within a larger moral context framed by canon law and ultimately the Bible. This is something we have now lost almost completely. In this way they were different from modern economics and social science which are frequently de-contextualized and dis-embedded from the social and moral context (*what are the mechanical working principles governing markets?* they ask), that is time–space indifferent. Medieval economics had a much stronger ethical component. They would ask: *how do I want markets to work?* Judgements as to the imputed superiority or scientific complexity of one model over the other ultimately represent a dead end, as they lead to value judgements and individual statements of opinion. But even so, many of the medieval scholastic works on economics could be as axiomatic and model-based as some of the more recent theories (one of the main differences being obviously that they contained less mathematics). Scholastic economic theory, as well as Luther's own peculiar stance, should therefore not be dismissed as either primitive or less modern, or in any way less refined, than contemporary models. It was simply different.

How do we place Luther's thinking, as borne out in his 1524 *Sermon on Commerce and Usury* in scholastic economic discourse? Luther's concept of 'Re-formation' bears a deeply conservative character. Luther's primary aim was to reform church and faith by *returning* to something much older than the status quo, something that lay far back in the past, even though one could argue that this idealized state was more like a discursive concept. It was as utopian as the return to the *Altes Recht* (ancient right) or godly right state of things demanded by the rebellious peasants in 1524–26 all across the German lands. Chances are that such idealized situations or 'natural states' had never existed in reality. Naturally, Luther disliked current scholastic theory; dismissing it as sophistry, that is argumentation for argumentation's sake, nit-picking, bending the truth here and there and ready to justify just about any circumstance as being in accordance with Scripture – if need be. By pointing backwards, he held up – in the Marxian view at least, and this is why some Marxist authors were very critical of him – the progress of history (see above). Rather than providing an analytical or model-based set of axiomatic points, Luther above all presented a *mirror* of current practices in economic life and financial markets during his days. Most of them he found utterly wrong. And by doing so he gave away a surprising range of insights into aspects and working mechanisms of the economy that deserve closer attention.

Even more important than the axiomatic *Weltfremdheit* aspect in Luther's teachings (see above) was his theology of *justification by faith alone* or *sola fide* principle. There were no detours from it, no possible little helpers on the road to salvation, such as indulgences or masses sung and other donations of money and material resources to churches and bishops (as in the Old 'Catholic' faith). It was faith in God alone which determined the individual's actions and position before God. Whoever acted in the faith of God would

---

36. Roy Bin Wong, *China Transformed: Historical Change and the Limits of European Experience* (Ithaca, NY: Cornell University Press, 1997), 139.

be automatically able to do well; anything that was done unfaithfully was doomed to fail. People would act justly as true Christians if they adopted these rules. They would implement the fundamental principles of charity, *Freigebigkeit* and *Mildigkeit* (large-handedness; charitableness). These principles come out clearly in the following words in his *Sermon von den guten Wercken* (1520), where he discussed the seventh commandment in principle (*Thou Shalt Not Steal*):

Mildickeyt: wilch ist eyn werck das von seynem gůtt yderman willig ist zcü helffen vnnd dienenn, ynnd streyttet nit alleyn widder den diebstall [vndd] raüberey. Ĝonndernn widder alle vorkurtzung ĝo ym zceytlichen gutt eyneĝ gegem dem andernn mag vbenn alĝ da seyn [geytz] Wücher: vbertheüren.vbirschlahen falsche ware: falsch maĝ. falsch gewicht, brauchen. vnnd Wer mochts alles ertzelenn. die behennden newen spitzigen sündlin: die sich teglich mehren: ynn aller hanthierŭng In wilchen yderman seyn vorteyll sucht mit des andernn nachteyll. vnnd vorgisset des gesetzes des do saget. Was du willt das dyr andere thun. Das thü du yhn auch Wer diĝe regell für aŭgen hielte. eyn iglicher ynn seynem handwerck. gescheffte vnnd handell gegen seynem nehstenn. wurd woll findenn. wie er sollt kauffen vnnd vorkeuffen. nehemen vnnd gebenn. leyhen vnnd vmbĝonst gebenn. (295)

[This commandment also has a work, which includes very many good works while opposing many vices. In German this work is called *Mildigkeit*[37], a willingness to help and serve all men with one's own means. Further, it fights not only against theft and robbery, but against every kind of sharp practice which men perpetrate against each other in matters of worldly goods. For instance, greed, usury, overcharging and counterfeit goods, short measure, short weight, and who could give an account of all the smart, novel, and sharp-witted tricks, which daily increase in every trade! In these sharp practices everybody seeks their own advantage through the disadvantage of the other, and forgets the law which says: 'What you want others to do to you, you do to them' [Matt. 7:12]. Everyone who keeps this rule before him, each man in his trade, in business, and dealings with his neighbour, would soon find out how he ought to buy and sell, give and take, lend and give without return, promise and keep his promise, and the like.]

The passage went on:

And when we look at the world as it really is and see how greed has the upper hand in all business, we would not only find enough to make a living with honour in the sight of God, but would also acquire a fear and dread of this dangerous and pitiable life which is so overburdened, entangled and caught up with the cares of earning a living and the dishonest pursuit of gain.[38]

---

37. My italics. The 1966 edition of Luther's works has suggested 'selflessness' as a translation, which I have not followed here.
38. *Luther's Works, Vol. 44: The Christian in Society* I, ed. James Atkinson and general ed. Hartmut T. Lehmann (Philadelphia, 1966), 106–7.

Again, this is timeless. It is not antiquated or in any way outdated reasoning but incorporates key principles of what made – and still makes – business and economic activity fair quite independent of context. Luther was formulating a model of (Christian) ethics here. The seventh commandment was another natural cornerstone of Luther's economics, especially his views on avarice, usury and the taking of interest, about which more below. Related to this was Luther's expressively stated *anti-materialism*. Money would never make you happy. As he said in his *Treatise on Good Works* a few lines further down:

> Such a man is absolutely certain that he is acceptable to God: therefore he does not cling to money; he uses his money cheerfully and freely for the benefit of his neighbour. He knows full well that he will have enough no matter how much he gives away.[39]

From this was derived his fundamental stance developed at length in the *Sermon on Usury* (1520) and the present treatise: 'we are also to know by this commandment that this kind of selflessness should extend even to enemies and opponents.'[40] Money would never induce you to do those works that led to individual salvation. Quite to the contrary, as Luther pointed out, for example, in his *Table Talk* on *Gott, und nicht Geld, erhält die Welt* (God, not money, keeps the world going): money and wealth would make people only greedier than they had already been before. Where there was much money around, it would only increase the people's appetite for goods and thus increase prices.[41] (Is this a crypto-version of the quantity theory, or potentially a monetarist stance? One may ask in haste.) You should put your full trust in God that everything would turn out right and be catered for in material terms. Here Luther's vision was that of an agrarian economy with serial plant growth that recurred yearly (or twice yearly) evolving around the harvest cycle of seed → tendering the plants → ripening → harvest → seed. Interestingly Luther had not much to say on harvest failures, which occurred frighteningly regularly and usually led to grotesque price increases every five to ten years on average, if we study existing grain price data which may give away the trend in output. Harvest failure would cause economic hardship, malnutrition and hunger for large groups of society. But when referring to the price increases towards the end of the 1530s, which can be corroborated on the basis of existing Leipzig and other cities' grain market data,[42] Luther usually attributed the causes to market failure, that is distributional effects, rather than absolute shortfalls of output over demand. He especially blamed farmers and merchants' malpractices such as forestalling and other speculative market manipulations, without questioning other possible economic origins of grain price inflation.

Whilst Luther entertained a somewhat idyllic and idealized vision of agriculture as the chief source of society's wealth, as economic actors he held peasants in decidedly low

---

39. Ibid., 108.
40. Ibid., 109.
41. The modernized German translation of the Latin original reads *Darum kann groß Geld und Gut den Hunger nicht stillen, noch ihm raten, sondern verursacht mehr die Teurung. Denn wo reiche Leute sind, ist es allezeit teuer.* See Mayers Volksbücher, *Tischreden*, vol. 1 (Leipzig: Bibliographisches Institut, 1906), 34.
42. See chap. 2, table 2.3.

regard; increasingly so after the events of the Peasants' War in 1524. This is the more paradox as in his stylized autobiographical reflections he would usually identify himself as of 'peasant stock' (chapter 2). But certainly he had the big fish in his mind, the upper classes of village society, the commercial farmers who drove hard bargains with ample surpluses. These peasants 'did not pray', he complained, but would rather have others do that for them. By their avaricious love for the damned Mammon and sheer profit motive, they drove up prices, Luther repeatedly said. This is impossible to corroborate; it may well be true but chances are that the phenomenon of price inflation he complained about repeatedly in the 1530s and 1540s was due primarily to real shortfalls in aggregate harvest supply, for instance, when he prayed for rain at a time of dearth in June 1532.[43] But again, grain markets and prices and Luther's comments upon these economic phenomena give away a very peculiar 'Lutheran' theological concept of avarice and the larger problem of salvation *in the world according to Luther*. To attempt a value judgement and call this more outdated or primitive than other developments in (scholastic) price theory of the time would mean to seriously misinterpret both Luther the theologian and Luther the economist.

'Just Prices' or Just Prices?

As seen above, Luther's basic parameters or economic principles rested upon the scholastic idea of the 'just' price and *distributive justice* in terms of chances and market participation.[44] But it has also been demonstrated in the previous section how more relaxed medieval scholastic price theory had become about the free market. Luther, on the other hand, with his ethical stance on economics – manifested especially in his (1529) preface to the *Oikonomics/ Hausvater* book by Justus Menius – added something to an existing discourse that was quite peculiar.

High medieval scholastic definitions of just prices varied; some of them, however, came quite close to what we would nowadays identify as a 'free market price'. Aquinas and Augustinus had, in the thirteenth century, defined the price as something that was determined by utility (*indigentia omnia mensurat*). Others, such as Petrus Johannes Olivi (d.1298) and Buridanus or Bernardino di Siena would define it according to *virtuositas*, *complacibilitas* and *raritas*. Roman law (Corpus Iuris Civilis) had known the stance *multitudo civilis, prout scilicet in civitate sunt multa artificial ad quae una domus sufficere non potest*.[45] Here the connection was made between economic differentiation, specialization and division of labour. Once a community had reached a threshold size, that is had turned into *society*, exchange of goods and services would have become a necessity. And where there were many goods and buyers around there would have been some sort of competition, which would influence processes of price formation. This did not mean that incomes and

43. For example, *Tischreden, vol 3. Von guten Werken – vom Gebet* (Leipzig: Bibliographisches Institut, 1906), 37s.
44. See works cited in note 29.
45. All examples taken from Otto Gerhard Oexle, 'Wirtschaft. III: Mittelalter', in Brunner, Conze and Koselleck, eds, *Geschichtliche Grundbegriffe*, 526–50 (547).

wealth should be distributed equally. Rather, economic *chances* should be harmonized and stay in line with the general features of a just profit and a just price of things the medieval authors had in mind. Regulating prices by applying maximum or target prices for select ranges of goods set by the government was a key feature in pre-modern political economy. But scholastic economics also had an eye on market prices where they could – or would – not be fixed by the state but should be governed by a principle we may call the Christian ethic.

As in many scholastic texts in Luther's *Kauffshandlung und Wucher*, the just price already comes across, if weakly so, as a market price, that is the (f)actual price as the result of individual bargaining processes; apart from market distortions and commercial malpractices which Luther discussed extensively in part I of the present sermon and which will be discussed in more detail in chapter 5 below. In the 1540s Luther said, for instance, when consulted on current practices in the grain trade, that it was difficult if not impossible to a priori determine just what a just price was. Too many sorts and types (of grain) were around; moreover prices may be subject to variation according to time and space. Price formation should be left to the individual's conscience based on natural law, Luther said.[46] Price regulation, in terms of maximums and thresholds, should be something the state should deal with – at times of crisis, and/or for those goods that were considered essentials, that is whose production and exchange could not be left to the free market forces.

Therefore, Luther was, at least within the present sermon, clearly much less laissez-faire than the scholastic economists of the thirteenth and fourteenth centuries who had argued in a rather abstract and quite theoretical way that free and partly competitive markets were necessary and some sort of natural given. Luther's market price on the other hand was framed in a more ethical stance; he brought morals back into the field where the scholastics had apparently left it. The fixing of not only maximum or target prices for essentials such as bread, grain and meat but also wages was a cornerstone of medieval and early modern political economy. In the German lands, prices were frequently fixed for essentials – especially grain, usually in terms of a maximum (or less frequently a threshold) level at which the market should clear. Such target or set prices were known by the name of *Preistaxen* (for prices); literally 'tax prices' or 'set rates'. In the German context such set rates were known for a different array of goods, mainly foodstuffs including beer, fish and meat, but sometimes also drugs (medicine), iron, timber, wine, etc.[47] Such regulations frequently also extended to wages, insurance and freight rates, that is those very activities that kept the market running and the distribution of goods in motion. To maintain the common good, general welfare as well as economic, political and social order, worldly authorities habitually published edicts and legislation relating to price regulation. These forms of market intervention can be documented as early as the thirteenth century; chances are that they were much older than that.[48]

46. Rieth, *'Habsucht' bei Martin Luther*, 205.
47. Hans-Jürgen Gerhard, *Wesen und Wirkung vorindustrieller Taxen: Preishistorische Würdigung einer wichtigen Quellengattung* (Stuttgart: Franz Steiner, 2009).
48. Ibid., esp. 17–29.

For these reasons, pre-industrial society may – and has – come across as somewhat 'über-regulated'. At least that is what scholars have called it at times.[49] Upon second thought, this stance should come across as fallacious. One need only remember to what extent certain markets were (and sometimes still are) regulated even in the free market economies of the western European world during the twentieth century. The British and German coal industries were nationalized at some stage in the 1950s (the German coal industry has remained so until very late), and so were the big railway companies during most of the twentieth century. During the 1960s and 1970s British state ownership extended to major companies in manufacturing such as automotive flagships Rolls Royce or Jaguar, the latter part of British Leyland Motors, to be nationalized in 1975. In the case of the Scandinavian countries, the state has in the twentieth century usually contributed more than 50 per cent of gross national product. These countries can be said, with a pinch of salt, to be 'run' by the state. Or consider the Common Agrarian Policy of the European Union since the 1970s, which has, by the use of tariffs, quotas, bounties and subsidies, created an essentially un-free, highly regulated and heavily protected market. Market regulations and other rules governing our daily lives, from the DIN norms to food security measures, up to the proverbial angular shape of a 'norm' EU-banana, abound. Against such examples the early modern and largely 'traditional' economies of Europe should appear, if we look more closely at the matter in a long-term perspective, as rather laissez-faire and comparatively thinly regulated. The more so, because the grasp of the state was not nearly as intensive in terms of being able to tax, control and monitor its subjects' economic activity as it is today. Markets have always been regulated, especially for essentials, such as foodstuffs or energy. They have been so for a reason; even nowadays regulation extends much more deeply into the layers and multiple webs of human activity than we usually acknowledge. We should therefore perhaps give up the notion that early modern economy or society of Luther's day was in any way more 'governed' or significantly more regulated than ours nowadays. The opposite is true.

Much more difficult it is, accordingly, to determine ex post whether such 'set prices' as abounded in pre-modern economy, the German *Taxen* prices and other forms of market interventions, were always fixed on the basis of *real* transactions that had gone before, that is reflecting actual transaction prices (then the degree of intervention would have been comparably low); or whether they represented somewhat more rigid interventions in the shape of imperative-normative minimum or (more often) maximum values below/ above which transactions would be considered illegal and usurious. Be that as it may, *Taxen* or set rates were usually published – in the later eighteenth century in the emerging newspapers (*Intelligenzblätter*), serving as a general guideline for all other transactions within this particular market.[50] It is in either case impossible to determine the share of

---

49. Andrea Iseli, *Gute Policey. Öffentliche Ordnung in der frühen Neuzeit* (Stuttgart: Ulmer, 2009).

50. Gerhard, *Wesen und Wirkung*; also *id.* and Karl Heinrich Kaufhold, *Preise im Vor- und Frühindustriellen Deutschland. Nahrungsmittel – Getränke – Gewürze, Rohstoffe und Gewerbeprodukte* (Stuttgart: Franz Steiner, 2001), introduction. For Scotland the practice and nature of the so-called 'fiars prices' in the seventeenth and eighteenth centuries has been masterfully surveyed in A. J. S. Gibson and T. Christopher Smout, *Prices, Food and Wages in Scotland 1550–1780* (Cambridge: Cambridge University Press, 1995).

smuggling and evasion, that is the share of transactions carried out in violation of the legal norms. But during the early modern period, we find practically no documented resistance to such price fixation measures. They seem to have been commonly accepted, if not generally adhered to, not only by the writers and theorists of political economy but also by the general public at large – as a keystone and foundation pillar of the economy and the common good. Some historians have expressed their surprise at this, given the imputed high density of regulation inherent in the pre-industrial economy.[51] However, as a new study by Harcourt has made it clear, the seemingly high degree of 'policing' and market regulation in seventeenth- and eighteenth-century Europe would have appeared humble and quite laissez-faire compared to modern markets in the twentieth and twenty-first century. And what is true of the eighteenth century is, in this particular regard, also true of the sixteenth century, or Luther's time. Effectively, the markets of pre-industrial Europe at the time of Martin Luther were, compared to our modern ones, much more lightly and less densely regulated; not least because the state could not do much about it in terms of real control (and that is what Luther indirectly complains about).[52] Nevertheless, we must turn a more recent *communis opinio* on price fixation on early modern grain and victualing markets on its head. It was not in spite of but arguably *because of* the existence of such regulative frameworks including some intervention support that allocation mechanisms and European markets functioned so well serving a populace that was, over the centuries, almost continuously increasing. Otherwise, we should expect much more debate and common complaints, for instance, about the *Taxen* and their imputed failure to clear markets and advance the common good.

Very often the prices 'set' by the governments seem to have been very close to actual or current market prices, that is the somewhat elusive thing we have become accustomed to call the free market price. In fact, since the times of Bernardino di Siena scholastic economics had taken a more relaxed approach, arguing that price formation was happening, metaphorically clad into modern syntax, at the intersection of one imaginary supply and one imaginary demand curve. But we must be careful, still. Luther's remark that prices at his time were formed *wie lands gewonheyt ist zu geben und zunemen* (Strohm) may suggest that this was also the case in Saxony during his time. However, in Luther's time some markets, including grain, were sometimes quite strictly regulated. The practice of markets being embedded within either a 'moral economy'[53] (E. P. Thompson) or an 'economy of obligation'[54] (Muldrew) surely continued for a long time, even though some circumstantial evidence seems to suggest that regulation by the authorities had become less and less effective with more and more transactions during the sixteenth century representing the result of completely individualized negotiations. It is, of course, difficult to trace the degree of monetization and the evolution of a market economy in Luther's times. Contemporary

51. Gerhard, *Wesen und Wirkung*, 43.
52. Harcourt, *Illusion of Free Markets*.
53. Edward P. Thompson, *Customs in Common* (New York: New Press, 1991).
54. Craig Muldrew, *The Economy of Obligation: The Culture of Credit and Social Relations in Early Modern England* (New York: St Martin's Press, 1998); Martha C. Howell, *Commerce before Capitalism in Europe, 1300–1600* (Cambridge: Cambridge University Press, 2010).

sources such as municipal accounts are full of documented transactions and recorded prices, mostly for foodstuffs and timber or expenses relating to building works.[55] To what extent such transactions always involved completely free bargaining processes according to the rather modern notion of a market price, or to what extent they were still predominantly framed within a system of societally framed thresholds and maxima, that is influenced by government regulations aimed at keeping prices and wages within 'just' boundaries determined by the common good and the scholastic equilibrium theory, we will never know.

But the problem can be solved at least partly – and some light shed on it – by acknowledging that even nowadays there is hardly a single market that is completely free, that is without any regulation whatsoever or completely dis-embedded from its wider socio-cultural and psychological ramifications. Economic activity, exchange and price formation take place within a constant tension field framed by individual demand and supply curves, preferences of the consumer as well as the cost-efficiency schedule of the producer – and the rules, laws and regulations inserted into this competitive field by the government and the state, rules that are – usually – targeted at sustaining the 'common good'. Luther's many comments on markets may suggest, therefore, that a considerable share of such transactions had become *progressively de-contextualized* from their non-economic circumstances. Again the sermon *Von Kauffshandlung und Wucher* appears to be a powerful anti-pamphlet.

By the Sweat of Your Brow: Rank and Status

Social status in Luther's view was derived from one's own toil and physical expenses of labour and capital resources. Principally peasants and farmers had the same position within the godly order of things as artisans and craftsmen; even merchants were allowed a fair living and rank within this order. Everybody had to work so as to make a living. Private assets and wealth were nothing Luther disapproved of in principle, as long as they were modest and used to the good of others. Money was a necessary evil. Society couldn't do without it. And as long as it was used as a means of transaction and modest accumulation ('just' profit rather than just profit), it was not contrary to God's order. But whoever was wealthy enough was obliged to freely spend their surplus on charity or lend money at zero interest. To work, be that as a peasant, miner, artisan or merchant, was necessary in this world, because before consumption would come production: of viable resources, such as food, clothes and other necessities. In this way and in Luther's eyes, labour was a form of 'worship' to God which every true member of the Christian community had to engage in. This stance, which simply underlined a basic Christian command, that is to work and live according to one's status and position in society , must not be mistaken for a Puritan or Calvinist work ethic imputed by Max Weber or a

---

55. Rössner, *Deflation – Devaluation – Rebellion*, chap. 2.

more general sense of predestination which combined the idea of salvation with material success.[56]

Charity for the poor and a secure baseline income (*gerechte Nahrung*) were the main criteria defining 'just' behaviour and a 'just' configuration of the social landscape in Luther's view. Labour was the principal source of value. Principally, all activities were equivalent, be that the labours and pains of a smith, a farmer or the rather lush life of a nobleman. In terms of modern theory this would sound awkward. Ever since events turned sour during the Peasants' War in summer 1524 and 1525, Luther developed an increasingly negative view on farmers and farming. Later in his life, in his *Table Talk*, a genre reflecting the 'old Luther' as one scholar has aptly remarked,[57] he said about peasants that they were lazy, 'snoring and slumbering' away, careless of what the future may bring. Having been lulled into superficial security by the mere empirical observation of repetitive plant growth year after year (see above), Luther proposed that peasants lived without sorrow. They would sell their produce without much risk; having to pay only tithes and taxes to their feudal lords. Everything grew without their input and initiative (*wachse ohne ihr Zutun*).[58] This is of course plain nonsense, if taken literally, especially given the low average total factor productivity in agriculture these days, the highly work-intensive production process (the capital coefficient was low in agriculture) and regularly occurring harvest failures and subsistence crises. But again, Luther's apparently staunch negation of economic reality needs to be seen in the wider context. He was making a stylized point here. More likely he was referring to God's chosen order of the physical landscape, and how little the berated farmers, the 'big fish' in rural society on top of the village hierarchy could ever make out of it with their ungodly desire for earthly profit. 'A Christian peasant is like a wooden poker' he said, using the oxymoron as a rhetoric figure.[59] What Luther meant here were the big farmers of his day, in sixteenth-century nomenclature 'Meier' or 'Erbzinser' or in modern German *Vollbauern*. By gambling with the harvest in order to drive up prices and raise their mark-up, they gambled with something that was for God alone to steer.[60]

It follows from these lines, almost consequentially, that Luther had no differentiated understanding of the concept of *adding value* – a fundamental concept in fact in terms of modern growth and development theory, as well as European economic development in historical perspective.[61] In fact, he sometimes argued that only agriculture and mining were productive, which, when taken literally, sounds almost physiocratic.[62] Luther had no concept of productivity, as Schmoller pointed out. The very idea that the *quality* and not

---

56. Richard Sennett, *The Corrosion of Character: The Personal Consequences of Work in the New Capitalism* (New York: W. W. Norton, 2000); Koch, *Gerechtes Wirtschaften*, 236–40.

57. Kurt Aland, ed., *Luther Deutsch. Die Werke Martin Luthers in neuer Auswahl für die Gegenwart*, vol. 9, *Martin Luther Tischreden*, 3rd ed. (Stuttgart: Klotz, 1960).

58. Aland, ed., *Luther Deutsch* 9, 184.

59. Ibid., 264. A poker had to be made from iron, of course.

60. Ibid., 263.

61. Erik S. Reinert, *How Rich Countries Got Rich… And Why Poor Countries Stay Poor* (London: Constable 2007), chap. 3 and *passim*.

62. Strohm, 'Luthers Wirtschafts- und Sozialethik', 210.

only quantity of labour and capital input could co-determine total output and agrarian performance was apparently alien to Luther.[63] His 'labour theory of value' derived from his peculiar theology. Everyone who expended labour and pains for making a living should be entitled to a reward when operating in the Christian faith, at least a modest one: be that a wage or profit. Luther principally understood that even merchants and traders should be entitled to a modest profit, but only as long as this corresponded to the expenses and labours incurred in the process. Here he was in accordance with Thomas Aquinas (*Summa theologiae*, 2a2ae).[64] But as the late medieval scholars since the fourteenth century had already developed a quite sophisticated concept of the skill premium, that is the idea that everybody should be paid not chiefly according to status, but above all qualification and demand for and supply of their skills,[65] Luther again took things back much farther than the late medieval scholasticism consensus.

In commerce he saw the biggest evils or greatest temptation to slip from the realm of the 'just' profit (as a reward for one's time and labour spent on making a living) to 'unjust' or capitalist profit – *chrematistics* to use the Aristotelian terminus technicus, or profit for profit's sake. At times when the amount of labour and physical expenses on productive purposes was naturally limited by the individual's physical strength and ability and thus capacity to work, the duration of the working day or the productive capacity of the soil, commerce and business ranged very low on Luther's scale of appreciation. This is because in the commercial realm there existed no obvious upward limits to expansion. The Augsburg merchants involved in the first voyage of Vasco da Gama were said to have made a 150 per cent return on their investment.[66] Whilst such profit mark-ups are not unusual in international commerce nowadays, at Luther's time they were thought to be grossly exaggerated and perverse (even though the actual net profit rates of the total yearly business of the Augsburg companies may have been lower, they certainly surpassed the scholastic equilibrium benchmark of 5 per cent per annum, however. We know that the spice trades paid astronomic profits at times). With regard to commerce, Luther differentiated between good and bad trading. Distribution and trade were necessary, and commerce was not an incriminating activity per se. And a modest mark-up on goods was to be considered legitimate as there were, at any point in time and space, a certain range of goods that could not be produced locally, or which were in short supply or otherwise not available. Society needed the merchant to secure a stable and safe allocation of resources. Commerce was bad, however, when carried out purely for the sake of profit – that is profit that went beyond the legitimate desire to make a fair and equitable living. Here Luther was again more conservative than some of the contemporary theologians. In fact, at roughly the same time when he wrote his *Kauffshandlung* the late scholastic doctors of Salamanca developed the idea of capital as a productive factor, which prefigured a more

63. Schmoller, 'Zur Geschichte der national-ökonomischen Ansichten', 474.
64. Wood, *Medieval Economic Thought*, 153.
65. Ibid., 153.
66. Konrad Häbler, *Die überseeischen Unternehmungen der Welser* (Leipzig: C. L. Hirschfeld, 1903), 24, and Franz Hümmerich, *Die ersten deutschen Handelsfahrten nach Indien 1505 und 1506* (Munich: Oldenbourg: 1922), 142.

relaxed attitude towards commerce, entrepreneurial activity and the lending at interest in general.[67]

The Role of the State

On the role of the state, Luther maintained that princes and kings had the most difficult time on earth. Here we find roots of the charges levied against twentieth-century Lutheranism and its *Autoritätshörigkeit*, a sort of uncritical willingness to follow worldly authority, which led to the most dramatic consequences in the period of national socialism (1933–45) when Protestants seem, on balance, to have been slightly more prone to subscribe to Hitler's programme and ideology than other confessions of the Christian faith. It was practically impossible for those whom God had invested with the temporal sword, that is worldly authority, *not* to commit sin on a daily basis, Luther said. But evil deeds and wicked un-Christian people needed to be punished. Temporal law (judicative and legislative) needed to be upheld with a sharp sword (executive) so as to safeguard property rights, the continuation of public life and what may classify, put in modern words, as 'law and order'. In his *Ermahnung zum Frieden auf die zwölf Artikel der Bauerschaft in Schwaben* ('Admonition to Peace, A Reply to the Twelve Articles of the Peasants in Swabia', 1525), in which he was mildly in favour of the peasants' cause, he emphasized that the existence of serfdom and *villainage* (*Leibeigenschaft*) was legal and a God-given; it had been practiced amongst the Old Testament prophets (WA 18, pp. 326s.). Luther even went as far as stating that inequality was at the core of society and that one should not mistake Christian freedom for any personal or political freedom and total economic equality. This was something which the more radical reformers and political agitators of the 1520s, such as Thomas Müntzer at Mühlhausen, would disagree with; of course, this was the same *Autoritätshörigkeit* of some versions of the Lutheran faith mentioned above; be that in twentieth-century totalitarian Germany or nineteenth-century US, where the Norwegian Lutheran church during the Civil War (1861–65) opted in favour of slavery, as slavery was something known from Scripture.[68] Luther said, in reply to the Third Article on the peasants' demands (which called for the abolition of serfdom in general), 'This article would make all men equal, and turn the spiritual kingdom of Christ into a worldly, external kingdom; and that is impossible. A worldly kingdom cannot exist without an inequality of persons, some being free, some imprisoned, some lords, some subjects, etc.; and St. Paul says in Galatians 5 that in Christ the lord and the servant are equal.'[69] On the remaining and more specific points on the peasants' agenda Luther had

---

67. Francesco Boldizzoni, *Means and Ends: The Idea of Capital in the West 1500–1970* (Basingstoke: Palgrave Macmillan, 2008).

68. Erik S. Reinert and Francesca Lidia Viano, *Thorstein Veblen. Economics for an Age of Crises* (London: Anthem, 2012), 22. I am indebted to Erik Reinert for mentioning this to me.

69. *Luther's Works, Vol. 46: Christian in Society III*, ed. Robert C. Schulz, gen. ed. Hartmut T. Lehmann (Philadelphia: Fortress: 1967), 39. Original: *Es will dieser artickel* (i.e. the third of the twelve articles of the Upper Swabian Peasantry) *alle menschen gleich machen, wilchs unmueglich ist, Denn welltlich reich kan nicht stehen, wo nicht ungleichheyt ist ynn personen, das etliche frey seyn, etliche gefangen, etliche herren, etliche unterthan &c.* (WA 18, 327).

nothing to say, he said, implying that the existing worldly, that is politico-juridical and economic, order must not be touched or changed. In the early stages of the Peasants' War in 1524, he even admonished the rulers to be less oppressive towards the rebellious peasants, acknowledging that the latter had a cause. But as the events unfolded he took a completely different turn in his subsequent pamphlet *Wider die räuberischen und mörderischen Rotten der Bauern* (1525).[70] The peasants in Luther's opinion had challenged worldly authority and the God-given order; second, they had been robbing and pillaging churches, cloisters and estates; and third, they had deliberately misinterpreted the Gospel for their own purposes. All three aspects made the peasants blasphemous in Luther's mind.

New institutional economics has, following the path-breaking work by North and Weingast,[71] or more recently in a blockbuster survey on global inequality in historical perspective,[72] framed the state as a provider of public goods; safeguarding property rights, rules and algorithms relating to all matters of human interaction including economic exchange with the purpose of stabilizing expectations and thus setting up a framework that is beneficial to the development and flourishing of commercial life. Luther was far from a modern understanding of the state determining, by its choice of exclusive or inclusive political and economic institutions, whether the way forward would lead into development or underdevelopment. Luther's state was strong, but derived from the need to make the Gospel work within a world that was utterly un-evangelical. Luther replied, in another *Table Talk*, to the question whether government should rule according to reason or to law, that in theory reason should be the paramount principle of governance. Yet, due to the inherent character of the world and its corrupted habits, minds and practices, rule based on law and order was the only feasible way of implementing justice and security.[73]

Another interesting side remark was his famous comment on the Frankfurt Trade Fairs in the present *Sermon on Commerce and Usury* (1524). Frankfurt was, in Luther's words, the 'silver sink' that drained the Empire of money spent on superfluous imports. This remark has earned him the somewhat dubious classification as an early mercantilist.[74] A mercantilist he clearly wasn't, but his remarks bear close resemblance to a general bullionist stance which would have been shared by most contemporary thinkers on political economy during Luther's days. He only saw a strong need for the state to intervene where the market would not resolve existing problems of unjust distribution of chances and resources. This was something later cameralist and mercantilist authors would have shared during the seventeenth and especially the eighteenth century with

70. WA 18, 344–61.
71. Douglass C. North, John Joseph Wallis and Barry R. Weingast, *Violence and Social Orders: A Conceptual Framework for Interpreting Recorded Human History* (Cambridge: Cambridge University Press, 2009).
72. Daron Acemoglu and James A. Robinson, *Why Nations Fail: The Origins of Power, Prosperity, and Poverty* (New York: Crown, 2012).
73. Kurt Aland, ed., *Luther Deutsch. Die Werke Martin Luthers in neuer Auswahl für die Gegenwart, Vol. 9: Martin Luther Tischreden*, 3rd ed. (Stuttgart: Klotz, 1960), 186s.
74. Fabiunke, *Luther als Nationalökonom*, 88.

Justi's works on state regulation of markets; even Adam Smith was by no means an advocate of free markets generally, reserving a role for the state in this department (when markets went over the top). Luther had a rudimentary understanding of a negative balance of payments (due to his bullionist stance) and the problems this may cause in terms of employment of productive factors (capital, labour and land), as well as interest rates (see chapter 5).

But we may note a surprising detail here. Luther repeatedly referred to the princes and their 'calculations' as he phrased it, presumably regarding the nature and extent of tax yields and government income, and how God would eventually thwart their plans.[75] Apparently the time around 1530 had witnessed an early phase of proto-cameralist state craft with accounts and tax registers produced in Saxony that drew up a rough schedule of Saxony's districts and their relative (taxable) wealth.[76] A significant number of Latin schools were founded in the wake of the Reformation in every minor as well as major town in sixteenth-century Saxony. We may assume that these state-backed efforts made a valuable contribution to the promotion of useful knowledge. Luther also repeatedly emphasized the increased number of lawyers and law suits witnessed during his times, as though German society had not only become more commercialized but also progressively functionally differentiated. The obvious alternative was that the region had simply become more indebted; the more debt, bankruptcy and hardship there is the more lawyers are needed to handle property right transfers during times of crisis. Be that as it may, it was once reported, for instance, by means of *Table Talk*, how Luther, someone who had (briefly) trained as a lawyer himself, took the hands of his son Martin (who by that date would have been a toddler or little boy) and said to him that if he chose to become a lawyer, he would deliver him to the gallows with his own hands, in case he followed this plan. (We may hope that his son was too young to understand these words.) At another day, when a lawyer got awarded his LLD at the University of Wittenberg, the residence of the Albertine rulers of Saxony, Luther commented: 'yet another snake has been born that will act against the theologians', and that jurisprudence was the most abominable occupation in this world. No one would be following it, if not for the sake of money: *Juristen – böse Christen*, he would say ('jurists make false Christians').[77] We may interpret these utterings against the developments sketched out above, particularly the mining boom and structural changes in Saxony and Thuringia where population growth and specialization had led to a reconfiguration of the productive landscape (see chapter 2). Commercial litigation certainly increased in the wake of the mining boom and the subsequent post-1490–1500 crisis in the Erzgebirge mining districts; litigation was something Luther repeatedly picked up on. It is one of his *leitmotifs* in the present *Sermon on Commerce and Usury*.

---

75. Aland 189. 'The princes do not pray for God's help when they set out a plan or policy but will say "three times three makes nine; two times seven makes fourteen", and surely this calculation is correct. However, Our Lord will say: what do you make of me? Am I a simple number that does not count? Am I being here in heaven in vain? For this reason he overthrows all their plans and distorts all their calculations.'
76. Aland, ed., *Tischreden*.
77. Ibid., 199.

Usury

Luther's main economic concern, however, was *usury*. Usury was the root of all the evils he saw in his times. Avarice, one of the seven cardinal or 'deadly' sins, was intrinsically related to it. Avarice was in a sense the *motive*, usury its *figuration* in economic reality. It was part of a more general human desire to make money out of things whose primary purpose was not money to be made out of them. More specifically, and put in modern words, many of Luther's writings, as well as significant portions of his *Sermon on Commerce and Usury* were directed at what we would call 'financial capitalism'. Financial capitalism was not the exact equivalent, but was a representative figuration of the behavioural motives Aristotelian philosophy knew as *chrematistics*.

In his *Table Talk*, Luther referred to the Fugger merchants at Augsburg, the proverbial example and main scapegoat for all aspects where financial capitalism had gone mad. Jakob, and later on (after 1525) his nephew Anton Fugger, could with a wink provide several tons of gold and silver at a day's notice at Augsburg or anywhere else where they employed agents and factors. Allegedly Augsburg alone would provide 30 tons (*Tonnen*) of gold at once within three weeks' notice. Luther was certainly exaggerating here, and it is not clear (nor ultimately relevant) if he referred to a metric unit, or simply a *Fass* or vat of undetermined size and weight. But the bottom line is clear: Augsburg in the days of Luther was what Canary Wharf or Wall Street or the *Börsenviertel* in London, New York and Frankfurt-on-the Main, respectively, are nowadays for the financial economy: a global financial hub where millions of florins were handled every day. Hardly any other merchant, prince or king could draw such sums at such short notice and ease as Jakob Fugger the Elder, who headed the Fugger imperium until 1525. There were a few that came close, people perhaps such as Bartholomäus Welser or Ambrosius Höchstetter, Fugger's contemporaries and likewise powerful *Augsburger Handelsherren* (merchant princes). Luther repeatedly emphasized and discussed specifically the role played by the techniques of remitting large sums of money and obligations from one place to another without using cash. In order for large sums to circulate over thousands of kilometres, only written notes (*Zettel*) were required which would disappear discreetly in one's sleeve. Within Luther's world of a moral economy based on honesty, willingness to pay in cash and to 'lend expecting nothing in return' – or else let go (of interest charges, of loans advanced, etc.), these techniques represented the ultimate manifestation of financial capitalism. In modern terminology and according to recent research, we may identify these notes as some sort of letter of credit, most likely a *bill of exchange*.

Bills of exchange and related financial techniques (of cashless payment) had been developed in thirteenth-century Italy in close cooperation with the papal court. Many of the Italian merchant-bankers acted as financiers and bankers for the Curia. As the Church was the largest financial enterprise and business corporation in Europe these days, collecting dues and fees from all over Christian Europe which needed to be remitted to the Curia in Rome, it needed institutions and experts who would remit these moneys over wide distances at comparative ease, low risk and competitive cost. In sixteenth-century Germany, the Fugger merchants of Augsburg had taken up this role for the German lands. The Italian merchant bankers' financial techniques developed in the twelfth and thirteenth centuries, spread gradually outwards from Italy and, during the fourteenth and fifteenth centuries, found their way into the less-developed parts of northern and central Europe, where they were used by the larger merchant-bankers and financiers in the large Upper German financial markets, too. Around 1500 AD, Fugger's handwriting alone[78] would suffice to get the ball rolling, and hundreds of thousands, if not millions, of florins were transferred around Europe within weeks, if not days. When a balance was struck for the Fugger corporation upon patriarch Jakob Fugger the Elder's death (d. 1525) in 1527, the company was said to have had assets to the tune of more than three million florins (of which 1.6 million were liquid assets!), and liabilities came to ca. 867,000 florins. To provide just a rough dimension (even though modern comparisons are problematic): around 1500 AD, the yearly monetary wage for a maidservant was around five florins, excluding, of course, non-monetary components in lodging, clothing and food. An urban craftsman or master artisan who did well and had a flourishing workshop could expect to make around fifty florins or gulden per year.[79] What the Fuggers had amassed in terms of assets and wealth (under Anton the volume of assets of the firm is said to have doubled),[80] therefore, was way out of line with what the vast majority of contemporaries could possibly expect. At three million florins for assets (in 1527), this came to at least 60,000 ordinary working people's yearly income. Of course, the economic landscape of the 1500s was not in the same way monetized as our modern one; many forms of economic exchange, production and consumption either bypassed the market (for instance, when they belonged to the subsistence sector) or were not cleared using money and monetary figures (prices) as the syntax of exchange. So those monetary income figures we have from late medieval and early modern sources, often municipal accounts based on day labour ratios, are pretty meaningless when it comes to establishing average income figures where no such concept or the possibility of measuring it did exist. However, the above figures serve to sketch out the dimensions. Luther reported how 'the Fugger', presumably referring to Anton (as the quote refers to a time during the 1530s), when asked to pay taxes (*Schatzung*) to the City Council at Augsburg, replied that he did not even know how much money he had at Augsburg. His capital and assets were invested across 'the entire world, in Turkey, Greece, Alexandria, France, Portugal, England, Poland and just about any- and everywhere'.[81]

Money was sterile, as Luther emphasized,[82] following Aristotle (and many others to come yet, such as Karl Marx or J. Schumpeter). Money could never beget money. Nevertheless, the taking of interest had, during the Middle Ages, become regular practice, even though it was frowned upon by canon law and hefty discourses were waged repeatedly, if not continuously, about asking to give back more than had been given over

---

78. *Martin Luther, Tischreden*, vol 1, Meyers Volksbücher (Leipzig: Bibliographisches Institut, 1900), 59–60.

79. Jakob Strieder, ed., *Die Inventur der Firma Fugger aus dem Jahre 1527* (Tübingen: Lapp'sche Buchhandlung, 1905).

80. Mark Häberlein, *The Fuggers of Augsburg: Pursuing Wealth and Honor in Renaissance Germany* (Charlottesville: University of Virginia Press, 2012).

81. *Martin Luther Tischreden*, vol 1, 60.

82. For example, Aland, ed., *Table Talk*, 259–60.

in the initial transaction. This could be any transaction ranging from personal loan, a firm partnership (*societas*; *commenda*), marine insurance, a bill of exchange, a life annuity (*census*), etc. But rather than interpreting the canonical bans on usury as normative (which they were not; they were factually quite inefficient), we may perhaps interpret them as reflections of the degree or intensity with which they were broken. Whenever discourses on usury became more pronounced in terms of frequency and heftiness, for instance, during the thirteenth and fourteenth centuries, they served as a good indication that the credit economy had expanded, so people had something to complain about. Usury laws were a form of social criticism. They were, moreover, quite schizophrenic, as it was on top of all else, *churchmen* who regularly lent out capital at interest, especially in Luther's days. It had been churchmen who had developed the techniques of the modern credit economy to perfection. The large remittances of tithes and *servitia*, that is the papal dues collected all across European Christendom from Poland to Portugal, which had to be transferred to Rome using the bill of exchange as a safe means of cashless payment, would not have been possible without the financial instruments and assistance in the process by the Upper Italian merchant and banking houses of the thirteenth and fourteenth centuries.[83] Invariably, any such exchange transaction carried (an often concealed) interest.

In the fourteenth century, interest rates on loans provided to the English kings had ranged at up to 33 per cent per annum. Financial arrangements involving the charging of interest, such as partnership agreements (company finance) under the *commenda* and *societas* schedule, or early forms of marine insurance, likewise during the fourteenth century, were sealed at rates of up to 50 per cent per annum. Not all of them were deemed usurious.[84] According to Schmoller, a general ban on the taking of interest was lifted by Pope Martin V in 1425. The Frankfurt Jews were entitled to lend at 21.67 per cent per annum in 1491.[85] In 1540, when Luther wrote his last great economic pamphlet anent usury *An die Pfarrherren Vermahnung wider den Wucher zu Predigen*, he reported that interest rates stood at up to 40 per cent and that the Church was in the midst of the usury business. As usual, Luther was silent about the *exact* nature and type of transaction under consideration. Interest rates would have varied with the type of credit transaction or 'financial market segment', depending upon whether the transaction was a deposit, company share or loan. The terms and duration of the loan and the solvency or credit rating of the debtor also mattered. Such stray observations on interest rates as we have from the Middle Ages and the early modern period assembled in the classic pieces by

---

83. Markus A. Denzel, *Handbook of World Exchange Rates, 1590–1914* (Farnham: Ashgate, 2010), introduction, for the most recent history of the bill of exchange as a financial instrument and innovation in medieval and early modern Europe; *id.*, *Das System des bargeldlosen Zahlungsverkehrs europäischer Prägung vom Mittelalter bis 1914* (Stuttgart: Franz Steiner, 2008).

84. Wood, *Medieval Economic Thought*, 193.

85. Schmoller, 'Zur Geschichte der national-ökonomischen Ansichten', 556. According to Schmoller the calculus was based on 1 *heller* per florin interest per week.

Sylla[86] or Le Goff[87] or more recent surveys[88] are by and large chance observations that do not allow a systematic differentiation according to market segments or types of loans. Suffice it to say that during the later Middle Ages, church bans and prohibitions on usury should above else be interpreted as discursive tools and normative statements. They were not necessarily or always kept or adhered to by the economic actors.

In fact by the later fifteenth century in most areas of Europe, rates of interest around 5 or 6 per cent per annum were recognized as perfectly legal.[89] The Dutch urban *renten* markets had since the later fourteenth century settled at around 5 per cent in normal years.[90] In England state finance could be obtained at rates that were slightly higher, around 7 per cent p.a. In the Italian city states, the rates were lower.[91] Based on alternative market data, land rents, which were usually lower than rates on state finance, the picture is essentially confirmed. German rates were close to the northern European average of 5 per cent p.a. in the 1500s.[92] This was, however, neither a linear nor steady process. It had been marked by cycles and conjunctures but above all constant negotiation and re-negotiation in the religious discourse about what was considered legitimate and what was not. The actual level of interest did not matter at first, as the question had originally evolved around the problem whether interest was legitimate per se; only later did the theologians' debates evolve around the question of maximum rates. The thirteenth century had seen a tightening of usury laws (but no one seems to have cared that much, see above), when the taking of interest was generally blamed as a sin against fellow Christians and the community of God. The higher rates for urban and state finance in the twelfth and thirteenth century seem to reflect this generally negative stance.[93] In the High and later Middle Ages, the taking of interest then became exempt from the usury laws, and thus made legal, for certain cases such as late or deferred payment (*poena detentia*), the *damnum emergens* or compensation to the lender who incurred a loss after making a loan in consequence of parting with his/her money; or the *lucrum cessans*, which was compensation for foregone chances of investment (possibly carrying a higher return).[94] Endless scholarly treatises informed by Aristotelian and Platonic ideas combined with Biblical words were produced by the medieval scholars (scholasticism) reflecting an ever-changing dynamic relation between religious discourse and private

---

86. Sidney Homer and Richard Sylla, *A History of Interest Rates* (New Brunswick, NJ: Rutgers University Press, 1991).

87. Jacques LeGoff, *The Birth of Purgatory* (Chicago, IL: University of Chicago Press, 1984).

88. For example, Charles R. Geisst, *Beggar Thy Neighbor: A History of Usury and Debt* (Philadelphia: University of Pennsylvania Press, 2013).

89. Most recently Geisst, *Beggar Thy Neighbor*, chap. 2. I am following my piece Rössner, 'Money, Banking, Economy'.

90. Jan Luiten van Zanden, *The Long Road to the Industrial Revolution. The European Economy in a Global Perspective, 1000–1800* (Leiden: Brill, 2009), 22–23 (based on data by Jaco Zuijderduijn).

91. Stephen R. Epstein, *Freedom and Growth. The Rise of States and Markets in Europe, 1300–1750* (London: Routledge, 2000), 19, fig. 2.1.

92. David Stasavage, *States of Credit. Size, Power, and the Development of European Polities* (Princeton, NJ: Princeton University Press, 2011), 41, figs 2.3 and 2.4.

93. See graph in Van Zanden, *Long Road*, 23.

94. Wood, *Medieval Economic Thought*, chap. 8; Geisst, *Beggar Thy Neighbour*, chaps 1, 2.

entrepreneurship. The boundaries of what was legal – in a sense of conforming to Scripture – were fluid, and they seem to have been adjusted to changes in the material and economic environment.

This apparent malleability of the legal and institutional environment should, by the way, caution us against haphazard assumptions of the Christian usury and market doctrine as barriers to economic growth (which is sometimes said about modern Islamic law and finance). Men usually found ways of interpreting Scripture creatively or else found alternative strategies that conformed to the teachings of the Old and New Testament. The history of the bill of exchange and the rise of the European system of cashless payment, which was fundamentally based upon the concept of interest-bearing credit (by the time dimension it included, reflected, for example, in the technique of *discounting* as well as *endorsing*[95]), remains the most indicative and vivid testimony of how dynamic the relationship between faith, culture and economics could be, and how flexible people became in financial innovation and alternative interpretations of the words of the Gospel. Religion as such is never hostile to economic behaviour per se; it is people's interpretation of religious texts and their relation to economic activity which determines how market-friendly religious discourse becomes.

Coping strategies directed at circumventing the usury laws were and had been numerous (the invention of purgatory had been one of them, after all[96]), as a decree of the Imperial Diet in 1530 noted, ranging from a difference between nominal loan and the sum actually repaid (which would have been higher), the concealment of interest in the shape of a commodity transaction, in which the purchaser paid a higher price than originally stipulated in the contract, to regular payments in return for services made by the debtor. Sometimes, such techniques included the stipulation of credit repayment in money where the actual loan had been made in goods that were worth much less than their nominal or stipulated value; finally different types of money could be used by stipulating a different type of money or currency in the actual loan contract, say current money, or small change, whilst actual payment would be demanded in gold or full bodied coin. As the latter usually bore a premium on the nominal exchange rate, such operations fulfilled the criteria of 'more asked for in return compared to the amount given over originally'.[97]

Luther had no positive opinion on the scholastic authors of the fourteenth and fifteenth centuries who in his opinion had bent Scripture in ways that had made them arrive at a very relaxed stance on usury and the taking of interest. In a resolution of the Imperial Diet from 1500, a general ban on interest was still promoted,[98] even though at that time this would have been a more or less empty prescription, as canon law, as well as common practice had for long accepted interest as the cornerstone around which financial markets evolved. Interest rates were necessary for capital markets to exist; even

---

95. Denzel, *Handbook*, introduction.
96. Le Goff, *Birth of Purgatory*.
97. Fritz Blaich, *Die Wirtschaftspolitik des Reichstags im Heiligen Römischen Reich: Ein Beitrag zur Problemgeschichte wirtschaftlichen Gestaltens* (Stuttgart: G. Fischer, 1970), 161.
98. Ibid., 159.

the churchmen had realized this. Only consumptive credit, micro-credit so to speak, borne out of the immediate necessity to make a living, should remain completely interest-free. Moreover, the 1500 Imperial Decree specifically exempted *Rentenkauf* and *Wiederkauf* from the prohibition, two very common types of annuity or rent transaction (see chapter 5) which represented the flagship financial products of the age, as they were a perfectly legitimate way of gaining a secure income in the area of usually 5, but sometimes up to, 10 per cent per year.

Luther's meandering polemic on usury, especially the second part of the present treatise (originally the *Sermon on Usury* from 1520) should be understood in the light of the preceding remarks. Here Luther was not so modern, after all, as it seems. Current 'Catholic', that is Old Church, practice on markets, prices and credit was much more relaxed about usury in Luther's days, as the expert opinions produced by Dr Johannes Eck in and around 1514 demonstrate.[99] Whilst the bill of exchange had been the Italian bankers' means of circumventing usury bans, in the German lands the census, annuities and land rents (*Zins- und Rentenkauf, Gülte*) were accepted as a general coping strategy.[100] The same is true for late fifteenth- and early sixteenth-century Spain, where *censos* were used and legitimized in scholastic economic discourse as 'the sale of a right to a yearly payment of money or produce, secured on real estate'.[101] Spanish mercantilist development discourse around 1600 (the 'arbitristas') had it, in the words of Martín González de Cellorigo, *Memorial de la política necesaria y útil restauración a la República de España* (Valladolid, 1600), that the 'cause of the ruin of Spain is that the wealth has been and still is riding upon the wind in the form of papers and contracts, *censos* and bills of exchange, money and silver and gold, instead of in goods that fructify and by virtue of their greater worth attract to themselves riches from abroad, sustaining our people at home'.[102] Again the rather timeless notion of two types of capitalism comes to the fore in Luther's text here: good and bad, financial-speculative vs. productive capitalism, an important dichotomy in political economy which economists from Luther to Hilferding, Schumpeter and Sombart knew and were aware of. In the German lands the census or annuity business had been legitimized by papal bulls by Martin and Calixtus in the fifteenth century. By the late fifteenth century, this technique represented one of the cornerstones of urban (i.e. state) finance, particularly in the north German Hansa towns.[103]

---

99.   Johann Peter Wurm, *Johannes Eck und der oberdeutsche Zinsstreit 1513–1515* (Münster: Aschendorff, 1997).

100. Schmoller, 'Zur Geschichte der national-ökonomischen Ansichten', 557–58.

101. Marjorie Grice-Hutchinson, *Early Economic Thought in Spain 1177–1740* (London: G. Allen & Unwin, 1978), 52.

102. My italics. I am indebted to Erik Reinert for providing this reference.

103. See, for example, H.-P. Baum, 'Annuities in Late Medieval Hanse Towns', *The Business History Review* 59, no. 1 (1985), 24–48, and for a most recent and comprehensive survey, Eberhard Isenmann, *Die deutsche Stadt im Mittelalter, 1150–1550: Stadtgestalt, Recht, Verfassung, Stadtregiment, Kirche, Gesellschaft, Wirtschaft* (Vienna: Böhlau, 2012).

On the Leipzig financial market, annuities and municipal obligations could bear up to 10 per cent per annum.[104] Life rents could bear up to 20 per cent in some German imperial cities in the early sixteenth century.[105] Census or *Gült* (Zins-/Rentenkauf) transactions were usually sealed at 5 per cent per annum. Luther's second part of the *Sermon on Usury* (1520) and the present composite sermon *Von Kauffshandlung und Wucher* (1524) focused on this particular type of transaction, although his remarks make for a considerably wide range of possible transactions and interpretations. For these reasons, the original term *zinsskauff* should be left as it is: un-translated.[106] Luther himself avoided a final stance on the subject, as he grudgingly acknowledged certain scenarios in which the taking of interest might be considered legitimate, most notably in the concept of *Schadewacht*. This was a legitimate[107] payment of interest (*interesse*) in compensation for a situation in which the repayment of a loan was uncertain and the lender's ability to lead a decent lifestyle was jeopardized by his parting with the money. He had to live, after all. Similarly this applied to widows and orphans who had no other means of supporting themselves than by investing their savings at a profit (see below). Lest their humble savings were eaten up by their daily expenses, they should be allowed to lend and thus invest them at interest. Here Luther thought that 4 to 6 per cent per annum was acceptable.

Usury, however, covered more than the mere taking of interest. It was in Luther's teaching, intrinsically linked with the concept of *Freigebigkeit, Milde* – a counterpart to usury, something he called *gelindickeyt*, 'epijkia, equitas, clementia, comoditas', for instance, in his *Epistel am 4. Adventssonntag* (WA 10.I.2, 174) and the discussion of the seventh commandment (*Thou Shalt not Steal*). It generally related to circumstances where something was lent and more was asked upon return. Such scenarios, as Luther himself said in *Kaufshandlung und Wucher*, covered situations where *rye* (was) *to be repaid with wheat, bad money to be repaid with good, bad wares to be repaid with good wares* (75). Luther referred to such practices as asymmetrical bargains (*vngleiche hendel*). Any asymmetrical bargain that was based on inequality in exchange and difference in the value of things given and things received in return was to be deemed usurious.[108]

Luther's *Kauffshandlung und Wucher* may be called crypto-scholastic in outlook and scope but only upon first and very superficial glance. Mainstream scholastic economic theory taught as part of a larger theological curriculum at the universities of his time, for instance, by Gabriel Biel (c.1415–1495) in Tübingen, who wrote a treatise on monetary

---

104. Uwe Schirmer, 'Der Finanzplatz Leipzig vom Ende des 12. bis zur Mitte des 17. Jahrhunderts. Geldwesen – Waren- und Zahlungsverkehr – Rentengeschäfte', in Markus A. Denzel, ed., *Der Finanzplatz Leipzig* (Frankfurt, in preparation).

105. Schmoller, 'Zur Geschichte der national-ökonomischen Ansichten', 557.

106. See chapter 4.

107. *[S]chadewacht heissen die juristen bucher zu latein interesse, vnd solch leyhen ist freylich kein wucher, sondern* [...] *ehrlicher dienst*, see *An die Pfarrherrn Vermahnung wider den Wucher zu predigen* (1540), Luther WA, I, 345.

108. The original reads *Nu ist an allen zweyffel niemant, der do wolt, das yhm rocken auff korn, boeße muntze auff gutte, poße wahr auff gute wahr gelyhen wurd.* It should be *klar, das solche leyher widder die natur handelnn, todlich sunden, wucherer seyn* und *ungleych handelln mit yhrem nehstenn.* For Luther, usury was defined as scenarios of exchange where people *mehr odder eyn anders widder geben mussen, das besser ist, dan sie geporgett haben.* Martin Luther, *Gesammelte Werke*, vol. 6 (Weimar, 1888), 48–49.

economics,[109] or the Spanish theologians at the school of Salamanca, ca.1550, appears to have been more advanced in terms of accepting the market and credit economy as a fait accompli. Superficially, Luther went further back than that. But he had every reason for doing so. And upon second sight his economics was neither backward nor did it represent outdated scholastic stances of the pre-1300 era. Luther had created something new, as should by now have become apparent (and which will hopefully become even more apparent from the remaining chapters and the translation of the 1524 German original). Following Keynes,[110] the strict adherence to and emphasis of a general ban on usury would have made perfect sense within in an undeveloped agrarian world, where total factor productivity, as well as the means of effecting economic and technological change total were low. The old scholastic interest rate ceiling (of 5 per cent) would have kept capital's marginal productivity high, simultaneously providing affordable means of *both* increasing business turnover and generating means for investment, whilst at the same time preventing the common man from being bled by the loan shark.[111] And it may be remembered from most recent times that there is no iron law dictating that people *have* to charge interest on loans and related commercial transactions *at all* for the economy and financial markets to work. As mentioned previously in September 2014, the European Central Bank lowered its base rate to 0.05 per cent p.a., even charging private commercial banks a negative (or punitive) rate of minus 0.20 per cent for overnight deposits with the European Central Bank. This was the very biblical command: *mutuum date, nihil inde sperantes* – lending without expecting anything in return. To say that Luther's economics was underdeveloped or primitive or less well developed than 'High Scholasticism' simply means to completely misunderstand the man, his religious as well as his economic theory. The detailed comment of his great 1524 pamphlet (chapter 5) will make this very clear.

---

109. In his larger theological treatise, see Heiko A. Oberman, ed., *Gabrielis Biel, Collectorium circa quattuor libros Sententiarum* (Tübingen: Mohr, 1977).

110. Keynes, *General Theory*; after Blaich, *Wirtschaftspolitik des Reichstags*, 164 (who used the German edition, *Allgemeine Theorie*, 2nd ed. (1955), 297).

111. A similar point was made on Spain, see Grice-Hutchinson, *Early Economic Thought in Spain*, 53.

Chapter 4

THE GRIP OF THE DEAD HAND: CRISIS ECONOMICS FOR A PRE-INDUSTRIAL SOCIETY?

Monetary Shortage and Economic Crisis

One point which Luther touches upon rather in passing in the present sermon *Von Kauffshandlung und Wucher*, but which arguably represented a fundamental aspect of connection between his religious criticism, theology and his general economics, is the practice of hoarding money or, alternatively, putting it into unprofitable ventures such as indulgences or church interior for ritual purposes. Such practices seem to have become increasingly popular in Luther's age, as has been shown in chapter 1. And with his stance on indulgences, Luther also, wittingly or unwittingly, contributed something new to our modern knowledge in political economy regarding money and its speed in circulation – money's *velocity* of circulation.

The problem of velocity is important in at least two regards. First, it ties in with the hypothesis of, and the causal mechanisms triggering, a general depression as sketched in chapter 2. At times when profits and economic outlook are negative on balance, there will be fewer funds available for investment.[1] People will be reluctant to spend or invest; they will hold back much more money for precautionary motives than is healthy for the economy. They will put it away for an indeterminate amount of time; not withdrawing it from circulation entirely or forever (which would make the *amount* of money go down), but rather withholding it from the market. This will decrease money's velocity. The Keynesian notion of holding cash for precautionary motives comes to mind; and as the mercantilist and cameralist authors before him (since about mid-seventeenth century), Keynes never tired of stressing the importance of *spending* money in the economy. Here he stood at the end of a long line of economic thought which had developed similar ideas since the early sixteenth century at the very latest, as the present chapter will show. This thought will be developed as an afterthought on Luther's economics as sketched in chapters 2 and 3; it adds some new light and context to Luther's theological and economic ideas. What Luther – and numerous contemporary contributions to the public discourse of his days on the spending and hoarding of money – picked up on repeatedly, both directly and indirectly, was a scenario of monetary scarcity and a reduced speed of

---

1. See chapter 2, and for a full discussion and extended data survey, Philipp Robinson Rössner, *Deflation – Devaluation – Rebellion. Geld im Zeitalter der Reformation* (Stuttgart: Franz Steiner, 2012), chap. 2.

money's circulation. In his direct critique of indulgences, as well as indirectly at many other places, Luther framed his general views against what we may call a 'tragedy of hoarding'.

But secondly, the following will also have a bearing in terms of placing Luther the economist within a wider chronological framework of political economy and the development of economic thought on the question of money's velocity in the longer run. The *communis opinio* expressed, for instance, by Pribram or Schumpeter[2] has had it that velocity – as an independent variable – was discovered sometime around 1650 (perhaps by William Potter). The Spanish theologians of Salamanca, whilst aware of the primitive quantity theory and the aspect that a currency's exchange value fluctuated with changes in its demand and supply, seem to have interpreted velocity as constant.[3] The later cameralists, however, devoted increasing attention to *circulation*, i.e. the desire for a high velocity of money and a low demand for money to hold, because a low velocity (high demand for money to hold) may lead the economy into a cycle of deflation and depression. Frequently economic discourse used the metaphor of a turning wheel or sphere[4], but it is not easy to exactly disentangle M (money) from V (velocity) in this peculiar strand of mercantilist–cameralist discourse. Moreover, it is not usually acknowledged that the velocity of circulation can be interpreted as the inverse of hoarding, called *demand for money to hold* in modern nomenclature. But if we do so (and more on the formal aspects discussed below), we can trace scholarly discussions of velocity much further back than the 1650s when it is said to have first emerged as an independent variable in the political economy discourse. In fact, the discussions go as far back as Martin Luther and the humanists.

As noted above, the sixteenth century is generally held to be a century of economic expansion, and there is nothing wrong with the notion as such; as seen in the long run or c. 1470–1620, both population and prices increased yielding the proverbial age of the so-called Price Revolution.[5] But we must stress that the first two-and-a-half decades of the new century were different. They were marked by deflation and depression in wages and living standards. The inflationary processes which Sebastian Franck and many other publicists of the age noted and commented on did not set in prior to the end of the Peasants' War.[6] Luther's early works (between ca.1515 and 1525), which amounted to a

---

2. Karl Pribram, *Geschichte des ökonomischen Denkens*, vol. 1 (Frankfurt: Suhrkamp, 1998), 147–48; Joseph A. Schumpeter, *History of Economic Analysis* (Oxford: Oxford University Press, 1954).

3. Bertram Schefold, 'Spanisches Wirtschaftsdenken zu Beginn der Neuzeit', in *id.* (ed.), *Vademecum zu zwei Klassikern des spanischen Wirtschaftsdenkens* (Düsseldorf: Verlag Wirtschaft und Finanzen, 1998), 5–40; Marjorie Grice-Hutchinson, *The School of Salamanca. Readings in Spanish Monetary Theory, 1544–1605* (Oxford: Clarendon, 1952); *ead.*, *Early Economic Thought in Spain 1177–1740* (London: G. Allen & Unwin, 1978).

4. Wilhelmine Dreissig, *Die Geld- und Kreditlehre des deutschen Merkantilismus* (Berlin: Dr. Emil Ebering, 1939), 28.

5. Chapter 2.

6. Gustav (von) Schmoller, 'Zur Geschichte der national-ökonomischen Ansichten in Deutschland während der Reformations-Periode', *Zeitschrift für Gesamte Staatswissenschaft* 16 (1860): 461–16. Bauernfeind, in his study of the medieval and early modern grain market of Nuremberg, has made the same observation, see Walter Bauernfeind, *Materielle Grundstrukturen im Spätmittelalter*

new interpretation of Scripture, were developed, formulated and published at – and in the light of the following we may say against the background of – a time of *depression*. Admittedly, it is hard to reconstruct the configuration of the economic landscape and the conjunctures that would have been relevant in Luther's Germany in a way that would satisfy the modern econometrician. How do we grasp historical pre-industrial agrarian economies that are five hundred years away from us, and which not only functioned using technological parameters that were not only fundamentally different from ours – societies which had radically lower total factor productivity levels – but also followed different cultural belief systems and used different socio-economic mechanisms of resource allocation such as prestige, social, economic and cultural capital? Using modern interpretative frameworks of national income and growth accounting schedules – something which scholars have done in the not so distant past[7] – ultimately does not lead us very far in the present task. We should adopt a rather historical inductive and empirical approach, using what is available in terms of the limited data and non-quantitative, or better *not-so-quantitative-as-some-cliometricians-would-wish* evidence, to get as reliable a picture as possible.

Bad Money, Evil Coins: On the Economics and Social Costs of Coin Debasement

With all caveats in mind, the available historical evidence from the period around 1500 yields some unequivocal conclusions; some relevant economic data has been presented above (table 2.3, chapter 2), marking out the first twenty-five years or so of the sixteenth century as a period of economic crisis and depression. Whilst the price level, real wages and silver output speak for themselves, pointing towards deflation as a socio-economic phenomenon, a few of the other indicators require some explanation. The rate of depreciation of the leading south German penny currencies[8] (Vienna, Augsburg and Munich, column 4 in table 2.3) provides an indication of what we may with a lot of imaginative fantasy call the *general business climate*. Petty currency debasement rates serve as a very rough proxy measure for overall societal stability. The penny was the small man's everyday means of market-based transactions; the majority of people were living in the countryside with limited disposable income, which means that they were literally stuck within the low exchange sphere of the petty coins.[9] All money circulating in the German lands contained at least some precious metal, usually silver, as during that time people derived money's purchasing power from the market value of the metal contained

und der Frühen Neuzeit. Preisentwicklung und Agrarkonjunktur am Nürnberger Getreidemarkt von 1339 bis 1670 (Nuremberg: Schriftenreihe des Stadtarchivs, 1993).

7. See sources for Table 2.3 in chapter 2, as well as discussion ibid.
8. An enlarged database and analysis is presented in Philipp Robinson Rössner, 'Monetary Instability, Lack of Integration and the Curse of a Commodity Money Standard. The German Lands, c.1400–1900 A.D.', *Credit and Capital Markets* 47, no. 2 (2014): 297–340.
9. Rössner, *Deflation – Devaluation – Rebellion*, chaps 3 and 4 for an extended discussion of the monetary and social ramifications of coin use and differential types or segments of currency.

in each coin.[10] And since money usually also serves as a means of storing wealth, the rate of a coin's depreciation gives you a hint as to how the general economic or business climate evolves. If rates of depreciation (here: loss in terms of silver content measured in grams of silver per penny) were high, people tried to get rid of the money, rather than saving it, because they expected the value of their savings to deteriorate the longer they were held in debased small change coin. Moreover, people may be reluctant to make agreements and contracts if the precious metal content of circulating coins was persistently unstable and subject to change, and their coin exchange rate fluctuated over time. They may seek for alternatives such as virtual currencies, book money or the so-called ghost money – i.e. keep accounts and calculate sums in their head using coin substitutes for clearing remaining balances and obligations in real-life payments and settlement of obligation.[11]

However, this was no option for the small man on the street. The lesser folk who had to use bad debased small change were often charged a risk premium if they made payments in underweight coins, thus increasing transaction costs for the entire system. Also, peasant farmers and others *paid* in underweight coins would, in times of deflation, have experienced a further reduction in profits than warranted on the grounds of the decline in the general price level. When there was no adjustment in prices for coin debasement, i.e. when nominal price-level stability went together with deflation measured in terms of precious metal per coin handed over for payment, the purchasing power of the money in your hands would erode doubly, first by nominal deflation and second by silver content reduction.[12] The social consequences of bad or unstable money were immeasurably high.[13]

---

10. This is called a *commodity* standard of money. Contrary to the *fiduciary* standard where the intrinsic or material value of money is significantly below its exchange value or purchasing power, a commodity money standard or theory poses many coordination problems and increases transaction costs, a phenomenon which has been overlooked by most economists and historians and which has been addressed for the Reformation period in Germany *en detail* in Rössner, *Deflation – Devaluation – Rebellion*, chaps 2 (markets for money as a commodity), III (problems of monetary coordination and tension fields between monetary policy and societal welfare issues) and IV (social costs of bad money: economic rents; economic costs of bad money; transaction costs).

11. Frederic C. Lane and Reinhold C. Mueller, *Money and Banking in Medieval and Renaissance Venice, Vol. 1: Coins and Moneys of Account* (Baltimore: Johns Hopkins University Press, 1985). Good surveys on medieval and early modern coin use include Peter Spufford, *Money and its Use in Medieval Europe* (Cambridge, MA: Cambridge University Press, 1988); Philip Grierson, *Numismatics* (Oxford: Oxford University Press, 1975); Michael North, *Das Geld und seine Geschichte. Vom Mittelalter bis zur Gegenwart* (Munich: Beck, 1994); *id.* (ed.), *Von Aktie bis Zoll. Ein historisches Lexikon des Geldes* (Munich: Beck, 1995); *id.*, *Kleine Geschichte des Geldes. Vom Mittelalter bis heute* (Munich: Beck, 2009).

12. Eckart Schremmer and Jochen Streb, 'Revolution oder Evolution? Der Übergang von den feudalen Münzgeldsystemen zu den Papiergeldsystemen des 20. Jahrhunderts', *Vierteljahrschrift für Sozial- und Wirtschaftsgeschichte* 86 (1999): 457–76.

13. Rössner, *Deflation – Devaluation – Rebellion*, chaps 4 and 5; *id.*, 'Monetary Instability, Lack of Integration and the Curse of a Commodity Money Standard'.

This devaluation of petty coins, christened by some scholars the *big problem of small change*, was a phenomenon that haunted Germany, as well as most other parts of Europe, almost continuously between c. 1250 and 1870.[14] However, there were phases when devaluation rates were particularly high. John Day (1978) has established four periods of acute bullion famine for the Middle Ages; the last falling into the period of economic depression in the 1440s and 1450s.[15] But another period when coin debasement was marked was the first two decades of the sixteenth century, i.e. the time immediately preceding Luther's 95 Theses (1517). At that time silver remained high in price, as the American deposits around Potosí had not yet been tapped to sufficient extent and amounts so as to offset these shortages. Obviously, the monetary authorities, i.e. rulers, princes and their mint masters, either had to economize on silver or else adjust the circulating means of exchange to a changed market price of the base metal, which means that they would have had to debase their coins.[16] Debasement would also create social problems. These problems were virulent in the German lands, and the popular uprisings which seem to have increased in number and intensity between the 1470s and 1520s demonstrate how dramatic the situation was.

A rich economic discourse had evolved since the days of medieval scholastic author Nicolaus Oresmius (Oresme), who had produced a widely read treatise on coin debasement, arguing, basically, that debasement was a no-go and to be resorted to only in the most extreme case scenarios, when the common good was in danger (as in the case of war or an impending foreign invasion). Almost all economic writers of the pre-1800 period agreed that in theory money should always remain stable. In reality, however, it didn't. Why the rulers didn't adhere to the call is another story that is beyond the scope of the present book.[17] With the exception of the 'Ernestine' writer or pamphleteer in the 1530–31 Saxon currency dispute[18], and cameralist author Johann Joachim Becher (1635–1682), in his discourse on economic development (*Politischer Discurs: Von den eigentlichen Ursachen deß Auf- und Ablebens der Städt, Länder und Republicken*, 1668), in which he

---

14. Thomas J. Sargent and François R. Velde, *The Big Problem of Small Change* (Princeton, NJ: Princeton University Press, 2003); for the German lands with more detail and ample statistical evidence on coin exchange rates and silver content/debasement rates, see Rainer Metz, *Geld, Währung und Preisentwicklung. Der Niederrheinraum im europäischen Vergleich: 1350–1800* (Frankfurt: F. Knapp, 1990). For the central German lands, a comparable study is still wanting; some data, mainly on Saxony and adjacent territories has been presented and analysed in Rössner, *Deflation – Devaluation – Rebellion*, 311–30, 376–483.

15. John Day, 'The Great Bullion Famine of the Fifteenth Century', *Past & Present* 79 (1978), 3–54.

16. A full discussion of monetary policy within a situation of silver scarcity has been provided in Rössner, *Deflation – Devaluation – Rebellion*. A shorter model is in *id.*, 'Monetary Instability, Lack of Integration and the Curse of a Commodity Money Standard'.

17. Discussed within an unpublished paper, Philipp Robinson Rössner, 'Discourses on Development: Economic Divergence and German Economic Thought, 1500–1900', paper presented at the international workshop on 'Reconfiguring Divergence', Universität Leipzig, 11–13 April 2014. Available from the author upon request.

18. Bertram Schefold, 'Wirtschaft und Geld im Zeitalter der Reformation', in *id.* (ed.), *Vademecum zu drei klassischen Schriften frühneuzeitlicher Münzpolitik* (Düsseldorf: Verlag Wirtschaft und Finanzen, 2000), 5–58.

made the outspoken point that a modest debasement in the order of 5 per cent may be allowed so as to keep the money in the country and prevent currency speculation à la Gresham's law (good native coin exported from the domestic economy in exchange for bad coin that remained within the country), most German economic authors between the 1300s and 1800s would have agreed that coin debasement did more harm than good to society. German authors, from Oresmius to Biel and Copernicus as well as the cameralists, knew about the problem; sometimes so well that they did not spill much ink in terms of explaining what exactly the problem was. Spanish theologian and late scholastic author Juan de Mariana, in *De monetae mutatione* (1605) argued – still in line with medieval monetary theory going back to Oresmius – that the king must not alter the currency in terms of its precious metal content without consent of the commonwealth or *communitas regni*. This was in line with his general argument about 'no taxation without parliament', i.e. that taxes – which any coin debasement as a sort of inflation tax ultimately was – must not be altered without the subjects' consent.[19] By that time rulers had, however, violated this rule for centuries with devaluation rates being particularly marked during the fifteenth century – when German penny currencies lost 50 per cent in terms of precious metal; between the sixteenth and the nineteenth centuries, these rates appear to have come down to a – still high – centennial average rate of debasement or silver loss rate in the order of 25 per cent.[20] During the great hyperinflation in the early phase of the Thirty Years War 1619–23 – the German *Kipper- und Wipper-Inflation* – the implicit contractual arrangement between princes and subjects completely broke down: coin debasement – and thus general price inflation rates – reached into the hundreds of percentages within months.[21]

But coin debasement was also a significant feature of Luther's day and age. Luther, in fact, repeatedly commented on the problem of small change debasement and how clever people used different coins of different value yet similar denomination (say, *groschen*, of which hundreds of different types circulated in the Germany of Luther's day) to take advantage of the fragmented monetary landscape and financial or money markets, managing to get favourable coin exchange rates for their bad coin which they put into circulation forcing others to accept these coins at face value. This incriminating activity was known in contemporary discourse as coin usury (*Münzwucher*), representing one possible configuration of the deadly sin of avarice.

Germany: A Silver Sink?

As mentioned in previous chapters, the economic depression of the early sixteenth century was partly triggered by monetary shortage and an endemic strain on the Central

---

19. John Laures, *The Political Economy of Juan de Mariana* (New York: Fordham University Press, 1928). Erik Reinert drew my attention to this book.

20. Rössner, 'Monetary Instability, Lack of Integration and the Curse of a Commodity Money Standard'.

21. Most recently, Martha White Paas, John Roger Paas and George C. Schofield, *Kipper und Wipper Inflation, 1619–23: An Economic History with Contemporary German Broadsheets* (New Haven, CT: Yale University Press, 2012), 1–17.

European balance of payment. The German lands – apart from the north perhaps – were suffering from a heavy drain of silver to the south, north and east; contemporary discourse, as we will see below, repeatedly picked up on that. The available documentary evidence on a deflationary crisis around 1500 can be augmented by further evidence. In 1510–15, an oversupply of copper to European and African markets led to a series of collapses of some larger firms involved in the long-distance copper trade.[22] These copper trades linked the central European and especially the Upper German regional economies with the nascent global economy. In 1527–28, the lead mining business in the Harz Mountains came to a standstill when an army in the service of the Duke of Braunschweig/Brunswick besieged the mines of Rammelsberg near Goslar in pursuance of an old mortgage.[23] The year 1512 also saw a significant decline in cattle exports towards the west, the main source of demand for the Hungarian cattle export industry.[24] The *Augsburg Chronicle* reported a harsh contraction in fustian production. Chronicles and other proxy data confirm that the second decade of the sixteenth century was unusually cold. Winters were harsh, as *Clemens Sender's Chronicle* and many other contemporary accounts report.[25] In Marburg (Hesse), public expenditure, particularly on consumption and building activity (a component of expenditure that was particularly sensitive to fluctuations in the business cycle), fell by up to 80 per cent during 1500–20.[26] Such a grave reduction in public expenditure can be traced in many other cities in the southern part of the Empire and Switzerland.[27] In 1529, the giant firm of the Augsburg Höchstetter family dynasty collapsed and went bankrupt after a failed attempt at monopolizing European quicksilver supplies.[28] The Höchstetter had controlled significant shares of

22. Ekkehard Westermann, *Das Eislebener Garkupfer und seine Bedeutung für den europäischen Kupfermarkt, 1460–1560* (Cologne: Böhlau, 1971); *id.*, 'Zur weiteren Erforschung kommerzialisierter Agrargesellschaften Mitteleuropas und ihrer Konflikte im ersten Drittel des 16. Jahrhunderts', *Studia Historiae Oeconomicae* 15 (1980): 161–78.

23. Ian Blanchard, *The International Economy in the 'Age of the Discoveries', 1470–1570: Antwerp and the English Merchants' World*, ed. P. R. Rössner (Stuttgart: Franz Steiner, 2009), chap. 4.

24. Gusztáv Heckenast, 'Die mitteleuropäische Handels und Finanzkrise der Jahre 1512–1513 un (sic) der ungarische Bauernkrieg', in *id.,ed.*, *Aus der Geschichte der ostmitteleuropäischen Bauernbewegungen im 16–17. Jahrhundert* (Budapest: Akadémiai Kiadó, 1977), 107–12.

25. Historische Kommission bei der Bayerischen Akademie der Wissenschaften, ed., *Die Chronik von Clemens Sender, Die Chroniken der schwäbischen Städte, Augsburg*, vol. 4 (Leipzig: S. Hirzel, 1894), 132; Bayerische Akademie der Wissenschaften, ed., *Die Chroniken der baierischen Städte. Regensburg. Landshut. Mühldorf. München* (Leipzig: S. Hirzel, 1878), 28, 32, 55–56; Rüdiger Glaser, *Klimageschichte Mitteleuropas. 1200 Jahre Wetter, Klima, Katastrophen*, 2nd ed. (Darmstadt: Wissenschaftliche Buchgesellschaft, 2008), 94/fig. 31; Christian Pfister, 'Climate and Economy in Eighteenth-Century Switzerland', *Journal of Interdisciplinary History* 9, no. 2 (1978): 223–43; Franz Mauelshagen, *Klimageschichte der Neuzeit. 1500–1900* (Darmstadt: Wissenschaftliche Buchgesellschaft, 2010).

26. Bernd Fuhrmann, *Der Haushalt der Stadt Marburg in Spätmittelalter und Früher Neuzeit (1451/52–1622)* (St Katharinen: Scripta Mercaturae Verlag, 1996), 121–22/table 2; 264–65/table 11; 277/table 14; 326/table 19.

27. Rössner, *Deflation – Devaluation – Rebellion*, chap. 2, *passim*.

28 Most recently, Thomas Max Safley, 'The Höchstetter Bankruptcy of 1529 and its Relationship to the European Quicksilver Market', in Philipp Robinson Rössner, ed., *Cities – Coins – Commerce*.

the intercontinental silver and spice trades via Lisbon.[29] They were the main rivals of the proverbially rich and last medieval super-company of the Fuggers.[30] Their collapse led to a series of defaults of private investors who had invested their savings in the firm, down to members of the lower strata of society such as maidservants and others who had invested their precarious and humble savings in the flourishing company and aspiring quicksilver monopolist.

Around 1500, Spanish and Portuguese overseas expansion commenced (in the Spanish case) or reached new heights (Portugal). The evidence presented so far needs to be seen in this context, i.e. within an emerging proto-global economy. Silver production in the Saxon Erzgebirge Mountains and Tyrol faced a long-term decline between the 1490s and the 1540s. Between 1500 and 1525, aggregate output decreased by about 35 per cent. Most of what still came out of these mines went to Venice, Lisbon and ultimately to Asia. This link became particularly significant in the wake of the Portuguese discoveries, when the naval route to Asia along the West and East Coast of Africa was opened and developed in the wake of Vasco da Gama's return from Calicut in 1499. Around 1500, Portuguese investment in the Asian trades experienced an unusually fast growth.[31] A considerable share of silver produced in the German mines was, on top of the traditional drain via Venice and the Baltic, channelled into these new Asian trades (see chapter 2). Lisbon's urban fabric changed, as witnessed by such formidable buildings as the Mosteiro dos Jerónimos (extension commenced in 1501) financed out of the *Vintena da Pimenta*, levied at 5 per cent on the African and Oriental trade. This tax is said to have yielded the equivalent of up to 70 pounds of pure gold in the years after 1501 or the equivalent of close to 12,000 cruzados, which were roughly equal in purchasing power to one Rhenish florin or Thaler coins when using the gold–silver ratio as the basis for the calculation. At the same time, the proverbial renovation of Rome under the Renaissance popes transformed the physical outlook of the sacred city of Western Christendom. This was due not the least to the huge remittances from the North for religious services, pilgrimages and indulgences. During the first decades of the sixteenth century, more than half a million florins were handled by the Fugger merchants

---

Essays Presented to Ian Blanchard on the Occasion of his 70th Birthday (Stuttgart: Franz Steiner, 2012), 149–66.

29. See chapter 2.
30. See discussion in chapter 2.
31. Jorge Nascimento Rodrigues, *Portugal. O Pioneiro da Globalização. A Herança das Descobertas*. 2nd ed. (Lisbon: Centro Atlantico, 2009), 205, 211–32; Antonio H. de Oliveira Marques, *Geschichte Portugals und des portugiesischen Weltreiches* (Stuttgart: Kröner, 2001), *passim*, esp. 79–104, 134–84; Joaquim Veríssimo Serrão, *História de Portugal, Vol. 3: O Século de Ouro (1495–1580)*, 2nd ed. (Lisbon: Editorial Verbo), 95–119; 329–32; Armando Castro, *História Económica de Portugal, Vol. 3: Séculos XV e XVI* (Lisbon: Editorial Caminho, 1985), 155–212; Carlos A. da Silva Nogueira, *Elementos de História Económica Portuguesa (da integração na economia euro-atlântica à actualidade)*, 2nd ed. (Lisbon: Lusolivra, 1997), 65–75; Vitorino Magalhães Godinho, *Os descobrimentos e a economia mundial* (Lisbon: Editorial Presença, 1981–83); J. Romero Magalhães, 'A estrutura das trocas', in *id*. ed., *Historia de Portugal, Vol. 3: No Alvorecer da Modernidade (1480–1620)* (Lisbon: Estampa, 1993), 315–53 (esp. 336–53).

of Augsburg alone for transfers of indulgence money from Germany to Rome.[32] The Fuggers were the most important financial intermediaries providing this service to the German lands. They closely cooperated with the Pope and his financial representative in Germany, Albrecht of Brandenburg, Archbishop and Elector of Mainz, Halberstadt and Magdeburg. Accordingly, they received a fair share of negative acclaim in the public discourse of the day.[33]

This is not to say that all money spent in the German lands on indulgences went to Rome; much of it was actually spent by the churches and monasteries in the surrounding local and regional economies. Much of it was also, rather than being spent on consumption or economic investment, allocated to ceremonial purposes: for altarpieces, chalices, crosses coated with silver, silver plate and other equipment devoted to liturgical processes. But the indulgence remittances down south put a further drain on available silver resources, the main share of which at that time still came out of the central European, especially the Saxon, mines and the Mansfeld smelting district (chapter 2).[34] It is, of course, impossible to monitor silver flows precisely, but conservative estimates suggest that around 1480–1520 at least 70 per cent, if not much more, of yearly silver production in Europe was exported, predominantly via Venice or Lisbon, into the Levant and Indian Ocean and ultimately to India and China.[35] These connections have been discussed in chapter 2.

At times when the major part of European currencies contained at least some silver, such a silver drain was bound to have a negative impact upon aggregate monetary supply (and its composition in terms of different coins and their precious metal content). After about 1490–1500, most of the south German, Swiss and Austrian mints went through a protracted period of decline. Many mint masters were unable to obtain silver for coinage at a price that would have made it profitable turning this silver into coins. The larger mints in Crain, Vienna, Hall (Tyrol), Linz, Klagenfurt, Graz, Salzburg, Basle, Constance, Nuremberg, Augsburg, Baden-Baden, Swabia and Bavaria repeatedly stopped producing coins, as did lesser ones in the many smaller territories.[36] A growing population had to make ends meet with a decreasing per capita supply of silver and thus per capita supply of silver money in real (silver) as well as – in all likelihood – nominal terms (numbers of coins of particular denomination) since the 1490s.

If total population and overall economic activity increased faster than the monetary mass of the economy, consisting of the amount of money in circulation and its velocity, the overall price level for the whole economy, at least the goods handled using the somewhat elusive market, could be expected to fall, possibly triggering a depression. If there was less money around for investment and consumption, bigger projects as well as

---

32. Johannes Mötsch, 'Die Wallfahrt St. Wolfgang bei Hermannsfeld', in Enno Bünz, Stefan Tebruck and Helmut G. Walther, eds., *Religiöse Bewegungen im Mittelalter. Festschrift für Matthias Werner zum 65. Geburtstag* (Cologne: Böhlau, 2007), 673–702, (683).

33. See chapter 2.

34. See chapter 2.

35. Prasannan Parthasarathi, *Why Europe Grew Rich and Asia Did Not. Global Economic Divergence, 1600–1850* (Cambridge: Cambridge University Press, 2011).

36. Rössner, *Deflation – Devaluation – Rebellion*, 185–90.

items of expenditure would be put on hold or held back from the market. People would be cautious and investors reluctant to spend. But another effect reinforced the apparent contraction in per capita money supply around 1500: velocity also appears to have been declining.

You Spin Me Round, or Discovering Velocity

Scholars have long been aware that the *monetary component* of the Fisher equation (see below), which establishes a relation between changes in money supply and the price level (if not economic activity; Margaret Thatcher and the monetarists of the twentieth century were dogmatic about the money supply as government's chief means of economic intervention), consists of two things. One is the actual *amount* of it that is put in circulation, usually denoted M. The other is its *velocity*, usually denoted as V, i.e. the number of times this amount of money changes hands within a given period, usually a year. Thus, even a small stock of money can be made to go a longer way if velocity increases. On the other hand, when velocity decreases, this may have a considerable contracting effect on monetary mass, or the overall left-hand side of the Fisher equation (M times V, or MV), i.e. on 'what money really does', even when the *nominal amount of money* (M) remains the same. If the two effects combine, say M and V decline (or expand) in tandem, they will mutually reinforce each other.

But as V cannot be measured, and reliable data for those variables that would allow us to calculate it as a residual (M, P, T) are lacking, historians have tended to stay away from the problem and, for matters of simplicity and want of better data and ideas, have said – without providing much empirical evidence – that velocity (V) may be interpreted as a constant in the long run when formulating historical models of monetary changes and economic development. This assumption has led to a comparative dismissal of velocity as a possible historical actor and protagonist.[37] In the light of recent research on that matter, however, this assumption should be given up. With a little arithmetic trick, a whole new way of looking at V can be opened up. Velocity can indeed – for certain times – be said to have been a *protagonist* rather than just a walker-on. And Luther's writings, especially those connected with his theory of salvation, are partly linked to the problem of money's velocity as one of the main actors of the play. Velocity was M's *antagonist*, so to speak.

Quantifying or measuring money supply or mint output (M) for Germany around 1500 in a statistical way would be historically nonsensical. Neither a unified German state nor a standardized German monetary policy existed, let alone a common currency. Monetary policy was left to the five hundred or so independent territories that made up the Holy Roman Empire we call Germany around 1500 AD.[38] But we can say something

---

37. For a recent discussion, see Rössner, 'Monetary Instability, Lack of Integration and the Curse of a Commodity Money Standard'.

38. Most recently, Rössner, 'Monetary Instability, Lack of Integration and the Curse of a Commodity Money Standard'; David Chilosi and Oliver Volckart, 'Money, States, and Empire: Financial Integration and Institutional Change in Central Europe, 1400–1520', *The Journal of Economic History* 71, no. 3 (2011), 762–91; Oliver Volckart, 'Regeln, Willkür und der gute Ruf: Geldpolitik und Finanzmarkteffizienz in Deutschland, 14. bis 16. Jahrhundert',

on velocity. For this we can use data assembled by the ancient and venerable auxiliary historical science called *numismatics* – a discipline which has vanished almost completely from the academic landscape, and utterly sadly so.[39] We may approximate the decennial levels of hoarding on the modern territory of Germany by searching a database of coin hoards held by the Numismatische Kommission or the Board of Numismatists of the states of the Federal Republic of Germany, a semi-governmental institution.[40] Every coin find has to be reported to the authorities of the respective federal state in Germany on whose territory the coins are discovered. The commission of numismatists (Numismatische Kommission) keeps a database, including much data on older coin finds from the beginning of the twentieth century, which is constantly updated for new finds. Numismatists can then date (that is estimate the age of) a particular coin hoard by determining the age of the *most recently struck coin* found in this hoard. This gives us a tentative *post*-date or minimum age for the hoard. The logic is simple: if a particular hoard contains, say, a series of fourteenth-century Bracteates or *Hohlpfennige* (hollow pennies), fifteenth-century *Horngroschen* and also some Thaler coins struck by the Saxon Elector and Duke in 1525, the money cannot have been buried before 1525. Disregarding undeclared coin finds, an aggregate series of coin hoards dated accordingly is – with an appropriate dose of caution – therefore likely to capture the long-term trend in *hoarding*. The result of this query, based on data, part of which has been presented in table 2.3 in chapter 2, has been plotted in figure 4.1.

Jahrbuch für Wirtschaftsgeschichte 2009/2, 101–29. Older studies that are useful – and which go beyond those already mentioned in this chapter – include Joachim Schüttenhelm, 'Problems of Quantifying the Volume of Money in Early Modern Times. A Preliminary Survey', in Eddy H. G. Van Cauwenberghe, ed., *Precious Metals, Coinage and the Changes of Monetary Structures in Latin-America, Europe and Asia (Late Middle Ages–Early Modern Times)* (Leuven: Leuven University Press, 1989), 83–98; *id.*, 'Zur Münzprägung und Silberversorgung süddeutscher Münzstätten im frühen 16. Jahrhundert', in Werner Kroker and Ekkehard Westermann, eds., *Montanwirtschaft Mitteleuropas vom 12. bis 17. Jahrhundert. Stand, Wege und Aufgaben der Forschung* (Bochum: Vereinigung der Freunde von Kunst und Kultur im Bergbau, 1984), 159–69. That 'old is best' is demonstrated by the even more ancient but still highly useful numismatic works by Ferdinand Friedensburg, *Münzkunde und Geldgeschichte der Einzelstaaten des Mittelalters und der Neueren Zeit* (Munich: R. Oldenbourg, 1926); A. Luschin v. Ebengreuth, *Allgemeine Münzkunde und Geldgeschichte des Mittelalters und der Neueren Zeit*, 2nd ed. (Munich: R. Oldenbourg, 1926); as well as Friedrich Freiherr von Schrötter, 'Das Münzwesen des Deutschen Reichs von 1500 bis 1566', *Jahrbuch für Gesetzgebung, Verwaltung und Volkswirtschaft* 35 (1911) and 36 (1912), repr. in Friedrich von Schrötter, *Aufsätze zur deutschen Münz- und Geldgeschichte des 16. bis 19. Jahrhunderts (1902–1938)*, ed. Bernd Kluge (Leipzig: Reprintverl. im Zentralantiquariat, 1991), 3–76.

39. In 2014, there were two numismatic chairs in Britain and one in the German-speaking lands, that is full and institutionalized university professorial chairs that engaged in full-time teaching and researching what had once been a queen and flagship discipline of the auxiliary historical sciences (*Historische Hilfswissenschaften*). A lot of professional numismatists nowadays work in different academic environments or at temporary/non-tenured/personal chair level. This is a pity, because it means that we are beginning to lose valuable precarious knowledge.

40. I am grateful to the curator of the coin collections in the Moritzburg, Halle, Federal State of Saxony-Anhalt, Germany (where I obtained access to this database), Mr Ulf Dräger (Halle). He provided advice, coffee and cheerful company during the day I spent in his *Turmkabinett* in 2010.

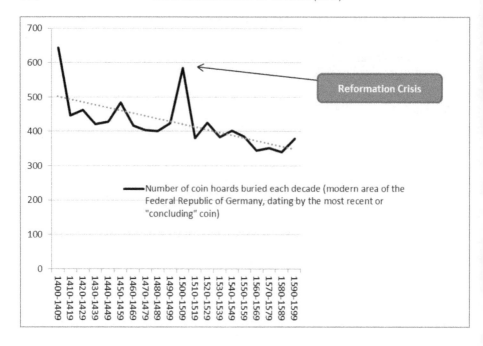

Figure 4.1 Number of coin hoards buried per decade in the area of today's Federal Republic of Germany (1400–1600). (*Source*: intranet database / Datenbank der Numismatischen Kommission der Länder in der Bundesrepublik Deutschland e. V., accessed 23 December 2010.)

It seems as though the long-term trend in hoarding money – i.e. keeping money back from the market where it was neither spent nor invested in interest-bearing assets – was decreasing. This is in line with a monetarist explanation of the sixteenth-century inflation (the so-called Price Revolution). An increasing amount of coin would have been dishoarded and put back into circulation, yielding in combination with some long-term expansion in mint output, mining and silver imports, the long inflation characteristic of the sixteenth century (which represented, as one has to bear in mind, no general economic expansion, i.e. per capita income growth in the German economy).[41] There was, however, one notable upswing or peak in the series during the first decade of the sixteenth century, when the long-term negative trend in hoarding was temporarily reversed (figure 4.1). The decade immediately preceding Martin Luther's 95 Theses was, according to these data, a period of *increased hoarding*. This matches with the notion of an economic depression towards the beginning of the sixteenth century.[42]

What are we to make of this and how does this tie in with Luther's economic writings? Whilst any answer to this is bound to remain tentative in many ways, it is nevertheless clear that hoarding – in any form – represented a form of saving disjointed from the

41. See chapter 2.
42. In detail Rössner, *Deflation – Devaluation – Rebellion*, chap. 2.

usual market mechanism as it lacked the transfer from savings to productive investment, including credit and other financial paper bearing interest. Burying money – often in churchyards and graveyards – may have economic, as well as many other cultural and social, ramifications. Usually, people hoard money when they are uncertain about the expected return of an investment, especially when neither any feasible means of consumption nor profitable investment alternatives exist. This could be the case in times of war, bad climate or economic depression. The pattern of coin hoards displayed and described above (figure 4.1) may perhaps, with a generous pinch of salt, be interpreted as one possible approximation of the *trend* in the otherwise unknown pattern of *holding cash* or *hoarding* in the German lands since the 1400s. And with the number of coin hoards buried during the first decade of the sixteenth century significantly above the long-term average, Luther and the economic discourse on hoarding and giving money to the church – where it was smelted into silver chalices and other items – may simply refer to a *decrease in the velocity of money*. How is this possible?

As shown above, economists such as Irving Fisher have established a basic tautological relationship between money supply (M), its velocity (V), total economic activity (T) and the overall price level (P) written as

$$MV = PT \tag{1}$$

Rearranging the simple Fisher equation ($MV = PT$), for the moment disregarding different types of coins with different segment-specific velocities[43], yields

$$V = \frac{PT}{M} \tag{2}$$

Because neither M nor T carry any historical meaning as *measurable* quantities for pre-industrial agrarian economies such as Germany at the time of the early Reformation for reasons outlined above as well as in chapter 2, it has been notoriously difficult, if not impossible, to *calculate* velocity (V) for the medieval and early modern period, although some historians have given in to the temptation, based on entirely speculative estimates for M as well as gross domestic product and only marginally better evidence on prices or P. This has led to grossly fantastical calculation results for V.[44] But there is an alternative at hand. The Cambridge School of Economics in the 1920s and 1930s approach, based

---

43. For this see Rössner, 'Monetary Instability, Lack of Integration and the Curse of a Commodity Money Standard'.
44. On England, see the earlier controversy between Mayhew and Miskimin over velocity in the EcHR: N. J. Mayhew, 'Money Supply, and the Velocity of Circulation in England, 1300–1700', *Economic History Review*, Second Series, XLVIII (1995), 238–57; Harry A. Miskimin, 'Not Sterling: A Comment on Mayhew's Velocity', *Economic History Review*, Second Series 49 (1996), 358–60; N. J. Mayhew, 'Not Sterling: A Reply to Prof. Miskimin', *Economic History Review*, Second Series 49 (1996), 361. Jack A. Goldstone, 'Lessons from the English Price Revolution of the Sixteenth and Seventeenth Centuries', *The American Journal of Sociology* 89 (1984): 1122–60 is also influential yet entirely speculative.

on earlier research by Marshall, defined velocity as the inverse of a variable called *demand for money to hold*, something that is well known also from Keynesian economics (*k*), thus:

$$V = \frac{1}{k} \qquad (3)$$

Accordingly velocity's inverse is

$$k = \frac{1}{V} \qquad (4)$$

If we interpret *k* as a dimensionless variable that gives away the share of, or preference for, demand for money to hold, *V* then, all of a sudden, changes from passive actor (calculative residual, if *M*, *T* and *P* are known) into a historical protagonist (or, rather, *antagonist* of *M*). Here, velocity is contingent upon millions of individual decisions of households and actors on how much money to spend or alternatively to hold back from the market: for transactions, speculation and safeguarding against instable economic circumstances in the near future. If *k increases* (meaning: less money is spent), *V* will *decrease* and vice versa.[45] And *k*, other than *V*, can be measured, or at least approximated, even for periods lacking reliable evidence on *M* and *T* (the price level, or *P*, usually is the only variable of the Fisher equation for which we can obtain half-way reliable historical data). The pattern of coin hoards displayed and described above (figure 4.1) may perhaps, with a generous pinch of salt, be interpreted as one possible method of approximating the *trend* in *k*, i.e. the pattern of holding cash. This was clearly increasing in the long run (1400–1600), but significantly above average during the first decades of the sixteenth century. Thus, velocity is likely to have declined during the first two decades of the sixteenth century, simultaneously to a contraction in the available amount of money in circulation (*M*).

Discourses on Silver Outflow and Money's Velocity

Suffice it to cite a few corroborative examples from contemporary economic and political discourse which point in the same direction as the conjectural remarks made in the previous section. The great German humanist authors of the 1510s and 1520s almost uniformly mocked the drain of silver that plagued central Europe those days. They were unanimous in blaming Rome and the Papacy for the situation, even if in a very satirical way and in places certainly overdrawn manner. Ulrich von Hutten, Imperial Knight and prominent intellectual, wrote in his *Vadiscus* dialogue (1519–20) about how the Romans (meaning the Curia/Papal Court), day after day, devised new means of taking away money from the Germans. It was three things in particular, von Hutten wrote,

---

45. This is somewhat at variance with the suggestion that '[i]ncreased use of money is thus usually combined with a *fall* in velocity, made possible by the availability of growing amounts of coin', which is certainly a very peculiar explanation, applying to early modern England perhaps but arguably not Germany (my italics). This explanation would also be at variance with an imputed increase in *k* (as a result of a decline in velocity). Quote taken from Nicholas Mayhew, *Sterling. The History of a Currency* (London: Penguin, 1999), 59.

that anyone returning from Rome would bring: 'bad conscience, an upset stomach, an empty purse'. There were three things everyone at Rome desired: 'short Mass, good coins, having a good time'.[46] Here von Hutten hinted at Gresham's law: the good money went away, the bad money stayed in Germany. Numerous other writings bear out an increasingly negative or at least cynical attitude towards forms of investment which were now identified as unproductive. The Old Granny, in the fictitious dialogue (1523) with Heinrich von Kettenbach[47], confessed that she burnt devotional candles to the tune of seven pennies (d) per week (*Ich verprenne all wuchen 7 pfenbart liecht*). For this she got the harsh reply by the reformed priest that by gambling or betting the money, or even simply burning it, she would have gotten a better deal out of it. The mere practice of spending money on devotional candles was deemed idolatrous by an increasing number of adherents to the reformed faith. By giving it to the priests, the money would be either transferred to Rome and exacerbate an already negative balance of payments, or else used in the most frivolous way, for vain pleasures, conspicuous consumption or whores.[48] Nothing, however, would be gained in terms of personal-individual salvation. Because luxurious clothes usually had to be imported, often from Italy, as Luther himself pointed out in the article 'Italian Clothing Is Better than German' (1538), in his *Table Talk*, possible multiplier effects of the spending on manufactures, to use modern language, were foregone.[49] The *haubt artickel durch welche gemeyne Christenheyt byßhere verfuret worden ist*[...], Wittenberg 1522,, another pamphlet of the 1520s, complained about indulgences, pilgrimages, shrines and monasteries. These were institutions where money, in the eyes of the contemporaries, was sunk without being retrieved within a productive framework.[50] Zwingli made similar remarks. During the Peasants' War in 1525, the grievances of the peasants in Salzburg in Austria mentioned the malpractice of confessors who habitually charged one florin to those who were terminally ill. This was a practice that harmed especially the poor descendants and widows and would increase their hardship even more than the loss

---

46. In the original, *scheren platt und kahl / Und nehmen stets von Teutschen Geld / Dahin ihr Praktik ist gestellt / Und finden täglich neue Weg / Daß Geld man in den Kasten leg / Da kommen Teutsche um ihr Gut.* [...] *Drei Ding hasset Rom, Jus patronatus, frei election und daß die Deutschen noch einen Pfennig haben.* [...] *Drei Ding bringt man gewöhnlich von Rom, böses Gewissen, bösen Magen, leere Säckel* [...]; *Drei Ding will jedermann haben zu Rom, kurze Messen, gute Münzen, bon tempo.* Rudolf Bentzinger, ed., *Die Wahrheit muß ans Licht! Dialoge aus der Zeit der Reformation* (Leipzig: Reclam, 1982), 46, 52, 72–74.

47. Hannelore Winkler, 'Der Wortbestand von Flugschriften aus den Jahren der Reformation und des Bauernkrieges in seiner Einheitlichkeit und landschaftlichen Differenziertheit', Univ. PhD Diss. (Leipzig, 1970), 61–62. Later published as *Der Wortbestand von Flugschriften aus den Jahren der Reformation und des Bauernkrieges* (Berlin: Akademie Verlag, 1975).

48. *Eyn gesprech Bruder Hainrich von Kettenbach mit aim fromen alte mutterlin von Vlm* [...] (1523), cited after Adolf Laube, Annerose Schneider and Sigrid Looss, eds., *Flugschriften der frühen Reformationsbewegung (1518–1524),* vol. 1 (Berlin [East]: Akademie Verlag, 1983), 201–03.

49 *Luther's Works*, ed. Hartmut Lehmann, vol. 54, *Table Talk*, ed. Theodore G. Tappert (Philadelphia: Holman, 1967), Nr. 3956, 298.

50. After Laube, Schneider and Looss, eds, *Flugschriften der frühen Reformationsbewegung*, 166. The original reads: *viel scheynender werck, mit wallfartten, ablas suchen, kirchen pawen, kloester, messen, jar tag, seelgereyth und anders stifften, grosse opffer thun, kirchen tziern, vasten und andern der gleychen eußerlichen wercken zu erdichten und sich darynn zu bemuhen.*

of the main bread winner.[51] Similar *topoi* abound in the early Reformation discourse. They often had a decidedly vitriolic and satirical outlook, but clearly singled out the unproductive manner in which money had been (and still was) spent under the Old Catholic pattern of purchasing salvation from purgatory. We need to be aware that not everyone would have condemned the practice of indulgences as generally unproductive; especially since productive and productivity are modern notions unknown (in this shape) to sixteenth century authors. Also, as we have seen in chapter 1, many contemporaries saw indulgences simply as an insurance policy against pains of burning in purgatory. It was Luther's own and very peculiar idea that salvation must be completely disentangled from monetary and economic contributions of the individual towards this peculiar goal. Donations to the poor and those in need, out of charity, were on the other hand always welcome! But ultimately this idea proved very powerful; it was accordingly adopted quite willingly by those on the reformed side of Christendom. And the *sale* of indulgences was finally banned by the Catholic Church in 1567–70.

Luther himself repeatedly picked up on the problem of religious donations, liturgical luxury and idolatry. And of course, his early works centre on the problem of indulgences. His sermons of the early 1520s are full of references to indulgences, luxurious chalices, monstrances, church bells and altar pieces. Rather, the money should be allocated to those in need, the poor and the hungry, he said. That his remarks were probably not so wide of the mark is demonstrated by the amounts of silver and gold that were retrieved from cloisters and churches when liturgical and devotional equipment was remonetized in the wake of the Reformation in Saxony and the dissolution of the former monasteries. Upon its dissolution in 1526, the *Kirchenschatz* (church treasure) in Torgau in Saxony amounted to 35 marks of gold and 831 marks of silver, the latter amounting to somewhere around 207 kilograms of pure silver (there were regional variations in the weight of one silver mark), representing the equivalent of close to 8,000 Thalers or Rhenish florins. Between 1526 and 1531, about 75,355 Rh fl of former church treasure were confiscated and put back into circulation upon government account in the Saxon lands.[52] Further confiscations followed towards the 1530s and 1540s; in 1539, the yields from confiscated church silver (and gold) amounted to 8,976 Rh fl.[53] It is clear that these church treasures had accumulated for decades, if not centuries, before the Reformation. Their freeing – in those regions where church treasure and monasteries were dissolved – would have provided a once-and-for-all stimulus to the amount of money in circulation, as all silver and gold could potentially be remonetized and put back into the monetary realm. We will never know for certain about the exact channels and flow mechanisms of this

51. The original reads: *wo ein mensch kranckh ist worden, so haben die peichtväter den kranckhen angehallten, und dem beichtvater ainen gulden schaffen, was arm wittib und waisen auch gellter abbruch haben und mangl muessen leiden.* A. Hollaender, 'Die vierundzwanzig Artikel gemeiner Landschaft Salzburg 1525', *Mitteilungen der Gesellschaft für Salzburger Landeskunde* 71 (1931): 65–88, (84).
52. Uwe Schirmer, 'Reformation und Staatsfinanzen. Vergleichende Anmerkungen zu Sequestration und Säkularisation im ernestinischen und albertinischen Sachsen', in Michael Beyer, Jonas Flöter and Markus Hein, eds, *Christlicher Glaube und weltliche Herrschaft. Zum Gedenken an Günther Wartenberg* (Leipzig: Evangelische Verlagsanstalt, 2008), 179–92, (183).
53. Ibid., 187.

reconfiguration of the monetary landscape, but it is known, for instance, that the English Tudor Kings profited considerably from the dissolution of the English monasteries in the 1530s. Some of the money in government hand (to which the dissolved Church treasures would have belonged in the first place) may well have found its way back into domestic monetary circulation.

Suffice it to cite just one possible yet entirely speculative and impressionistic transmission mechanism. As we have seen the so-called Price Revolution which has been discussed briefly in chapter 2, in the German lands – as well as across most parts of north-west Germany – did not set in before the 1530s.[54] Influxes of South American silver did not begin to manifest themselves in meaningful or significant quantities before the 1550s. We also know that large chunks of domestic or German silver production were exported prior to the 1530s. And even if velocity of money (V) would be slowly ascending post-1520 (see figure 4.1 above), a residual remains to explain the process of monetary and real economic expansion after 1530 that led to the long cycle of price inflation, 1530–1620. Because between the onset of the Price Revolution around 1530 and the recognizable inflow of the American silver – which is often held responsible for triggering the sixteenth-century inflation – in the 1550s there remained a lacuna, a gap to be covered, of about 20 years. Where did the inflation post-1525 and of the 1530s and 1540s which Luther and Sebastian Franck wrote about come from?[55] This should read: where did the monetary basis for price inflation originate? Perhaps part of the monetary input or boosting of the monetary sector on the eve of the American silver inflow, c. 1530–1550, was provided by the developments which have been discussed in this section, i.e. the injection of additional supplies of silver that had been buried in the church treasuries and monasteries for ages before Luther[56], and which were, during the 1530s and 1540s, gradually being dissolved within the areas where the Protestant faith was adopted.

Luther also picked up repeatedly on the practice of hoarding and burying money. In his *Sendbrief vom Dolmetschen* ('On Translation', 1530), as well as many other occasions, he would quote scripture whilst strictly condemning the practice of burying money: 'Thus is why the master in the gospel scolds the unfaithful servant as a slothful rogue for having buried and hidden his money in the ground [Matt. 25:25–26].'[57] The idea that money was misallocated, by indulgences and other similar practices such as pilgrimages, purchasing devotional candles, eternal masses, comes across, if indirectly, in Luther's 95 Theses, where he said (Nr. 43, 45 and 46) that money was not to be spent on indulgences but rather, if there was a surplus in savings, to be given to the poor (43, 45) or one's own family (46). On religious pilgrimages to Rome, which were connected with the problem

---

54. See chapter 2 for discussion and relevant literature.
55. See John H. A. Munro, 'Price Revolution', in Steven N. Durlauf and Lawrence E. Blume, eds, *The New Palgrave Dictionary of Economics*, 2nd ed., vol. 6 (Basingstoke: Palgrave Macmillan, 2008), 631–34, and Nicholas J. Mayhew, 'Prices in England, 1170–1750', *Past & Present* (2013), 219 (1), 3–39, for recent overviews on competing models explaining sixteenth-century inflation.
56. I am much indebted to Chris Close (St John's) for reminding me of this point.
57. *Luther's Works, Vol. 35: Word and Sacrament* I, ed. Helmut T. Lehmann and E. Theodore Bachmann (Philadelphia: Fortress Press, 1960), 81.

of indulgences, Luther said, in his address *To the Christian Nobility of the German Nation Concerning the Reform of the Christian Estate* (1520), that

> all pilgrimages should be dropped. There is no good in them: no commandment enjoins them, no obedience attaches to them. Rather do these pilgrimages give countless occasions to commit sin and to despise God's commandments. [...] Let priest and master show him how to use the money and effort for the pilgrimage for God's commandments and for works a thousand times better by spending it on his own family or on his poor neighbours.[58]

On the local shrines in Saxony and Thuringia, Luther commented, in his *Address to the Christian Nobility* (1520) that the

> chapels in forests and the churches in the fields, such as Wilsnack, Sternberg, Trier, the Grimmenthal, and now Regensburg and a goodly number of others which recently have become the goal of pilgrimages, must be levelled. [...] They do not see that the devil is behind it all, to strengthen greed, to create a false and fictitious faith, to weaken the parish churches, to multiply taverns and harlotry, to lose money and working time to no purpose, and to lead ordinary people by the nose.[59]

Jan Hus, the Bohemian heretic, had, long before Luther, specifically picked up the Wilsnack shrine in his indulgence critique around 1400 (chapter 1). In 1524, Luther said that people 'waste a great deal of money and property on indulgences, masses, vigils, endowments, bequests, anniversaries, mendicant friars, brotherhoods, pilgrimages and similar nonsense'. It would be better 'to contribute a part of that amount towards schools for the training of the poor children. That would be an excellent investment'.[60]

Burying Money: Luther and the Tragedy of Hoarding

What Luther and the satirical discourse of the years around 1517 referred to, and what Luther called avarice, both the *desire to have more* (*Habsucht*) and the *disinclination to give away money* (*Geiz*) may be rephrased, metaphorically speaking, as a *decrease in velocity* of money. We all use metaphors as a discursive and linguistic strategy to approximate a reality around us which is too complex to be accurately described directly, let alone comprehended in its entirety. So this somewhat partisan interpretation of Luther's views on avarice may be permitted here, as the traditional explanations are not particularly satisfactory. Indirectly Luther and the contemporary discourse on hoarding and spending during the early Reformation had developed the idea that money was an economic resource. Money was more than its *amount* (*M*); *velocity* mattered as well. Therefore, one

---

58. *Luther's Works, Vol. 44: The Christian in Society* I, ed. Hartmut T. Lehmann and James Atkinson (Philadelphia: Fortress, 1966), 171.

59. Ibid., 185.

60. *To the Councilmen of all Cities in Germany that they Establish and Maintain Christian Schools, Luther's Works, Vol. 45: The Christian in Society* II, ed. Hartmut T. Lehmann and Walther I. Brandt (Philadelphia: Fortress, 1962), 351.

means of economizing on money as a scarce resource, especially when M was declining, would be to increase its velocity: by dishoarding of treasure or decreasing the demand for money to hold when framed in Keynesian lingo. The practice of indulgences, as well as the overburdening of churches with valuable silver equipment, something which had become immensely popular around 1500, surely was one means that kept monetary circulation low, as much of the indulgence money eventually ended up in the mortmain, the *dead hand*, in the shape of altarpieces and silver (and gold) equipment in churches, cloisters and monasteries. On top of that, a lot of money was buried underneath the ground. Luther would not have any of that.

Chapter 5

VON KAUFFSHANDLUNG UND WUCHER (1524): ANALYTICAL SUMMARY

A Declaration of War

After invoking the gospel as a guideline to good deeds [1],[1] Luther comes straight to the point by identifying the evils of his time. These may be captured under the catch-all term *avarice* [1, 2 and *passim*]. As avarice (or *greed*, Latin *avaritia*) is one of the capital vices or cardinal sins, it is – in Luther's view – the main danger posed to contemporary society [1, 2]. Avarice can be generally defined as the desire to have more, but after that the story becomes tricky. What does more mean? It could mean, for instance 'more than due', as justified in terms of the just profit or reward to one's labour and effort spent on procuring a specific bundle of goods or making a just and honest living. Even though Luther disliked the medieval scholastic theologians, he is, at least implicitly, using the schoolmen's distributional concept of justice here; figuratively speaking the geometrical (as opposed to an arithmetical) mean as a benchmark for distributing capabilities, rewards and resources. Everyone should be rewarded a fair wage, profit and income, commensurate with one's occupation and status within society. Fair in this model does not mean equal as in the later communitarian and proto-communist utopias of the age, for instance, Thomas Müntzer's movement in Mühlhausen or the Anabaptists' design of egalitarian communities in some other regions of contemporary Germany in the wake of the Reformation. It means, rather, 'according to one's contribution and rank within society'. But more, in the theological notion of *avaritia* entertained by Luther, could also mean 'more *and* more', that is transforming the desire for a just reward or profit, which even honest Christian merchants were entitled to, into the desire for 'profit for profit's sake'. This was the Aristotelian concept of χρηματιστική (*chrematistike*, chrematistics). It had many figurations in daily life and commercial exchange; the taking of interest was one of them (and arguably the most prominent one). The Christian tradition since Late Antiquity had identified chrematistics as base motives charged up with the notion of *metaphysically evil*.[2] But notions and definitions of chrematistics had changed and adapted over the ages, which makes the placing of Luther's text in the overall scholarly tradition on usury and undue commercial profits somewhat tricky.

---

1. The basis for translation is the old American translation in *Luther's Works*, vol. 4 (Philadelphia: Holman, 1915–1931), trans. Charles M. Jacobs. The text has been considerably revised by the present author. The paragraphs of the translation have been numbered [in square brackets] for the reader's convenience.
2. See previous chapter for a discussion of scholastic economics.

Chrematistics classified as an unnatural activity because it did not fit the figurative design or what we may call the visual theory (*Anschauung*) of the economy according to scholasticism and late medieval views on economic activity and behaviour. Luther's visual theory[3] was, as we have seen in chapter 3, based on agriculture and agrarian environments evolving around plant growth and yearly re-growth, manifested by a harvest yield which usually outpaced the seed sown by a multiple of perhaps three or four, a common ratio in landlocked central and mid-central and eastern Europe. This ratio increased only when you moved towards the more productive agrarian economies in the north-west of Europe near the North Sea coastline, for instance, in the Netherlands or the German marshes in Schleswig where seed productivity may go into the area of seven, eight and more corns yielded per seed sown. The idea that significant gains could be made by activities such as borrowing and lending which involved neither physical labour and toil nor any expenses of significance, nor the inherent and constant risks of harvest failure all agrarian economies were exposed to, was a notion that was almost diametrically opposed to the economic configurations the medieval scholastic authors had in mind (and with whom Luther shared a lot in common – even though he'd usually deny it). Money as a physical thing was sterile in their view, as it could not beget or produce anything material or physical out of itself (as opposed to plants or the soil, for instance). Indeed, Luther identified merchants and certain commercial practices as the evil of his times which needed addressing [1, 2 and passim]. In this way his text is above all a study in polemic and theology, before it turns to business ethics and economics, containing a wealth of insights into contemporary society in the same way as a hefty dose of Luther's personal opinion and his very peculiar theory of salvation. *Von Kauffshandlung und Wucher* was a pamphlet, not a textbook, an impulse, a challenge, in short, a declaration of war.

Apart from that it also sketched a very abstract, even pure model or theory of the economy according to Luther's new interpretation of Scripture (chapter 3). This is something we should keep in mind, lest we arrive at total misjudgements of Luther's theoretical achievements both in theology and in economics. As shown in the previous chapters, all too often Luther and the present treatise have been taken literally, *as though they represented an actual sketch of the working mechanisms of the economy*. That would be simplistic. If measured against more market-friendly and mechanistic-technical economic theories of the past two centuries in the wake of the Scottish Enlightenment philosophers and their French counterparts around Quesnay and the Marquis de Condorcet, then, of course, Luther's 1524 text will come across as rather unrefined and primitive in places. But contrary to Adam Smith and his *Wealth of Nations* and many subsequent developments in classical and neoclassical economics, especially general equilibrium theory, Luther never set out to describe or analyse abstract laws and functional mechanisms of the economy. To him the very idea that an economy could be modelled completely de-contextualized from its idiosyncratic conditions of time and space (as we have learned to understand the economy nowadays) would have sounded silly as would the idea that unrestrained self-

---

3. See, for example. Bertram Schefold, 'Edgar Salin and his Concept of "Anschauliche Theorie" ("Intuitive Theory") during the Interwar Period', *Annals of the Society for the History of Economic Thought* 46 (2004) 1–16.

interest was a better economic driving force than an economy of self-restraint, respect and mutual obligation. Luther must have known Conrad Peutinger's economic sketches and models of the 1520s (chapter 3 and present chapter, section 5.5) which came quite close to Smithian and Mandevillian mechanistic reasoning about natural order, self-interest and optimal allocation by unregulated markets. In fact, Peutinger and Luther did meet in person, at least once during their lifetime, at the Imperial Diet.[4] Luther simply had a different viewpoint on things, not necessarily for the worse, as should have become clear by now. Because if we accept (we don't have to, but recent research in the history of political economy suggests we should) that the natural order idea/natural law theory of the economy as found in classical and neoclassical economics, is only one alternative amongst several epistemologies in the economic sciences, and that Luther simply had a different epistemology here – something which Roscher and Schmoller acknowledged, then we may be able to appreciate better the important insights buried in this 1524 text.

The discussion will follow, as far as possible, the original arrangement of the text as delivered in 1524. However, as is well known, the *Sermon on Commerce and Usury* is a composite, consisting of the first part *On Commerce* (*Von Kauffshandlung*, 1524) which was newly written in 1524, a second part *On Usury*, which is identical to the earlier *Great Sermon on Usury* that had been delivered in 1520 and which in turn picked up on the initial and shorter *Sermon on Usury* dating from 1519 and a brief final or third section which, as the first part, was newly written in 1524. Since Luther incorporated the *Sermon on Usury* somewhat verbatim into his 1524 pamphlet, using a copy-paste approach – very common practice then, as it is today, keeping to the original strictly as delivered in 1524 would make the argument look less stringent and slightly more muddled than it really is because of the duplications and reiterations within the 1524 text. Moreover, Luther makes a lot of analytical–theological digressions. Therefore, to retain the inherent theoretical stringency, which is fairly apparent in Luther's text, the following list of topics has been mildly rearranged so as to achieve a topical order rather than following the original textual sequence. Numbers [in square brackets] indicate the separate paragraphs of the pamphlet which have been, for matters of convenience, given numbers by the present author. Quotes are rendered in *italics* when incorporated into running sentences and indented when extending over several sentences.

Balance-of-Payment Constraints and Economic Development

One cannot deny that buying and selling are necessary [3], Luther says, acknowledging that every society of a certain size and stage of development (in terms of division of labour) must have a certain level of distribution and economic specialization. Lest every member of society be entirely self-sufficient, commerce is necessary. But Luther finds the emerging global trade disturbing. He calls it *auslendische kauffs handel*, literally 'foreign trade', *which brings from Calicut, India, and such places, wares such as costly silks, gold-work and spices, which minister only to luxury and serve no useful purpose, draining away the wealth of land and people* [3]. All modern English editions have – wrongly – translated the German original *Kalikut*

---

4.   I am grateful to Chris Close for reminding me of this aspect.

as 'Calcutta', whereas the actual location Luther had in mind certainly was *Calicut*, a city state ruled by native princes at the Indian Malabar Coast where the Portuguese had established a trading fort by 1513, which was recaptured by the Zamorin rulers of the area in 1526. Since the early 1500s and in the wake of several voyages by Vasco da Gama after 1498, the Portuguese operated a string of trading posts for their spice trades along the Malabar Coast and in the Indian Ocean area.[5] This stance on spices and the concept of superfluous luxury is something Luther shared with the early mercantilists and cameralist authors of the late sixteenth and seventeenth centuries, particularly in England, Italy and the German lands, before high and late mercantilism developed, from the later seventeenth century, a more relaxed and positive outlook on the virtues of luxury and foreign exchange.[6] This, as well as the following paragraph [4], has sometimes earned him the dubious qualification as an 'early mercantilist', as well as the even more senseless label as an early bourgeois author,[7] neither of which Luther was, of course. But as always, there is a grain of truth even in such gross misclassifications, as we shall see. In this famous and oft-quoted passage he said:

> God has cast us Germans off. We have to throw our gold and silver into foreign lands and make the whole world rich while we ourselves remain beggars. England would have less gold if Germany let it keep its cloth; and the king of Portugal, too, would have less if we let him keep his spices. You calculate yourself how much gold is taken out of Germany, without need or reason; from a single Frankfurt fair, and you will wonder how it happens that there is a single *heller*[8] left in German lands. Frankfurt is the gold and silver sink, through which everything that springs and grows, is minted or coined here, flows out of the German lands. If that hole were stopped up we should not now have to listen to the complaints that there are debts everywhere and no money; that all lands and cities are burdened with rent charges and ruined with interest payments. [4]

This paragraph is most interesting in at least three ways. First, with the allusion to the *heller* or half-penny, named after the Tyrolean mining and minting town of Hall as the smallest coin within the central German currency landscape – which knew an utmost variety of different penny, *groats* and *heller* coins minted by the Saxon Dukes and Electors,

---

5. Of course, the city of Calcutta did not exist in Luther's days. What Luther refers to here is the town of Kalikut/Calicut (today, Kozhikode). I am indebted to Prasannan Parthasarathi (Boston) for pointing me to this translational slip.
6. Where particular trade balances may be negative and luxury goods allowed into the country as long as they could not be produced domestically and as long as the aggregate or overall balance of trade remained positive, causing an influx of bullion. See, for example, Karl Pribram, *Geschichte des ökonomischen Denkens*, vol. 1 (Frankfurt: Suhrkamp, 1994), 93–180.
7. For example, Günter Fabiunke, *Martin Luther als Nationalökonom* (Berlin: Akademie, 1963).
8. The *heller* or half-penny was the smallest coin or denomination in those regions of early modern Germany that used the penny-groschen-gulden accounting ratio. At Luther's time (until the 1530s), one heller amounted to the 504th part of a gulden or florin. Thus one *gulden* (Rhenish florin) = 21 *groschen* (groats) = 252 d (pennies) = 504 *heller* (half-pennies; at 12 pennies to the groat). For detailed discussion of monetary relations and monetary policy in central Germany during Luther's age, see Philipp Robinson Rössner, *Deflation – Devaluation – Rebellion. Geld im Zeitalter der Reformation* (Stuttgart: Franz Steiner, 2012), chap. 3.

the Counts of Mansfeld, of Schwarzburg, of Henneberg and many, many more – Luther underlines his argument of monetary shortage. Due to the frequently debased nature and low purchasing power of most *hellers* in his days, these coins were the least likely to be exported by any merchant or financial speculator. Heller coins represented the bottom of the currency hierarchy. Some of them were old and worn and would have, in Luther's days, circulated for several decades and human generations. Their value varied from type to type; their exchange rate of half penny was only a notional one, as the pennies circulating in the Saxon and central German realms exchanged anywhere between the notional or the official rate of 12 and up to 20 (and sometimes even more) pennies to the next denomination, the *Groschen* (groat). The same was true for the *hellers*.[9] We may invoke a financial market operation colloquially known as Gresham's law or spontaneous debasement.[10] This will, according to its basic assumption, usually cause full-bodied or good money (i.e. money whose intrinsic silver or gold content comes close to its nominal value or imputed purchasing power) to be exported or hoarded in exchange for 'bad' money which is left in circulation and everyday transactions (if individuals act economically rationally).[11] Thus, the *hellers* Luther is mentioning in the text would have represented the very type of money that stayed in the German lands until the very last. If no *hellers* were left, there would be no money left at all in Germany – full stop. Luther made equivalent remarks in his address to the Christian nobility *An den Christlichen Adel Deutscher Nation* (1520), and in many other instances. Imperial Knight and humanist scholar Ulrich von Hutten struck the same chord. The debates on the Imperial Diet of 1522 picked up on the export of good money, as did the complaints of the Imperial Knights (*Reichsritterschaft*) in 1523.[12] If we believe these discourses – of course, we don't have to, but they are pretty close to each other and non-ambivalent enough so as to suggest that the humanists had a point here – there would have been an endemic shortage of silver and reliable money in the German lands. This did not only cause some economic disequilibrium and deflationary tendencies, and credit levels to contract, as discussed in chapters 2 and 4, but moreover also social problems. 'Good' coins were traded at a premium even though official currency legislation said that no such premiums should exist and that all coins ought to circulate at face value. The door would be thrown open for usurious currency manipulations. But in a system of free minting, that is a system where the market determined the amount of money in circulation as well as its composition (in terms of full bodied gulden/florins compared to small change coins) and

---

9. Rössner, *Deflation – Devaluation – Rebellion*, chap. 3, 381–86, table 4 for coin or spot exchange rates of several types of domestic as well as foreign coins admitted into circulation in the Saxon lands around 1511.

10. John H. Munro, 'Deflation and the Petty Coinage Problem in the Late-Medieval Economy: The Case of Flanders, 1334–1484', *Explorations in Economic History* 25, no. 4 (1988), 387–423.

11. Philipp Robinson Rössner, 'Monetary Instability, Lack of Integration and the Curse of a Commodity Money Standard. The German Lands, c.1400–1900 A.D.', in *Credit and Capital Markets* 47, no. 2 (2014), 297–340.

12. Gustav (von) Schmoller, 'Zur Geschichte der national-ökonomischen Ansichten in Deutschland während der Reformations-Periode', *Zeitschrift für Gesamte Staatswissenschaft*, 16 (1860), 461–716, (635–38).

factually also exchange rates, boundaries between coin usury and coin arbitrage were fluid, to say the very least.[13] Suffice it to say that Luther had a point when complaining about the outflow of silver: this created considerable *economic* as well as *social* costs.

Thus in this apparent 'fear of goods', a term coined by E. Heckscher,[14] Luther followed a rather common bullionist stance, which some historians of economic dogma have called, rather ambiguously and following K. Marx, 'monetarist'. As a political-economy principle, the idea can be found in southern and western Europe from the fourteenth century.[15] But Luther made two further interesting turns in this small paragraph [5]. With his remark on a net outflow of money or negative balance of payment, he established a possible connection with a monetary and credit contraction which has been discussed in detail in chapter 4. If liquid funds available for credit contracted vis-à-vis-demand for loans, which is indirectly hinted at here (*If that hole were stopped up we should not now have to listen to the complaint that there are debts everywhere and no money; that all lands and cities are burdened with charges and ruined with interest payments*), that is by a leftward shift in credit supply that was not met by a commensurate decline in demand for credit, this would cause interest rates to increase, if we interpret the interest rate to be a market price, that is the price for capital. Luther obviously referred to an acute monetary and credit shortage here.

But thirdly, Luther – in this very same paragraph on the Frankfurt Fairs – also touched upon a larger question of what we may call, with all due simplification and retaining due scepticism towards applying modernisms to historical analysis, *economic development*. Contrasting the German lands with England, which enjoyed a positive trade balance with the continent (Luther said) in terms of manufactured cloth exports, immediately illustrated his point. Six years later, the 'Ernestine' (1530), an anonymous pamphleteer in the Saxon currency dispute (*Münzstreit*) about a proposed devaluation of the Saxon currency argued that devaluation by means of coin debasement should stimulate exports and thus bolster the domestic economy.[16] The 'Ernestine' essentially confirmed Luther's view by saying, 'the same kingdoms, countries and islands (*referring above all to England and France, PRR*) have orientated their business, commerce, order of things, economic policy and practical economic activity thus that they export their and other countries' goods predominantly to us Germans, as well as Hungarians and Bohemians, thereby bringing our money into their country, which enriches them and makes their wealth increase.'

---

13. Rössner, *Deflation – Devaluation – Rebellion, passim.*
14. Eli F. Heckscher, *Der Merkantilismus*, 2 vols, trans. G. Mackenroth (Jena: G. Fischer, 1932).
15. See, for example, Diana Wood, *Medieval Economic Thought* (Cambridge: Cambridge University Press, 2002), 125–31.
16. Historically minded economists studying the pedigree of modern economic theory have known these writings for more than 150 years. Roscher called the pamphlets 'some of the most noteworthy economic writings of the period', see Wilhelm Roscher, *Geschichte der Nationaloekonomik in Deutschland* (Munich: Oldenbourg, 1874), 102–6. See also Hans-Joachim Stadermann, *Der Streit um gutes Geld in Vergangenheit und Gegenwart. Enthaltend drei Flugschriften über den Münzstreit der sächsischen Albertiner und Ernestiner um 1530 nach der Ausgabe von Walther Lotz* (1893) (Tübingen: Mohr, 1999); Bertram Schefold, 'Wirtschaft und Geld im Zeitalter der Reformation', in *id.*, ed., Vade*mecum zu drei klassischen Schriften frühneuzeitlicher Münzpolitik* (Düsseldorf: Verlag Wirtschaft und Finanzen, 2000), 5–58, for a most recent contextualization and clearly the best survey on this topic so far.

And 'Our domestic industry is geared towards accumulating and exporting money and wealth (*silver being Saxony's main export, PRR*) and take (manufactured) imports in return. This enriches about a hundred people, whilst driving princes and the common man, numbering more than one hundred thousand, to ruins.'[17]

Thus, Luther and his contemporaries had developed quite a refined outlook on the question of development which was based on empirical observation. England had improved her export position with regard to cloth manufactures only very lately, and partly due to a new economic policy or outlook, as we may call it; there was no economic policy these days in the modern sense of the word, neither in England nor on the continent, which would deserve the name. But a new economic outlook which went into the direction of protecting the nascent English woollen cloth industry by prohibitive–protective measures, for instance, a general ban on the export of unprocessed wool, became manifest in the customs reform upon the ascent of Henry VII in 1485.[18] By the early sixteenth century, the process of substituting manufactured woollen cloth, the famous *New Draperies*,[19] for raw wool exports was already in full swing. The accumulation of useful knowledge in a textile sector which became, between the late 1400s and later 1700s, increasingly sheltered by a protectionist state and accordingly designed tariff legislation, arguably laid the foundations for later export-led growth in Britain's textile industries, not only within the woollen sector but also in the linen and, more importantly, the cotton industry.[20] Luther may or may not have been aware here, if very implicitly, that having a native cloth industry with a positive net contribution to exports would have been a *desideratum*, although in the present example, he does not distinguish between spice imports from Portugal (something which did Portugal no great service in the long run, as spices were primary and unprocessed goods with little potential for adding value) and cloth imports from England, which were manufactured and thus carried a higher share of added value in the final good's price. Modern development textbooks have long known the axiom and very basic truth that different types of economic activity have different potentials to generate economies of scale and thus added value; it was one of the main lines of seventeenth- and eighteenth-century mercantilist and cameralist discourse in Spain, Italy and the Germanic lands.[21] The idea as such may well be traced

---

17. My translation, based on Schefold, 'Wirtschaft und Geld', 41. Original pag. in the Ernestine pamphlet, p. 56.

18. Ha-Joon Chang, *Kicking away the Ladder: Development Strategy in Historical Perspective* (London: Anthem, 2003), 19–21; Erik S. Reinert, *How Rich Countries Got Rich... And Why Poor Countries Stay Poor* (London: Constable, 2007).

19. See Ian Blanchard, *The International Economy in the 'Age of the Discoveries', 1470–1570: Antwerp and the English Merchants' World*, ed. P. R. Rössner (Stuttgart: Franz Steiner, 2009).

20. Prasannan Parthasarathi, *Why Europe Grew Rich and Asia Did Not. Global Economic Divergence, 1600–1850* (Cambridge: Cambridge University Press, 2011), esp. chap. 5; Giorgio Riello, *Cotton. The Fabric that Made the Modern World* (Cambridge: Cambridge University Press, 2013), chaps. 5, 8, but esp. 10.

21. This is because the elasticity of demand for manufactured goods is higher than for primary goods (such as food or raw material inputs). Modern development economics textbooks have this as a common stance, see, for example, A. P. Thirlwall, *Growth and Development. With Special Reference to Developing Economies*, 7th ed. (Houndmills: Macmillan, 2003), 78–79.

back to Giovanni Botero's (ca. 1544–1617) bestselling volumes on *Sulla grandezza delle città* (first edition 1588), the *Della ragion di stato* (1589) and his *Relazioni universali* (1591), which all went through multiple editions, totaling 45 before 1671 (with two late imprints until 1839); some of the basic ideas on manufacturing and good governance may be traced back to the medieval *Fürstenspiegeln* (Princes' Mirrors).[22] This insight, however, flies in the face of modern neoclassical trade theory developed along the lines of Ricardian comparative advantage and Heckscher–Ohlinian relative factor endowment in the wake of the post-1800 rise of 'Enlightened' or classical economics. Smithian–Ricardian theory, as is well known, advocates economic specialization according to comparative advantage regardless of the *actual type* of production (industry, services, agriculture and raw materials), assuming that all economic activities are alike. Naturally, this is not the case; it never has been.[23] There are fundamental differences across the commodity spectrum in terms of productivity, economies of scale and demand elasticities – and thus the potential to generate added value – for products that originate in the primary sector (agriculture, raw materials), as compared to manufacturing/industrial activities, where more value is generated than in agriculture.[24] The appropriate choice of menu within the productive landscape determines the relative growth potential of an economy in the long run.[25]

Whilst Luther, contrary to Botero and other contemporaries, shows no apparent understanding here of the concept of added value in development and the differential capacities of the several types of production (spices, cloth production) to generate differential economies of scale, his overall observation still ties in with later German voices

---

22. Reinert, *How Rich Countries Got Rich*; id. with Ken Carpenter, 'German Language Economic Bestsellers before 1850, with two chapters on a common reference point of Cameralism and Mercantilism', in Philipp Robinson Rössner, ed., *Economic Growth and the Origins of Modern Political Economy: Economic Reasons of State, 1500–2000 Milton Park and New York: Routledge, 2016* (forthcoming).
23. A manifestation of which is the classic textbook by Paul R. Krugman, Maurice Obstfeld and Marc J. Melitz, *International Economics. Theory and Policy*, 15th ed., forthcoming (Boston, MA: Pearson, 2015), which used, in its older editions, to be in line with the Ricardian mainstream.
24. The service sector is ambiguous in terms of the potential to generate added value, as well as raising productivity levels; mainly because this is a very inhomogeneous branch of economic activity. Some occupations within that sector will naturally appear very unproductive on paper simply because there is no physically remaining output to be measured adequately, and, accordingly, competing and ambiguous proxies for measuring output in this sector exist. Usually incomes are taken as a proxy, but this suggests measurability where no such thing exists. How does one put a monetary value on the output of a BBC symphony conducted by Sir Simon Rattle and how does this compare to a haircut at the local barber shop? And why is a haircut that takes thirty minutes so much cheaper than a chat with a notary lasting for the same amount of time, who meanwhile drafts up a property sale contract for the house you are going to move into? Both work within services, but their pay scales will differ radically. But it is difficult to say that the one is more productive than the other based on their financial reward. Salary and skill premium are weak proxies for either productivity or value generated within each occupational branch of the service sector. From a sociologist's viewpoint: Gösta Esping-Andersen, *Social Foundations of Postindustrial Economies* (Oxford: Oxford University Press, 1999).
25. Reinert, *How Rich Countries Got Rich*.

on the question of underdevelopment. This is why we must make a little digression here and take a brief glimpse forward in order to contextualize Luther and his contribution to economic thought more firmly in the *longue duree*. One of the next German economists to pick up on Luther's remarks in 1524 was German-Austrian cameralist Philip Wilhelm von Hornick (sometimes Hörnigk; also Horneck, 1640–1714), who developed the idea of relative development and accordingly underdevelopment in more detail in his major work *Oesterreich über alles, wann es nur will* ('Austria above all else if only it wills so', 1684) – a title sounding truly gruesome to anyone familiar with the German language and the twentieth-century pre-history of dictatorship and totalitarian abuses of the phrase 'über alles'. What Hornick and his contemporaries had in mind, however, was different.[26] In this classic pamphlet, Hornick identified something which may be called a small divergence within Europe since the later Middle Ages. Whilst beginning with the lament about the loss of specie and foreign exchange for luxury imports, especially to France (*Oesterreich über alles, wann es nur will*, 18s) – very similar to Luther – Hornick said that about a hundred years ago, France, England and the Netherlands would have stood at about the same level of wealth as the German lands. This would place the reference point for Hornick's analysis somewhere in the middle of the sixteenth century, although naturally he does not give away the quantitative evidence on which his claim should rest. It ties in with what recent research on urbanization and real wages, in the wake of an older thesis by F. Braudel, has established regarding an economic divergence within the European lands in the wake of the sixteenth-century shift of economic power towards the north-western rim; something which also comes across clearly from the available urbanization and comparative real wage date presented in tables 2.1 and 2.2 in chapter 2.[27] After the mid-sixteenth century, the native woollen industries of Austria and Germany developed into poverty, Hornick says, a process exacerbated by the Thirty Years' War (1618–1648). It is worth quoting Hornick in full:

Dann wo heutigen Tags eine Nation mächtig und reich sey oder nicht/hangt nicht ab der Menge oder Wenigkeit ihrer Kräffte oder Reichthum/sondern fürnehmlich ab deme/ob ihre Nachbarn deren mehr oder weniger/als sie / besitzen. Dann mächtig und reich zu seyn/ist zu einem Relativo worden/gegen diejenige/so schwächer und ärmer seynd. Waren nun vor anderthalb hundert oder mer Jahren/ Franckreich/Engelland / Holland und andere/weit nicht so reich und mächtig/ als jetzo: da konte sich Teutschland gegen sie starck und wohlhäbig preisen/und unsere Voreltern mit ihrem Zustand billig zufrieden seyn. Indeme nun aber unsere Nachbarn uns/und gleichsam sich selbst/so unvergleichlich überstiegen und angewachsen; so will uns wenigst/wann wir rechtschaffene Leute seynd/und unser Verfahren künfftig zu verantworten gedencken/gebühren/es auch nicht bey dem Alten bleiben zu lassen/sondern darob zu seyn/daß wir in Gegenhaltung unserer

---

26. Ibid., for a good recent introduction to seventeenth-century cameralist economics in modern perspective.
27. See chapter 2 for the tables and accompanying literature.

Nachbahrn wieder auf den alten Fuß/das ist/wenigst auf einen mit der Wohlfahrt unserer Nachbahrn gleichen/wo nicht höheren Grad kommen. (20)

[The wealth of today's countries does not depend upon their affluence or lack of powers and wealth as such, but above all from what their neighbours possess in terms of power and wealth. Wealth and power have turned into relative variables, compared to those who are weaker and poorer. About a hundred and fifty or more years ago France, England, Holland and others were by no means as rich and wealthy as they are today; and Germany could praise itself strong and affluent compared to the others; our forefathers could be quite content with their situation. But as our neighbours have in the meantime surpassed us – as well as themselves – and grown so considerably over time in terms of wealth this should give us occasion to rethink where we are and, provided we are respectable to ourselves considering our future chances, not to let the matter rest as it stands, but to take all measures necessary to attain at least the same level of wealth as our neighbouring countries and thus move back to where we used to be, if not much further ahead.]

Hörnigk's formulation *und gleichsam sich selbst* ('as well as themselves', see above quote) is interesting inasmuch as it may have referred to growth in per capita product *over time*, rather than cross-sectional development differentials. Whilst Luther's writings do not bear out the idea of *growth* in the modern sense, he certainly had, as many German economists to follow, an understanding of *relative* economic development and underdevelopment.

Public discourse picked up on this. The *Reichspolizeyordnung* of 1548 (literally Imperial Economic Policy Ordinance) issued a general export ban on raw wool, as well as the admonition to 'wear only domestically manufactured cloth'. The Imperial Resolution of 1555 sounded similar.[28] In England such measures had been enforced since the 1480s as we have seen in the previous section; under the early Tudors they were in full swing.[29] To what extent such laws and edicts were ever enforced effectively in the German lands is a totally different matter; we have every reason to suspect that they were by and large unenforceable. What counts, however, is that Luther and his contemporaries *had this idea*, in the wake of the imperial reform movement (*Reichsreform*), which included a whole range of economic policy matters, from currency and cloth production to trade policy and restrictions to be coordinated and regulated, that is managed on the imperial level. The early sixteenth-century 'Reformers' were quite aware of the idea of development and relative wealth. They had an increasingly refined, an abstract notion of the economy as a *Volkswirtschaft*, a national economy that was not an *oikonomy* anymore[30], that is a figurative household in the traditional sense, but something larger, more complex, a

---

28. Schmoller, 'Zur Geschichte der National-ökonomischen Ansichten', 650–51.

29. Hubert Hall, *A History of the Custom-revenue in England: From the Earliest Times to the Year 1827* (London: E. Stock, 1892).

30. The Greek οἶκος or *oikos* translates as 'Haus' or *house*, with a peculiar political economy attached to it. See Johannes Burkhardt and Birger P. Priddat, eds, *Geschichte der Ökonomie* (Frankfurt: Deutscher Klassiker Verlag, 2009), 645–72 (esp. 650–51), with text samples of the *Hausväterliteratur* or *Oikonomics/Economics* genre which stood somewhat between neo-Aristotelian thought and mercantilism–cameralism in the German-speaking lands.

more abstract system. What we find emerging here in the early sixteenth-century texts by Luther, von Hutten and others partaking in the public discourse on the common good, including protectionist measures on the imperial level is the emergence of the abstract concept of a *national economy* in our modern sense, or *oiko*-nomics turning – gradually – into proper *economics*.

The Role of the State

Of course, the state in the modern sense did not exist around 1500, but we find political authorities and patterns of government that attained 'proto-state' qualities, increasingly resembling what would soon emerge as the early modern fiscal–military states of Europe. For matters of convenience – and because again the text is quite timeless here again – the term 'state' will be retained. Luther and most of the humanists were also convinced that this state could, and should, do something to steer the process of economic development. It is also significant that England was identified as the main counterpart, if not rival. As noted previously, due to the peculiar composition of the 1524 pamphlet *Von Kauffshandlung und Wucher*, Luther's argument contains replications and duplications, as well as numerous theological digressions. Luther does, in fact, make some comments on the role of the state, which may for reasons of convenience and stringency follow the previous paragraph on the balance of payments and economic development. These remarks were placed between the sections on the four Christian ways of doing business [20–24] and the discussion of commercial malpractice (see section 5.3 below; in Luther's text these are the paragraphs [27ff]).

Luther's rather short digression of the state [25, 26] has been interpreted by some scholars as another crypto-mercantilist (or cameralist) stance.[31] The idea is not completely out of this world; however, it is not really correct or entirely sensible, either. Luther's concept of the state should be seen in the context of his wider theory of salvation and governance which has become known as the *Two Sword Doctrine*. As there were too many un-Christian people in this world, Luther said, you needed a strong government, not only in regard to economic and commercial matters [25]. With this, as well as the conclusions that *We must, therefore, keep the roads open and in good order, preserve peace in the towns, and enforce law in the land, and let the sword hew brisky and boldly against the transgressors* [ibid.], or that *It is the princes' duty to keep the roads safe for the sake of the wicked as well as of the good* [50], Douglass North and Barry Weingast and the new institutional economists' state[32] seems to shine through these lines. This state monopolizes violence, justice and legislation, thus safeguarding individuals' property rights, reducing transaction costs and stabilizing economic expectations. The degree or extent to what these property rights were designed so as to *favour* or discourage commercial and economic expansion, that is whether the set of property rights was good or bad, was another matter. Luther does not touch

---

31 Fabiunke, *Luther als Nationalökonom*, 158–60 on the genealogy of bourgeois economics within a Marxist frame of interpretation. Its political propaganda notwithstanding, Fabiunke's work still contains some valuable insights.

32. See chapter 3 for discussion and select references.

upon these matters, however, which again must caution us against using an overdose of modernisms. The main purpose of the state Luther had in mind was to uphold good Christian order, even if this involved the use of violence [25]. With his postulate that *if there are no Christians, the temporal authorities ought to compel everyone to repay what they have borrowed; if the authorities are negligent and do not compel repayment, the Christian ought to put up with the robbery* [26] Luther makes an interesting case that the three Christian ways of exchange (see below) only apply to Christians and that therefore the state, or – in Luther's words – the 'temporal authorities' should indeed enforce contracts and repayments of loans, even in those cases where they clearly were usurious! Otherwise, economic life would simply come to a standstill [37].

In his reference to Genesis and the forestalling and the passages of grain purchases by Joseph Son of Jacob [35–38], Luther makes an important comment on the interventionist role of the state [37]. Here he referred to a common practice of urban municipal governments of his time to buy up reserve supplies of grain in order to have them redistributed to the poor in times of need. Joseph *did right and well, for Joseph was conducting the temporal government in the king's stead* [37]. If government engaged in market manipulations that were very similar to forestalling and related speculative transactions, this was perfectly legitimate, even obligatory, Luther said. It is not known why he drew up this contrast here. He contrasted two types of economic behaviour or transactions that look similar on paper yet had followed fundamentally different ethical motives with radically different market impacts. On the one hand, there was the profit-seeking merchant buying up grain supplies before they reached the common market (forestalling, German *Fürkauf*) at times of crisis with the aim at *driving up* its price, thus raising his profit margin by *increasing* the shortage. On the other hand, there was the state doing something very similar, by pre-emptive purchases of grain at the time of crisis, yet with the entirely different motive of *lowering* its price, by subsequently offering it to those in need and thus attempting to *alleviate* the shortage. A recent account has called the biblical practice of building up emergency supplies of foodstuffs an early example of quasi-Keynesian anti-cyclical policy.[33] Such practice was common in early modern Europe, not only in the German lands.

'Just' Prices or Just Prices? Two Competing Notions of Equilibrium

Luther then goes on to list some of the more obvious malpractices in commerce and business dealings that were common in his days. He does not mince his words. He calls them sins. The first of these misgiven principles is: *I may sell my goods as dear as I can* [6], the desire for profits that know no boundaries. This is chrematistics again. Luther plays on the idea that profits and prices as a composite of costs plus reward or modest mark-up are justifiable on the ground that everyone was entitled to make a decent living; even the merchant who was a necessary actor in the economic configuration as an agent clearing demand and supply, by bringing those goods into the domestic realm of circulation which

---

33. On this see the controversial yet stimulating Tomáš Sedláček, *Economics of Good and Evil: The Quest for Economic Meaning from Gilgamesh to Wall Street* (Oxford: Oxford University Press, 2011).

could not be produced or procured domestically. But there should be ceilings, upper limits, maximum values. Profits should be capped. They ought to be in line with the medieval ideal of social equilibrium (not equality!) which general scholastic equilibrium theory had established and during the course of the High Middle Ages developed into a full theory, and which Luther, even though he had a negative view on scholastic thought in general, acknowledged, if implicitly, as a guideline to his model.[34]

We may recall from the discussion in chapter 3 that the 'just' price of the later scholastic authors of the thirteenth, fourteenth and fifteenth centuries was akin to the 'free market price', where 'free' was defined as 'free of asymmetries' such as monopoly, arbitrage, speculation and usury – the usual suspects in terms of market distortions. In this way, the scholastic notion of free markets actually came quite close to our modern concept, that is markets that are regulated with numerous laws and ordinances prohibiting and sanctioning inappropriate behaviour directed at market domination and price setting by single individuals or monopolist companies and firms. Of course, the modern notion of equilibrium is very different and usually relates to Walrasian neoclassical, especially micro-economic concepts of balance and market order, for instance, where prices settle at the intersection of imputed demand and supply curves. This notion of equilibrium, however, is value-free but not objective, because the stipulation of being non-judgemental or 'value-free', inherent to modern neoclassical price theory, *does* reflect a strong position that is in itself very value-laden carrying an overdose of subjectivism.[35] The scholastic theorists, as we have seen above, employed a different notion of equilibrium. Theirs was a social equilibrium, a harmonized and fair distribution of chances and capabilities. Neither Luther nor most of the other scholastic theologians ever dared to quantify in exact terms just what (or how much) a 'just profit' or 'just price' should be. Only superficiality or a modernist view would identify this stance as symptomatic of a wishy-washy approach; in fact, the opposite was the case. Everybody who was a true and faithful Christian would simply *know* what was just and

---

34. See chapter 3 for full discussion.

35. One may invoke Nietzsche's dictum here that ultimately science and scientific observation cannot be value free but have to depend upon perspective: 'Hüten wir uns nämlich, meine Herren Philosophen, von nun an besser vor der gefährlichen alten Begriffs-Fabelei, welche ein "reines, willenloses, schmerzloses, zeitloses Subjekt der Erkenntnis" angesetzt hat, hüten wir uns vor den Fangarmen solcher kontradiktorischer Begriffe wie "reine Vernunft", "absolute Geistigkeit", "Erkenntnis an sich"; – hier wird immer ein Auge zu denken verlangt, das gar nicht gedacht werden kann, ein Auge, das durchaus keine Richtung haben soll, bei dem die aktiven und interpretierenden Kräfte unterbunden sein sollen, fehlen sollen, durch die doch Sehen erst ein Etwas-Sehen wird, hier wird also immer ein Widersinn und Unbegriff vom Auge verlangt. Es gibt nur ein perspektivisches Sehen, nur ein perspektivisches "Erkennen"; und je mehr Affekte wir über eine Sache zu Worte kommen lassen, je mehr Augen, verschiedne Augen wir uns für dieselbe Sache einzusetzen wissen, um so vollständiger wird unser "Begriff" dieser Sache, unsre "Objektivität" sein. Den Willen aber überhaupt eliminieren, die Affekte samt und sonders aushängen, gesetzt, daß wir dies vermöchten: wie? hieße das nicht den Intellekt kastrieren?', Friedrich Nietzsche, *Genealogie der Moral*, 361, quoted after Oliver Garbrecht, *Rationalitätskritik der Moderne: Adorno und Heidegger* (Munich: Utz, 2002), 64. Erik Reinert brought this quote to my attention.

what wasn't – by heart that is, if not as the result of careful and reflexive-introspective examination that should guide each of the individual's actions, including one's economic *trans*-actions. Because acting on the market meant interacting with others; this automatically entailed considerations of what was fair and what was not (if you were a true and faithful person). Markets can never be value-free, that is. To look for a simple formula guarding price formation and profits would have been foolish in the eyes of the schoolmen. The Spanish theologian Domingo de Soto, a contemporary of Luther, made the point that the very posing of the question did not lead anywhere in particular, because, in the words of the authority on this matter, 'if someone asks you how much he can sell for, and you answer "What justice dictates," you tell him nothing that he did not already know'.[36] This was a remarkable peculiarity in pre-classical, particularly scholastic, economic thought. It made, apparently, for relatively great flexibility in terms of interpretation. Potentially it left the door open for those who took the opportunity to bend the rules. Potentially it even gave way to a certain laissez-faire, almost liberal thinking on markets and price formation which the late medieval schoolmen seem to have reached in the 1400s, and this is something with which Luther seems to have disagreed. Too much freedom on the market was not good.

Luther acknowledged that fixing the 'just' price was *indeed a thing that will never be governed either by writing or speaking, nor has anyone ever undertaken to fix the price of every sort of wares* [9]. He reiterated this point in [12]. Price formation was contingent, dependent upon circumstances of time, space and type of transaction. In order for everyone to receive at least a fair, if small, slice of the cake the *state* should jump in and manage the process, for instance, by setting upper price limits for the necessities of everyday life when and where necessary, and which should be enforced as rigorously as possible (*Preistaxen* or set prices). This has been analysed in chapter 3. With this stance Luther was in line with both contemporary political economy and economic policy regarding (urban) markets. But he was far from advocating a general regulation mechanism for all types of goods and all markets. Again, this is perhaps not all too different from twentieth-century European visions of coordinated capitalism (or *Soziale Marktwirtschaft* in post-war Germany).[37] Reality frequently worked differently; the state's means of enforcing price controls and market regulation remained imperfect, to say the very least, even in Luther's days. Arguably sixteenth-century economic exchange frequently attained the characteristics of modern free market exchange. Generally we should acknowledge that the oft-imputed modern dichotomy between free vs. regulated markets probably never existed. In fact, modern markets that are usually held to be free belong to the most heavily regulated fields of human interaction you can imagine. That is because in order to be free (of asymmetry and usury) they *have to* be regulated.[38] Luther and the medieval scholastic authors were well aware of this.

36. Odd Langholm, *The Legacy of Scholasticism in Economic Thought. Antecedents of Choice and Power* (Cambridge: Cambridge University Press, 1998), 80.
37. See chapter 3 for a detailed discussion and references.
38. Bernard E. Harcourt, *The Illusion of Free Markets. Punishment and the Myth of Natural Order* (Cambridge, MA: Harvard University Press, 2011).

But the merchants of Luther's days would not comply with scholasticism's guideline of what a just price (and profit) should look like. They were bent on making and enforcing their own rules. They were the main culprits of this sermon, his main goal of attack. They would, as Luther states, rather price the wares according to the level of what the market would take, which he calls 'one's neighbour's need' – this is the perfectly free market, where no regulations exist to safeguard the individual against risks of hardship, arbitrage, speculation and usury: *not that he may relieve it, but that he may use it for his own profit, to raise the price of goods, which he would not have raised if it had not been for his neighbour's need* [7]. Unfortunately we do not have enough market data from the sixteenth century to formulate a reliable model about how markets *really* worked in Luther's days; scholars have debated the extent to which market relations guarded economic exchange at the time. But that is not even the point. As has been shown above in chapters 2 and 3, the question as such is ill-posed, in the sense that it is neither helpful nor illustrative of the actual problems of market exchange. Economic exchange is and always has been culturally framed and embedded into wider social contexts. And this is no different today from how it was 500 years ago. And whilst admittedly within the so-called feudal economies the non-market, that is both the reciprocal 'moral' or 'economy of obligation' and the redistributive components of exchange (feudal or manorial economy; someone taking away something from you just because they can or, for instance, because it has been laid down in ancient statutes) took up a large chunk of total output, in those branches where the market reigned – meaning free bargaining processes about prices and quantities purchased – the market process followed working mechanisms that were very similar to today's. Therefore, it is difficult to settle on a definitive interpretation of Luther's words here. He said: *The rule ought to be, not: I may sell my wares as dear as I can or will, but: I may sell my wares as dear as I ought to, or as is right and proper* [8]. This represents a time–space-indifferent stance, in fact, but certainly not a question of imputed primitivism or less sophisticated economic theory.

The idea of 'right and proper' obviously mingled Christian theology and scholastic economics with the idea of a strong, pro-active state or government (see above), which should intervene whenever price formation and market mechanisms violated the 'just' price. In Luther's words price formation should follow the rule that *now it is fair and right that a merchant take as much profit on his wares as will pay the cost of them and repay him for his trouble, his labour, and his risk* [9] – something to be found in many a scholastic textbook. But Luther went on further, purporting that the best rule of thumb merchants should use when calculating their profits was by *estimating the amount of time and labour you have put on it and comparing it with that of a day labourer* [14]. This dictum has earned him amongst others, Schmoller's admiration,[39] for Adam Smith in his *Inquiry into the Nature and Causes of the Wealth of Nations*, Book 1, chap. 5, apparently sounds similar:

The real price of everything, what everything really costs to the man who wants to acquire it, is the toil and trouble of acquiring it. What everything is really worth to the man who has acquired it, and who wants to dispose of it or exchange it for

---

39. Schmoller compared this passage with Adam Smith, *Wealth of Nations*, chap. 5, and found it 'sharp and modern economic reasoning for his time'.

something else, is the toil and trouble which it can save to himself, and which it can impose upon other people.[40]

Again we should be careful not to read too many modernisms into Luther's words. But indeed one paragraph further down Luther makes an astonishing admission that *the next best thing is to hold our wares at the price which they fetch in the common market, or which is customary in the neighbourhood* [10]. Again it is only with a considerable portion of fantasy and interpretation that we could call this a 'free market price' in the sense of modern micro-economic or price theory, because yet another paragraph later he reiterates that consciousness and good Christian faith should be the guiding principles behind price formation [11]. And in making pricing decisions, even the most honest merchant or true Christian trader will make mistakes, even if small in relation to the good's hypothetical just value [12]. This is why we ask God for forgiveness even for those sins we commit when leading the most Christian life one could possibly lead. True. But Christian merchants would have been in control in terms of *limiting* the amount of potential damage and inherent risk to society inherent to any of their transactions [12, 13]. Most merchants of Luther's day were, however, in his interpretation, acting un-Christian-like.

At Luther's time proverbs, satirical works and other references to market exchange and the inroads the market had made into sectors of life where it should not belong had become numerous. The proverb *Sobald das Geld im Kasten klingt, die Seele in den Himmel springt* ('When the coin in the chest rings, the soul forth to heaven springs')[41] had been known since the 1470s; as has been shown in chapter 1, it attained refreshed prominence in the public debate in the wake of the general indulgence campaign spearheaded by Cardinal Albrecht of Brandenburg and his faithful servant in the central German lands, Dominican Friar Johann Tetzel in 1516 and 1517. The proverb *Schlechtes Geld kommt immer wieder* ('bad money always comes back') referred to a higher velocity for debased small change compared to better high-value or full-bodied coins, colloquially known as Gresham's law, or more technically *spontaneous debasement*[42], whereas *Was soll Geld, das nicht wandert durch die Welt* ('what use is money that does not travel?') drew an analogy to the somewhat negative impact of buried or treasured money, that is money that was kept from the market and was neither spent nor invested into some profitable venture (see chapter 4). *Geld macht aus Sauer Süß* ('money turns sour into sweet') and *Geld macht krumme gerade* ('money transforms uneven into even') echoed money's versatility and fungible nature, as did *Ein Goldener Schlüssel öffnet Herz und Schüssel* ('a golden key opens heart and bowl') or *Gold macht hold* ('gold makes you look attractive'). *Wo es Geld regnet, hören die Gesetze auf* ('The rule of law ends where it is raining gold') another proverb went.[43] Luther's

---

40. Adam Smith, *The Wealth of Nations, Books I–III*, ed. Andrew S. Skinner, new ed. (London: Penguin Classics, 1999), 133.

41. See also chapter 1 on indulgences.

42. Thomas J. Sargent and François R. Velde, *The Big Problem of Small Change* (Princeton, NJ: Princeton University Press, 2003).

43. All examples from *Die deutschen Volksbücher, gesammelt und in ihrer ursprünglichen Echtheit wiederhergestellt*, ed. Karl Simrock, vol. 5: *Deutsche Sprichwörter* (Frankfurt, 1846), 3252–53, 3317, 3328, and the *Neue Scheidemünze* collection.

wrangling and seemingly inconsistent theory of what the market price should actually be, as reflected in the above-mentioned passages in the sermon *Von Kauffshandlung und Wucher*, give away his powerful normative model, on the one hand, and an obvious capitulation before economic reality, on the other hand. Whilst the theological and political discourse not only on just prices but also on governance and price controls in the interest of the common good (called *Gute Policey* in the German lands[44]) had it that price formation – for a certain range of goods – belonged in the hands of the state, which may be a prince, duke, or an urban municipal,[45] reality looked very different and perhaps more akin to what modern micro-economics and price theory have to say on price formation. In many ways Luther's remarks seem to come very close to the simple admission that in many cases there was not much one (or the state) could do.

This line of thought culminates in the following passages on commercial malpractice of his days.

Get Rich or Die Tryin': Monopoly and Big Business

The discussion of merchants' tricks commences with six paragraphs on the practice of standing *surety* [15–20][46] or in modern German *Bürgen*.[47] These are passages that sound a bit strange and out of context to the modern ear,[48] especially when considering the overall composition and discursive strategy of the text. They can be properly appreciated only when seen in context with the subsequent sections [22–32], but, more importantly, the second part of the treatise, the (1520) *Great Sermon on Usury* [present edition: 56–96]. In fact, it was quite congenial for Luther to commence his discussion of commercial malpractice with a short treatise of the practice of surety or bail. Because this was a practice in which a person, by testifying for another man's *soul* and reputation (because that is what *bürgen* or standing surety ultimately is), assumed powers that belonged in God's hands alone. Your soul was something that was negotiated within the virtual space extending between you and God. To throw it in business and financial market transactions in return for monetary payment (credit, surety) meant to put it somewhere it didn't belong. Again the problem of intermingling spheres – economics on the one hand and salvation and trust on the other hand – shines through these lines as one of Luther's main themes and tunes, similar to the problem of indulgences (chapters 1 and 4).

44. See, for example, Achim Landwehr, *Policey im Alltag: Die Implementation frühneuzeitlicher Policeyordnungen in Leonberg* (Frankfurt: Klostermann, 2000); Alf Lütdke, *Herrschaft als soziale Praxis: Historische und sozial-anthropologische Studien* (Göttingen: Vandenhoeck & Ruprecht, 1991); Andrea Iseli, *Gute Policey. Öffentliche Ordnung in der frühen Neuzeit* (Stuttgart: Ulmer, 2009).

45. From the legalist-normative viewpoint, a good recent introduction is Iseli, *Gute Policey*.

46. On surety, see Christian Hattenhauer, 'Bürgschaft', in Albrecht Cordes et al., eds, *Handwörterbuch zur deutschen Rechtsgeschichte*, 2nd ed., 4th delivery (Berlin: Schmidt, 2008), col. 770–74. On the likely type of surety alluded to by Luther, the *Zahlungsbürge*, see Werner Ogris, *Elemente europäischer Rechtskultur* (Vienna: Böhlau, 2003), 517–21. I am indebted to Anja Amend-Traut (Würzburg) for pointing out the recent literature on surety in the legal historical context.

47. Which in modern German is both noun and verb.

48. As Burkhardt and Priddat, eds, *Geschichte der Ökonomie*, say.

In medieval German legal practice, several configurations of standing surety existed for different spectrums of transactions, ranging from economics and business to politics with the *hostage* being one extreme form of it.[49] In general terms, standing surety meant that a third party assumed full liability for the obligations of a debtor to their creditor. This was a *personalized* form of debt collateralization, as opposed to pledging where debt was backed up by some physical property or economic asset (capital). It appears as though standing surety was a credit operation or action taken when the debtor had no collateral to offer, that is no or only little private wealth, when he was literally penniless.[50] But we do not know the exact scenario Luther was referring to here. Obviously, in the practice of surety economy intermingled with the non-economic realm particularly closely – too closely for Luther's liking. One's personal reputation, *Trew und Glauben*, one's social capital, trust and trustworthiness were thrown into the balance to collateralize something that was supposed to be economic: a *loan*. Naturally, whenever the social intermingled with the economic, things were bound to become awkward. Luther acknowledged this. He immediately illustrated the complex web of interactions between the social and the economic sphere, with feelings, emotions, and the last thing that one could take away from you when everything else had already been gone: your *reputation*. Your soul; the very traits that *made you* as a person. How could something such as trust and character ever be thrown into the same balance as a sum of money? How could you possibly measure reputation? If you agreed to stand surety for someone else, you at least implicitly agreed that this would also extend to the creditor's *Trew und Glauben*, their character and reputation as individuals.[51] As a surety or bailsman you would not only assume their economic obligations but also stand in as a person with *your* own reputation, *your* credibility as a human individual and honourable member of society for an obligation incurred by someone else. In a world that knew no centralized institutions monitoring and enforcing contracts and property rights in the same way as law courts and formalized rules do nowadays, social networks and informal sanctions were favoured for solving economic coordination problems relating to contract enforcement, safeguarding of property rights and dealing with existing information asymmetries. They did so alongside more formalized open-access institutions such as law courts (which also existed, of course), albeit the balance frequently was in favour of the former.[52] In this way sociology, culture and economics intermingled. In a world where habitus, honour and reputation may have carried a larger weight in economic exchange than they do today (which is to an extent debatable), the practice of standing surety carried double significance. You assumed

49. Ogris, *Elemente europäischer Rechtskultur*, 501–2, 507–8. More recently Hattenhauer, 'Bürgschaft'.
50. E. Kaufmann, 'Bürgschaft', in Adalbert Erler and Ekkehard Kaufmann, eds, *Handwörterbuch zur Deutschen Rechtsgeschichte*, vol. 1 (Berlin: Erich Schmidt Verlag, 1971), 565–69.
51. Thomas Max Safley, 'Bankruptcy: Family and Finance in Early Modern Augsburg', *Journal of European Economic History* 29 (2000), 43–76.
52. See, for example, Avner Greif, *Institutions and the Path to the Modern Economy: Lessons from Medieval Trade* (Cambridge: Cambridge University Press, 2006); J. L. Goldberg, 'Choosing and Enforcing Business Relationships in the Eleventh-Century Mediterranean: Reassessing the "Maghribi Traders"', *Past & Present* 216 (2012), 3–40.

liability not only for the creditor's financial obligations but also for their character as a person, as a human being.

The other problem Luther indirectly hinted at here, whilst picking up on the credit economy and financial markets of his days, was that the act of providing surety resembled a form of credit transaction itself. Therefore, it was potentially linked to the usury discourse; through the obvious question whether someone standing surety for someone else was entitled to a financial reward for this service. Because, if that was the case, the transaction would have resembled the very act of giving credit (which potentially carried interest).[53] Be that as it may, with the passages on surety Luther found quite an apt introduction to the main problem he attacked within the present sermon: the modern credit economy.

He was certainly right inasmuch as that most economic, social and cultural historians would nowadays agree that the pre-modern economy was an economy that ran, above anything else, on credit. Credit was given on consumption and production alike. In the putting-out system or *Verlag*, many branches of the industrial sector and particularly woollen and linen cloth production, long lines of credit both on raw materials and on purchases of the final goods were not only regular but also represented a necessary requirement for the industry and its complex web of producers and customers to survive. *Der schöpferische Kredit*[54] – productive investment in the sense of *schaffendes Kapital* (creative capital) – arguably represented a *conditio sine qua non* for the flourishing of medieval and early modern business and commerce. Coin changed hands to clear balances after mutual obligations had, in the first place, been settled by exchanging goods. The money economy came on top of what superficially has sometimes been portrayed as more of a barter economy or economy of obligation than a straight market economy. But whilst the notion of barter strictly speaking implies that the actors do not prima facie have the motivation to exactly or simultaneously clear one debt against the other, or else have only limited means of exactly specifying the monetary value of the goods involved, transactions on credit on the other hand do involve an exact quantification of claims and obligations. And whilst many of the cashless transactions may have been morally embedded in some form – as all economic transactions, in fact, are ultimately, if you think about it – credit was the first and foremost an economic, not a social or cultural, thing, even in Luther's times. Therefore, we should not *über-culturalize* early modern society and economics,[55] but rather acknowledge that the market played a similar role in economic life as it does today, the major difference being that nowadays much more money is circulating on the market

---

53. Wilhelm Endemann, *Studien in der romanisch-kanonistischen Wirthschafts- und Rechtslehre bis gegen Ende des siebenzehnten Jahrhunderts*, vol. 2 (Berlin, 1883), 343.
54. Clemens Bauer, 'Wirtschaftsgeschichtliche Probleme des fünfzehnten Jahrhunderts', in *Die Welt zur Zeit des Konstanzer Konzils*, ed. Th. Mayer (Konstanz / Stuttgart: Thorbecke, 1965), 83–98 (90–91).
55. As is sometimes done, see Martha C. Howell, *Commerce before Capitalism in Europe 1300–1600* (Cambridge: Cambridge University Press, 2010) and Francesco Boldizzoni, *The Poverty of Clio. Resurrecting Economic History* (Princeton, NJ: Princeton University Press, 2011) for recent powerful restatements.

than in earlier centuries.[56] There are ample references that a money economy had taken hold of English rural society as early as the thirteenth century.[57] We should, therefore, probably replace terms such as barter economy or economy of obligation with *cashless* or *cash-scarce economy*, because – regardless how much money (as in *cash* or *coins*) actually did or did not change hands – chances are high, based on ample medieval and early modern documentary evidence, that people reckoned in money *in a similar way we do nowadays*. People used money for the same range of motives and transactions as we do nowadays, even though they comparatively seldom used it *physically*. But that is also something that is perhaps not so radically different from today if we consider how much money being used or circulating within the economy today is virtual money.

In fact, if there was anything that characterizes Luther's world at the time he was writing, it would be what the modern German has as *Leben auf Pump*, to 'live on tick', capturing, very remotely of course, the foundations of the American consumer revolution of the 1920s, the explosion of credit card transactions, especially in Britain and the US since the 1980s, and the subprime mortgage boom of the 2000s. Both the lender, Luther says, and the debtor gain from the credit economy, but only superficially so. The debtor does so because she will get the superficial yet treacherous fulfilment of her current or immediate wants and the lender because of the grotesquely enhanced interest rate (*usury*). Luther mentions how the practice of standing surety has become so ubiquitous *not only among merchants but throughout the world* [15]. This is the other side of the coin. He lists a series of biblical quotes condemning the practice because *it causes the ruin of many and brings them irrevocable injury* [ibid.]. He even invokes an old German proverb *Burgen soll man wurgen* ('bailsmen should be slain' or alternatively, as the phrase is ambiguous and laden with double meaning, 'bailsmen should be held responsible for the debtor's obligations') [16]. The proverb, apparently reflecting ancient Germanic law,[58] has two translation opportunities. The transitive as well as intransitive translation for the German *würgen* would be 'to choke', that is both to choke *someone* and to choke *on* something. In the present instance, the proverb obviously means that in terms of commercial law sureties can – and should – be held fully liable for the debtors' obligations, as though it was they who had incurred the financial obligations themselves. The other possible meaning is that bailsmen – or anyone standing surety for someone else – should be severely punished for what Luther held to be a reckless, silly and totally purpose-free practice. Standing surety means to usurp powers that are in the hands of God alone. Only God can be the source of trust, reputation and faith [17]. The German term, *Bürge*, it should be noted, also carries a protective notion, with the bailsman protecting, literally by covering or harbouring the culprit. Thus, the practice of standing surety means to usurp powers that are not for mankind to wield. Standing surety is not only against God's will but also a haphazard and senseless *presumption about the future* [18–20]. The credo that *everything*

---

56. Fernand Braudel, *Civilization and Capitalism, Vol. I: The Structures of Everyday Life*, pbk. ed. (London: Phoenix, 2002), 436–78.

57. Ian Blanchard, *Mining, Minting and Metallurgy in the Middle Ages, Vol. 3: Continuing Afro-European Supremacy 1250–1450* (Stuttgart: Franz Steiner, 2005), 1089–1107.

58. Ruth Schmidt-Wiegand, 'Bürgen muss man würgen, aber nicht an den Leib reden', in Cordes et al., eds, *Handwörterbuch zur Deutschen Rechtsgeschichte*, vol. 1, col. 737–38.

is in God's hand only [ibid.] was, as we have seen in chapter 3, a cornerstone of Luther's theology.

This brings Luther to an elaboration of one of his favourite topics that were also important in the 1520 *Great Sermon on Usury* (the second part of the 1524 pamphlet in the present edition): the four Christian ways of doing commerce or business. The first is the command *let them rob us of our property and take it from us* [21]. It invokes Matthew 5:50, meaning that whenever something is taken from you by force, or else – a more realistic scenario in business – if anyone will overcharge you and make an undue profit out of a particular transaction, then simply let go of it without mourning your loss or thinking twice about it, or even thinking of commercial litigation! God caters for you on Earth as well as in Heaven. There are more important things than to worry about foregone profit. The second command is to '*give freely to everyone*' [22]. This was a general Christian command relating to the basic principle of charity. The third way was *lending; that is, I give away my property and take it back if it is returned to me; if not, then I must do without it* [23]. This is the medieval principle of *mutuum date nihil inde sperantes*, based on Luke 6:35: *But love ye your enemies, and do good, and lend, hoping for nothing again.*[59] Luther explains that *when we make a loan, we take the risk that it may be a gift* [23]. Instead, we should give only according to our means and capabilities: *thus the best rule to follow is that if the amount asked as a loan is too great, you give something outright, or lend as much as you would be willing to give, taking the risk of losing it* [27]. In the same way as a credit/debt relationship must not lead to the debtor's invalidity, no one willing to extend a loan should be economically ruined by altruism taken too far.

Luther finds the credit economy of his days disturbing. It is unfounded, economically as well as spiritually. Consequentially, the postulate derived from his three Christian principles of doing business is that *in this way everything is paid in ready cash* [24] or in kind, something which Luther picks up four paragraphs further down after the digression on the state [28]. Because

[I]f there were none of this becoming surety and lending on security, many a man would have to remain humble and be satisfied with a moderate living, who now aspires day and night after the high places, relying on borrowing and standing surety. This is the reason that everyone now wants to be a merchant and get rich [29].

In 2005 German politician Franz Müntefering, then party leader of the Social Democratic Party of Germany (SPD) coined the term *locusts* for private equity investors who would buy companies at cheap prices only to tear them apart, recapitalize and streamline those branches of the business that were promising and then sell off the pieces quickly at inflated profit. Other examples of recent financial malpractice would include the unsecured debt/hypothecary market in the United States the collapse of

---

59. See sections on usury and discussion in chapter 3.

which triggered a worldwide recession in 2007.[60] In the 1524 pamphlet, Luther discusses practices which seem, on the surface, very similar.

He gives practical examples of the *three errors* or main evils of his time, namely *that everyone may sell what is his own as dear as he will, borrowing, and becoming surety* [30]. In Luther's days and age, such manipulations included the merchants *selling their goods on credit for a higher price than if they were sold for cash* [32], introducing a speculative element on top of the fact that (in all likelihood) interest would be charged on all transactions made on credit. Modern commercial practice of offering a *disagio* or deduction of the final price for goods and services delivered upon cash payment, a very common practice, for instance, in building and construction, would not see anything wrong with this. But for Luther *goods should not be sold for a higher price on credit than for cash* [33]. Arguably such a practice would be doubly usurious, comprising of the enhanced price (which may represent a concealed interest rate), as well as the credit transaction itself, which would also have carried interest.

The following paragraphs cover situations that were in contemporary linguistics and public discourse often framed as *monopoly*. This was a fluid term to say the least, and not completely overlapping with the modern technical definition of it. Here we come to a most interesting aspect of the political and economy discourse of the day. In the early 1500s, the term monopoly captured a variety of commercial malpractices and other incriminations identified by the public discourse as violations of the common good. Our modern definition of monopoly as the securing of the major share or entire supply of one particular good or service, putting the respective actor, firm or cartel in the position to dictate its price, was only one of them.[61] Perhaps, a more apt if wider definition may be *practices directed at gaining maximum control over the market* for a peculiar commodity. According to such a general definition, society and economy of the day were in many ways organized around natural monopoly, due to the peculiar economic configuration or *Wirtschaftsordnung* or *Wirtschaftsstil* (economic style) in the words of influential economists Edgar Salin, Alfred Müller-Armack or Bertram Schefold.[62] Some branches of production

---

60. Harold James, *The Creation and Destruction of Value: The Globalization Cycle* (Cambridge, MA: Harvard University Press, 2009).

61. The basic study still remains Fritz Blaich, *Die Reichsmonopolgesetzgebung im Zeitalter Karls V. Ihre ordnungspolitische Problematik* (Stuttgart: G. Fischer, 1967), esp. 17–37. Id., *Die Wirtschaftspolitik des Reichstags im Heiligen Römischen Reich: ein Beitrag zur Problemgeschichte wirtschaftlichen Gestaltens* (Stuttgart: G. Fischer, 1970), 135–53. On the monopoly debate, see also Bernd Mertens, *Im Kampf gegen die Monopole. Reichstagsverhandlungen und Monopolprozesse im frühen 16. Jahrhundert* (Tübingen: J. C. B. Mohr, 1996); Eberhard Isenmann, *Die deutsche Stadt im Mittelalter 1150–1550* (Cologne: Böhlau, 2012), 972–77; Heinrich Crebert, *Künstliche Preissteigerung durch Für- und Aufkauf. Ein Beitrag zur Geschichte des Handelsrechts* (Heidelberg: Carl Winter, 1916); Josef Höffner, *Wirtschaftsethik und Monopole im fünfzehnten und sechzehnten Jahrhundert* (Jena: G. Fischer, 1941); Karin Nehlsen-von Stryck, 'Das Monopolgutachten des Rechtsgelehrten Humanisten Conrad Peutinger aus dem frühen 16. Jahrhundert. Ein Beitrag zum frühneuzeitlichen Wirtschaftsrecht', *Zeitschrift für Neuere Rechtsgeschichte* 10 (1988), 1–18.

62. Bertram Schefold, *Wirtschaftsstile, Vol. I: Studien zum Verhältnis von Ökonomie und Kultur* (Frankfurt-on-the-Main: Fischer, 1994), esp. 73–110, and *id.*, ed., *Wirtschaftssysteme im historischen Vergleich* (Stuttgart: Franz Steiner, 2004); Alfred Müller-Armack, *Religion und Wirtschaft. Geistesgeschichtliche*

such as mining, alum or the amber trades were thought to be incapable of existing within a competitive market; they were *natural monopolies*.[63]

But the debates of the 1520s evolved around a different question of far wider socio-economic relevance. They were waged mostly on the Imperial Diet, specifically relating to certain Augsburg and Nuremberg businesses, such as the Fugger and Welser firms which were usually organized around the extended family; family-run but quite different from what most modern family (middle class) businesses look like. Partnerships were formed for specified periods of time, usually for the short run (two to seven years) and mostly by members of one family dynasty who would accept some silent participation or capital deposits by outsiders, who were more often than not related to the core family in some form, if not by blood then by marriage, godparentship and other types of weak social ties that were used to establish trust and security in business outside the strong ties marked by consanguinity. At a time when reliable information, particularly on a debtor's creditworthiness, was scarce and motives of defaulting on existing contracts apparent, weak ties and private order or informal enforcement institutions were used to create social capital and trust (*Trew und Glawben*).[64]

As early as 1439, the *Reformatio Sigismundi*, one of the famous reform pamphlets and socio-political agendas of the day, had demanded that big companies should be dissolved (*zerschlagen*), because 'they do harm to the people' (*denn sie tun allen Ländern weh*).[65] In 1519 Emperor Charles V, in his *Wahlkapitulation*, the political programme he promised upon his pending election as emperor, obliged himself to abolish the big companies (*die grossen geselschaften der kaufgewerbsleut, so bisher mit irem gelt regirt, gar abethun*[66]). Of course, the attempts came to nought; in the end, when the monopoly debate was sealed in the 1530s the big Augsburg and Nuremberg firms, headed by the Fugger imperium under Anton Fugger, emerged Phoenix-like out of the ashes bigger and stronger than ever. The discourse on merchant capitalism quickly became centre part on the agenda of the Imperial Diets at Worms in 1521 and in Nuremberg, 1522–25, frequently handled within the very same time slot allotted to the Luther case (*Causa Lutheri*). Before that, in 1512 an Imperial Diet at Trier/Cologne had defined the practice of monopoly in the wider sense as *Fürkauf* or forestalling – speculative purchases of a particular commodity with the aim at limiting supply and thus increasing its price. Practices of limiting the market to certain purchasers only, as well as minimum sales prices, were included in the definition of monopoly as a statutory offense.[67] Price dumping as a means of driving rivals out of business was also discussed widely in 1521–22. Luther picked up each of these practices in the present pamphlet.

Hintergründe unserer europäischen Lebensform, 3rd ed. (Berne: Haupt, 1981), esp. 46–244; Heinrich Bechtel, *Wirtschaftsstil im Spätmittelalter. Ausdruck der Lebensform in Wirtschaft, Gesellschaftsaufbau und Kunst von 1350 bis um 1500* (Munich: Duncker & Humblot, 1930).

63 Höffner, *Wirtschaftsethik und Monopole*, 49 et *passim*.

64. See above.

65. I am following Isenmann, *Die deutsche Stadt im Mittelalter*, 972–77.

66. After Blaich, *Wirtschaftspolitik des Reichstags*, 137.

67. Isenmann, *Die deutsche Stadt im Mittelalter*, 973.

In 1522–23 negotiations were held about a formal prohibition of large companies or monopolies by imperial decree (*Ratslag der Monopolien halb*). References and reports were produced both in favour of and against the large companies. They have incensed some historians to interpret the pamphlets written in connection with this discourse as belonging to a new age and the dawn of competitive capitalism. Monopoly, it was said in the most comprehensive statement of the *Kleine Ausschuss* on the Nuremberg Imperial Diet in 1522, damaged the common good. The companies charged outlandish prices on spice imports, in collusion with the King of Portugal (until 1521 Dom Manuel I, succeeded by John/Dom João III) who put up the selling prices at a grossly exaggerated level. The big south German companies would offer a price that was even higher than the one demanded by the king (the import of spices from the Portuguese realms to which Luther refers early in his sermon were put under royal monopoly and limited to a small range of actors, mostly German companies).[68] The companies would then habitually manipulate the market by charging prices and increasing or decreasing the prices for particular types of spices completely at their own discretion.[69] The smaller territories and Imperial Knights, when asked for their statement regarding the big companies, referred to the problem that the big trading companies damaged fiscal income on customs, tolls, as well as smiths, carriers and haulers and inn-keepers, who drew their major proceeds from travelling non-incorporated merchants. The larger imperial cities (the five or six companies that were concerned by this debate operated from the big and rich imperial cities of Augsburg and Nuremberg) argued in turn for the necessity of big firms. Who else would supply the empire with goods that had to be procured outside Germany, in Asia and other world regions, such as spices, if not the big companies? Single merchants would not be able to provide the same degree of capitalization and business scale necessary for the existence of long-distance inter-regional and international trades. These trades would collapse, if big firm partnerships and cartels were forbidden, passing into the hands of French and Italian merchants. The German economy would have less profit and taxable income to draw on.[70] The compromise reached was somewhat schizophrenic. The Diet acknowledged that although big business did many harms to the common good, the damages would be more considerable if it were completely abolished.

The Augsburg judiciary and official representative of the Augsburg City Council representing Augsburg's high society and governing class, a man who went by name of Dr Conrad Peutinger, provided a series of reports on why monopoly and big business were necessary.[71] In his reply to the *Ratslag der Monopolien halb* and his 'Denkschrift' in 1530, Peutinger mentioned the interdependency of economic processes, creating a picture of economic dynamics that were essentially the consequence of institutions securing private property rights and individual entrepreneurship striving for profit. Peutinger opposed fixed or set prices determined by the government (*Taxen*), providing

---

68. Rössner, *Deflation – Devaluation – Rebellion*, 251–90.
69. Isenmann, *Die deutsche Stadt im Mittelalter*, 974–75.
70. Blaich, *Wirtschaftspolitik des Reichstages*, 138–39.
71. Blaich, *Reichsmonopolgesetzgebung*, 74–81. A lucid and more recent discussion is Schefold, 'Wirtschaft und Geld', at 9–16.

a detailed analysis of price formation on markets which testify to a quite well-developed and sophisticated concept of micro-economic analysis.[72] He said that *the richer the merchants, the more they are in number, the larger will be their business volume and turnover and accordingly the benefit of the common good*.[73] Peutinger's reports have been said to represent a 'break-through of modern economic thought', a separation of economics as a mode of thinking that was separated from general social theory (scholasticism), including the acknowledgement of the national economy as a distinct configuration, somewhat implying that the opponents of monopoly did not have such a concept.[74] Peutinger, the idea sometimes goes, even anticipated Adam Smith's concept of the invisible hand,[75] promoting individual entrepreneurial strife for profit as the general *movens* and best-possible schedule of allocation for a healthy economy. New research on this matter has suggested, however, that one should be careful here, not least because between Peutinger and Smith at least two other writers mentioned similar mechanisms, namely Leonhard Fronsperger[76] (1564) and, of course, Bernard de Mandeville, in his *Fable of the Bees* (1705/24). More importantly the monopoly opponents were neither backward nor did they entertain a more primitive view of the economy. In fact, they had the same configuration of the national economy in mind as Peutinger did.[77] Only their goals and views on what represented a just distribution of resources and factors of allocation were somewhat different. Modern research has dismantled Peutinger's pamphlet as a work of lobbyism rather than scientific analysis; informed by the motives of the small yet powerful range of actors he served, attempting neither to model objectively the working mechanisms of the economy nor to promote anything that would have resembled a general and independent theory of it.[78] But to Peutinger's credit it must be said that he was a humanist and well-educated scholar, debating with Luther and the other public figures of the day at eye level. In the 1520s, the public's attitude towards the Augsburg and Nuremberg big companies had turned vicious in places, as borne out by the case waged on the Imperial Diets. Peutinger argued his – and the companies' case – with his back to the wall.[79]

---

72. Blaich, *Wirtschaftspolitik des Reichstages*, 139; Clemens Bauer, 'Conrad Peutingers Gutachten zur Monopolfrage', *Archiv für Reformationsgeschichte* 45 (1954), 1–43; 145–96; *id.*, 'Conrad Peutinger und der Durchbruch des neuen ökonomischen Denkens an der Wende zur Neuzeit', in Hermann Rinn, ed., *Augusta 955–1955* (Munich: Rinn, 1955), 219–28.
73. After Isenmann, *Die deutsche Stadt im Mittelalter*, 976.
74. Clemens Bauer, *Gesammelte Aufsätze zur Wirtschafts- und Sozialgeschichte* (Freiburg i. B.: Herder, 1965), 253.
75. Isenmann, *Die deutsche Stadt im Mittelalter*, 976.
76. Schefold, 'Wirtschaft und Geld', 16–20.
77. Mertens, *Monopole*, 158–60.
78. Ibid., 160. Heinrich Lutz, *Conrad Peutinger. Beiträge zu einer politischen Biographie* (Augsburg: Die Brigg, 1958), 140, however, states that Peutinger's reports did not evolve around self-interest as a prime mover but the *city* as a politico-economic configuration distinct from others (such as the rural environment or rural society).
79. I am much indebted to Chris Close (St John's, USA) for this very careful and differentiated interpretation of Peutinger.

One must, however, note the specific location of this discourse under its idiosyncratic conditions of time and space in order to appreciate that Peutinger's model was somewhat different from the market dynamics at work in eighteenth-century Britain which Adam Smith and David Hume above everyone else developed into a more formal model of general equilibrium which has subsequently become known as classical economics. In Bauer's words, 'His father was a merchant [...] and so were his brothers; the father of the great tycoon Ambrosius Höchstetter (*who became one of the accused in the monopoly case, PRR*) was his power-of-attorney; above all his marriage into the Welser dynasty, after the Fuggers the wealthiest and most powerful merchant dynasty of Augsburg, catapulted Peutinger into the social and economic elite of his age.'[80] To label Peutinger an economic theorist of the sixteenth century would, therefore, be akin to calling George Soros an influential contributor to twentieth-century economic knowledge. Nevertheless, the contrast is apparent. German economic discourse during the 1520s and 1530s evolved around the question: *what role should markets play in society and economy?* To what extent must markets and some business practices be earmarked as harmful to the common good? Again this is a very modern question. Peutinger, and less so Dr Johannes Eck, 'Dreck' (German for *dirt*) as he was pointedly called by Luther in his pun by omitting the commonly used full stop in the German language after the doctoral title, thus transforming *Dr. Eck* into *DrEck*, the Catholic theologian who produced a series of reports on the legitimacy of interest, was the biggest counterpart to Luther in the debate on economics and sociology. Whilst Peutinger marked one extreme pole of the continuum – some prototype of economic liberalism, perhaps (but very remotely so) – Luther marked the other end of the debate.

At the same time as the monopoly debates increased in steam, *Von Kauffshandlung und Wucher* was published. A few months earlier, in 1523, the Fugger, Welser and Höchstetter firms had been officially accused by the *Reichsfiskal*, the fiscal-general, of having formed a monopoly – which was defined as a criminal offense. They would be the companies Luther had in mind when writing the respective passages on commercial malpractice in his sermon on commerce (part I of the present document). Emperor Charles V, as is well known, finally cancelled the monopoly charge in the 1530s. Charles needed the money; it was as simple as that. In 1525 the emperor had complied still, by signing an edict (*Constitutio de illicitis mercimoniis*) which made monopoly practices a punishable offence, but only to lift it subsequently, by an Imperial Decree in 1530, for the mining and metal trades. The Fugger, Welser and Höchstetter firms had their biggest stakes in the mining and metal/silver trades (see chapter 2). The monopoly question was finally solved in their interest in 1530. In 1526 the emperor even exempted the Fuggers and gave them carte blanche for all possible monopoly charges, which represents one of the weirdest (in the words of Fritz Blaich) yet ultimately understandable moves in the whole game. The Fuggers were the main lenders to Charles V, after all. The door was opened for further erosion of what had originally, that is in and around 1520, appeared as a hard stance on monopoly and market distortion.[81] As usual, the deal was framed in the language of compromise, but effectively it was a victory for the big southern firms. Large

80. Bauer, *Gesammelte Aufsätze*, 255.
81. See also Bauer, *Gesammelte Aufsätze*, 236–37.

corporations were allowed to continue but boundaries should be set, both in terms of total capitalization (suggestions for upper limits reached from 20,000 to 50,000 florins) and in terms of (hard to enforce) prohibition of accepting foreign shares and deposits. The big firms and companies literally got away with impunity.

Practices of *monopoly*, then, in Luther's words extended to the following activities:

- *Profiteering* [33];
- Forestalling [34]. Luther contrasts the practice of forestalling with the charitable actions by Joseph in Genesis 41:48 [35]. These practices have been discussed in section 5.3.
- Another crucial malpractice was price dumping [39].
- On futures [40] Luther remarked: Again, it is a fine piece of sharp practice when one man sells to another, by means of promises ('Mit worten ym sack' in the German original), goods which he himself has not, as follows. This included an element of arbitrage and speculation, as it involved insider information of where and when to buy the goods more cheaply before reselling them.
- Undercutting, using straw men [41, 47].
- Price cartels [42, 43]. In paragraph [43], Luther mentions as a prime example of a price cartel the Company of Merchant Adventurers of London, a company that existed between the early thirteenth and the early nineteenth century and which controlled English broad cloth exports to the continent, wielding not only considerable commercial but also some political influence.[82] This company sent, in 1600 still, about three quarters of their cloth exports to the Netherlands and German markets.[83]
- Ruinous competition by selling the same good at a higher price upon credit to someone from whom I will buy it back at a discount [44].
- Bankruptcy.[84] Business turnover will be grotesquely inflated by loans most of which the merchant will be unlikely to ever repay. By declaring bankruptcy and fleeing the country or seeking refuge in a church asylum, the merchant returns afresh into business with the main share of his liabilities cancelled [45].
- *Manipulation or adulteration of merchandize*. Several ways of violating contracts due to changes in the outer appearance of goods put up for sale [48].

The taking of interest, something which Luther discussed at length in his *Great Sermon on Usury* (part II of the present treatise), extended to activities such as shareholding and other means of corporate finance, which Luther analysed within the sections on commercial malpractice [46, 55]. Monopoly and usury went hand in hand. Both were about market control and undue power over other individuals. Big business always

---

82. In a broader social and political context: Robert Brenner, *Merchants and Revolution: Commercial Change, Political Conflict, and London's Overseas Traders, 1550–1653* (Princeton, NJ: Princeton University Press, 1993), chap. 1.
83. Ibid.
84. Thomas Max Safley, ed., *The History of Bankruptcy: Economic, Social and Cultural Implications in Early Modern Europe* (New York: Routledge, 2013), esp. introductory chapter; *id.*, 'Bankruptcy: Family and Finance in Early Modern Augsburg'.

made a profit, even when prices kept alternating [53]. *They hang thieves who have stolen a florin or half a florin and do business with those who rob the whole world and steal more than all the rest* [54]. How timeless do these lines sound! Luther closes the part on commerce (*Von Kauffshandlung*, 1524) with a bloomy polemic and the statement that it was not in his own hands to look into these things, but rather the duty of the state [55]. *If the companies are to stay, right and honesty must perish; if right and honesty are to stay, the companies must perish* [55]. The *Great Sermon on Usury* follows, which had already been delivered in 1520.

Time is Money: Avarice, Usury and Financial Markets

Usury was – as practically all other economic topics in Luther's oeuvre – framed by the concept of *avarice*. Following Aquinas and the medieval churchmen, avarice was a sin of excess, of wanting more: just for the sake of it. As such it could originate only out of base motives. Avarice was 'a sin against God, just as all mortal sins, in as much as man condemns things eternal for the sake of temporal things'. This explains why Luther takes such a complicated digression in his *Sermon on Usury* (1520), the second part of the 1524 *Von Kauffshandlung und Wucher*, by developing at length the three principles of giving. Whilst on many other occasions strongly denying any adherence to scholasticism, Luther here adopted a standard scholastic stance derived from Aquinas and other medieval authors. This applies especially to the stance on *risk* which, according to many scholastic authors, passed from lender to borrower, once a loan was made; therefore, the creditor or lender should not be asking for interest as a charge for risks incurred.[85]

In this part of the sermon, Luther identifies *avarice* as the primeval vice jeopardizing the true Christian nature and natural order of things. Luther reiterates the three ways of giving providing, first, a more detailed exegesis of the biblical command 'be prepared to let go' as well as its possible circumvention strategies [57, 58, 59]. Principally *you must pray for him and do well to him who does evil to you* [58]. Of course, in Luther's times people did not adhere to Christian commands. Quite to the contrary; law courts were over-burdened with claims and cases for litigation, disputes about property rights and contract enforcement [60–63]. These practices had by no means excluded the Church, since *throughout the Church the greatest and holiest and commonest work these days is suing and being sued* [60]. And again Luther sees this as an expression of a *mentalité* that has charged up business and commerce with a more positive connotation than ever before. The

> bright young boys look on this (i.e. *business and commerce*, PRR) as a good thing to do, and regard it with equanimity […]. Hence it comes that lawsuits and litigations, notaries, officials, jurists, and that whole noble riff-raff, are as numerous as flies in summer. [60]

It should be remembered that Luther had been on the way towards becoming a professional lawyer-administrator himself, by means of his liberal arts studies 1501–5 and his brief spell at the Law Faculty of Erfurt University in 1505. He knew what he was talking about. Throughout his oeuvre and later career, his views on jurists and lawyers

---

85. Wood, *Medieval Economic Thought*, 192–93.

remained spiteful. On the present matter, he said that God's law would always come before temporal law: *the things that human laws command and forbid matter little; how much less the things that they permit or do not punish* [61]. No one should become plaintiff or litigator on their own. Rather the 'brotherly Christian community' should act in a concerted way and bring evil-doers and wicked people to the attention of the temporal authorities, to be tried and punished according to law and custom, with proof of evidence provided by everyone in good faith. What Luther seeks to avoid are endless cases and sequences of commercial litigation: *if peace is to be kept, one party must be quiet and suffer* [63]. Litigation is a waste of time, money and valuable resources. It corrupts people's minds, because it means clinging to temporal goods, giving up the true Christian and thus unconditional confidence in God in all matters earthly as well as spiritual. This confidence should make us safe and secure in this world: *and even though everything were taken from us, there is no reason to fear that God will desert us and not provide for us even in temporal matters* [64]. From a modern point of view of *über* regulation of many a commercial and economic sector, Luther's words sound somewhat reassuring. Where there is place for informal law and property rights enforcement procedures – we may say: arbitration and mediation, it will be better for society at large, not only economically. Litigation on the other hand, that is formalized practice of enforcing property rights using a law court, increases transaction costs, and arguably also the mental-emotional rifts within society. Where people fight over goods, there will also be animosity about other matters. Recent comparative studies on governance, commercial litigation, arbitration and private order enforcement mechanisms as alternatives governing exchange relations and decreasing transaction costs in international trade essentially confirm that litigation was, in the rise of the Flemish and Dutch commercial cities between 1250 and 1650, always used as the means of last resort when it came to settling commercial disputes.[86]

These passages are followed by a detailed discussion of the *second commandment* regarding exchange. These passages are similar, if more detailed, to the respective sections in the first part of the treatise *Von Kauffshandlung / On Commerce* (part I) [21–24, 27–28]. Everyone should give lavishly [65]; if everyone did so, there should be no beggars any more [66]. People should be more altruistic and not subject their patterns of spending and giving to motives of private profit and one's own advancement in terms of honour, social prestige and reputation. Rather than holding feasts for *their friends, the rich and powerful, who do not strictly speaking need them, and forget the needy about it* [67], one should give to people even if they are not your friends but your enemies [68]. What seems like a rather theoretical if not hypothetical postulate about Christian norms turns into a most interesting aspect, in two ways.

First, the argument regarding beggars [66] works in both directions: *there should be no beggars any more* – full stop! as one may add. Here Luther addresses an apparently recent rise in begging by people who were neither incapacitated nor poor and destitute enough to qualify as 'honest' beggars as defined by medieval social theory. Strictly speaking begging should always be a strategy of last resort. Only then it could be an effectual target for

---

86. Oscar Gelderblom, *Cities of Commerce: The Institutional Foundations of International Trade in the Low Countries, 1250–1650* (Princeton, NJ: Princeton University Press, 2013).

the true Christian's command to act charitably. But: *now, however, there is so much begging that it has even become an honour; and it is not enough that men of the world beg, but the spiritual estate of the priesthood practices it as a precious thing* [66]. In Schmoller's interpretation Luther was referring here chiefly to the mendicant friars.[87] According to the contemporary Eberlin von Günzburg, who wrote a short book entitled *I Wonder Why There Is So Little Money in Germany*,[88] up to 300,000 florins would have left the German lands annually for remittances to Rome, thanks to the friars alone.[89] Whether or not such a figure is accurate does not matter; Günzburg's remarks carry a wider relevance. As a general practice, begging witnessed an increase during the sixteenth century. In the wake of the population rise since the 1470s and the progressive reduction of available per capita resources compared to the mouths that needed to be fed during the long sixteenth century or Price Revolution (chapters 2 and 4), real wages declined and poverty levels increased, ca. 1470–1620.[90] The numbers of beggars shot up as well, as did visual depictions of begging in contemporary art. Whilst late medieval scholastic equilibrium theory had identified begging as constitutional for Christian community and society and manifestly important for the opportunity of giving alms and thus fulfilling the charity commandment, public discourse after 1500 increasingly identified begging as a problem. Now, the strong beggar appeared as a discursive figure. Beggars and vagrants were now depicted increasingly as parasitical. Whoever was physically capable, or thought to be so, of working with one's own hands should not be begging. This image and perception of the beggar prefigured the origin of the *work house*, a prototype in mercantilist social theory and employment policy.[91]

The second component – which works only within the general concept of salvation and true Christian life as manifested in the three degrees or ways of giving discussed above – is Luther's critique of contemporary practices of alms giving.

> The way things now go, they apply the high title of 'alms,' or 'giving for God's sake,' to giving for churches, monasteries, chapels, altars, church towers, church bells, organs, paintings, statues, silver and gold ornaments and vestments, and for masses, vigils, singing, reading, testamentary endowments, sodalities, and the like. [...] Where there are a hundred altars or vigils, there is not one man who feeds a tableful of poor people, let alone gives food to a poor household. [69]

This passage ties in with Luther's notion of avarice and the misallocation of productive resources by burying treasure in the dead hand of the church (see chapter 4 for a full discussion). The cornerstone of his teachings on giving, which is partly related to

---

87. Schmoller, 'Zur Geschichte der national-ökonomischen Ansichten', 526–27.

88. *Mich wundert, dass kein Gelt ihm land ist. Ein schimpflich doch vnschedlich gesprech dreyer landtfarer vber yetz gemelten tyttel. Eylemburg durch Jac. Stöckel* (1524).

89. Schmoller, 'Zur Geschichte der national-ökonomischen Ansichten', 669.

90. See chapter 2.

91. Philipp Robinson Rössner, 'Das friderizianische Preußen (1740–1786) – eine moderne Ökonomie?', *Vierteljahrschrift für Sozial- und Wirtschaftsgeschichte*, 98, 2 (2011), 143–72; *id.*, 'Das Friderizianische Wirtschaftsleben – eine moderne Ökonomie?', in Bernd Sösemann and Gregor Vogt-Spira, eds, *Friedrich der Große in Europa. Geschichte einer wechselvollen Beziehung*, 2 vols (Stuttgart: Franz Steiner, 2012), 375–90.

Luther's understanding of indulgences, is manifested in the following paragraph: *it would be sufficient, if we gave the smaller portion to churches and the like, and let the lion's share flow toward God's commandment, so that among Christians good deeds done to the poor would shine more brightly than all the churches of stone or of wood* [70]. If every parish, every district, provided for their own poor and those in need, rather than erecting lavish buildings and over-burdening ritual and church interior with unnecessary luxury, this would be a better world, in accordance with the true principles of charity towards your neighbour [71].

To Luther, the clearest manifestations of beggars are the churchmen and clerics who ply the country, pledging for indulgences. Whilst people seem to be unwilling to extend their charitable alms beyond the utter minimum to keep the poor and needy people alive or at bare subsistence, no one will strike the same balance when it comes to deciding how much money should be invested in maintaining and improving church buildings and other property, Luther remarks grimly [72]. And after criticizing the monopolist position of the Curia in selling *canonization, pallia, bulls, and breves*, he makes the characteristic remark: *well for you, dear Rome, that even though the Germans run short of money, they still have chalices, monstrances, and images enough; and all of them are still yours!* [72]. Here Luther strikes the same chord regarding the outflow of silver from the German lands, which the satirical discourse of the day, such as the Vadiscus dialogue by Ulrich von Hutten picked up (chapter 4).

Luther then moves on to lending which should be interest free [73], *since there is no lending except lending without charge, and if a charge is made, it is not a loan* [74]. Contemporaries may have felt differently. In paragraph [75] there follows a brief but interesting definition of usury as to *give back more, or something else that is better than he has borrowed.* Usury therefore has, alongside the quantitative element, also a qualitative component. No one would wish, if asked for their opinion or given a choice, *good wares to be repaid with bad, or with equally good wares, but without charge* [77]. At another place Luther refers to coin usury (repayment in bad coin of a loan that had been made in good coin). He then goes on to identify some common objections to his, that is the argument of foregone profit opportunities, which the lender would suffer from if they had invested their money otherwise, as well as the 'everybody does it' argument – especially the church [78]. The former is one of the four standard reasons advanced by medieval scholastic theory on usury on why the taking of interest should be considered legitimate (*lucrum cessans*).

Luther then moves on to the *other part* of the *Sermon on Usury*, where he discusses a type of financial market transaction which he obviously considered emblematic and characteristic of his age and which he had discussed at length in the first part of the sermon (*Von Kauffshandlung*): the *Zinss kauff*. A literal and somewhat clumsy translation of this term would be 'purchase of interest'. The older English translation of Luther's *Kauffshandlung* has it that way; the revised (1962) version has retained, in a much more careful fashion, the original German term (*zinss kauff*[92]). No modern equivalent exists[93],

---

92. *Luther's Works, Volume 45: Christian in Society II*, ed. Walther I. Brandt, gen. ed. Helmut T. Lehmann (Philadelphia: University of Philadelphia Press, 1962), 295ff. and comments on the revised translation in ibid., 237ff.

93. David Wayne Jones, *Reforming the Morality of Usury: A Study of Differences that Separated the Protestant Reformers* (Dallas: University Press of America, 2004), 53.

but scholars have suggested close resemblance between *zinss(kauf)* and Latin *census* or rent or annuity, with *zinsskauff* accordingly denoting the trade in such financial market products, that is the annuity business in general. Caution obliges us to remain careful and say that this terminus technicus is likely to have referred to a potentially wide variety of fixed payments upon loans that were – frequently but not by necessity – given against some sort of hypothecary or real estate as collateral. Luther's usage of the term *zinsskauff* meanders and is profoundly ambiguous throughout; this makes a definite translation impossible. The problem is a historical one: Grimm's *Dictionary*, the main reference point for historical technical and legal terms of early modern Germany, defines *Zinskauf* as 'in der regel ein verzinsliches gelddarlehen auf grundstücke', that is a mortgage/ hypothecary.[94] However, in the same volume, the Brothers Grimm defined *Zinskäufer*, that is the purchaser of zins, as *darlehensgläubiger*, that is, in more generic terms, the person providing credit or a loan in general. Thus *zinss kauff* may have principally extended to most other forms of interest-bearing assets as well, such as rents, (life) annuities, obligations and shares in companies, with a whole spectrum of possible interest rates. In modern German, *Zins* and *Zinsen* translate as 'interest'/'interest rate(s)', or any regular income stream resulting from real estate and other forms of productive capital investment, including rented flats and houses for which *Mietzins* (rent) is to be paid. We find the latter type of *zinss* mentioned frequently in sixteenth-century documents.[95] The term, however, also includes (in the more modern usage) not only current and savings accounts, state obligations as well as corporate bonds but also the interest one has to *pay* on a loan and other types of credit, such as bank overdraft charges. In sixteenth-century sources, *zinss* could therefore literally cover many different types of transactions, incomes and financial market products. In the pre-industrial agrarian economies of Luther's days, *Zins* could also refer to the payment of a feudal rent or other charges and obligations that arose from the usufruct of land within the non-market or redistributive allocation arrangements of the feudal economy (feudal dues, Ger. *Grundabgaben*). *Zinss kauff* therefore remains one of the trickiest and likewise most interesting and significant *termini technici* in Luther's oeuvre. We should avoid a definite translation. We may say, however, with an appropriate degree of caution that it covered – in Luther's understanding – the general practice of financial market transactions. *Zinss kauff* in Luther's day and age was the archetypical catch-all term for the modern financial business.

In the *rentes* or annuity business (*Rentengeschäft*)[96] in the wider sense, which would in any case have been fairly close to the sort or sorts of transactions Luther had in mind in the present sermon, the creditor lent a specified sum of money (*Hauptgut, capitale,* capital) to the debtor in return for a sum of interest paid annually. Interest could be paid in money or kind, or a combination of the two. This type of credit transaction was frequently collateralised by a specified piece of real estate, usually a plot of land that bore some

---

94. Jacob and Wilhelm Grimm, *Deutsches Wörterbuch*, 16 vols (Leipzig: Deutscher Taschenbuch Verlag, 1854–1971), vol. 31, col. 1527–29.

95. For example, Günter Zorn, ed., *Akten der Kirchen- und Schulvisitationen in Zwickau und Umgebung 1529 bis 1556* (Langenweissbach: Beier & Beran, 2008), 18, referring to a type of (house?) rent due to the Zwickau pastor in 1529.

96. Isenmann, *Deutsche Stadt im Mittelalter*, 949.

sort of regular income or rent payment, which was signed over to the creditor. The transaction was effected by the debtor transferring the usufruct of a certain and specified piece of land or other real estate that carried a fixed income stream or rent charge, to the creditor. Contemporary synonyms for such transactions (we may say different types of financial market products) were *census, pension, canon, merces, redditus, Gült, Ewiggeld, Leibzucht*. They may all have covered transactions that were similar or even identical in terms of type and nature to the transaction Luther had in mind here (but we cannot be ultimately sure). Rents and annuities belonged amongst the commercial papers and securities that were traded on the emerging financial markets of the day. Due to the usury laws, it was imperative that a rent was collateralized by some sort of revenue-bearing real estate, a plot of land, a rented house or a landed estate, therefore, introducing a hypothecary element to the deal. This way the transaction remained a *commodity transaction* (sale → purchase) without turning into a pure *credit operation*. What was sold was a regular stream of physical revenue of something that could re-grow or renew itself, such as a plot of land where seed was sown and would bear a yearly fruit.

Therefore, contrary to straight credit upon interest, annuities and other forms of hypothecary credit, when shaped in the *zinss kauff* or census contract, did not violate the Aristotelian and scholastic sterility-of-money doctrine. The interest payments gained from them were not deemed usurious.[97] *Ewigrenten*, that is irredeemable annuities, as well as *Leibrenten*, which terminated with the death of the creditor or purchaser of the rent, were particularly popular with the middle strata of society as they represented a means of generating a regular income stream even for widows, orphans and others who were incapable of working or making a decent living from the toil of their own hands on the grounds of illness, disability or old age. In modern lingo, *zinss kauff* would have represented gilt-edged securities eligible for trust investment. But for someone who had money as well as good health and physical stamina and who was thus capable of working, they represented a quick way of making money without any effort. Too quick for Luther's liking. The money would work for you. This is why Luther was so furious about the *zinss kauff*, making it the cornerstone of his usury discourse. *Leibrenten*, which included an element of invisible amortization, bore twice as much interest as the legal maximum interest rate of 5 per cent. They could be traded at 10 per cent per annum.[98] *Ewigrenten* had initially been traded at up to 15 per cent per annum; this rate had equilibrated at 3–5 per cent p.a. at Luther's time, suggesting a slow but significant growth of the financial market over the fifteenth century in terms of volume and depth. As more and more people would use financial markets, accordingly not only the supply of financial paper but also the security of trading (property rights) improved. In Luther's times, rents and annuities were used even by peasants in order to bridge temporary financial bottlenecks around harvest time.[99] The collateral for rents and annuities was often spread across a different spectrum of land plots and real estate so as to spread the risk of default.

---

97. Ibid., 950–1.
98. Ibid., 952.
99. Immediately prior to the harvest around July/August, the farmer's liquid reserves and savings would have run down to precarious levels; see ibid., 952.

Annuities had been legalized by an Imperial Decree in 1500,[100] evoking a host of public debates. Luther was virtually uniformly negative about it. *Zinss kauff* in Luther's words was something *by which a man can burden others without sin and grow rich without worry or trouble* [79]; something which *is now established as a proper trade and a permitted line of business*, and which *is a new and slippery invention* [80]. By calling it a recent innovation, Luther presumably referred to the 1500 Imperial Decree (see above), presumably also a recent spurt in the volume of financial market transactions in the wake of the central European mining boom of the 1470–90 period. *Zinss kauff* to him represented an invention that was exclusively directed at circumventing the canonical ban on usury; it could not be good per se.[101]

The way *zinss kauff* is handled, Luther says, makes it a business that serves the investor or lender more than the person taking up credit [ibid.]. It is made for people who are on the lookout for a safe investment; for profit without risk. This can be no good [ibid.]. *Zinss kauf* is 'offensive', Luther says, because debtor and lender are unequal. Luther implicitly evokes the scholastic concept of equilibrium in transactions. The risk, for instance, of being unable to meet the regular interest payments, is entirely devolved to the debtor; the creditor or purchaser of the census will be legally entitled to a regular payment even at times when the seller of *zinss* (i.e. the debtor) is unable to meet the payments, for reasons of bankruptcy, damage to his assets, incapability or general economic hardship. The whole transaction favours the lender [ibid.]. *Zinss kauf*, therefore, *lays burdens upon all lands, cities, lords, and people, sucks them dry and brings them to ruin, as no usury could have done* [ibid.]. There are *some avaricious fellows* (original German: 'geytzige blaßen'), *who collect their incomes from zinss at the prescribed or agreed time, and quickly invest it again in another interest-bearing asset – so that the one income always drives the other along, as water drives the millwheel*. Again: no comment! We find here, again, the dichotomy between investment or productive vs. financial or speculative capital. *Zinss kauf* is against natural law and the golden rule, framed in Matthew 7:12: *therefore all things whatsoever ye would that men should do to you, do ye even so to them: for this is the law and the prophets*. *Zinss kauf*, Luther says, *gives free rein to avarice* [81]. Luther turns to some of the more common legitimations for *zinss kauf* (the money may have been invested more profitably elsewhere, so the lender–investor should be entitled to a reward), stressing the asymmetry between borrower and lender. The latter will always get, or be entitled to, his income whilst the former faces economic risk. Luther clearly invokes commerce and business as the main field where *zinss kauff* is practised as a means of generating circulating capital and keeping the ball rolling [82].

---

100. Schmoller, 'Zur Geschichte der national-ökonomischen Ansichten', 578.

101. The subprime mortgage crisis in the US after 2007, which was based on an increasingly complex set of financial market papers, mortgage-backed securities (MBS) and collateralized debt obligations (CDOs), looks strangely similar to what Luther complains about here. It has triggered a worldwide recession the full consequences of which are as yet unknown. It has cost the EURO-zone not only a lot of money but also GDP growth; the financial loss of the banking sector within the European Monetary Union is estimated at more than 900 billion Euros alone. J. Benchimol, 'Risk Aversion in the Eurozone', *Research in Economics* 68, no. 1 (2014): 39–56.

Here Luther introduces his main objection against this transaction: the concept of negative interest. The creditor or lender – the buyer of *zinss* or rents, obligations, annuities or other interest-bearing assets – can only make a profit, so to speak (fixed income), due to the fact that this transaction represents an investment, and he has a legal claim to the interest payment. The risk of loss or economic hardship is passed on to the debtor, who uses the money to make a living or carry on a business. Luther contrasts positive against negative interest, the former being the simple price of capital; the other being the (hypothetical) fair share of the creditor in the debtor's profit as well as loss, that is the participation in the debtor's economic risks as an entrepreneur and the performance of his business which is bound to go up and down – if the world was a just and truly Christian one [82, 83]. This is because *when I buy zinss, rent or any other sort of income from a particular piece of land, I do not buy the grounds as such, but the toil of the seller whilst working the ground, by which he is to bring me my income* [89]. It is against God's law and nature of things if no risk is involved where business and trade and most economic activity, above all agriculture, carry numerous inherent risks, but the fortunes of merchants and other businessmen rise and decline with the economic climate, the state of the market and shifting relations between demand and supply [83–84, 87–89]. Luther then criticizes *zinss kauff* as a strategic investment completely detached from the land market, that is the demand for and supply of real property [85], as well as the real economy. He points out the dangers of unsecured debt, that is those cases where the collateral is not specified in exact terms, say so many square metres of land, this particular house or farmstead [ibid.]. Unlimited use of this operation may, in Luther's dramatized words, result in whole communities becoming over-indebted and insolvent [86]. The whole *zinss* mentality is to make quick money without incurring any risk [87, 96].[102]

The only permissible exception from the rule that *zinss kauff* should be deemed usurious was when *both buyer and seller need their property, and therefore neither of them can lend or give, but they have to help themselves with such a transaction (kauffs wechsel)*.[103] Then an interest rate of up to 6 per cent per annum should be acceptable. Those charging more than that, *seven, eight, nine, ten per cent* [90] should be prosecuted. The Church practised such financial market operations in particular [92].

This, as well as Luther's subsequent statement, *as I said above, if all the world were to take ten per cent per annum, the church endowments should keep strictly to the law, and take four or five, with fear* [93] may be (and have been) interpreted as evidence that Luther thought interest to be permissible under certain conditions.[104] Later on in his *Table Talk*, he reiterated this stance that up to 6 per cent per annum may be acceptable on honourable loan types.[105] He also said this in his letter to the councilmen of Danzig in 1525. In fact, it is

---

102. Once again the similarities with the global financial and economic crises of the first decade of the twenty-first century, especially the unsecured debt crisis of 2007, are striking.

103. I have not been able to shed further light on the term *Kauffswechsel* here. Most likely it refers to commercial credit, that is lines of credit granted in business for bridging short-term liquidity gaps.

104. Most recently, for example, Charles R. Geisst, *Beggar Thy Neighbor: A History of Usury and Debt* (Philadelphia: University of Pennsylvania Press, 2013), 75–76.

105. Schmoller, 'Zur Geschichte der national-ökonomischen Ansichten', 570.

quite vain to look for either broken or continuous patterns, or evidence of consistency or inconsistency in Luther's thinking here: the letter to the Danzig City Council of 1525 was a pragmatic expert opinion demanded for an ad hoc solution in practical matters. Apparently, it was slightly more relaxed about interest and usury. But *Von Kauffshandlung und Wucher* was a programmatic, an axiomatic pamphlet. It was a *theory*. Here Luther developed his theoretical principles of economics. We must not forget this. Many of the things Luther discussed in the present sermon must be understood in a more figurative than literal way. Moreover, as mentioned above, we should also be careful distinguishing between what Luther considered *legal* and what he considered to be *legitimate*. The two did obviously not coincide. Whilst interest could be perfectly *legal* even in canon law under certain conditions – in fact in many scenarios within the outer world – it was certainly not legitimate in terms of being in accordance with God's chosen order. But no one would have maintained that God's chosen order was even near during the 1520s. And within the real world of the 1520s, bad and corrupted as it was, dogma and theory had to be adjusted to current circumstances so as to make them work in very basic and pragmatic terms. So Luther in practice well admitted that interest may be taken, but he never accepted it as a principle or good in itself that should govern human interaction. He did not like interest at all. It should be noted that there is no iron law or axiomatic whatsoever that would suggest, or even worse, determine, that capital *must* bear interest or that interest would be a necessary or useful thing for the economy to work. Interest was, and is, above all a concept. It is not only a financial market price but also a human invention. Human agency determines about the price for capital, not eternal laws. In fall 2014, the European Central Bank, for instance, lowered the base rate to 0.05 per cent per annum (and negative interest on overnight deposits), which was far below the rate of inflation. In many branches of the financial business, interest practically disappeared from the landscape, but certainly no one would have labelled the early twenty-first century European economy non-capitalistic.

Throughout the entire pamphlet, Luther makes an implicit analytical separation of what was legal in terms of temporal law and what was in accordance with God's (or natural) law. These two states of affair did not necessarily coincide or overlap. True Christians would not usually charge interest, regardless of their peculiar situation or specific nature of the transaction. They would not even charge moderate or superficially legit rates such as 5 or 6 per cent. But if society had been truly Christian, according to Luther's definition, there would have been no need to write such a treatise as the present *Sermon on Commerce and Usury*. This feeling or sentiment comes across on literally every page in *Von Kauffshandlung und Wucher*.

The final six paragraphs (part III of the 1524 composite pamphlet) were written in 1524 [97–102]. Here Luther identified one further commercial malpractice relating to the *zinss* market, that is to lend out a nominal sum quoted in terms of a specific currency or money whilst the actual loan was paid out in kind, that is goods that were valued at a price higher than what they would have fetched on the market [97]. This was clearly usurious. The consequential and most important, if profoundly utopian, solution to the whole problem of *Zinss kauff* or credit business suggested by Luther was to substitute interest or *zinss* with the tithe (*Zehnt*) as a price for capital, varying with the individual fortune of the debtor and the business the loan is allocated to, *or in case of need a ninth, or an eighth, or a sixth. Thus everything would be fair, and all depend on the grace and blessing of God* [98–100]. In modern words, Luther's alternative to fixed interest charges would be *participating bonds* or *profit-sharing*, especially where the *zinss* transactions related to business finance. Whoever lent money at interest should share equitably in the debtor's losses and profits. This was of course purely hypothetical.

In accordance with the Old Testament, Luther finally advocates the concept of a 'Jubilee year' [102]. *Von Kauffshandlung und Wucher* closes with a final call for the state, condemning the Pope and lamenting the weakness and hesitation of the worldly authorities to enforce true Christian practice: *God give them His light and grace. Amen* [102].

Chapter 6

CONCLUSION: WHAT CAN WE LEARN FROM LUTHER TODAY?

What can we learn from Luther today? Here are a few clues, tentative and certainly selective, and by all means subjective. They are answers, which the material presented in the preceding pages can – but by no means has to – offer especially in the light of the issues of our times (this is one but by no means the main or exclusive function of history). Times will move on and situations change; therefore, the following points are above all a snapshot. However, as has been argued in previous chapters, the crucial points Luther made in this text are timeless, and chances are that they will be equally important to economic reasoning in future decades if not centuries to come, in a similar way as they applied to Reformation Germany at the dawn of the modern age. They are by no means exhaustive or authoritative; the reader is left to choose her own interpretation by reading the original pamphlet *Von Kauffshandlung und Wucher* (On Commerce and Usury, 1524) herself which is presented in a new translation at the end of the present volume.

LESSON NUMBER ONE: We do not have to accept the economy and financial markets as a given. This does not mean that free markets in general, and deregulated financial markets in particular, are bad things per se. But rather than working to some often invoked eternal economic laws, the economy and markets are *malleable*. We are – that means we ought to be – in control of markets and not the other way round. In recent years, especially with the recent elections to the European Parliament (May 2014) people have, for instance, voiced their anxiety relating to specific problems of governance vs. agency. There seems to be an increasing awareness of the power we have taken away from the states over the past thirty years or so and handed over to supra-territorial institutions which are not under democratic control any more but will implement major decisions that are likely to affect the well-being of society at large without much possibility of the community or society to control or respond to these things. Supra-territorial institutions such as the GATT, the World Bank and International Monetary Fund have taken over branches of governance traditionally reserved for 'the state'. Once again this is nothing bad per se, but an increasing number of people have become aware of the possible negative consequences of this. The state must be re-invested as a protagonist, some people say. Ironically, that is exactly what Luther says in his great economic pamphlet *Von Kauffshandlung und Wucher* (1524) – *passim*. He finds that markets, not only financial markets, have gotten out of control and that the state should do something against it. Luther indeed hints at globalization as a problem, in his paragraph on the spice trade, the Frankfurt fairs and the drain on the balance of payments; he repeatedly urges 'the Princes', i.e. the state, to have a 'look into' things. Therefore, modern essays by heterodox economists such as Dani Rodrik's *Globalization Paradox*[1] or sociologist Ulrich Beck's *Society of Risk*[2] and Anthony Giddens' studies[3] on the paradoxes and rifts of globalization are not so radically new, as it appears. People voiced concerns that were essentially similar 500 years ago (under different idiosyncratic conditions of time and space, of course). Sure, no time in history is ever the same; nor does history repeat itself in any way. Nor are there any linear or cyclical patterns which would determine history's rhythm in any meaningful way. History is idiosyncratic and each society, culture and economy needs to be studied within its own specific conditions of time and space. Yet there are strikingly similar patterns of human *behaviour* which have not changed so much over time, giving rise to insights that are timeless. Luther was well ahead – or on top – of his time. He knew about the potential dangers, for instance when financial markets lost touch with the real economy and developed logics on their own. The same thing has happened during the latest global financial and economic crisis since 2007.

LESSON NUMBER TWO: There is no such thing as free markets.[4] This may sound more radical than it really is; in fact, the point is very trivial if you look at it closely. For once, it has not been possible to trace the free market anywhere yet (at least not on the historical record) – if we define the 'free market' as largely or completely deregulated and perfectly competitive as it is often portrayed in the textbooks. Second, in order for markets to behave well and function properly, they need a certain degree of regulation, sometimes very strict rules, because otherwise there will be people reaping undue advantages (rent seeking, usury, speculation and arbitrage), whilst others lose out – the classical market distortions. The recent financial crisis of the post-2007 years which has led to a grave destruction of private wealth and even individual health (with AIDS infection rates in Greece going up) has seen a worldwide contraction of economic activity. It has witnessed even some of the stronger European governments struggling with budgets, public investment and state finance. Most would probably agree that the crisis took off in the financial market sector in the US which had in the early 2000s gotten out of control. And parts of the mishaps seem to be due to a skewed thinking or meta-theory about what free markets (should) look like. Eighteenth-century discourse on natural order and self-enforcing market mechanisms was a specific product of its time. The French and Scottish Enlightenment discourse, or *Enlightenment economics* as we may call it following Joel Mokyr,[5] developed into what is nowadays known as

1. Dani Rodrik, *The Globalization Paradox: Democracy and the Future of the World Economy* (New York: W. W. Norton, 2011).

2. Ulrich Beck, *Risikogesellschaft: Auf dem Weg in eine andere Moderne* (Frankfurt: Suhrkamp, 1986); *id.*, *Macht und Gegenmacht im globalen Zeitalter: Neue weltpolitische Ökonomie* (Frankfurt: Suhrkamp, 2009).

3. Anthony Giddens, *Runaway World: How Globalization is Reshaping Our Lives* (New York: Routledge, 2000); *id.*; *The Consequences of Modernity* (Stanford, CA: Stanford University Press, 1990).

4. Bernard Harcourt, *The Illusion of Free Markets: Punishment and the Myth of Natural Order* (Harvard: Harvard University Press, 2011).

5. Joel Mokyr, *The Enlightened Economy: An Economic History of Britain, 1700–1850* (New Haven, CT: Yale University Press, 2009), chap. 4. Sophus Reinert, *Translating Empire: Emulation and the Origins of Political Economy* (Cambridge, MA: Harvard University Press, 2011), takes a different turn, calling 'enlightenment economics' a broader school of mainly eighteenth-century thought which others have called mercantilism.

neoclassical theory and which has represented the mainstream social and economic paradigm during the twentieth century. Many a theorist, journalist and public figure have argued, especially during the second half of the twentieth century, in favour of economic deregulation, suggesting that self-regulating markets are the optimum schedule of allocation. Recourse is often made in this discourse to the above-mentioned eighteenth-century Scottish (and French) philosophers. Markets were understood to clear spontaneously and to the optimum outcome of everybody when left free from government intervention (which may include taxation, protectionism, direct investment, subventions, etc.). But recent research has deconstructed this discourse as mythical. Even the freest markets one can think of nowadays, such as the New York Stock Exchange or the Chicago Wheat Exchange, are usually tightly regulated by a set of transaction-specific rules and laws that frequently number into the hundreds if not thousands, and which would have made eighteenth-century policy makers envious.[6] It is *because* – rather than *in spite* of – state regulation that markets function properly, i.e.in a Pareto-optimal sense, achieving the degree of freedom necessary to rule out practices of rent seeking and usurious behaviour.

Lesson Number Three: Markets should be controlled, supervised and regulated where appropriate. The degree of intervention should be at the discretion of the public that formulates the super-ordinate welfare goal (called in contemporary discourse around 1500 the common good). *Markets should primarily serve our interests; not the other way round.* The state may interfere in the economy and the working mechanisms of markets wherever necessary to retain – or re-attain – social and economic equilibrium. This was what late medieval scholastic economics was about; Luther's present treatise picks up on this repeatedly. Markets need rules to work efficiently in terms of a just and optimal allocation of societal and economic resources. This was the general credo of the late medieval scholastic theologians such as Bernardino di Siena or the schoolmen of Salamanca around 1500–50. It was at the core of eighteenth-century cameralist theory, the nineteenth century 'historical school' in economics and the twentieth-century models of coordinated capitalism (*Soziale Marktwirtschaft*, Ordo-Liberalism) à la Schumpeter, Eucken or Müller-Armack.[7] Market efficiency cannot be measured by the merchant's profit or well-being, as Luther points out. In this way he sharply positioned himself against more market-friendly or laissez-faire voices of his age, such as Conrad Peutinger, the Augsburg notary who produced, in 1530, a pamphlet heralding unrestrained entrepreneurial activity and generally unrestrained markets as the best way to achieve economic health, clouded in the deceptive model of self-interest as the general-purpose optimum allocation strategy. It is interesting to see how the notion of an invisible hand and unrestrained self-interest as the optimum schedule of resource allocation has cropped up so often in European history (not so much in Adam Smith's *Wealth of Nations*) – and much earlier than most scholars have usually assumed. We find it in the reports and expert references produced by Dr Peutinger in

---

6. Harcourt, *Illusion, passim.* Harcourt commences his discussion with the eighteenth-century *police des grains* in France.
7. See brief discussion in chapter 1.

the 1520s (and in his 1530 pamphlet) which he wrote for the big Augsburg merchant companies that were heavily involved in monopolistic business practices, and which exerted what contemporaries saw as an unduly high influence on market behaviour and price formation. The idea recurred in the 1560s with the pamphlet by Leonhard Fronsperger and, of course, in 1714 with Mandeville's proverbial *Fable of the Bees*. Adam Smith only mentions the invisible hand once in his *Wealth of Nations*, apparently, but scholars have supposed that it stood behind the entire system of economics he sketched out with his magnum opus.

In his earlier *Theory of Moral Sentiments* (1759), however, Adam Smith had been less dismissive towards the model of coordinated capitalism which he in his later *Wealth of Nations* (1776) identified as the 'mercantile system' and which has, in the wake of this slight misnomer, become known to us as mercantilism (including its 'German' variant *cameralism*).[8] In his *Theory of Moral Sentiments* (1759), shortly before he set out for Paris to meet with the physiocrats, Smith had said:

> The same principle, the same love of system, the same regard to the beauty of order, of art and contrivance, frequently serves to recommend those institutions which tend to promote the public welfare. When a patriot exerts himself for the improvement of any part of the public police (*as in the German* Policey *– meaning economic policy, PRR*), his conduct does not always arise from pure sympathy with the happiness of those who are to reap the benefit of it. It is not commonly from a fellow-feeling with carriers and waggoners that a public-spirited man encourages the mending of high roads. When the legislature establishes premiums and other encouragements to advance the linen or woollen manufactures, its conduct seldom proceeds from pure sympathy with the wearer of cheap or fine cloth, and much less from that with the manufacturer or merchant. The perfection of *police*, the extension of trade and manufactures, are noble and magnificent objects. The contemplation of them pleases us, and we are interested in whatever can tend to advance them. They make part of the great system of government, and the wheels of the political machine seem to move with more harmony and ease by means of them. We take pleasure in beholding the perfection of so beautiful and

---

8. Lars Magnusson, 'Mercantilism – A Useful Concept Still?', in Moritz Isenmann, ed., *Merkantilismus. Wiederaufnahme einer Debatte* (Stuttgart: Franz Steiner, 2014), 19–38. See also Lars Magnusson, *Mercantilism: the Shaping of an Economic Language* (London: Routledge, 1994); Donald C. Coleman, ed., *Revisions in Mercantilism* (London: Methuen, 1969). Major recent studies include Steven Pincus, 'Rethinking Mercantilism: Political Economy, the British Empire, and the Atlantic World in the Seventeenth and Eighteenth Centuries', *The William and Mary Quarterly* 69, no. 1 (January, 2012), 3–34; Terence Hutchison, *Before Adam Smith. The Emergence of Political Economy 1662–1776* (Oxford: Oxford University Press, 1988); Philip J. Stern and Carl Wennerlind, eds, *Mercantilism Reimagined: Political Economy in Early Modern Britain and Its Empire* (Oxford: Oxford University Press, 2014). Earlier writers such as Eli F. Heckscher, *Mercantilism*, 2 vols (London: Allan & Unwin, 1935), but specifically Robert E. Ekelund and Robert D. Tollison, *Mercantilism as a Rent-seeking Society: Economic Regulation in Historical Perspective* (College Station: Texas A&M University Press, 1981) sketched a negative assessment of mercantilism, which many historians still share, see, for example Mokyr, *Enlightened Economy*, chap. 4. Works such as Ha-Joon Chang, *Kicking Away the Ladder: Development Strategy in Historical Perspective* (London: Anthem, 2003), and Erik Reinert, *How Rich Countries Got Rich… And Why Poor Countries Stay Poor* (London: Constable, 2007), have painted a more positive picture.

grand a system, and we are uneasy till we remove any obstruction that can in the least disturb or encumber the regularity of its motions.

Adam Smith, *Theory of Moral Sentiments* (1759), Pt. 4, Chap. 1.[9]

This was Smith the mercantilist, Smith the interventionist – briefly before history, as well as his encounter with the physiocrats – turned him into a (rather unintended) advocate and propaganda-man of laissez-faire free-market capitalism, which he almost certainly never was, but for which he has remained famous until today. So even the man who is generally acknowledged to have acted as the founding father of the classical paradigm in economics – however unwittingly, was not without sympathy for government intervention or coordinated capitalism (Eichengreen) which – with the promotion of domestic industry – clearly went beyond the 'night-watchman state' for which he became, deservedly or undeservedly, known only in subsequent years and centuries.

LESSON NUMBER FOUR: We are in control – ultimately, that is; meaning we should take (back) control where appropriate. It is up to us to determine how markets should work, how much freedom they should enjoy, how this freedom is defined and what markets are meant to achieve. Markets do not dictate how economy and society work – it is exactly the other way round. Markets do not follow an abstract, inherent or time–space-indifferent working mechanism, nor do they function well automatically or by definition. The economy is a living *organism*, not a *mechanism* (as it has often been portrayed in neoclassical theory). First, we must formulate *goals*. Then we can develop *means* to achieve them – not the other way round. We should never succumb to the idea that the economy, as well as all other realms of human (inter)action, such as love, marriage and feelings – are governed – and can be analysed and then designed a priori by using the tools of general equilibrium theory or utility maximization. This would be akin to putting the cart before the horse. Markets are not value free. And neither can economics ever be free of subjectivism.

LESSON NUMBER FIVE: Economics, the scientific study of the economy, is no child of the Enlightenment. This is an almost banal insight; especially given the advances made in the field of the history of political economy over the past decades. However, the current major undergraduate economics and history of economic thought textbooks designed for future MBAs and economists still pretend that everything started with a certain moral philosopher born in a humble coal exporting port at the Scottish east coast in 1723 (A. Smith the younger; his father was a customs officer at the port of Kirkcaldy). As a scientific, if theoretical, discipline, economics has a much longer tradition, much older even than Martin Luther and the German Reformation economists. Some of the cornerstones of Luther's economics are as valid today as they were 500 years ago; several millennia ago in fact.[10]

---

9. My italics. I am indebted to Erik Reinert for pointing me towards this passage.
10. See, for example Tomáš Sedláček, *Economics of Good and Evil: The Quest for Economic Meaning from Gilgamesh to Wall Street* (Oxford: Oxford University Press, 2011).

LESSON NUMBER SIX: Economics must be fair. Nobel-Prize winner Amartya Sen has developed the concept of capability. It provides a holistic approach to the idea of economic inequality, which may be the result of income inequality, market distortion, information asymmetry, but also gender- and caste-specific barriers to entry which decisively influence an individual's *chances* to lead a humane life. Luther's concept of *gerechte Nahrung*, a *topos* borrowed from medieval social theory which includes the physical act of eating and being nourished, as well as the more metaphorical-figurative notion of 'making a living', still represents as valid a guideline today as it did half a millennium ago – even though we must not believe Luther would have made a particularly valuable contribution to either gender-specific or general social equality. As we have seen, he was quite misogynous in some of his writings, but he was also ironical at times, so we should not take literally everything he wrote, specifically on women. Yet, he never favoured a more equal distribution of income, and he never argued in favour of the abolition of serfdom and *villainage* – a form of slavery – and its wider institutional-legalist framework of the manorial economy. We must be clear that Luther had his negative sides as well – as any human being, scholar and contributor to theoretical and academic knowledge. But even so, the principle of charity and *gerechte Nahrung* has lost some of its appeal during the last two centuries or so which saw Europe's transformation into an industrial economy. In Luther's world, paupers, at least as long as they were principally willing to work but could not, due to adverse conditions of health or the economy, such as the labour market, were entitled to charity. Charity was not only a fundamental theological commandment but also the fundament upon which society should rest. Some modern governments have transformed this principle into absurdity; just consider the British Conservatives' recent *Big Society* propaganda in the election campaign of 2010, a clever ideology that was directed at legitimizing the retreat of the state out of its core areas of governance and which has received some ideological backing even by professional academics. Heart-warming is the story of eminent popular historian and confessed neo-conservative Niall Fergusson collecting litter at the seashore near his weekend domicile on the Welsh coast as a manifestation of private initiative taking back its territory which the predatory interventionist state had usurped in the past half-century or so but where it has allegedly failed to perform (such as collecting rubbish).[11] Not everyone would share the free market enthusiasm of Fergusson and the British Conservatives nowadays. According to recent sociological studies it has become, even in the western world, increasingly difficult for the 'working' middle classes, i.e. people living on an income which used to classify as 'full', to make a decent living.[12] And, given these dangerous scenarios which are in many ways likely to destabilize societal cohesion and solidarity, it is unclear whether the state can afford to progressively withdraw from the economy and society, as many of the more liberal and 'neo-con' voices in the discourse still demand.

LESSON NUMBER SEVEN: Contrary to a still widely-held popular opinion, the market is no good or reliable indicator of an individual's value and worth. The idea of a general

---

11. Niall Fergusson, *The Great Degeneration. How Institutions Decay and Economies Die* (London: Allen Lane, 2012).
12. *Der Spiegel*, 5 May 2014.

ceiling on incomes is still alien to most of us today. Minimum wages on the other hand are currently a fashionable tool and quick-fix to the solution of short-term political problems (and they also represent a fishing for votes), but why should there not be a maximum wage (or reward to efforts) also? Tabloid coverage and news of hedge fund managers earning yearly salaries approaching the gross domestic product of the poorer sub-Saharan countries have kept circulating in recent years. Why should there be an open end to a stock broker's or funds manager's yearly salary, even if she works 80 hours per week, is successful and always has the right hand in making the right decision? Do people really or always *have* to earn what they are worth on the market? To what extent can the market be a valid guideline of what people – humans – are worth? Do we have to accept that the market price, i.e. salary, is a reliable measurement of an employee's value? Why do CEOs in leading US corporations *have* to make more than 475 times as much as their employees?[13]

LESSON NUMBER EIGHT: Persistent differentials in the growth rates of income from capital (interest, profit) vs. labour (wages) increase social tension and may lead to revolt. A recent and not uncontroversial study by French economist Thomas Piketty argues that there has been, the past fifty years or so, a fundamental growth rate differential between profits and wages in the north-west European economies, which has led to a skewed distribution of incomes received from capital and investment compared to labour incomes.[14] Incomes from capital, including business profits, have grown much faster than wages. In Britain and the US, the upper decile of the population have increased their share in national product by about a third. In the US, as we speak, the upper 10 per cent of the population hold 50 per cent of the national wealth, whilst the lowest decile hold only 20 per cent. It is a moot point to speculate about the future; however, it is unlikely that such a skewed income distribution will increase these societies' capacity to sustain balanced economic growth and general welfare.

Luther, in his 1524 *Sermon on Commerce and Usury*, attacked principally the same problem: an inflated rate of profit growth vis-à-vis stagnant or much lower capacities for average incomes, especially labour, to grow – especially in his critique of merchant malpractice and grossly inflated business profits. When Luther published his piece *Von Kauffshandlung und Wucher*, the most dramatic social revolt ever experienced in German history had already broken out – the Peasants' War (1524–25). It was fought over a redistribution of gross national income or agrarian product along more equitable and fair lines which were usually framed in the words of 'Ancient Law' (which, of course, had never existed in that form). In the *Twelve Articles of the Upper Swabian Peasantry* (1524), a formalized agenda or political programme was set that was adopted in many other regions of the empire. In the German Peasants' War, the farmers and rural workers took things into their own hand by proving Luther, in his general assessment of the societal

---

13. William T. Cavanaugh, *Being Consumed. Economics and Christian Desire* (Grand Rapids, MI: Wm. B. Eerdmans Publishing Co, 2008), 20–21. The data relate to 1999 figures compared to 1980 figures (when the ratio had been at 42 times to 1).

14. Thomas Piketty, *Capital in the Twenty-First Century* (Cambridge, MA: The Belknap Press of Harvard University Press, 2014).

imbalances he identified in this sermon, right. Had he published this pamphlet earlier, he might have earned himself the notion of a prophet.

Many more questions may be raised. Ultimately, the issue comes down to value judgement – something that has been absent from the modern social sciences for too long. This has frequently led to a proposed objectivism as the guideline and imputed starting point for many a model in modern economics and sociology (and other social sciences). It has frequently been overlooked that this objectivism in itself reflects a strongly subjectivist position. It would be time to admit that science cannot be value free – lest it becomes entirely meaningless in the literal sense. Then, perhaps, our models will become more realistic again. The scholastic theologians had a clear understanding of this philosophical problem. And so had Luther who, as we have seen, was in many ways much more radical (and only the naïve would say that he was *backward*) than the medieval schoolmen. By all means we can learn something from him; especially, perhaps, in times of social and economic crisis.

ON COMMERCE AND USURY

Von Kauffshandlung und Wucher
1524

Martin Luther

NOTES ON THE TEXT

Gulden   florin/Rhenish florin, common currency and money of account in south-central Germany

Pfennig   penny (d.)

In 1500 the ratio between gulden and groschen (groat) was fixed at 1 florin or gulden (abbr. fl Rh) = 21 groats or groschen (abbr. gr.), and 1 groschen nominally exchanged at 12 pfennige or pennies (abbr. d for Lat. *denarius*). In 1542 the ratio or (exchange rate) of the florin to the groat was officially raised to 24, but this ratio had existed much earlier than that. The commonly accepted standard of money was a metallist, commodity money or non-fiduciary one, as opposed to our modern notion of money which is 'chartalist'/nominalist/fiduciary, meaning that the intrinsic value of the currency (coins, bank notes) is insignificant compared to its official or imposed purchasing power or circulating value. Around 1500 the coin exchange rates, i.e. the ratio of pennies to the groat or groats to the florin, were flexible and often re-negotiable, notwithstanding what the official legislation would say. For further information and technical discussion of currency matters, see Philipp RobinsonRössner, *Deflation – Devaluation – Rebellion. Geld im Zeitalter der Reformation* (Stuttgart: Franz Steiner, 2012), chap. 3.

Paragraph numbers have been added by the present author in [*square brackets*].

The text *Von Kauffshandlung und Wucher* (1524) consists of three parts. The first part – which we may call *Von Kauffshandlung* (henceforth: *I. On Commerce*) – was newly written and delivered in 1524.[1] Luther added, as *Part II. On Usury*, a more or less verbatim version of his earlier work *Great Sermon Anent Usury* (1520),[2] which in turn is an extended version of his (short) *Sermon Anent Usury* which he had delivered in 1519.[3] These two parts were followed by a brief *addendum (Part III)* to the *Great Sermon on Usury* which Luther wrote in 1524. The first edition was delivered sometime between April (on 8 April 1524 the text was as yet unknown) and September 1524.[4]

According to the compilation of editions provided by the editors in vol. 15 (284–86) of the *Luther Werke* (Weimar ed.), as well as information retrieved from worldcat.org, the pamphlet went through at least the following editions:

A. *Vuittemberg* (Wittenberg) 1524, printed by Hans Luft, with 62 copies preserved (as of 1899) in Kiel, Lübeck, Vienna, Halle, Berlin, Arnstadt, Altenburg, Dresden,

---

1. Martin Luther Gesamtwerke, Weimarer Ausgabe, vol. 15 (Weimar, 1899), 279–322; text: 293–313.
2. Martin Luther Gesamtwerke, Weimarer Ausgabe, vol. 6 (Weimar, 1888), 33–60; text: 36–60.
3. Ibid., 1–8; text: 3–8.
4. Martin Luther Gesamtwerke, Weimarer Ausgabe, vol. 15, 321–322.

Erfurt, Görlitz, Zwickau, Leipzig, Weimar, Wernigerode, Wolfenbüttel, Munich, Münster, Stuttgart,Königsberg (Kaliningrad), Olmütz (Olomuc), Breslau (Wroclaw), Amsterdam, London, Strasbourg and many more.

B. Wittenberg 1524, printed by Wolf Köpffel at Strasbourg.

C. Wittenberg 1525, another edition which is otherwise identical to (B).

D. Wittenberg 1524.

E. Wittenberg 1524 (with copies inter alia in London).

F. Wittenberg 1535 (with copies inter alia in London).

G. *Hamborch*/Hamburg 1579 *Auff das Newe Gedruckt Anno 1579* (new imprint).

Version (A) provided the basis for (B) and (D), (C) was a new imprint of (B), (E) and (F) were based on (D) and (G) was based on the Wittenberg *Urdruck* (A) with only a handful of alterations. Within each edition minor alterations can be found in terms of word spelling. It seems as though the pamphlet was reprinted and circulated widely amongst printers and readers across the major cities of Germany.

As heylig Euange-
lion / nach dem es an den tag ko-
men ift / ftrafft vnd zeygt allerley
werck der finfternis / wie die S.
Paulus nennet Ro.13. Denn es ift
eyn helles liecht / das aller wellt
leucht vnd leret / wie böfe die werck
der wellt find / vnd zeyget die rech
te werck fo man gegen Gott vnd den nehiften vben foll.
Daher auch ettliche vnter den kauffleuten aufferwacht
vnd gewar worden find / das vnter yhrem handel man-
ch böfer griff vnd fchedliche fynantze ym brauch find /
vnd zu beforgen ift / es gehe hie zu / wie der Ecclefiafti-
cus fagt / Das kauffleut fchwerlich on funde feyn mü-
gen / Ja ich acht es treffe fie der fpruch S. Pauli .1. Ti-
mo. vlt. Der geytz ift eyne wurtzel alles vbels. Vnd aber
mal / Wilche reych wollen werden / die fallen dem teuffel
ynn den ftrick vnd ynn viel vnnutze fchedliche begirde /
wilche die leutt verfencken yns verderben vnd verdam-
nis.

Wie wol ich aber dencke / dis meyn fchreyben wer-
de faft vmbfonft feyn / weyl der vnfal fo weyt eyngerif-
fen / vnd aller ding vberhand genomen hat / ynn allen
landen . Dazu die ienigen / fo das Euangelion verfte-
hen / felbft aus eyggenem gewiffen wol kunden vrteylen /
ynn folchen euferlichen leichten fachen / was billich vnd
vnbillich fey. Bin ich doch ermanet vnd gebeten / folche
fynantze zu rüren vnd ettliche an den tag zu bringen / ob
yhe der hauffe nicht recht wolle / das doch ettliche / wie
wenig auch der felben fey / aus dem fchlund vnd rachen
des geytzs erlöfet wurden / Denn es mus ya fo feyn / das
man noch etliche finde vnter den kauffleuten fo wol / als

vnter

ON COMMERCE AND USURY

Part I. On Commerce

[1] The Holy Gospel[5], since it has come to light, rebukes and reveals all 'the works of darkness,' as St. Paul calls them, in Romans 13:13. For it is a brilliant light, which lightens all the world and teaches how evil are the world's works and shows the true works we ought to do for God and our neighbour. Therefore some of the merchants, too, have been awakened, and have become aware that in their business and commercial dealings many a wicked trick and hurtful financial practice[6] is in use, and it must be feared that the word of Ecclesiasticus applies here, and that 'merchants can hardly be without sin.' Nay, I think St Paul's saying in the last chapter of 1 Timothy 6:10, fits the case, 'Avarice is a root of all evil,' and 'Those that are minded to get rich fall into the devil's snare and into many profitless and hurtful lusts, which sink men in destruction and perdition.'

[2] I think, to be sure, that this book of mine will be quite in vain, because the mischief has gone so far and has completely got the upper hand in all lands; and because those who understand the Gospel ought to be able in such easy, external things to let their own conscience be judge of what is proper and what is not. Nevertheless I have been urged and begged to touch upon these doubtful financial manipulations of late and to expose some of them, so that even though the majority may not want to do right, some, if only a few, may yet be delivered from the gaping jaws of avarice.[7] For it must be that among the merchants, as among other people, there are some who belong to Christ and would rather be poor with God than rich with The Devil, as says Psalm 37:16, 'Better is the little that the righteous hath than the great possessions of the godless.' For their sake, then, we must speak out.

[3] One cannot deny that buying and selling are necessary. These activities cannot be dispensed with. But they can be practiced in a Christian manner; especially when the articles of trade serve a necessary and honourable purpose. For in this manner even the patriarchs bought and sold cattle, wool, grain, butter, milk and other goods. These are gifts of God, which He bestows out of the earth and distributes among men. But

---

5. For quotations from the Old and New Testament, the *King James Bible* version has been used.
6. The original has *fynantze*, which is a pejorative term for financial operations, usually expressively correlated with the incriminatory practice of usury.
7. Church doors frequently depicted monster-like figures with open mouths; presumably in allegory to the gaping jaws of avarice.

those foreign trades, which bring from Calicut[8], India, and other such places, wares such as costly silks, gold-work and spices, which minister only to luxury and serve no useful purpose, draining away the wealth of land and people – these trades ought not to be permitted, if we had government and princes. But of this it is not my present purpose to write, for I think that like overdressing and overeating, it will have to stop of itself when we have no more money left. Until then neither writing nor teaching will do any good. We must first feel the pinch of want and poverty.

[4] God has cast us Germans off. We have to throw our gold and silver into foreign lands and make the whole world rich while we ourselves remain beggars. England would have less gold if Germany let it keep its cloth; and the king of Portugal, too, would have less if we let him keep his spices. You calculate yourself how much gold is taken out of Germany, without need or reason; from a single Frankfurt fair, and you will wonder how it happens that there is a single *heller*[9] left in German lands. Frankfurt is the gold and silver sink, through which everything that springs and grows, is minted or coined here, flows out of the German lands. If that hole were stopped up we should not now have to listen to the complaints that there are debts everywhere and no money; that all lands and cities are burdened with rent charges and ruined with interest payments. But let that pass. So it will go anyhow. We Germans must be Germans; we never stop unless we must.

[5] It is our purpose here to speak about the abuses and the sins of trade inasmuch as they concern the conscience. The injury they work to the merchant's purse we leave to the care of princes and lords, that they may do their duty.

[6] First. The merchants have among themselves one common rule or chief maxim which is the basis of all their sharp practices and financial operations. They say: 'I may sell my goods as dear as I can.' This they think their right. Lo, that is giving place to avarice and opening every door and window to Hell. Because what can it mean? Only this: 'I care nothing about my neighbour; so long as I have my profit and satisfy my greed, what affair is it of mine if it does my neighbour ten injuries at once?' There you see how shamelessly this maxim flies squarely in the face not only of Christian love, but of natural law. Now, what good is there in trade? How can it be without sin when such injustice is the chief maxim and the rule of the whole business? On this basis trade can be nothing other than robbing and stealing other people's property.

[7] For when this rogue's eye and cheapskate of a merchant finds that people must have his wares; or that the buyer is poor and desperately in need of these, he takes advantage of him and raises the price. He considers, not the value of the goods or what

---

8. The 1931 as well as the revised 1962 translation of Luther's works have rendered the German original *Kalikut* as 'Calcutta', which is very obviously incorrect. See introductory essay, chapter five.

9. The *heller* or half-penny was the smallest denomination coin in the central German lands in Luther's time. Until the later 1530s one *heller* would have exchanged at 1/504th of a Rhenish florin or gulden, as the official ratio was 1 florin (gulden) = 21 groschen = 252 pennies (d) = 504 heller. After the 1530s the ratio increased to 1 florin/gulden = 24 groschen = 288 pennies = 576 heller. Philipp Robinson Rössner, *Deflation – Devaluation – Rebellion. Geld im Zeitalter der Reformation* (Stuttgart: Franz Steiner, 2012), esp. ch. III, for a detailed analysis of monetary policy and monetary relations in Saxony in the early sixteenth century.

he has earned by his trouble and risk, but only the other man's need; not that he may relieve it, but that he may use it for his own profit; so as to raise the price of goods, which he would not have raised if it had not been for his neighbour's need in the first place. Because of his greed, therefore, the wares must have a price proportioned to his neighbour's need; and his neighbour's need, in the same way as his own wares, must have a value put on it. Pray, is not that unchristian and inhuman? Is this not equal to selling a poor man his own poverty? If, because of his need, he has to buy his wares so much the dearer, it is just the same as if he had to buy his own need; for what is sold is not the wares as they are, but the wares plus the fact that he must have them. This and similar abominations are the necessary consequence when the rule is: I may sell my wares as dear as I can.

[8] The rule should be, not: I may sell my wares as dear as I can or will, but: I may sell my wares as dear as I ought to, or as is right and proper. For your selling ought not to be a work that is entirely within your own power and will, without law or limit, as though you were a god and beholden to no one; but because this selling of yours is a work that you perform toward your neighbour, it must be so governed by law and conscience, that you do it without harm and injury to your neighbour, and that you be much more concerned to do him no injury than to make large profits. But where are such merchants? How few merchants would there be and how would trade fall off, if they were to amend this evil rule and put things on a Christian basis!

[9] You ask, then, how dear may I sell? How am I to reach at what is fair and right, so as not to overreach or overcharge my neighbour? I answer: That is, indeed, something that will never be governed either by writing or speaking. Nor has anyone ever undertaken to fix the price of every sort of wares. The reason is that wares are not all alike: one sort comes from a greater distance than another; one sort costs more than another. On this point, therefore, everything is, and must remain, uncertain. And no fixed rule can be made, any more than one can set a certain city as the place from which all wares are to be brought; or establish a definite cost price for them, since it may happen that the same wares, brought from the same city by the same road, cost vastly more one year than another, because, perhaps, the weather is bad or the road is worse, or something else happens that raises the cost at one time above that at another time. Now it is fair and right that a merchant take as much profit on his wares as will pay the cost of them and repay him for his trouble, his labour, and his risk. Even a farmhand must have food and hire for his labour. Who would serve or labour for nothing? As the Gospel[10] says, 'the labourer is worthy of his hire.'

[10] But in order not to leave this question entirely unanswered, the best and safest way would be for the temporal authorities to appoint over this matter wise and honest men who appraise the cost of all sorts of wares and fix accordingly the target price[11] at which the merchant would get his due share and have an honest living, just as at certain places they fix the price of wine, fish, bread and the like. But we Germans are

---

10. Luke 10:7.
11. The original has *das mas und zill, was sie gellten sollt* (WA 15, 296), which suggests a sort of target price, perhaps a maximum price (German: *Taxe*). Jacobs (1931) translated this as 'outside price'.

so busy drinking and dancing that we cannot bear any such regulation. Since, then, we cannot hope for such an institution or edict, the next best thing will be to hold our wares at the price which they fetch in the common market, or which is customary in the neighbourhood. In this matter we can accept the proverb: 'Do like others and you are no fool.' Any profit made in this way, I consider honest and well earned, since there is risk of loss in wares and outlay, and the profits cannot be all too great.

[11] But when the price of goods is not fixed either by law or custom, so that you must fix it yourself, then indeed no one can give you any other instructions except to lay it upon your conscience to be careful and not overcharge your neighbour, and seek not avaricious gain, but only an honest living. Some have wished to make it a rule that a man may take a profit of one half on all wares; some say one-third; others say something else; but none of these things is a safe rule unless it be so decreed, either by the temporal authorities or by common law; what they would determine would be safe. Therefore you must make up your minds to seek in your business only your commensurate and just[12] living; count your costs, trouble, labour and risk on that basis, and then fix, raise, or lower the price of your goods; so that you are repaid for your labour and trouble.

[12] To be sure, I would not have anyone's conscience so perilously restrained or so closely bound on this point as to insist that one must strike the right measure of profit to the very *heller*; for it is not possible to get at the exact amount that you have earned with your trouble and labour. It is enough that with a good conscience you seek to arrive at the exact amount; for it lies in the very nature of commerce and business that the thing is impossible. The saying of the Wise Man will hold in your case too: 'A merchant will hardly deal without sin, and a publican[13] will hardly keep his tongue from evil.'[14] If you therefore take a little too much profit, unknowingly and unintentionally, let that go into your Lord's Prayer, where we pray, 'Forgive us our debts'; for no man's life is without sin. Besides, the time will come when you will get too little for your trouble; throw that in the scale to balance the times when you have taken too much.

[13] For example, if you had a business of a hundred gulden (florins) a year, and above all the costs and honest returns which you had for your trouble, labour, and risk, you were to take an extra profit[15] of one or two or three gulden – that I should call a mistake which could not well be avoided, especially on a whole year's business. Therefore you should not burden your conscience with it. But bring it to God in the Lord's Prayer, as another of those inevitable sins that cleave to all of us. It is not done on purpose[16] or out of greed that you have made this mistake; it goes with the very nature of your occupation (I am

---

12. The original has *zymliche narunge* (WA 15, 296), which alludes to the Scholastic distributional or equilibrium theory of the geometrical mean.

13. Original (WA 15, 297) has *kretzmer*, which is derived from the Czech-German for village publican or licensed victualler. On Saxon village life and institutions, see e.g. Karlheinz Blaschke, 'Dorfgemeinde und Stadtgemeinde in Sachsen zwischen 1300 und 1800', in: Peter Blickle (ed.), *Landgemeinde und Stadtgemeinde in Mitteleuropa* (Munich: Oldenburg, 1991), 119–143.

14. Psalm 34:13 reads 'Keep thy tongue from evil, and thy lips from speaking guile.'

15. The original reads *zween odder drey zu viel gewunst*. Jacobs (1931) ambiguously translated 'zu viel' as 'excessive'.

16. Original has *muttwille* (WA 15, 297).

speaking now of good-hearted, God-fearing men, who would not willingly do wrong), just as the marriage duty is not performed without sin, and yet because of its necessity God winks at it, for it cannot be otherwise.

[14] In determining how much profit you ought to take on your business and your labour, there is no better way than to reckon it by estimating the amount of time and labour you have spent on it and comparing it with that of a day labourer[17], who works at another occupation, and seeing how much he earns in a day. On that basis reckon how many days you have spent in getting your wares and bringing them to your place of business, how great the labour has been and how much risk you have run, for great labour and much time ought to have so much the greater returns. That is the most accurate, the best and the most definite advice that can be given in this matter. If anyone dislikes it, let him do better at it. My ground is, as I have said, in the Gospel, 'A labourer is worthy of his hire,' and Paul also says, 'He that feedeth the flock shall eat of the milk; who goeth to war at his own cost and expense?' If you have a better ground than that, you are welcome to it.

[15] Second – there is a common error, which has become a widespread custom, not only among merchants but throughout the world, by which one man stands surety for another; and although this practice seems to be without sin looking like a virtue springing from love, nevertheless it causes the ruin of many and brings them irrevocable injury. King Solomon often forbade it and condemned it in his Proverbs. He says in Proverbs 6:8, 'My son, if thou be surety for thy neighbour, thou hast bound thine hand, thou art snared with the words of thy mouth and taken with the words of thy mouth. Do this now, my son, and deliver thyself, for thou art come into the hand of thy neighbour; go, hasten, and urge thy neighbour; give not sleep to thine eyes nor slumber to thine eyelids; deliver thyself as a roe out of the hand and as a bird out of the hand of the fowler.' So also in Proverbs 20:16, 'Take his garment that becomes surety for a stranger, and take a pledge of him for the stranger's sake.' Likewise, in Proverbs 22:26, 'Be not of those that strike hands and become surety for debts.' And again in Proverbs 27:13, 'Take his garment that becomes surety for another and take a pledge of him for the stranger's sake.'

[16] See with what strictness and vehemence the wise king forbids in Holy Scripture that one become surety for another, and the German proverb agrees with him, *Burgen soll man wurgen*; as if to say, 'Bailsmen (or anyone standing surety for someone else) should be choked – that is to be held responsible.'[18] It serves the surety right when he is caught and has to pay, for he acts thoughtlessly and foolishly in standing surety for someone else's debt. Therefore it is decreed in Scripture that no one shall become surety for another man unless he is able and entirely willing to assume the debt and pay it up himself. It seems strange that this practice should be wrong and be condemned, though many have

---

17. Schmoller compared this passage with Adam Smith, *Wealth of Nations*, ch. 5, and found it 'sharp and modern economic reasoning for his time'. See chapter three.
18. There is a double translation possibility here which lends itself to ambiguity. The phrase may be rendered as either (a) 'to be choked' or, alternatively, (b) 'to be held fully accountable for the debtor's obligations.' For detailed comments see chapter five.

discovered the folly of it when it has made them scratch their heads. Why, then, is it condemned? Let us see.

[17] Standing surety is a work that is too lofty for a man; it is unseemly, for it is presumptuous and an invasion of God's rights. For, in the first place, the Scriptures bid us to put our trust and place our reliance on no man, but only on God; for human nature is false, vain, deceitful, and unreliable, as the Scriptures say and as experience teaches every day. But he who becomes surety puts his trust in a man, and risks life and property on a false and insecure foundation; therefore it serves him right when he falls and fails and goes to ruin. In the second place, a man puts his trust in himself and makes himself God (for that on which a man puts his trust and reliance is his god). But of his life and property a man is not sure and certain for a single moment, any more than he is certain of the man for whom he becomes surety, but everything is in God's hand only, and He will not allow us a hair's breadth of power or right over the future or have us for a single moment sure or certain of it. Therefore the man who becomes surety acts in an unchristian way, and deserves what he gets, because he pledges and promises something that is not his and is not in his power, but in the hands of God alone.

[18] Thus we read in Genesis 43:9 and Genesis 44:14 how the patriarch Judah became surety to his father Jacob for his brother Benjamin, promising that he would bring him back or bear the blame forever; but God finely punished his presumption so that he could not bring Benjamin back until he gave himself up for him, and afterwards was barely freed by grace. It served him right, too; for these sureties act as though they did not need to be on speaking terms with God or to consider whether they were sure of a tomorrow for their life and property. They act without fear of God, as though their life and property were their own, and were in their power as long as they wished to have it; and this is nothing but a fruit of disbelief. James in his Epistle, James 4:13, calls this pride and says, 'Go to, now, ye who say, Today or tomorrow we will go into this or that city and there trade and get gain; whereas ye know not what shall be on the morrow. For what is your life? It is even a vapour which endureth a little time and then vanisheth. For that ye ought to say, If we live and God will, we shall do this or that; but now ye glory in your pride.'

[19] Moreover, God has condemned this presumption about the future and disregard of Him in more places, such as Luke 12:16, where the rich man had so much grain one year that he wanted to pull down his barns and build greater, and bestow his goods therein, and said to his soul, 'Good soul, thou hast much goods for many years; eat, drink and be merry.' But God said to him, 'Thou fool, this night thy soul shall be required of thee, and whose shall that be which thou hast laid up?' So it is with all that are not rich toward God. So He answers the apostles also in Acts 1:7, 'It is not for you to know the time or the hour which the Father hath in his own power'; and in Proverbs 27:1, 'Boast not thyself of the morrow, for thou knowest not what may yet happen today.' Wherefore He has bidden us, in the Lord's Prayer, to pray for nothing more than our daily bread today, so that we may live and act in fear and know that at no hour are we sure of either life or property, but may await and receive everything from His hands. This is what true faith does. Indeed we daily see in many of God's works that things must happen thus, whether it suits us or not.

[20] Solomon has devoted almost the whole of that book of his that is called Ecclesiastes to this teaching, and shows how all man's planning and presumption are vanity and trouble and misfortune, unless God is brought into them, so that man fears Him and is satisfied with the present and rejoices in it; for God is the enemy of that secure and unbelieving presumption which forgets Him, wherefore He opposes it in all He does, lets us fail and fall, snatches away life and property when we least expect it, and 'comes at the hour when we think not'; so that the godless, as the Psalter says, never live out half their days, but always, unexpectedly and just when they are getting started, must depart and leave it, as Job also says in many places.

[21] If you say, however, 'How then are people to trade with one another, if surety is not appropriate? Many would have to stay back who can otherwise get on well'? To which the answer is: There are four Christian ways of commerce and handling business matters with others. The first way is to let them rob us of our property and take it from us, as Christ says in Matthew 5:40, 'If any man take thy cloak, let him have the coat also, and ask it not of him again.' This way of dealing counts for nothing among the merchants, and besides it has been neither held nor preached as a general Christian teaching, but as a counsel and as good intention for the clergy and the perfect, though they keep it even less than the merchants. But true Christians keep it, for they know that their Father in heaven has assuredly promised, in Matthew 6:11, to give them this day their daily bread. If all of us were to act thus, not only would numberless abuses in all kinds of business be avoided; but very many people would not become merchants at all, because reason and human nature flee and avoid that sort of risk and damage above all things else.

[22] The second way is to give freely to everyone in need, as Christ teaches in the same passage. This is a lofty Christian work and therefore counts for little among people. The number of merchants and volume of business would decline if it were put into practice; for the man who does this must truly lay hold on heaven and look always to God's hand and not to his accumulations of property, knowing that it is God's will to support him, even though all his corners be bare. He knows that it is true, as He said to Joshua, 'I will not forsake thee, nor take away my hand'. And as the proverb puts it, 'God has more than ever He gave away.' But that takes a true Christian, and a true Christian is a rare animal. The world and nature pay no heed to them.

[23] The third way is lending; that is, I give away my property and take it back if it is returned to me; if not, then I must do without it. Christ Himself, in Luke 6:35, makes a rule for this kind of lending and says, 'Lend, hoping for nothing again'; that is, Ye shall lend freely and run the risk that it may not be returned; if it comes back, take it; if not, make it a gift. The Gospel makes only one distinction between lending and giving, viz., a gift is not taken back and a loan is taken back if it is returned; but when we make a loan, we take the risk that it may be a gift. He who lends expecting to get back something more or something better than he has loaned, is an obvious and damned usurer, since even those who lend demanding or expecting to get back just what they have lent, and taking no risk of its return, are not acting in a Christian way.

[24] This too (as I should think), is a lofty Christian work and a rare one moreover, when the way of the world is considered; if it were practiced it would greatly lessen and destroy trade of all sorts. For these three ways of dealing, then, are a masterly keeping

of the commandments not to presume upon the future nor to put trust in any man or in oneself, but to depend solely on God. In this way everything will be paid in ready cash, and the word of James is applied, 'If God will, so be it.' In this way we deal with people as with those who may fail and are unreliable; we give our money without profit and take the risk that what we lend may be lost.

[25] But at this point you may ask: 'Who then can be saved and where shall we find Christians? Nay, in this way there would be no business in the world at all; everyone would have his property taken or borrowed and the door would be thrown open for the idle gluttons, of whom the world is full, to take everything with their lying and cheating.' I reply: I have already said that Christians are rare in the world; therefore the world needs a strict, hard temporal government that will compel and constrain the wicked not to steal and rob and to return what they borrow, even though a Christian ought not demand it, or even hope to get it back. This is necessary lest the world may become a desert, peace will perish, and business, commerce and society come to a halt: all of which would happen if we were to rule the world according to the Gospel and not drive and compel the wicked, by laws and the use of force, to do and suffer what is right. We must, therefore, keep the roads open and in good order[19], preserve peace in the towns, and enforce law in the land, and let the sword hew in a brisk and bold way against the transgressors, as Paul teaches in Romans 13:4. For it is God's will that those who are not Christians shall be held in check and kept from doing wrong, at least with impunity. Let no one think that the world can be ruled without blood. The sword of the ruler must be red and bloody; for the world will and must be evil. And the sword is God's rod and vengeance upon it. But of this I have said enough in my little book *On the Temporal Authorities*.

[26] Borrowing would be a fine thing, if it were practiced between Christians. In that case everyone would return what he had borrowed and the lender would willingly do without it if the borrower could not pay; for Christians are brethren and one does not forsake the other; nor would any of them be so lazy and shameless as not to work, but to depend on another man's wealth and labour, or else be willing to consume in idleness another fellow's goods. But where there are no Christians, the temporal authorities ought to compel everyone to repay what they have borrowed; if the authorities are negligent and do not compel repayment, the Christian ought to put up with the robbery, as Paul says, in 1 Corinthians 6:7, 'Why do ye not rather suffer wrong?' But if a man is not a Christian, you may exhort him, demand of him, treat him as you will; he pays no attention, for he is not a Christian and does not heed Christ's doctrine.

[27] There is a grain of comfort for you in the fact that you are not bound to make a loan except out of your surplus and what you can spare from your own necessities, as Christ says of alms, 'What you have left over, that give in alms; so are all things clean unto you.' If, therefore, someone wanted to borrow from you an amount so great that you would be ruined if it were not returned, and you could not spare it from your own necessities, then you are not bound to make the loan; for your first and greatest duty is to provide for the necessities of your wife and children and servants, and you must not

---

19. Original has *reyn* (WA 15, 302), which again lends itself to double interpretation of either (a) 'open' (b) or 'clean'.

divert from them what is due them from you. Thus the best rule to follow is that if the amount asked as a loan is too great, you give something outright, or lend as much as you would be willing to give, taking the risk of losing it. John the Baptist did not say, 'He that hath one coat, let him give it away,' but 'He that hath two coats, let him give one to him that hath none, and he that hath food, let him do likewise.'

[28] The fourth way of doing business is buying and selling, and that with ready cash or payment in kind. If a man wishes to practice this method, he must make up his mind not to rely on anything in the future but only on God, and to deal with men who will certainly fail and lie; often deliberately so.[20] Therefore the first piece of advice to such a man is that he shall not borrow anything or accept any security, but take only cash. If he wishes to lend, let him lend to Christians, or else take the risk of losing it and lend no more than he would be willing to give outright or can spare from his own necessities. If the government will not help him get his loan back, let him forfeit it; and let him beware of becoming surety for any man, but let him far rather give what he can. Such a man would be a true Christian merchant and God would not forsake him, because he trusts Him finely and gladly takes a chance, in dealing with his risky neighbour.

[29] Now if there was no such thing in the world as becoming surety, and the free lending of the Gospel were in practice and only cash money or ready wares were exchanged in trade, then the greatest and most harmful dangers and faults and failings in business and commerce would be well out of the way; it would be easy to engage with all sorts of merchants and traders[21], and the other sinful faults could the better be prevented. For if there were none of this becoming surety and lending on security, many a man would have to retain their due and humble status and be satisfied with a moderate living, who now aspires day and night after the high places, relying on borrowing and standing surety. This is the reason that everyone now wants to be a merchant and get rich.[22] Out of this come the countless dangerous and wicked tricks and wiles that have become a jest among the merchants nowadays. There are so many of them that I have given up on the hope that these mishaps can be entirely corrected. The business world is so overladen with all sorts of wickedness and deception that it cannot drag its own length; by its own weight it must fall in upon itself.

[30] In what has been said I have wished to give a bit of warning and instruction to everyone about this great, nasty, widespread world of business and commerce. If we were to accept the principle that everyone may sell his wares as dear as he can, and were to approve the custom of borrowing and lending upon interest and standing surety as described above, and yet try to advise men how they could act the part of Christians and keep their consciences good and safe – well, that would be the same thing as trying to teach men how wrong could be right and bad good, and how one could live and act according to Scripture and against Scripture at the same time. For these three errors – that

---

20. The original has the ambiguous term *gewisslich*, which may translate, according to context, as either (a) 'deliberately' or (b) 'surely/certainly' (WA 15, 303).

21. Original has *kauffmanschafft* (WA 15, 303).

22. Compare the positive notion business and finance still carry in British society even after the financial crashes post-2007.

everyone may sell what is his own as dear as he will, borrowing, and becoming surety[23] – are the three sources from which the stream of abomination, injustice, treachery and guile flows far and wide: to try to stem the flood and not stop up the springs, is simply a waste of labour and effort.

[31] At this point, therefore, I wish to analyse in detail some of these tricks and evil doings which I have myself observed and which pious, good people have described to me, to make it apparent how necessary it is that the rules and principles which I have set down above be established and put in practice, if the consciences of merchants and other businessmen are to be counselled and aided; also in order that all the rest of their evil doings may be derived and measured by these; for how is it possible to tell them all? By the three aforementioned sources of evil, door and window are thrown wide to greed and to wicked, wily, selfish nature; room is made for them, occasion and power is given them to practice unhindered all sorts of trickery and wiles, and daily to think out more such schemes, so that everything stinks of avarice, nay, is drowned and drenched[24] in avarice as in a great new deluge.

[32] First, There are some who have no conscientious scruples against selling their goods on credit for a higher price than if they were sold for cash: nay, there are some who wish to sell no goods for cash but everything on credit, so that they may make large profits. You can see that this way of dealing – which is plainly against God's Word, against reason and all fairness, and springs from sheer wantonness and greed – is a sin against your neighbour, for it does not consider his loss, but robs and steals from him that which belongs to him; it is not a seeking for an honest living, but only for avaricious gain. According to divine law[25], goods should not be sold for a higher price on credit than for cash.

[33] Again, there are some who sell their goods at a higher price than they command in the common market, or than is customary in the trade; and raise the price of their wares for no other reason than because they know that there is no more of that commodity in the country, or that the supply will shortly cease, and people must have it. That is a very rogue's eye of greed, which sees only one's neighbour's need, not to relieve it but to make the most of it and grow rich on the neighbour's losses. All such people are manifest thieves, robbers and usurers.

[34] Again, there are some who buy up the entire supply of certain goods or wares in a country or a city, so that they may have those goods solely in their own power and can then fix and raise the price and sell them as dear as they like or can. Now I have said above that the rule that a man may sell his goods as dear as he will or can is false and unchristian. It is far more abominable that one should buy up the whole supply of a particular good for that purpose. Even the Imperial and temporal laws[26] forbid this and call it 'monopoly,' i.e., purchase for self-interest, which is not to be tolerated in city

---

23. Not in the original text; insertion by the original translator Charles M. Jacobs.
24. Original reads *erseufft und erteufft* – here Luther is using specialist mining terminology relating to the draining of shafts; something which he must have been familiar with due to his upbringing and family background in the Mansfeld mining business. See introductory essay, chapter two.
25. Here WA 15, 305 has a reference to Moses 25,36s.
26. See introductory essay, chs. two and five.

or country alike. And princes and lords should stop and punish it if they did their duty properly. Because those merchants who do this act just as though God's creatures and God's goods were made for and given to them alone; and as though they could take them from or give them to other people at whatever price they chose.

[35] If anyone wishes to cite the example of Joseph in Genesis 41:48, how the holy man gathered all the grain in the country and afterwards, in the time of famine, bought with it for the king of Egypt all the money, cattle, land and people – which seems, indeed, to have been a monopoly, or practice of self-interest – here comes the answer: This purchase of Joseph's was no monopoly, but a common and honest purchase, such as was customary in the country. He prevented no one else from buying during the good years, but it was his God-given wisdom which enabled him to gather the king's grain in the seven years of plenty, while others were accumulating little or nothing. For the text does not say that he alone bought in the grain, but that he 'gathered it in the king's cities.' If the others did not do likewise, it was their loss, for the common man usually devours his living unconcernedly and sometimes, too, he has nothing to accumulate.

[36] We see the same thing today. If princes and cities do not provide a reserve supply for the benefit of the whole country, there is little or no reserve in the hands of the common man who supports himself from year to year on his yearly income.[27] Accumulation of this kind is not self-interest, or monopoly; but a right and good Christian providence for the community and for the good of others. It is not practiced in such a way that they seize everything for themselves alone, like these merchants, but out of the amounts supplied to the common market, or the yearly income which everyone has, they set aside a treasury, which others either cannot or will not accumulate, but get out of it only their daily support. Moreover the Scriptures do not tell us that Joseph gathered the grain to sell it as dear as he would, for the text clearly says that he did it not for greed's sake, but in order that land and people might not be ruined. But the merchant, in his greed, sells it as dear as he can, seeking only his own profit, careless about the land's and the people's ruin.

[37] But that Joseph used this means to bring all the money and cattle, and all the land and people beside, into the king's possession, does not seem to have been a Christian act, since he ought to have given to the needy for nothing, as the Gospel and Christian love bid us do. Yet he did right and well, for Joseph was conducting the temporal government in the king's stead.[28] I have often taught that the world ought not and cannot be ruled according to the Gospel and Christian love, but only by strict laws, with sword and force, because the world is evil and accepts neither Gospel nor love, but lives and acts according to its own will unless it is compelled by force. Otherwise, if only love were applied, everyone would eat, drink and live at ease on someone else's goods and expenses, and nobody would work; nay, everyone would take from another that which was his, and there would be such a state of affairs that no one could live because of the others.

[38] Therefore, because God so disposes things, Joseph did right when he got possession of everything by such fair and honest purchase as the time permitted, and following the

---

27. The German original actually has *eynkomen(s)*.
28. On this see the sections in Tomáš Sedláček, *Economics of Good and Evil: The Quest for Economic Meaning from Gilgamesh to Wall Street* (Oxford: Oxford University Press, 2011).

temporal law, allowed the people to remain under restraint and sell themselves and all they had; for in that country there was always a strict government and it was customary to sell people like other goods. Besides, there can be no doubt that as a Christian and a good man, he let no poor man die of hunger but as the text says, after he had received the king's law and government, he gathered, sold, and distributed the grain for the benefit and benefit of land and people alike. Therefore the example of the faithful Joseph is as remote from the doings of the unfaithful, selfish merchants as heaven is far from earth. So far this digression; now we come back to the merchants' tricks.

[39] When some see that they cannot establish their monopolies and other selfish trades[29] in any other way because other people have the same goods, they proceed to sell their goods so cheap that the others can make no profit, and thus they compel them either not to sell at all, or else to sell as cheap as they themselves are selling and so be ruined. Thus they get their monopoly after all. These people are not worthy to be called men, or to live among other men; nay they are not worth exhorting or instructing; for their envy and greed is so open and shameless that even at the cost of their own losses they cause loss to others, so that they may have the whole place to themselves. The authorities would do right if they took away from such people everything they had and drove them out of the country. It would scarcely have been necessary to tell of such doings, but I wanted to include them so that it might be seen what great knavery there is in commerce, and that it might be plain to everybody how things are going in the world, in order that everyone may know how to protect himself against such a dangerous class and social practice.[30]

[40] Again, it is a fine piece of sharp practice when one man sells to another, by means of promises[31], goods which he himself has not, as follows. A merchant from a distance comes to me and asks if I have such and such goods for sale. I say, Yes, though I have not, and sell them to him for ten or eleven gulden when they could otherwise be bought for nine or less, promising him to deliver them in two or three days. Meanwhile I go and buy the goods where I knew in advance that I could buy them cheaper; I deliver them and he pays me for them. Thus I deal with his – the other man's – money and property, without risk, trouble or labour, and I get rich. That is called 'living off the street,' on someone else's money and goods[32]; without having to travel over land and sea.

[41] Another thing that is also called 'living off the street' is when a merchant has a purse filled with money but wishes no longer to subject his goods to the risks of land and sea traffic, but to have a safe business, settling down in a large commercial city. Then, when he hears of a merchant who is pressed by his creditors and must have money to satisfy them and has none, but has good wares, he gets someone to act in his stead in buying the wares and offers eight gulden (florins) for what is otherwise worth ten. If this offer is not accepted, he gets someone else to offer six or seven, and the poor man begins to be afraid that his wares are depreciating and is glad to take the eight florins so as to

---

29. The original has *monopolia und eygennuetzige keuffe* (WA 15, 307).
30. Original has only *ferlichen stand* (WA 15, 307), which in this context refers to either social status (in the sense of a merchant class), or general practice.
31. Original reads *Mit worten ym sack*.
32. Original has *eygen gellt und gut* (WA 15, 307).

get cash without having to stand too much loss and disgrace. It happens, too, that these needy merchants seek out such tyrants and offer their goods for cash with which to pay their debts. They drive hard bargains and get the goods cheap enough and afterwards sell them at their own prices. These financiers are called 'cutthroats,' but they pass for very clever people.

[42] Here is another example of selfishness and greed. Three or four merchants have in their control one or two kinds of goods that others have not, or have not ready for sale. When these men see that the goods are valuable and advancing in price day after day, because of war or some other disaster, they join forces and pretend to others that the goods are much in demand and that not many people have them on sale. If, however, there are some who do have these goods for sale they put up a stranger or dummy to buy up all these goods, and when they have them entirely in their own control they make an agreement to this effect: Since there are no more of these goods to be had we will hold them at such and such a price, and whoever sells cheaper shall forfeit so and so much.

[43] This trick, I hear, is practiced chiefly and mostly by the English merchants in selling English or London cloth. It is said that they have a special council for this trade[33], like a city council, and all the Englishmen who sell English or London cloth must obey this council on penalty of a fine. The council decides at what price they are to sell their cloth and at what day and hour they are to have it on sale and when not. The head of this council is called the 'court-master' and is regarded as little less than a prince. See what avarice can and dare do.

[44] Again, I must report this little trick. I sell a man pepper or the like on six months' credit and know that he must sell it again by that time to get ready money. Then I go to him myself, or send someone else, and buy the pepper back for cash, but on these terms. What he bought from me for twelve gulden I buy back for eight and the market price is ten. So I purchase the goods two florins cheaper than the market gives, whilst he has purchased the goods off me for two florins or gulden above the common market price.[34] So I make profit going and coming, so that he may get the money and maintain his credit; otherwise he might have the disgrace of having no one extend him credit in the future.

[45] Those people who buy on credit more than they can pay for, practice or have to practice this kind of trickery (*fynantze*) – a man, for example, who has scarcely two hundred gulden obligates himself for five or six hundred instead. If my creditors do not pay, I cannot pay; and so the mischief goes deeper and deeper and one loss follows another, the farther I go in this kind of dealing, until at last I see the shadow of the gallows and I must either abscond or go to jail. Then I keep my own counsel and give my creditors good words, telling them I will pay my debts. Meanwhile I go and get as much merchandize on credit as I can and turn these goods into money, or get money otherwise on a bill of exchange or other type of letter of credit, or borrow as much as I can. Then, when it suits me, or when my creditors give me no rest, I close up my house, get up and run away, hiding myself in some monastery; where I am as free as a thief or murderer in a church yard. Then my creditors are glad that I have not fled the country

---

33. The Court of the English Merchant Adventurers. See discussion in chapter five.
34. This sentence was left out of the original translation by Charles M. Jacobs.

and release me from a half or a third of my debts on condition that I pay the balance in two or three years, giving me letter and seal for it. Thus I come back to my house and am a merchant again who has made two or three thousand gulden by getting up and running away, and that is more than I could have got in three or four years either by running or trotting. Or if that plan will not help and I see that I must abscond, I go to the Court of the Emperor or to his regents and gubernators[35], and for one or two hundred gulden I get a *Quinquernell*.[36] This is a letter bearing the Imperial Seal permitting me to be at large for two or three years despite my creditors; because I have represented that I have suffered great losses. For the Quinquernells, too, make a pretence at being godly and right. These are knaves' tricks.

[46] Again there is another practice that is customary in the companies. A citizen deposits with a merchant one or two thousand gulden for six years. The merchant is to do business with this and pay the citizen annually two hundred gulden (florins) fixed interest, for profit or loss. What profit he makes above that is his own, but if he makes no profit he must still pay interest (*zinss*). In this way the citizen is doing the merchant a great service, for the merchant expects with two thousand gulden to make at least three hundred; on the other hand, the merchant is doing the citizen a great service, for otherwise his money must lie idle and bring him no profit. That this common practice is wrong and is true usury I have shown sufficiently in the Sermon on Usury.[37]

[47] I must give one more illustration to show how this bad type of borrowing and lending[38] leads to great misfortune. When some people see that a buyer is unreliable and does not meet his payments, they can repay themselves finely in this way. I get a stranger or foreign merchant to go and buy that man's goods to the amount of a hundred gulden or so, and say: 'When you have bought all his goods, promise him cash or refer him to a certain man who owes you money; and when you have the goods bring him to me, as though I owed you money and act as though you did not know that he is in my debt; thus I shall be paid and will give him nothing.' These sorts of financial operations and fraudulent manipulations are[39] called 'finance' (*fynantze*); they ruin the poor man entirely together with all whom he may owe. But so it goes in this unchristian borrowing and lending.

[48] Again, they have learned to store their goods in places where they increase in bulk. They put pepper, ginger and saffron in damp cellars or vaults so that they may gain

---

35. In the 1530s, Ferdinand I, Archduke of Austria, brother of Charles V would have been the emperor's viceroy or regent as King of the Romans since 1531, and regent in the Hereditary Lands (Austria) since 1521.

36. *Quinquennale* or debt moratorium, usually for five years.

37. See below, Part II.

38. Original (WA 15, 309) has *das falsche borgen und leyhen* ('wrong borrowing and lending').

39. I am following the suggested translation of the term *fynantzen* in Johannes Burkhardt and Birger P. Priddat (eds), *Geschichte der Ökonomie* (Frankfurt: Deutscher Klassiker Verlag, 2009), 689, i.e. 'to raise money by manipulation'. Jakob Grimm and Wilhelm Grimm, *Deutsches Wörterbuch*, III, col. 1641 suggests that *Finanzerei* is equal to usury and all other sorts of fraudulent behaviour in commerce and economic activity (*fraudatio*).

in weight; woollen goods, silks, furs of martin and sable, they sell in dark vaults or sealed[40] booths, keeping them from the air, and this custom is so general that almost every kind of goods has its own kind of air, and there are no goods that some way is not known of taking advantage of the buyer, in the measure, or the count, or the weight. They know, too, how to give the goods a false colour; or the best looking are put top and bottom and the worst in the middle. Of such cheating there is no end and no merchant dare trust another out of his sight and reach.

[49] Now the merchants make great complaint about the nobles or robber barons[41] – saying that they have to transact business at great risk; that they are imprisoned and beaten and taxed and robbed etc. If they suffered all this for righteousness' sake the merchants would surely be saints of our age because of all their sufferings. To be sure, it may happen that one of them suffers some wrong before God, in that he has to suffer for another in whose company he is found and pay for another man's sins; but because of the great wrong that is done and all the unchristian thievery and robbery that is practiced by the merchants themselves all over the world, even against one another, what wonder is it if God causes this great wealth, wrongfully acquired, to be lost or taken by robbers, and the merchants themselves to be beaten over the head or imprisoned besides? God must administer justice, for He Himself has been called a Righteous Judge, see Ps. 10.[42]

[50] Not that I would excuse the highwaymen and bushwhackers or approve of their thievery! It is the princes' duty to keep the roads safe for the sake of the wicked as well as of the good; it is also the princes' duty to punish such unfair business practices and to protect their subjects against the shameful skinning done by the merchants. Because they fail to do it, God uses the knights and the robbers to punish the wrongdoing of the merchants, and they have to be His devils, as He plagues Egypt and the entire world with devils or destroys it with enemies. Thus He flogs one knave with another, but without giving us to understand that the knights are less robbers than the merchants, for the merchants rob the whole world every day, while a knight robs one or two men once or twice a year.

[51] Of the big trading companies and firms I ought to say much, but that whole subject is such a bottomless abyss of avarice and wrong that there is nothing in it that can be discussed with good conscience. For what man is so stupid as not to see that companies are nothing else than straight and pure monopolies? Even the temporal law of the heathen forbids them as openly injurious, to say nothing of the divine law and Christian statutes. They have all commodities under their control and do what they want with them[43] and practice without concealment all the tricks that have been mentioned above. They raise and lower prices as they please and oppress and ruin all the smaller

---

40. Added based on the etymological discussion of *kreme* (booths sealed by some sort of cloth or tent) in WA 15, 310–11, n. 4.
41. Of which German roads and forests abounded in the days of Luther, see Heinz Schilling, *Aufbruch und Krise: Deutschland, 1517–1648*, pbk ed. (Berlin: Siedler, 1988).
42. Also Ps. 11.
43. Original (WA 15, 312) *und machens damit wie sie wollen*, left out from the translation by Charles M. Jacobs.

merchants, as pike devour the little fish in the water; just as though these merchants were lords over God's creatures and free from all the laws of faith and love.

[52] Thus it comes that all over the world spices must be bought at their price, which they set and vary at their discretion. This year they put up the price of ginger, next year they do the same with saffron, or vice versa; so that all the time the bend may be coming to the crook and they need suffer no losses and take no risks. If the ginger spoils or fails, they make it up on saffron and vice versa; so that they remain sure of their profit. All this is against the nature, not only of commerce with any merchandise, but of all temporal goods in very general terms, which God wills should be subject to risk and uncertainty. But they have found a way to make sure, certain, and perpetual profit out of insecure, unsafe, temporal goods, though all the world must be sucked dry and all the money sink and flow into their gullet.

[53] How could it ever be right and according to God's will that a man should in a short time grow so rich that he could buy out kings and emperors? But they have brought things to such a state that the whole world must do business at a risk and at a loss, winning this year and losing next year, while they always win, making up their losses by increased profits, and so it is no wonder that they quickly seize upon the wealth of all the world; for a penny as a permanent and sure income is better than a gulden that is temporary and uncertain. But these companies make permanent and sure gulden (florins) out of their transactions, whilst we have to make do with temporary and uncertain pennies. No wonder, then, that they become kings and we beggars!

[54] Kings and princes ought to look into these things and forbid them by strict laws. But I hear that they have an interest in them, and the saying of Isaiah is fulfilled, 'Thy princes have become companions of thieves.' They hang thieves who have stolen a florin or half-florin and do business with those who rob the whole world and steal more than all the rest, so that the proverb may hold true: Big thieves hang the little thieves, and as the Roman senator Cato said: Only the petty and stupid thieves lie in prisons and in stocks, whilst public thieves walk around dressed in gold and silk. But what will God say to this at last? He will do as He says by Ezekiel; princes and merchants, one thief with another, He will melt them together like lead and brass, as when a city burns, so that there shall be neither princes nor merchants anymore. That time, I fear, is already at the door.[44] We do not think of amending our lives, no matter how great our sin and wrong may be, and He cannot leave any wrong unpunished.

[55] No one need ask, then, how he can hold shares in or be co-partner within the said companies with good conscience. The only advice to give him is: Let them alone, they will not change. If the companies are to stay, right and honesty must perish; if right and honesty are to stay, the companies must perish. 'The bed is too narrow,' says Isaiah, 'one must fall out; the cover is too small, it will not cover both.' I know full well that this book of mine will be taken ill, and perhaps they will throw it all into the winds and remain as they are. But it will not be my fault, for I have done my part to show how richly

---

44. Many works have stressed the millenarian fears and apocalyptic moods of the age before the enlightenment, especially in the sixteenth and early seventeenth century. See Achim Landwehr, *Geburt der Gegenwart: Eine Geschichte der Zeit im 17. Jahrhundert* (Frankfurt: Fischer, 2014).

we have deserved it if God shall come with a rod. If I have instructed a single soul and rescued it from the jaws of avarice, my labour will not have been in vain; though I hope, as I have said above, that this thing has grown so high and so heavy that it can no longer carry its own weight and will have to stop at last. To sum up, let everyone look to himself. Let no one stop as a favour or a service to me, nor let anyone begin or continue to spite me or to cause me pain. It is your affair, not mine. May God enlighten us and strengthen us to do His good will. Amen.

Part II. On Usury (*Great Sermon on Usury*, 1520)

First part

[56] First. It should be known that in our times (of which the Apostle Paul prophesied that they would be perilous) avarice and usury have not only taken a mighty hold in all the world, but have undertaken to seek certain cloaks under which they would be considered right and could thus practice their wickedness freely. And things have gone almost so far that we hold the Holy Gospel as of no value. Therefore, it is necessary, in this perilous time, for everyone to see well to himself, and in dealing with temporal goods, to make true distinctions and diligently to observe the Holy Gospel of Christ our Lord.

[57] Second. It should be known that there are three different degrees and ways of dealing well and rightly with temporal goods.[45] The first is that if anyone takes some of our temporal goods by force, we shall not only permit it, and let the goods go; we should even be ready to let him take more, if he will. Of this our dear Lord Jesus Christ says, in Matthew 5:40, 'And if any man will sue thee at the law, and take away thy coat, let him have thy cloak also.'[46] This is the highest degree of dealing well with temporal goods. And is not to be understood to mean, as some think, that we are to throw the cloak after the coat, but rather that we are to let the cloak go, and do not resist or become impatient about it, or demand it back again. For He does not say, 'Give him the cloak also,' but 'Let him have thy cloak also.' So Christ Himself, before the High Priest Annas[47], when He received a blow on the cheek, offered the other cheek also, and was ready to receive more such blows; nay, in His entire Passion we see that He never repays or returns an evil word or deed, but is always ready to endure more.

---

45. Luther discussed these things in the first part.

46. King James Bible has 'cloke' rather than cloak.

47. The original (WA 6, 36) uses Bischoff; Luther frequently 'translated' biblical technical terms and titles into the nomenclature of his day. The same is true with the *Zinsgroschen* which Luther introduced into the biblical story as his idiosyncratic translation of the Greek original δηναριος or νομισμα του κηνσου (Mt 22:19: επιδειξατε μοι το νομισμα του κηνσου οι δε προσηνεγκαν αυτω δηναριον/ *Shew me the tribute money. And they brought unto him a penny*). The *Zinsgroschen* or literally 'groat intended for census payment' was, rather than a penny, the standard Saxon *groat* nominal and legal tender money and money-of-account that circulated at 1/21 (and from the 1540s on 1/24) florins or gulden. This relation was used for official purposes (accounting) as well as for tax and tithe payments; it was important for the legalistic / property rights framework.

[58] Third. It is true, indeed, that He said to the servant Malchus, who struck Him, 'If I have spoken evil, prove the evil; but if well, why smitest thou me?' Some even of the learned stumble at these words, and think that Christ did not offer the other cheek, as He taught that men should do. But they do not look at the words rightly; for in these words Christ does not threaten, does not avenge Himself, does not strike back, does not even refuse the other cheek; nay, He does not judge or condemn Malchus, but as Peter writes of Him, He did not threaten, or think to recompense evil, but committed it to God, the just Judge, as if to say, 'If I have spoken rightly or you are right in smiting me, God will find it out, and you are bound to prove it.' So Zechariah said, when they killed him, *Videat dominus et judicet*, 'God will see it and judge.' So He did also before Pilate, when He said, 'He that hath given me over to thee hath a greater sin than thou.' For that is Christian and brotherly fidelity, to terrify him, and hold his wrongdoing and God's judgement before him who does you wrong; and it is your duty to say to him, 'Well, then, you are taking my coat and this and that; if you are doing right, you will have to answer for it.' This you must do, not chiefly because of your own injury, and also not to threaten him, but to warn him and remind him of his own ruin. If that does not change his purpose, let go what will, and do not demand it back again. See, that is the meaning of the word that Christ spoke before the court of Annas. It follows that, like Christ on the Cross, you must pray for him and do well to him who does evil to you. But this we leave now until the proper time.

[59] Fourth. Many think that this first degree is not commanded and need not be observed by every Christian, but is a good counsel, laid upon the perfect for them to keep just as virginity and chastity are counselled, not commanded. Therefore they hold it proper that everyone shall take back what is his own, and repel force with force according to their ability and knowledge; and they deck out this opinion with pretty flowers, and prove it, as they think, with many strong arguments; namely, First, as Canon Law (to say nothing of the temporal) says, *Vim vi pellere jura sinunt*, that is, 'The law allows that force be resisted with force.' From this comes, in the second place, the common proverb about self-defence; i.e. that it is not punishable for what it does. In the third place, they bring up some illustrations from the Scriptures, such as Abraham and David and many more, about whom we read that they punished and repaid their enemies. In the fourth place, they bring in Reason, and say, *Solve istud* (explain that); if this were a commandment, it would give the wicked permission to steal, and at last no one would keep anything; nay, no one would be sure of their own body. In the fifth place, in order that everything may be firmly proved, they bring up the saying of St Augustine who explains these words of Christ to mean that one must let the cloak go after the coat, *secundum praeparationem animi*, that is, 'he shall be ready in his heart to do it.' This noble, clear exposition they interpret and darken with another gloss, and add, 'It is not necessary that we give it outwardly and in deed; it is enough that we be inwardly, in the heart, ready and prepared to do it.' As though we were willing to do something that we were not willing to do, and 'yes' and 'no' were one thing!

[60] Fifth. See, these are the masterpieces with which the doctrine and example of our dear Lord Jesus Christ, together with the Holy Gospel and all His martyrs and saints, have hitherto been turned around, made unknown, and entirely suppressed, so

that nowadays those spiritual and temporal prelates and subjects are the best Christians who follow these rules, and yet resist Christ's life, teaching, and Gospel. Hence it comes that lawsuits and litigations, notaries, *officiales*[48], jurists, and that whole noble riff-raff[49], are as numerous as flies in summer. Hence it is that we have so much war and bloodshed among Christians. Suits must also be carried to Rome, for over there money is the thing most needed – and much money, that is![50] And throughout the Church the greatest and holiest and commonest work these days is suing and being sued. That is resisting the holy and peaceful life and doctrine of Christ, and the cruel game has gone to the point where not only is a poor man, whom God has redeemed with His blood, cited many miles for the sake of a trifling sum of three or four *groschen* (groats), put under the ban, and driven away from wife and children and family; but even the bright young boys look on this as a good thing to do, and regard it with equanimity. So shall they fall who make a mockery of God's commandments; so shall God blind and put to shame those who turn the brightness of His holy Word into darkness with *Vim vi repellere licet* and with letting the cloak go *secundum praeparationem animi*! For thus the heathen, too, keep the Gospel; nay, the wolves and all the unreasoning beasts; men need no longer be Christians to do it.

[61] Sixth. Therefore, I want to do my part and, so far as I can, to warn everyone not to be led astray, no matter how learned, how mighty, how spiritual, or how many of these things all at once they may be who have made, and still make, a counsel out of this decree; no matter how many are the flowers and the colours with which they decorate it. No excuses! This is simply a commandment that we are bound to obey, as Christ and His saints have confirmed it and exemplified it. God does not approve of laws – spiritual or temporal – which permit force to be resisted with force. And by no means do the Laws permit precious things exclusively – quite to the contrary! They permit common brothels, though they are against God's commandment, as well as many other wicked things which God forbids; and they have to permit secret sin and wickedness. The things that human laws command and forbid matter little, how much less the things that they permit or do not punish. Thus, whilst self-defence is not subject to prosecution before temporal law, before God it has no merit. Suing at law courts is condemned by neither Pope nor Emperor; but it is condemned by Christ and His doctrine. That some of the Old Testament fathers punished their enemies was never due to their own choice in the matter, and it was never done without God's express command, which punishes sinners, and punishes, at times, both good and bad, angels and men. For this reason they never sought revenge or their own profit, but only acted as obedient servants of God, just as Christ teaches in the Gospel that at God's command we must act even against father and mother, whom He has commanded us to honour. Nevertheless, the two commandments are not contradictory, but the lower is ruled by the higher. When God commands you to take revenge or to defend yourself, then you shall do it; and not before then.

---

48. Judges in bishops' courts, see Luther's Works, 1962 Am. ed., 276, n. 76.
49. Note that Luther himself had been near to becoming a trained jurist and professional administrator himself, before turning into a monk in 1505.
50. Here Luther picks up on a familiar topic in the satirical discourse of his day. See introductory essay, chapter five.

[62] Seventh. Nevertheless, it is true that God has instituted the worldly sword and the spiritual power of the Church, and has commanded both authorities to punish the evil and rescue the oppressed, as Paul teaches in Romans 13:3, and Isaiah in many places, and Psalm 82:3. But this should be done in such a way that no one would be plaintiff and litigator in his own case, but that others, in their brotherly fidelity and their care for one another, would tell the rulers that this man was innocent and that man wrong. Thus the authorities would resort to punishment in a just and orderly way, on proof furnished by the others; indeed, the offended party ought to ask that his case be not avenged, and ought to do his best to prevent it. The others, for their part, ought not to desist until the evil was punished. Thus things would be conducted in a kindly, Christian and brotherly way, with more regard to the sin than to the injury. Therefore Paul rebukes the Corinthians, in 1 Corinthians 6:16, because they took each other to court, and did not rather suffer themselves to be injured and defrauded, though because of their imperfection, he did permit that they appoint the least of themselves as judges. He did this to shame them and make them aware of their imperfection. In like manner we must still tolerate those who sue and are being sued, as weak and childish Christians whom we must not cast off, because there is hope for their improvement, as the same Apostle teaches in many places. We ought to tell them, however, that such conduct is neither Christian nor in any way meritorious, but human and earthly; a hindrance to salvation and not a help.

[63] Eighth. Christ gave this commandment in order to establish within us a peaceful, pure, and heavenly life. Now for everyone to demand what is his and be unwilling to endure wrong, that is not the way to peace, as those blind men think of whom it is said, in Psalm 13:1, 'They know not the way to peace,' which goes only through suffering. The heathen, too, know this by Reason, and we by daily experience. If peace is to be kept, one party must be quiet and suffer; and even though quarrels and litigations may last for a long while, they must finally come to an end, after injuries and evils that would not have been, if people had kept this commandment of Christ's at the start and had not allowed the temptation, with which God tries us, to drive them from the commandment and overcome them. God has so ordered things that he who will not let go a little because of the commandment, must lose much, perhaps everything, through lawsuits and dispute. It is fair that a man should give to the judges, proctors, and clerks, and receive no thanks for it, twenty or thirty or forty florins in serving the Devil, when he will not let his neighbour, for God's sake and for his own eternal credit, have two florins, or six. Thus he loses both his temporal and eternal goods, when, if he were obedient to God, he might have enough for both time and eternity. It happens, at times, that in this way great lords must lose a whole country in war and consume great sums of money on soldiers for the sake of a small advantage or only a small liberty. That is the perverted wisdom of the world; it fishes with golden nets and the cost is greater than the profit; there are those who win the little and squander the much.

[64] Ninth. It would be impossible to become dissolved of our attachment to temporal goods, if God did not decree that we should be unjustly injured, and exercised thereby in turning our hearts away from the false temporal goods of the world, letting them go in peace, and setting our hopes on the eternal goods which are invisible and unbeknownst to us. Therefore he who requires that which is his own, and does not let the cloak go

after the coat is resisting his own purification and the hope of eternal salvation, for which God would exercise him and to which He would drive him. And even though everything were taken from us, there is no reason to fear that God will desert us and not provide for us even in temporal matters; as it is written in Psalm 37:25, 'I have been young and have grown old, and have never seen that the righteous was deserted or his children went after bread.' This is proved in the case of Job also, who received in the end more than he had before, though all that he had was taken from him. For, to put it briefly, these commandments are intended to detach us from the world and make us desirous of heaven. Therefore we ought peacefully and joyfully to accept the faithful counsel of God, for if He did not give it, and did not let wrong and unhappiness come to us, the human heart could not maintain itself; it entangles itself too deeply in temporal things and attaches itself to them too tightly, and the result is satiety and disregard of the eternal goods in heaven.

[65] Tenth. So much for the first degree of dealing with temporal goods! It is also the foremost and the greatest, and yet, alas! it has not only become the least, but it has come to nothing and, amid the mists and clouds of human laws, practices and customs, has become quite unknown. Now comes the second degree; that is that we should give freely to everyone in need or asking us for help. Of this also our Lord Jesus Christ speaks in Matthew 5, 'He who asks of thee, to him give.' Although this degree is much lower than the first, it is, nevertheless, hard and bitter for those who have more taste for the temporal than for the spiritual goods; for they have not enough trust in God to believe that He can or will maintain them in this wretched life. Therefore, they fear that they would die of hunger or be entirely ruined if they were to do as God commands, i.e. to give to everyone who asks for it. How, then, can they trust Him to maintain them in eternity? For, as Christ says, 'He who does not trust God in a little thing will never trust Him in a great.' And yet they go about thinking that God will make them eternally blessed; believing that they have good confidence in Him, though they will not heed this commandment of His, by which He would exercise them, and drive them to learn to trust Him in things temporal and eternal. There is reason to fear, therefore, that he who will not hear and obey the doctrine will never acquire the art of trusting, and as they do not trust God for the little temporal goods, so they must at last despair about those that are great and eternal.

[66] Eleventh. This second degree is so small a thing that it was commanded even to the simple, imperfect people of the Jews, in the Old Testament, as it is written in Deuteronomy 15:4, 'There will always be poor people in the land, therefore I command thee that thou open thy hand to thy poor and needy brother, and give to him.' Besides, He commanded them severely that they must allow no one to beg, and says, in Deuteronomy 15:4, 'There shall be no beggar or indigent man among you.' Now if God gave this commandment in the Old Testament, how much more ought we Christians be bound not only to allow no one to suffer want or to beg, but also to keep the first degree of this commandment, and let everything go that anyone will take from us by force. Now, however, there is so much begging that it has even become an honour; and it is not enough that men of the world beg, but the spiritual estate of the priesthood practice it as a precious thing. I will quarrel with no one about it, but I consider that it would be more fitting that there should be no more begging in Christendom under the New Testament,

than among the Jews under the Old Testament; and I hold that the spiritual and temporal rulers would be discharging their duty if they did away with all the beggars' sacks.

[67] Twelfth. There are three practices or customs among men that are opposed to this degree of dealing. The first is that men give freely and present gifts to their friends, the rich and powerful, who do not strictly speaking need them, and forget the needy about it. And if they thus obtain favour, advantage, or friendship from these people, or are praised by them as pious folk, they go carelessly about, satisfied with the praise, honour, favour, or advantage that comes from men, and do not observe, meanwhile, how much better it would be if they did these things to the needy, and therefore obtained God's favour, praise, and honour of whom Christ tells us in Luke 14.[51] Of such men Christ says, 'If thou make a midday or an evening meal, thou shalt not invite thy friends or thy brethren, or thy relatives, or thy neighbours, or the rich, so that they may invite thee again, and thus take thy reward; but when thou makest a meal, invite the poor, the sick, the lame, the blind; so art thou blessed, for they cannot recompense it to thee; but it shall be recompensed to thee among the righteous, when they rise from the dead.' Although this doctrine is so clear and plain that everyone sees and knows that it ought to be so, we never see an example of it among Christians anymore. There is neither measure nor limit to the inviting and entertaining of people, the high living, the eating, drinking, giving, presenting; and yet they are all called good people and Christians, and nothing comes out of it except that giving to the needy is forgotten. O what horrible judgment will fall upon these carefree spirits, when it is asked, on the Last Day, to whom they have given and done well!

[68] Thirteenth. The second custom is that people refuse to give to enemies and opponents. For it comes hard to our false nature to do good to those who have done it evil. But that does not help. The commandment is spoken for all men alike, 'Give to him that asketh,' and it is clearly expressed in Luke 6:30, 'To everyone that asketh of thee, give.' Here no exception is made of enemies or opponents; nay, they are included, as the Lord Himself makes clear in the same passage, and says, 'For if ye love them which love you, what thank have ye? for sinners also love those that love them. And if ye do good to them which do good to you, what thank have ye? for sinners also do even the same. But love ye your enemies, and do good, and lend, hoping for nothing again; and your reward shall be great, and ye shall be the children of the Highest: for he is kind unto the unthankful and to the evil.' These wholesome commandments of Christ have so fallen into disuse that men not only do not keep them, but have made of them a mere counsel[52] which one is not necessarily bound to keep, just as they have done with the first degree. They have been helped in this by those injurious teachers who say that it is not necessary to lay aside the *signa rancoris*, that is, the signs of enmity, and bitter, angry attitudes toward an enemy, but that it is enough to forgive him in one's heart. Thus they apply Christ's commandment about external works to the thoughts alone, though He Himself extends it, in clear words, to works, saying, 'Ye shall do good (not merely think good) to your

---

51. Original (WA 6, 42) has *von denen sagt Christus Luce xiiij*, which Charles M. Jacobs did not translate.

52. Original reads *eyn radt drauß macht*; WA 6, 43.

enemies.' So, too, in Romans 12:20, Paul, in agreement with King Solomon, says, 'If thine enemy hunger, feed him; if he thirst, give him drink; for thereby thou shalt heap coals of fire on his head'; that is, you will load him with good deeds, so that, overcome with good, his love for you will be incensed. From these false doctrines has sprung the common saying, 'I will forgive, but not forget.' Not so, dear Christian! You must forgive and forget, as you desire that God shall not only forgive and forget, but also do you more good than before.

[69] Fourteenth. The third custom is pretty and showy, and does most injury to this giving. It is dangerous to speak about it, for it concerns those who ought to be teaching and ruling others, and these are the folk who, from the beginning of the world to its end, can never hear the truth or suffer others to hear it. The way things now go, they apply the high title of 'alms,' or 'giving for God's sake,' to giving for churches, monasteries, chapels, altars, church towers, church bells, organs, paintings, statues, silver and gold ornaments and vestments, and for masses, vigils, singing, reading, testamentary endowments, sodalities, and the like. Giving has taken hold here, and the real stream of giving is on this side, to which men have guided it and where they wanted to have it; no wonder, therefore, that on the side to which Christ's word guides it, things are so dry and desolate that where there are a hundred altars or vigils, there is not one man who feeds a tableful of poor people, let alone gives food to a poor household. Not what Christ has commanded, but what men have invented, is called 'Giving for God's sake'; not what one gives to the needy living members of Christ, but what one gives, in terms of stone, wood, and paint[53] is called 'alms.' And this giving has become so precious and noble that God Himself is not enough to recompense it, but it has to be done with *breves*[54], bulls, parchments, lead, metal, cords large and small, and wax, green, yellow and white. If it is not glittering, it has no value. And it is all bought at great cost, 'for God's sake,' from Rome, and such great works are rewarded with indulgences, here and there, over and above the reward of God. But giving to the poor and needy, according to Christ's commandment, this miserable work must be robbed of such splendid reward, and be satisfied with the reward that God gives alone. Thus the latter work is pushed to the rear and the former is put out in front and the two, when compared, shine with unequal light. Therefore, St Peter of Rome must now go begging throughout the world for the building of his church, and gather great heaps of 'alms for God's sake,' and pay for them dearly and richly with indulgences. And this work suits him well, and he can easily attend to it, because he is dead; for if he were alive, he would have to preach Christ's commandments and could not attend to the indulgences. His lambs follow diligently after their faithful shepherd, go about with the indulgences in every land, and wherever there is an annual or parish fair in the village or town these beggars gather like flies in summer, and they all preach the same song, 'Give to the new building that God may recompense you, and the holy lord, St Nicholas.'

---

53. I.e. decoration for ritual purposes and ceremonial equipment in churches, cloisters and monasteries. Which seems to have increased towards the time when Luther put forth his views in 1517. See introductory essay.
54. A *breve* (literally *Brief*, 'letter') was a certificate that someone had paid a certain sum for giving alms, indulgences and other donations.

Afterwards they will have beer or wine, also 'for God's sake'; and the commissaries[55] are made rich – also 'for God's sake.' But we don't need commissaries or legates in order to preach to us that we shall give to the needy according to God's commandment.

[70] Fifteenth. What shall we say to this?[56] If we reject these works, the Holy See at Rome puts us under the ban and the high scholars will quickly call us heretics, for the place to which the stream of money is directed makes a mighty difference. We would not prevent the building of suitable churches and the adornment of them, for we cannot do without them, and without doubt the worship of God ought to be conducted in the finest way; but there should be a limit to it, and we should have a care that the appointments of worship should be pure, rather than costly. It is pitiable and lamentable, however, that by these clamorous practices we are turned away from God's commandments and led only to the things that God has not commanded, and without which God's commandments can well be kept. It would be sufficient, if we gave the smaller portion to churches and the like, and let the lion's share flow toward God's commandment, so that among Christians good deeds done to the poor would shine more brightly than all the churches of stone or of wood. To speak out boldly, it is sheer trickery, dangerous and deceptive to the simple-minded, when bulls, *breves*, seals, banners, and the like are hung up for the sake of dead stone churches, and the same thing is not done a hundred times more for the sake of those living Christians who are in need. Beware, therefore, O man! God will not ask you, at your death and at the Last Day, how much you have left in your will, or whether you have given so much or so much to churches; but He will say to you, 'I was hungry and ye fed me not; I was naked and ye clothed me not.' Let these words go to your heart, dear man! Everything will depend on whether you have given to your neighbour and done him good. Beware of all the show and glitter and colour that draw you away from this!

[71] Sixteenth. Pope, bishops, kings, princes and lords ought to labour for the abolition of these intolerable burdens and impositions. It ought to be established and decreed, either by their own statute or in a general council, that every town and village should build and maintain its own churches and care for its own poor folk, so that beggary would cease entirely, or at least that it would not be done in such a way that any place should beg for its churches and its poor in all other cities, according to the present unhappy custom; and the Holy See at Rome ought to be left to enjoy its own bulls, for it has enough other things to do, in order to perform its office properly, without selling bulls and building churches which it does not need. God has expressed it plainly in His law, in Deuteronomy 15:11, 'For the poor shall never cease out of the land.' Thus He has committed to every city its own poor, and He will not have men running hither and thither with beggars' sacks, as men now run to St James and to Rome. Although I am too small a man to give advice to popes and all the rulers of the world in this case, and although I myself think that nothing will come of it; nevertheless, it ought to be known what the good and needful course would be, and it is the duty of the rulers to consider and to do the things that are necessary for the best ruling of the common people, who are committed to them.

---

55. Such as the Dominican friar Johann Tetzel, upon whom Luther's indulgence critique focused.
56. Luther uses the *pluralis maiestatis* here, certainly referring, above all, to himself.

[72] Seventeenth. A device has been invented which teaches in a masterly way, how this commandment can be circumvented and the Holy Ghost deceived. 'People maintain that no one should be bound to give to the needy unless they are in extreme want.' Besides, they have reserved the right to investigate and decide what 'extreme want' is. Thus we learn that no one is to give or help until the needy are dying of hunger, freezing to death, ruined by poverty, or running away because of debts. But this knavish gloss and deceitful addition is confounded with a single word which says, 'What thou wilt that another do to thee, that do thou also.' Now no one is so foolish as to be unwilling that anyone should give to him until the soul is leaving his body or he has run away from his debts, and then help him, when he can be helped no more. But when it comes to churches, endowments, indulgences and other things that God has not commanded, then no one is so keen or so careful in reckoning out whether we are to give to the church before the tiles fall off the roof, the beams rot, the ceiling fall in, the dispensation letters mould, the letters of indulgence decay – though all these things could wait more easily than people who are in need – but in these cases every hour is one of 'extreme want,' even though all the chests, and the floor itself, were full, and everything well-built. Nay, in this case treasure must be gathered without ceasing, not to be given or lent to the needy on earth, but to the Holy Cross, to our Dear Lady, to the holy patron, St. Peter, though they are in heaven. All this must be done with more than ordinary foresight, so that if the Last Day never came, the church would be taken care of for a hundred or two hundred thousand years; and thus, in case of need, the canonization of a saint, or a bishop's *pallium*, or other like wares can be bought at the fair in Rome. I truly think that the Romans are very great fools not to sell canonization, *pallia*, bulls, and *breves*[57] at a higher price and not to get more money for them, since these fat German fools come to their fair and obligate themselves to buy them; though, to be sure, no Antichrist could collect these treasures more fittingly than the bottomless bag at Rome, into which they are all gathered and set in order.[58] It would grieve one to the heart, if these damned goods, taken from the needy, to whom they properly belong, were spent for anything else than Roman wares. St Ambrose and Paulinus, in former times, melted the chalices and everything that the churches had, and gave the wealth away to the poor. Turn the page, and you find how things are now. Well for you, dear Rome, that even though the Germans run short of money[59], they still have chalices, monstrances, and images enough; and all of them will eventually be yours!

[73] Eighteenth. We come now to the third degree of dealing with temporal goods. It is that we willingly and gladly lend without charges or interest. Of this our Lord Jesus Christ says, in Matthew 5:42, 'from him that would borrow of thee turn not thou away,' that is, 'do not refuse him.' This degree is the lowest of all and is commanded even in the Old Testament, where God says, in Deuteronomy 15:7, 'If there be among you a poor man of one of thy brethren within any of thy gates in thy land which the LORD thy God giveth thee, thou shalt not harden thine heart, nor shut thine hand

---

57. See above.
58. Again Luther develops an idea which was seized upon by the satirical discourse of the day, see introductory essay, chapter five.
59. See introductory essay, chapter five.

from thy poor brother; But thou shalt open thine hand wide unto him, and shalt surely lend him sufficient for his need, in that which he wanteth'; and they have allowed this degree to remain a commandment, for all the doctors agree that borrowing and lending shall be free, without charge or burden, though all may not be agreed on the question to whom we ought to lend. For as was said about the previous degree, there are many who gladly lend to the rich or to good friends, more to seek their favour or put them under obligation than because God has commanded it; especially if it is given the high title, spoken of above, viz., 'for God's service,' or 'for God's sake.' For everybody gladly lends to the Holy Cross and our Dear Lady and the patron saint, but where God's command points the way there is always trouble and labour. No one wants to lend on these conditions, except in cases of extreme want, where lending does no good, as has been said above.

[74] Nineteenth. Christ, however, excluded no one from His commandment; nay, He included all kinds of people, even one's enemies, when He said, in Luke 6:34, 'if ye lend *to them* of whom ye hope to receive, what thank have ye? for sinners also lend to sinners, to receive as much again'; and also 'lend, hoping for nothing again.' I know very well that very many *doctores* have interpreted these words as though Christ had commanded to lend in such a way as not to make any charge for it or seek any profit by it, but to lend gratis. This opinion is, indeed, not wrong, for he who makes a charge for lending is not lending and neither is he selling. It must therefore be usury, because lending is, in its very nature, nothing else than to offer another something without charge, on the condition that one get back, after a while, the same thing, or its equivalent, and nothing more. But if we look the word of Christ squarely in the eye, it does not teach us that we are to lend without charge, for there is no need for such teaching, since there can be no lending except lending without charge, and if a charge is made, it cannot be a loan. Christ wants us to lend not only to friends, the rich, and those to whom we are well disposed, who can repay us again, by returning this loan, or with another loan, or by some other benefit; but also that we lend to those who cannot or will not repay us, such as those in need, and our enemies. It is just like His teaching about loving and giving; our lending is to be done without selfishness and without self-seeking. This does not happen unless we lend to our enemies and to those in need; for all that He says is aimed to teach us to do good to everyone, that is, not only to those who do good to us, but also to those who do us evil, or cannot do us good in return. That is what He means when He says, 'lend, hoping for nothing again,' that is, 'you should lend to those who cannot or will not lend to you again.' But he who lends expects to receive back the same thing that he lends, and if he expects nothing, then, according to their interpretation, it would be a gift and not a loan. Because, then, it is such a little thing to make a loan to someone who is a friend, or rich, or who may render some service in return, that even sinners who are not Christians do the same thing, Christians ought to do more, and lend to those who do not the same, i.e., to those in need, and to their enemies. Thus, too, the doctrine fails which says that we are not bound to lay aside the *signa rancoris*, as has been said above; and even though they speak rightly about lending, yet they turn this commandment into a counsel and teach us that we are not bound to lend to our enemies or to the needy, unless they are in extreme want. Beware of this!

[75] Twentieth. It follows from this that they are all usurers who lend their neighbour wine, grain, money, or the like, in such a way that he obligates himself to pay interest on it in a year or at a given time; or that he burdens and overloads himself with a promise to give back more, or something else that is better than he has borrowed. And in order that these men may themselves perceive the wrong that they are doing – though the practice has, unfortunately, become common – we set before them three laws. First, this passage in the Gospel which commands that we shall lend. Now lending is not lending unless it be done without charge and without advantage to the lender, as has been said. Crafty avarice, to be sure, sometimes paints itself a pretty colour and pretends to take the surplus as a present, but that does not help if the present is the cause of the loan; or if the borrower would rather not make the present, provided he could borrow gratis. And the present is especially suspicious, if the borrower makes it to the lender, or the needy to the wealthy. For it is not natural to suppose that the needy would make a present to the wealthy out of his own free will; it is necessity that forces him to do so. Second, this is contrary to Natural Law, which the Lord also announces in Luke 6:31 and Matthew 7:12 'And as you would that men should do to you, do you also to them likewise'. Now, beyond all doubt, there is no one who would that men should lend him rye to be repaid with wheat, bad money to be repaid with good, bad wares to be repaid with good wares; indeed, he would much rather that men should lend him good wares to be repaid with bad, or with equally good wares, but without charge. Therefore it is clear that these usurers are acting against nature, are guilty of mortal sin, and seek their neighbour's injury and their own profit, because they would not put up with such treatment from others, and are thus dealing unfairly with their neighbour. Third, it is also against the Old and the New (Testament) Law, which commands, 'Thou shalt love thy neighbour as thyself.' But such lenders love themselves alone, seek only their own, or do not love and seek their neighbour with such fidelity as they love and seek themselves.

[76] Twenty-First. Therefore no better or briefer instruction can be given about this, and about all dealing with temporal goods, than that everyone who is to have business of some sort with his neighbour set before him these commandments, 'Whatsoever thou wilt that another do to thee, that do thou to him also,' and 'Thou shalt love thy neighbour as thyself.' If, beside this, he were to think what he would have for himself, if he were in his neighbour's place, he would learn for himself and find for himself all that he needs to know. There would be no need for law books or courts or accusation and court cases; nay, all the cases would be quickly and simply decided. For everyone's heart and conscience would tell him how he would like to be dealt with, what sort of allowances and abatements he would like to be given, what to be received and what forgiven, and from this he must conclude that he ought to do just that for everyone else. But because we leave these commandments out of view, and have eyes only for business, and its profit or loss, we must have all the countless books, courts, judges, law suits, blood, and all misery, and thus, upon the violation of God's commandments, must follow the destruction of God's kingdom, which is peace and unity, in brotherly love and faithfulness. And yet these wicked men go about, begging at times and fasting, giving alms at times, but in this matter, on which salvation depends, they are quite heedless and carefree, as if this commandment did not concern them at all, though without it they cannot be saved, even if they did all the other works of all the saints.

[77] Twenty-second. Here we meet two objections. The first is that if lending were done in this way, the *interesse* would be lost, that is, the profit which they could make meanwhile with the goods that were lent. The second is the great example, which they cite, that everywhere in the world it has become custom to lend for profit, and especially because scholars, priests, clergy, and churches do it, seeing that the improvement of the church's spiritual goods and of the worship of God is sought, and without these there would be very few Christians in the world, and everyone would be reluctant to lend.

[78] To which the answer is: there is nothing in all of that. In the first place, you must lose the interest and the profit if it be taken from you or if you give to someone outright; why, then, will you seek it and keep it in lending? He who decides to give and lend must give up the interest in advance, otherwise it is neither to be called giving nor lending. In the second place, whether it is a good custom or a bad custom, it is not Christian or divine or natural, and no example helps against that fact. For it is written, 'Thou shalt not follow the crowd to do evil, but honour God and His commandments above all things.' That the clergy and the churches do this is so much for the worse. For spiritual goods and churches have neither authority nor freedom to break God's commandments, rob their neighbour, practice usury, and do wrong. Moreover, the service of God is not improved by it, but corrupted. For keeping God's commandments is improving the service and worship to God; even knaves can improve the church property; and even if the whole world had the custom of lending with this kind of a charge, the churches and the clergy should act the other way, and the more spiritual their possessions were, the more Christian should be the manner in which, according to Christ's command, they would lend, give away, and let go of worldly goods. He who does otherwise, is doing so, not for the improvement of the churches or of their spiritual goods, but for his own usury-seeking avarice, which decks itself out with such good names. It is no wonder, then, that Christians are few; for here we see who they are that practice really good works, though many blind and deceive themselves with their own self-imposed and voluntary good works, which God has not commanded them to do. But if anyone finds that this makes it hard for him to lend to his neighbour, it is a sign of his great unbelief, because he despises the comforting assurance of Christ, who says, 'If we lend and give, we are children of the Highest, and our reward is great.'[60] He who does not believe this comforting promise and does not make it a guide for all his works, is not worthy of it.

Second part of this sermon

[79] First. Beneath these three degrees are other degrees and types of transactions, such as buying, inheriting, transfers, etc., and these are governed by temporal and spiritual law. By these no one becomes better or worse in the sight of God, for there is no Christian merit in buying anything, getting it by inheritance, or acquiring it in some other honest way, since the heathen, Turks, and Jews can be this good. But Christian dealing and the right use of temporal goods consist in the three above-mentioned degrees or ways –

---

60. Luke 6:35: *But love ye your enemies, and do good, and lend, hoping for nothing again; and your reward shall be great, and ye shall be the children of the Highest: for he is kind unto the unthankful and to the evil.*

giving away, lending without charge, and quietly letting go when your goods are taken by force. Let us put aside all other practices for the moment, and focus attention on the matter of certain types of purchases, especially the *zinss kauff* [61]; since this makes a pretty show and seems to be an easy way by which a man can burden others without sin and grow rich without any worry or trouble. For in other dealings it is manifest to everybody if a man sells too dear, or sells false wares, or possesses a false inheritance, or wealth that is not his, but this slippery and newly invented business very often makes itself the pious and faithful protector of damnable greed and usury.

[80] Second. Although the *zinss kauf* is now established as a proper trade and a permitted line of business, it is, nevertheless, something to be hated and opposed for many reasons. Firstly, because it is a new and slippery invention, especially in these last, perilous times, where nothing good is invented anymore and the thoughts of all men are bent upon wealth and honour and luxury, without any limit. We cannot find any example of this business among the ancients, and Paul says of these times that many new, evil practices will be invented. Secondly, because, as they must themselves admit, however right it may be in theory, it still makes a bad show and has an offensive outward appearance, and St. Paul bids us avoid all evil and offensive appearances, even though the thing itself were right and proper – *ab omni spetie mala abstinete* (Thessalonians ult.), 'Abstain from all appearance of evil.' Now in this business the advantage of the buyer, or receiver of *zinss*, is always looked upon as greater and better, and is more sought after by everyone than that of the seller, or payer of *zinss*; and this is a sign that the business is never conducted for the seller's, but always for the buyer's sake. For every man's conscience fears that it cannot be right to 'buy' such income, but no one has any doubt that he can sell what is his own at any risk that he cares to take. So close and dangerous does this business become to the conscience. Thirdly, this business, even if it may be conducted without usury, can scarcely be conducted without violation of the natural law and the Christian law of love. For it is to be supposed that the buyer never, or very seldom, seeks and desires the welfare and advantage of his neighbour, the seller, more than or equally with his own, especially if the purchaser of *zinss* is the richer man and does not need to buy it. And yet the natural law says, What we wish and desire for ourselves, we shall wish and desire for our neighbour also; and it is the nature of love, as St Paul says in 1 Corinthians 13:5, not to seek its own profit or advantage, but that of others. But who believes that, in this business, anyone buys *zinss* (unless he absolutely needs it) with a view to giving his neighbour, the seller, a profit and advantage equal to his own? Thus it is to be feared that the buyer would not like to be in the seller's stead, as in other kinds of trade. Fourthly, everyone must admit that, regardless whether this business be usurious or not, it does exactly the same work that usury does; that is to say, it lays burdens upon all lands, cities, lords, and people, sucks them dry and brings them

---

61. In the original *zinsskauf*. This is one of the trickiest – and most interesting and significant – *termini technici* in Luther's oeuvre, a term which may translate, according to context, as the purchasing of all sorts of interest-bearing assets; most likely referring to a financial market transaction known today as annuity, rent or mortgage / hypothecary. The original has been retained, as modern financial terminology is only ill-suited for capturing the possible ranges and scenarios of transactions Luther had in mind in 1524. See introductory essay, chapter five.

to ruins, as no usury could have done. We see this plainly in the case of many cities and principalities. Now the Lord taught, not that the fruit is to be known by the tree, but the tree by the fruit. Thus I cannot possibly think you a sweet fig-tree, when you bear nothing but sharp thorns, and I cannot reconcile the claim that this commerce in *zinss* is right when land and people are ruined by it. Fifthly, let us imagine, then, or dream, or force ourselves to think that this business is right, as it is now conducted; nevertheless, it deserves that pope, bishops, emperor, princes and everybody else endeavour to have it abolished, and it is the duty of everyone who can prevent it to do so, if only on account of its wicked and damnable fruits, which burden and ruin the whole world.

[81] Third, therefore it is not enough that this business should be rescued by canon law from the reproach of usury, for that does not rid it of or secure it against avarice and self-love; and from the canon law we find that it is not directed toward love, but toward self-interest. Money won by gambling is not usury either, and yet it is not won without self-seeking and love of one's self, and not without sin. The profits of prostitution are not usury, but they are earned by sin. And wealth that is acquired by cursing, swearing and slander is not usury, and yet it is acquired by sin. Therefore I cannot conclude that those who buy *zinss* which they do not need are acting rightly and properly. I boldly state and give warning that the rich, who use this business only to increase their incomes and their wealth by means of burdening others[62], are in great danger. Moreover, I do not think it permissible to act as some avaricious fellows do in fact (*geytzige blaßen*), who collect their incomes from *zinss* at the prescribed or agreed time, and quickly invest it again in another interest-bearing asset – so that the one income always drives the other, as water drives the millwheel. This is such an open and shameless practice of avarice that no man, however stupid, can deny it to be so; and yet all that is upheld as just. If there were no other reason to regard this *zinsskauff* as usury or plain wrong dealing (especially in such a case as I have mentioned), this one reason would be enough, viz., that it is a cloak for such manifest and shameless avarice, which allows men to do business without risk. Whatever is of God avoids sin and every kind of evil; but this sort of transaction gives free rein to avarice; therefore – the way it is conducted now – it cannot be of God.

[82] Fourth. We will now look at the arguments by which this tender business is justified. There is a little Latin word called *interesse*. This noble, precious, tender, little word may be rendered in German this way: 'If I have a hundred florins with which I can trade, and by my labour and trouble make in a year five or six florins or more, I place it with someone else, on a productive property, so that not I, but he, can trade with it, and for this I take from him five gulden (florins), which I might have earned; thus he is selling me the zinss – five gulden (florins) per hundred – and I am the buyer and he the seller. Here they say, now, that *zinss kauff* is proper because, with these florins, I might perhaps have made more in a year, and the interest is just and sufficient. All that is so pretty and shining that no one can see any fault in it at any point. But it is also true that it is not possible to have such interest on earth, for there is another, counter-interest, which goes like this: If I have a hundred florins or gulden, and am to do business with this money, I

---

62. Original (WA 6, 53) has *das andere da durch beschweret werden*, which has been left out from the 1915 translation by Charles M. Jacobs.

may run a hundred kinds of risk of making no profits at all, nay, of losing four times as much on top of it all. Because of the money itself, or because of illness, I may not be able to do business; or there may be no wares or goods on hand. Hindrances of this kind are innumerable, and we see that failures, losses, and injuries are greater than profits. Thus the potential losses may be as large, perhaps even larger, than the profits gained upon interest.

[83] Fifth. Now if *zinss* is bought on the first kind of interest only, so that these risks and the trouble are not assumed, and it can never happen that the buyer loses more than he invests, and thus the money is invested as though all of it could always be without the other interest[63], then it is clear that the trade is based on nothing, because there cannot be any such interest, and it cannot be invented. For in this business, goods are always on hand, and one can transact it sitting still; a sick man can do it, a child, a woman; indeed, it matters not how unfit the person is, though no such persons can engage in trade, and earn profits, with bare money. For these reasons those who look upon this kind of interest, and who deal in it, are worse than usurers; nay, they buy the first interest with the second interest, and win in order that other people may lose. Again – since it is not possible to regulate, compute, and equalize the second interest (for it is not in man's power) – I do not see how this business can last. For who would not rather invest a hundred gulden for safe income than do business with it, since in business he might lose twenty gulden in a year, and his capital on top, while in this business he cannot lose more than five, and keep his capital? Moreover, in trade his money must often lay idle because of the market (*Der wahr halben*), or because of his own physical condition, while in this business it is moving and earning all the time. Is it any wonder, then, that a man gets control of all the wealth in the world, when he has goods always at hand, with constant safety and less risk, and when his capital is protected in advance? One's profits cannot be small at times when one can always procure goods, just as one's losses cannot be small when one cannot get rid of goods, or cannot procure them. Therefore, money invested in trade and money invested in some interest-bearing asset are two different things; the one cannot be compared with the other. For money invested in *zinss* has a foundation that constantly grows and produces profit out of the earth, while money in trade has no certainty; the interest it yields is accidental, and one cannot count on it at all.

[84] Here they will say, perhaps, that, because they place money on land[64], there is an 'interest of loss,' as well as an 'interest of profit,' for the *zinss* stays or falls depending upon whether the land yields or not. This is all true, and we shall hear more about it below. But the fact remains that money invested in land increases the 'first interest' too much whilst carrying much lesser 'second interest' or risk of loss as compared with money that is invested in trade and commerce; for, as was said above, there is more risk in trade than in land. Since, then, one cannot just purchase any amount or piece of land with one's disposable sum of money, neither can one just purchase *zinss* infinitely or with zero risk.

---

63. I.e. the risk of making a *loss*.

64. Many transactions upon interest or *zinss kauff* took the shape of *Leib-* or *Ewigrenten*, i.e. (life) annuities that were tied to one specific piece of land or landed property which yielded a yearly payment, rent or income stream.

Therefore, it is not enough to say, 'With so much money I can buy so much *zinss* from some given piece of land, and therefore it is right for me to take so much income for it and let someone else look after the grounds.' For this would mean assigning a definite value or price to a chosen piece of land. That is impossible, and great hardship must result for land and people.

[85] Sixth. Therefore it is no wonder that those noble 'Knights of the Interest' (*zinss junckern*) grow rich so quickly and much faster than everybody else, for since the others keep their money in trade, they are subject to the two kinds of interest. But the Knights of the Interest, by this little trick, get out of the second interest and fall entirely into the first category; thus their risk is greatly reduced and their safety increased. For these reasons it should not be permitted to buy *zinss* with cash money, without specifying and defining the particular piece of ground from which the *zinss* is derived, as is now the custom, especially among the great merchants, who place money on some land in very general terms, without specification. By so doing they ascribe to the nature of money that which is only accidental to it. It is not in the nature of money that it buys land without a purpose, but it may happen that a piece of ground is up for sale upon rent or some other income stream when some money is at one's disposal; but that does not happen with all land or with all money; therefore the land or collateral for the debt ought to be named and exactly specified. If that were done, it would be evident how much money would remain unused for investment and have to remain in commerce or in the coffers, though it now produces income with neither right nor pretext except that one says (in a general way), 'By placing it on a piece of land, I can buy so much *zinss* with it, and that will be interest.'[65] Yes, my dear fellow, my money can buy my neighbour's house; but if it is not for sale, the ability of my money to buy has no effect on his obligation to pay me interest. In the same way, it is not the luck of all money to buy *zinss* or be invested in pawn-breaking and mortgaging; and yet some people want to buy or derive *zinss* from everything that can be used for that purpose. They are usurers, thieves, and robbers, for they are selling the luck of the money, which is not theirs and is not in their power. 'Nay,' you say, 'it can buy *zinss* from a piece of ground.' I answer, 'it does not do so yet, and perhaps it never will. Hans can take a Gretchen, but he has her not yet, and so he is not yet married. Your money can buy *zinss*; that is half of it, but the deal depends on the remaining part of it – the acceptance and the other half. I will not take half for full'.[66] But now the rich merchants want to sell the good fortune of their money, and that without any bad fortune, and sell the will and intentions of other people besides, because it rests with them whether the sale can be made. That is counting chickens before they are hatched.[67]

[86] Seventh. I say, further, that it is not enough that the grounds be there and be named, but the land must be described parcel by parcel and the money placed on it and the income to be got from it indicated, as, for example, the house, the garden, the

---

65. Here Luther uses the term *interesse*.
66. Original (WA 6, 56) has ßo *nym ich nit halb fur gantz*.
67. Original (WA 6, 56) has *das heyst die dreytzehende bern haud vorkaufft*, literally 'selling the bear skin before the bear has been killed'.

meadow, the pond, the cattle, and all this free and unsold and unencumbered. They must not play blind-man's-buff in the community and place a burden on the whole property. If this provision is not made, a whole town, or a poor man, must be sold in a sack and utterly ruined by the blind bargain, as we see happening now in many cities principalities and estates. The reason is this – the commerce of a city may decline, citizens become fewer, houses burn down, fields, meadows and all the ground run down and the goods and the cattle of every householder grow less, more children be borne; or it may be burdened with some other misfortune. Thus the wealth slips away, but the blind bargain, made with the whole property of the community, remains. Thus the poor and small remnant of wealth must bear the burden and expense of the whole former lot; and this can never be right. The buyer is sure of his *zinss* and has no risk, and this is against the nature of any real bargain; and it would not be so, if the property were described parcel by parcel, and the income were to fluctuate with the value of the ground, as is right.

[87] Eighth. The only way of defending this business against the charge of usury – inasmuch as it would do more than all other forms of *interesse* (financial market transactions discussed at present) – would be if the buyer of *zinss* had the same risk and uncertainty about his income that he has about all his other property. For with his property the provider of *zinss* (i.e. the one rendering the payment) is subject to the power of God – death, sickness, flood, fire, wind, hail, thunder, rain, wolves, wild beasts, and the manifold losses inflicted by wicked men. All these risks should be transferred to the lender or purchaser of *zinss*, for upon this, and on nothing else, the *zinss* rests; nor has he any right to receive *zinss* for his money, unless the payer of *zinss*, or seller of the property, specifically agrees, and can have free and entire and unhindered use of his own labour. This is proved from nature, reason, and all laws, which agree in saying that in a sale the risk lies with the buyer, for the seller is not bound to guarantee his wares to the buyer. Thus when I buy *zinss*, rent or any other sort of income from a particular piece of land, I do not buy the grounds as such, but the toil of the seller whilst working the ground, by which he is to bring me my income. I therefore take all the risk of hindrance that may come to his labour, insofar as it does not come from his fault or neglect, whether by the elements, beasts, men, sickness, or anything else. In these things the seller of the *zinß* has as great an interest as the buyer, so that if, after due diligence, his labour is unprofitable, he ought and can say freely to the receiver of the *zinss*, 'This year I owe you nothing, for I sold you my labour for the production of *zinss* from this and that property; I have not succeeded; the loss is yours and not mine; for if you would have interest on my profits, you must also have an interest in my losses, as the nature of a bargain requires.' The receivers of *zinss* payment (*zinss herrn*), who will not put up with that are just as pious as robbers and murderers, and wrest from the poor man his property and his living. Woe to them!

[88] Ninth. From this it follows that the blind *zinss kauff* which is based not on a designated piece of property, but on the land of a whole community, or many properties taken together, is wrong. The purchaser of *zinss* cannot show on what property the charge rests; he has, moreover, no risk, never accepts the possibility that income may fail here or there, and wants to be sure of his own rent payment.

[89] But perhaps you will say, 'If this were to be the case, who would buy *zinss?*' I answer: See there! I knew very well that if human nature were to do the right thing, it would turn up its nose. Now it comes out that in this trade in *zinss* the only things that are sought are safety, avarice, and usury. O how many cities, lands, and people must pay these charges upon interest, when it has long since been men's duty to remit them! For if there is no risk in this particular transaction, the purchase of *zinss* is, put simply, usury. With all ease and tranquillity they go about endowing churches and monasteries and altars and this and that, and yet there is no limit to the *zinss kauff*, just as though it were possible for wealth, people, luck, products, and labour to be alike in all years. However equal or unequal or irregular these things may turn out year after year, the charge upon interest (*zinss*) must go on at the same rate. Is this not bound to ruin land and people? I am surprised that the world still stands, with this boundless usury going on! It is thus that the world has improved! What in earlier days used to be called lending, has now been transformed into an interest-bearing asset transaction (*zinss kauff*).

[90] Tenth. The *zinss kauff* is sometimes made in such a way that *zinss* is bought from those to whom the buyer should rather lend or give something. That is utterly worthless, for God's commandment stands in the way, and it is His will that the needy shall be helped by (*interest-free, PRR*) loans, or gifts. Furthermore it happens that both buyer and seller need their property, and therefore neither of them can lend or give, but they have to help themselves with some sort of credit transaction (*kauffs wechsel*).[68] If this is done without breaking the church-law which provides for the payment of four, five, or six gulden on the hundred, it can be endured; but respect should be always had for the fear of God, which fears to take too much rather than too little, in order that avarice may not have its way into a decent business deal.[69] The smaller the percentage the more divine and Christian the deal. It is not my affair, however, to point out when one ought to pay five, four, or six per cent. I leave it for the law to decide when the property (*grund*) is so good and so rich that one can charge six per cent. It is my opinion, however, that if we were to keep Christ's command about the first three degrees, the *zinss kauff* would not be so common or so necessary, except in cases where the amounts were considerable and the properties large. But the practice has got down to *groats* (*groschen*) and pennies and deals with little sums that could easily be taken care of by gifts or loans in accordance with Christ's command. And yet they will not call this avarice.

[91] Eleventh. There are some who not only deal in petty sums mostly, but who also take too much interest – seven, eight, nine, ten per cent. The rulers ought to look into this. Here the poor common people are secretly imposed upon and severely oppressed.

---

68. It is not entirely clear whether Luther here refers to the *zinss kauf* including a mortgage aspect – as the older translations have assumed – or to any transaction settled upon credit (consumption or micro-credit), or even to the opportunity to clear obligations and extend credit for a transaction using bills of exchange or related transfer instruments. The phrase further on in the said paragraph, *wo der grund ßo gutt und reych ist* suggests that Luther meant above all the *zinss kauff*.

69. This passage has sometimes been taken as evidence of Luther acknowledging the legitimacy of interest in the order of up to six per cent per annum as legitimate – on certain transactions and specified circumstances.

For this reason these robbers and usurers often die an unnatural and sudden death, or come to a terrible end (as tyrants and robbers deserve); for God is a judge for the poor and those in need, as He often says in the Old Law.

[92] But then they say, 'The churches and the clergy do this and have done so, because this money is used for the service of God.' Truly if a man has nothing else to do than to justify usury, a worse thing could not be said about him; for he would take the innocent church and the clergy with him to the devil and lead them into sin. Leave the name of the Church out of it, and say, 'It is usury-seeking avarice that does not like to work to earn its bread, and so makes the name of the Church a cloak for idleness.'

[93] What sort of service to God are you doing? The service of God is to keep His commandments, so that no one steals, robs, overreaches and defrauds, or the like, but gives and lends to those in need. You would tear down this service of God in order to build churches, endow altars, and have masses read and prayers sung; though God has commanded none of these things, and with your 'service' to God you bring the true service to God to naught. Put in the first place the worship and service God has commanded, and let your chosen version of it come along behind. As I said above, if all the world were to take ten per cent per annum, the church endowments should keep strictly to the law, and take four or five, with fear; for they ought to let their light shine, and give an example to the worldly. Thus they turn things around, and would have freedom to leave God's commandments and His service in order to do evil and practice usury. If you would serve God your way, then serve Him without doing injustice to your neighbour, and without failing to keep God's commandments. For He says in Isaiah 61, 'For I the LORD love judgment, I hate robbery for burnt offering.'[70] The Wise Man also says, 'Honour the LORD with thy substance, and with the first fruits of all thine increase.'[71] But these overcharges are stolen from your neighbour, against God's commandment.

[94] Twelfth, But if anyone is afraid that the churches and endowments will go down, I say that it is better to take ten endowments and make of them one that is according to the will of God, than to keep many against God's commandment. What good does a service do you if it is against God's commandment and contrary to the true serving of God? You cannot serve God with two kinds of service that contradict one another, any more than you can serve two masters.

[95] There are also some simple folk who sell these *zinss* without having ground or other securities as collateral; or else sell more than the ground can bear. This leads to evident ruin. This matter is very dangerous and goes so far that it is hard to say enough about it. The best thing would be to turn back to the Gospel, approach it, and keep to Christian practices in commerce and business as has been said.

[96] There is also in this business a dangerous tendency, from which I fear that none of the buyers of *zinss* – at least very few of them – are free. That is that they want their income and their property to be sure and safe, and therefore place their money with others, instead of keeping it and taking risks. They very much prefer that other people

---

70. Isaiah 61:8.
71. Proverbs 3:9.

shall work with it and take the risks, so that they themselves can be idle and lazy, and yet stay rich or become rich. If that is not usury, it is very much akin to it. Briefly, it is against God. If you seek to take an advantage of your neighbour which you will not let him take of you, then love is gone and the natural law is broken. Now, I fear that, in this purchasing of *zinss*, we pay little heed to the success of our neighbour, if only our income and our property are safe, though safety is the very thing we ought not to seek. This is certainly a sign of greed or laziness, and although it does not make commerce worse, it is, nevertheless, sin in the eyes of God.

Part III. Addendum to the *Great Sermon on Usury* (1524)

[97] But down there in Saxony and Luneburg and Holstein, the thing is done so crudely that it would be no wonder if one man were to devour another. There they not only take nine or ten per cent, or whatever they can get, but they have also hitched a special device on to it. It goes this way – if a man lets me have a thousand florins upon *zinss*, I have to take, instead of cash, so many horses or cows, so much bacon, wheat, etc., which he cannot get rid of otherwise, or cannot sell for so high a price. Thus the money that I get amounts to scarcely half of the sum named in the obligation, say, to five hundred florins, though the goods and the cattle are of no use to me, or may bring me in scarcely one or two hundred florins. Behold! These fellows are not highway robbers, but common house thieves. What shall we say about this? These men are not men at all, but wolves and senseless beasts, who do not believe there is a God.

[98] In sum, for all this usury and unfair securing of income there is no better advice than to follow the law and example of Moses. We ought to bring all these *zinss* and other interest-bearing transactions under the ordinance that that which shall be taken or sold or given shall be a tithe, or in case of need a ninth, or an eighth, or a sixth. Thus everything would be fair, and all depend on the grace and blessing of God. If the tithe turned out well in one year, it would bring the creditor a large sum; if it turned out badly, the creditor would bear the same risk as the debtor, and both would have to look to God. In that case, the interest payment could not be fixed at any given amount, nor would that be necessary; it would always remain uncertain how much the tithe would yield and yet the tithe as such would be certain.

[99] The tithe, therefore, is the best of all fixed charges (*zinss*) and it has been in use since the beginning of the world. In the Old Law it is praised and established as the fairest of all arrangements according to divine and natural law. By it, if the tenth did not reach, or were not enough, one could take and sell a ninth, or fix any amount that the land or house could stand. Joseph fixed the fifth as the amount to be taken, or found it so fixed and customary in Egypt. For by this arrangement the divine law of fairness constantly abides, that the lender take the risk. If things turn out well, he takes his fifth; if they turn out badly, he takes so much less, as God gives, and has no definite and certain sum.

[100] But now that the *zinss kauff* is based on definite and specified amounts, which are to be paid equally, year after year, good and bad alike, it is clear that land and people must be ruined. The purchaser buys the same *zinss* for unequal and equal years, poor years and rich years alike; nay, he buys a blessing that God has not yet given for a blessing

that is already given. That can never be right, for by that means one sucks out another one's sweat and blood. Therefore it is no wonder that in the few years that the *zinss kauff* has been practiced, i.e., about a hundred years, all princedoms and lands have been impoverished and pawned and ruined.

[101] But if the purchase or *zinss* were based, not on produce, but on houses or places that were gained and acquired by manual labour, it could be justified by the law of Moses, by having a 'jubilee year'[72] in these things and not selling incomes from *zinss* in perpetuity. For I think that, since this business is in such a disordered state, we could have no better examples or laws than the laws which God provided for His people, and with which He ruled them. He is as wise as human reason can be, and we need not be ashamed to keep and follow the law of the Jews in this matter, for it is profitable and good.

[102] Emperor, kings, princes and lords ought to watch over this matter and look to their lands and peoples, to help them and rescue them from the horrible jaws of avarice, and things would be so much the better for them. The imperial diets should deal with this as one of the most necessary things, but they let this lie, and serve, meanwhile, the pope's tyranny, burdening lands and people more and more, until at last they must be destroyed because the land can no longer endure them, but must spew them out. God give them His light and grace. AMEN.

---

72. See Sedláček, *Economics of Good and Evil*, passim.

BIBLIOGRAPHY

Abel, Wilhelm. *Agrarkrisen und Agrarkonjunktur in Mitteleuropa vom 13. bis zum 19. Jahrhundert*, 3rd ed. Berlin, 1935; repr. Hamburg: Parey, 1978.
———. *Agricultural Fluctuations in Europe from the Thirteenth to the Twentieth Centuries*. London: Methuen, 1980.
———. 'Zur Entwicklung des Sozialprodukts in Deutschland im 16. Jahrhundert', *Jahrbücher für Nationalökonomie und Statistik* 173 (1961): 448–89.
———. *Massenarmut und Hungerkrisen im vorindustriellen Deutschland*. Göttingen: Vandenhoeck, 1971.
Acemoglu, Daron, Simon Johnson and James A. Robinson. 'The Rise of Europe: Atlantic Trade, Institutional Change, and Economic Growth', *American Economic Review* 95, no. 3 (2005): 546–79.
Acemoglu, Daron and James A. Robinson. *Why Nations Fail: The Origins of Power, Prosperity, and Poverty*. New York: Crown, 2012.
Acham, Karl, Knut Wolfgang Nörr and Bertram Schefold, eds. *Erkenntnisgewinne, Erkenntnisverluste. Kontinuitäten und Diskontinuitäten in den Wirtschafts-, Rechts- und Sozialwissenschaften zwischen den 20er und 50er Jahren*. Stuttgart: Franz Steiner, 1998.
Aland, Kurt, ed. *Luther Deutsch. Die Werke Martin Luthers in neuer Auswahl für die Gegenwart, Vol. 9, Martin Luther Tischreden*, 3rd ed. Stuttgart: Klotz, 1960.
Appleby, Joyce O. *The Relentless Revolution: A History of Capitalism*. New York: W. W. Norton, 2010.
Arena, Richard, and Christian Longhi, eds. *Markets and Organization*. Berlin: Springer, 1998.
Atkinson, James, ed. *Luther's Works, Vol. 44, Christian in Society I*. Philadelphia: Fortress, 1966.
Backhaus, Jürgen G., ed. *The Reformation as a Precondition for Capitalism*. Münster: LIT Verlag, 2010.
Backhouse, Roger. *A History of Modern Economic Analysis*. London: Basil Blackwell, 1985.
Barge, Hermann. *Luther und der Frühkapitalismus*. Gütersloh: C. Bertelsmann, 1951.
Bauer, Clemens. 'Conrad Peutingers Gutachten zur Monopolfrage', *Archiv für Reformationsgeschichte* 45 (1954): 1–43, 145–96.
———. 'Conrad Peutinger und der Durchbruch des neuen ökonomischen Denkens an der Wende zur Neuzeit'. In *Augusta 955–1955*. Edited by Hermann Rinn. Munich: Rinn, 1955.
———. *Gesammelte Aufsätze zur Wirtschafts- und Sozialgeschichte*. Freiburg i. B. : Herder, 1965.
———. 'Wirtschaftsgeschichtliche Probleme des fünfzehnten Jahrhunderts'. In *Die Welt zur Zeit des Konstanzer Konzils*. Edited by T. Mayer, 83–98. Konstanz: Thorbecke, 1965.
Bauernfeind, Walter. *Materielle Grundstrukturen im Spätmittelalter und der Frühen Neuzeit. Preisentwicklung und Agrarkonjunktur am Nürnberger Getreidemarkt von 1339 bis 1670*. Nuremberg: Schriftenreihe des Stadtarchivs, 1993.
Baum, H. -P. 'Annuities in Late Medieval Hanse Towns', *The Business History Review* 59, no. 1 (1985): 24–48.
Bayerische Akademie der Wissenschaften, eds. *Die Chroniken der baierischen Städte. Regensburg. Landshut. Mühldorf. München*. Leipzig: S. Hirzel, 1878.
Baylor, Michael G. *The German Reformation and the Peasants' War. A Brief History with Documents*. Boston: Bedford/St Martin's, 2012.
Bechtel, Heinrich. *Wirtschaftsstil im Spätmittelalter. Ausdruck der Lebensform in Wirtschaft, Gesellschaftsaufbau und Kunst von 1350 bis um 1500*. Munich: Duncker & Humblot, 1930.
Beck, Rainer. *Mäuselmacher oder die Imagination des Bösen. Ein Hexenprozess 1715–1723*. Munich: C. H. Beck, 2011.
Beck, Ulrich. *Risikogesellschaft: Auf dem Weg in eine andere Moderne*. Frankfurt: Suhrkamp, 1986.
———. *Macht und Gegenmacht im globalen Zeitalter: Neue weltpolitische Ökonomie*. Frankfurt: Suhrkamp, 2009.

Becker, Christoph, and Hans-Georg Hermann, eds. *Ökonomie und Recht – historische Entwicklungen in Bayern*. Münster: Lit, 2009.

Becker, Gary S. *The Economic Approach to Human Behavior*. Chicago, IL: University of Chicago Press, 1976.

Benchimol, J. 'Risk Aversion in the Eurozone', *Research in Economics* 68, no. 1 (2014): 39–56.

Bentzinger, Rudolf, ed. *Die Wahrheit muß ans Licht! Dialoge aus der Zeit der Reformation*. Leipzig: Reclam, 1982.

Beyer, Michael, Jonas Flöter and Markus Hein, eds. *Christlicher Glaube und weltliche Herrschaft. Zum Gedenken an Günther Wartenberg*. Leipzig: Evangelische Verlagsanstalt, 2008.

Blaich, Fritz. *Die Reichsmonopolgesetzgebung im Zeitalter Karls V. Ihre ordnungspolitische Problematik*. Stuttgart: G. Fischer, 1967.

———. *Die Wirtschaftspolitik des Reichstags im Heiligen Römischen Reich: Ein Beitrag zur Problemgeschichte wirtschaftlichen Gestaltens*. Stuttgart: G. Fischer, 1970.

Blanchard, Ian. *The International Economy in the 'Age of the Discoveries', 1470–1570. Antwerp and the English Merchants' World*. Edited by P. Rössner. Stuttgart: Franz Steiner, 2009.

———. *International Lead Production and Trade in the 'Age of the Saigerprozess'*. Stuttgart: Franz Steiner, 1995.

Blaschke, Karlheinz. 'Dorfgemeinde und Stadtgemeinde in Sachsen zwischen 1300 und 1800'. In *Landgemeinde und Stadtgemeinde in Mitteleuropa*. Edited by Peter Blickle, 119–43. Munich: Oldenbourg, 1991.

Blaug, Mark. ed. *Pioneers in Economics 4, The Early Mercantilists: Thomas Mun (1571–1641), Edward Misselden (1608–1634), Gerard de Malynes (1586–1623)*. Aldershot: E. Elgar, 1991.

———. ed. *Pioneers in Economics 5, The Later Mercantilists: Josiah Child (1603–1699) and John Locke (1632–1704)*. Aldershot: E. Elgar, 1991.

———. ed. *St. Thomas Aquinas (1225–1274)*. Aldershot: E. Elgar, 1991.

Blickle, Peter. *Der Bauernkrieg. Die Revolution des Gemeinen Mannes*. 4th ed. Munich: Beck, 2012.

———. ed. *Landgemeinde und Stadtgemeinde in Mitteleuropa*. Munich: Oldenbourg, 1991.

———. *Die Reformation im Reich*. 3rd ed. Stuttgart: Ulmer, 2000.

———. *Die Revolution von 1525*. 4th ed. Munich: Oldenbourg, 2004.

———. *Unruhen in der ständischen Gesellschaft 1300–1800*. 2nd ed. Munich: Oldenbourg, 2010.

Block, Fred L., and Margaret R. Somers. *The Power of Market Fundamentalism: Karl Polanyi's Critique*. Cambridge, MA: Harvard University Press, 2014.

Boldizzoni, Francesco. *Means and Ends: The Idea of Capital in the West, 1500–1970*. Basingstoke: Palgrave Macmillan, 2008.

———. *The Poverty of Clio. Resurrecting Economic History*. Princeton, NJ: Princeton University Press, 2011.

Brady, Thomas A., ed. *Die deutsche Reformation zwischen Spätmittelalter und Früher Neuzeit*. Munich: Oldenbourg, 2001.

Brandt, Walther I., and Helmut T. Lehmann, eds. *Luther's Works, Vol. 45: Christian in Society II*. Philadelphia, : University of Philadelphia Press, 1962.

Braudel, Fernand. *Civilisation matérielle, économie et capitalisme (XVe–XVIIIe siècles)*, Engl. trans. S. Reynolds, *Civilization and Capitalism, 15th–18th century*. New York: Harper & Row, 1982–84.

Brecht, Martin. *Martin Luther, Vol. 1. Sein Weg zur Reformation: 1483–1521*. Stuttgart: Calwer Verlag, 1994.

Brenner, Robert. *Merchants and Revolution: Commercial Change, Political Conflict, and London's Overseas Traders, 1550–1653*. Princeton, NJ: Princeton University Press, 1993.

Brunner, Otto, Werner Conze and Reinhart Koselleck, eds. *Geschichtliche Grundbegriffe. Historisches Lexikon zur politisch-sozialen Sprache in Deutschland*. Vol. 7. Stuttgart: Klett-Cotta, 1992.

Bünz, Enno, Stefan Tebruck and Helmut G. Walther, eds. *Religiöse Bewegungen im Mittelalter. Festschrift für Matthias Werner zum 65. Geburtstag*. Cologne: Böhlau, 2007.

Burkhardt, Johannes. 'Wirtschaft, IV–VII'. In *Geschichtliche Grundbegriffe. Historisches Lexikon zur politisch-sozialen Sprache in Deutschland*. Edited by Otto Brunner, Werner Conze and Reinhart Koselleck. Vol. 7, 550–59. Stuttgart: Klett-Cotta, 1992.

—— and Birger P. Priddat, eds. *Geschichte der Ökonomie*. Frankfurt: Deutscher Klassiker Verlag, 2009.

Cameron, Euan. ed. *The European Reformation*. 2nd ed. Oxford: Oxford University Press, 2012.

——. *The Short Oxford History of Europe: The Sixteenth Century*. Oxford: Oxford University Press, 2006.

Cassone, Alberto and Carla Marchese. 'The Economics of Religious Indulgences', *Journal of Institutional and Theoretical Economics (JITE) / Zeitschrift für die gesamte Staatswissenschaft* 155, no. 3 (Sept. 1999): 429–42.

Castro, Armando. *História Económica de Portugal, Vol. 3: Séculos XV*-*XVI*. Lisbon: Editorial Caminho, 1985.

Cauwenberghe, Eddy H. G. Van. ed. *Precious Metals, Coinage and the Changes of Monetary Structures in Latin-America, Europe and Asia (Late Middle Ages–Early Modern Times)*. Leuven: Leuven University Press, 1989.

Chang, Ha-Joon. *Kicking Away the Ladder: Development Strategy in Historical Perspective*. London: Anthem, 2003.

Chilosi, David, and Oliver Volckart. 'Money, States, and Empire: Financial Integration and Institutional Change in Central Europe, 1400–1520', *The Journal of Economic History* 71, no. 3 (2011): 762–91.

Classen, Albrecht, ed. *Medieval Culture: A Compendium of Critical Topics*. Berlin and New York: De Gruyter, forthcoming, 2015.

Coleman, Donald C., ed. *Revisions in Mercantilism*. London: Methuen, 1969.

Cordes, Albrecht, et al., eds. *Handwörterbuch zur deutschen Rechtsgeschichte*. 2nd ed., 4th delivery, Berlin: Schmidt, 2008.

Crebert, Heinrich. *Künstliche Preissteigerung durch Für- und Aufkauf. Ein Beitrag zur Geschichte des Handelsrechts*. Heidelberg: Carl Winter, 1916.

Day, John. 'The Great Bullion Famine of the Fifteenth Century', *Past & Present* 79 (1978): 3–54.

——. 'The Question of Monetary Contraction in Late Medieval Europe'. In *Coinage and Monetary Circulation in the Baltic Area, c. 1350–c. 1500*. Edited by Jørgen Steen Jensen, 12–29, Copenhagen: Nordisk Numismatisk Unions Medlemsblad, Nationalmuseet, 1982.

Denzel, Markus A. *Handbook of World Exchange Rates, 1590–1914*. Farnham: Ashgate, 2010.

——. *Das System des bargeldlosen Zahlungsverkehrs europäischer Prägung vom Mittelalter bis 1914*. Stuttgart: Franz Steiner, 2008.

——, ed. *Wirtschaft – Politik – Geschichte. Beiträge zum Gedenkkolloquium anläßlich des 100. Geburtstages von Wilhelm Abel am 16. Oktober 2004 in Leipzig*. Stuttgart: Franz Steiner, 2004.

Dietrich, Richard. *Untersuchungen zum Frühkapitalismus im mitteldeutschen Erzbergbau und Metallhandel*. Hildesheim: Olms 1991.

Dinzelbacher, Peter. *Das fremde Mittelalter. Gottesurteil und Tierprozess*. Essen: Magnus, 2006.

Dirlmeier, Ulf. *Untersuchungen zu Einkommensverhältnissen und Lebenshaltungskosten in oberdeutschen Städten des Spätmittelalters* (Mitte 14. bis Anfang 16. Jh.). Heidelberg: Winter, 1978.

Dreissig, Wilhelmine. *Die Geld- und Kreditlehre des deutschen Merkantilismus*. Berlin: Dr. Emil Ebering, 1939.

Drelichman, Mauricio, and Hans-Joachim Voth. *Lending to the Borrower from Hell: Debt, Taxes, and Default in the Age of Philip II*. Princeton, NJ: Princeton University Press, 2014.

DuPlessis, Robert S. *Transitions to Capitalism in Early Modern Europe*. Cambridge: Cambridge University Press, 1997.

Durlauf, Steven N., and Lawrence E. Blume, eds. *The New Palgrave Dictionary of Economics*. 2nd ed. Vol. 6. Basingstoke: Palgrave Macmillan, 2008.

Ebner, Herwig, et al., eds. *Festschrift Othmar Pickl zum 60. Geburtstag*. Graz: Leykam, 1987.

Eibach, Joachim, and Günther Lottes, eds. *Kompass der Geschichtswissenschaft. Ein Handbuch.* Göttingen: Vandenhoeck & Ruprecht, 2002.

Eichengreen, Barry J. *The European Economy since 1945: Coordinated Capitalism and Beyond.* Princeton, NJ: Princeton University Press, 2007.

Ekelund, Robert E., and Robert D. Tollison. *Mercantilism as a Rent-seeking Society: Economic Regulation in Historical Perspective.* College Station: Texas A&M University Press, 1981.

Ekelund, Robert B., Jr., Robert F. Hebert and Robert D. Tollison. 'An Economic Model of the Medieval Church: Usury as a Form of Rent Seeking', *Journal of Law, Economics, & Organization* 5 (1989): 307–31.

Elsas, Moritz J. *Umriss einer Geschichte der Preise und Löhne in Deutschland vom ausgehenden Mittelalter bis zum Beginn des neunzehnten Jahrhunderts.* 3 vols. Leiden: A. W. Sijthoff, 1936–49.

Emig, Joachim. Volker Leppin and Uwe Schirmer, eds. *Vor- und Frühreformation in Thüringischen Städten (1470–1525/30).* Cologne: Böhlau, 2013.

Endemann, Wilhelm. *Studien in der romanisch-kanonistischen Wirthschafts- und Rechtslehre bis gegen Ende des siebenzehnten Jahrhunderts.* Berlin, 1883.

Epstein, Stephen R. *Freedom and Growth. The Rise of States and Markets in Europe, 1300–1750.* London: Routledge, 2000.

Erikson, Erik H. *Young Man Luther: A Study in Psychoanalysis and History.* London: Faber & Faber, 1958.

Erler, Adalbert and Ekkehard Kaufmann, eds. *Handwörterbuch zur Deutschen Rechtsgeschichte.* Vol. 1. Berlin: Erich Schmidt Verlag, 1971.

Esping-Andersen, Gösta. *Social Foundations of Postindustrial Economies.* Oxford: Oxford University Press, 1999.

Evans, Eric J. *Thatcher and Thatcherism.* 2nd ed. London: Routledge, 2004.

Fabiunke, Günter. *Martin Luther als Nationalökonom.* Berlin [East]: Akademie Verlag, 1963.

Feinman, G. M., and C. P. Garraty. 'Preindustrial Markets and Marketing: Archaeological Perspectives', *Annual Review of Anthropology* 39 (2010): 167–91.

Fergusson, Niall. *The Great Degeneration. How Institutions Decay and Economies Die.* London: Allen Lane, 2012.

Flynn, Dennis O., Arturo Giráldez and Richard von Glahn, eds. *Global Connections and Monetary History, 1470–1800.* Aldershot: Ashgate, 2003.

Friedensburg, Ferdinand. *Münzkunde und Geldgeschichte der Einzelstaaten des Mittelalters und der Neueren Zeit.* Munich: R. Oldenbourg, 1926.

Friedman, Thomas L. *The World Is Flat: A Brief History of the Twenty-first Century.* New York: Farrar, Straus and Giroux, 2005.

Fuchs, Walther Peter, ed. *Akten zur Geschichte des Bauernkriegs in Mitteldeutschland.* Vol. 2. Leipzig: Teubner, 1942.

Fudge, Thomas A. *Jan Hus, Religious Reform and Social Revolution in Bohemia.* London: Tauris, 2010.

———. *The Trials of Jan Hus. Medieval Heresy and Criminal Procedure.* Oxford: Oxford University Press, 2013.

Fuhrmann, Bernd. *Der Haushalt der Stadt Marburg in Spätmittelalter und Früher Neuzeit (1451/52–1622).* St Katharinen: Scripta Mercaturae Verlag, 1996.

Garbrecht, Oliver. *Rationalitätskritik der Moderne: Adorno und Heidegger.* Munich: Utz, 2002.

Gauci, Perry, ed. *Regulating the British Economy, 1660–1850.* Farnham: Ashgate, 2011.

Geertz, Clifford. 'The Bazaar Economy: Information and Search in Peasant Marketing', *American Economic Review* 68 (1978): 28–32.

Geisst, Charles R. *Beggar Thy Neighbor: A History of Usury and Debt.* Philadelphia: University of Pennsylvania Press, 2013.

Gelderblom, Oscar. *Cities of Commerce: The Institutional Foundations of International Trade in the Low Countries, 1250–1650.* Princeton, NJ: Princeton University Press, 2013.

Gerhard, Hans-Jürgen. 'Miszelle: Neuere deutsche Forschungen zur Geld- und Währungsgeschichte der Frühen Neuzeit. Fragen – Ansätze – Erkenntnisse', *Vierteljahrschrift für Sozial- und Wirtschaftsgeschichte* 83 (1996): 216–30.

———. 'Preise als wirtschaftshistorische Indikatoren. Wilhelm Abels preishistorische Untersuchungen aus heutiger Sicht'. In *Wirtschaft – Politik – Geschichte. Beiträge zum Gedenkkolloquium anläßlich des 100. Geburtstages von Wilhelm Abel am 16. Oktober 2004 in Leipzig*. Edited by Markus A. Denzel, 37–58, Stuttgart: Franz Steiner, 2004.

———. 'Ein schöner Garten ohne Zaun. Die währungspolitische Situation des Deutschen Reiches um 1600', *Vierteljahrschrift für Sozial- und Wirtschaftsgeschichte* 81 (1994): 156–77.

———. 'Ursachen und Folgen der Wandlungen im Währungssystem des Deutschen Reiches 1500–1625. Eine Studie zu den Hintergründen der sogenannten Preisrevolution'. In *Geld und Währung vom 16. Jahrhundert bis zur Gegenwart*. Edited by Eckart Schremmer, 69–84, Stuttgart: Franz Steiner, 1993.

——— and Alexander Engel. *Preisgeschichte der vorindustriellen Zeit. Ein Kompendium auf Basis ausgewählter Hamburger Materialien*. Stuttgart: Franz Steiner, 2006.

———. *Wesen und Wirkung vorindustrieller Taxen: Preishistorische Würdigung einer wichtigen Quellengattung*. Stuttgart: Franz Steiner, 2009.

——— and Karl Heinrich Kaufhold, *Preise im Vor- und Frühindustriellen Deutschland. Nahrungsmittel – Getränke – Gewürze, Rohstoffe und Gewerbeprodukte*. Stuttgart: Franz Steiner, 2001.

Gibson, A. J. S., and T. Christopher Smout. *Prices, Food and Wages in Scotland 1550–1780*. Cambridge: Cambridge University Press, 1995.

Giddens, Anthony. *Capitalism and Modern Social Theory. An Analysis of the Writings of Marx, Durkheim and Max Weber*. Cambridge: Cambridge University Press, 1971.

———. *The Consequences of Modernity*. Stanford: Stanford University Press, 1990.

———. *Runaway World: How Globalization is Reshaping Our Lives*. New York: Routledge, 2000.

Glaser, Rüdiger. *Klimageschichte Mitteleuropas. 1200 Jahre Wetter, Klima, Katastrophen*. 2nd ed. Darmstadt: Wissenschaftliche Buchgesellschaft, 2008.

Godelier, Maurice. *The Enigma of the Gift*. Chicago: University of Chicago Press, 1999.

Godinho, Vitorino Magalhães. *Os descobrimentos e a economia mundial*. Lisbon: Editorial Presença, 1981–83.

Goldberg, J. L. 'Choosing and Enforcing Business Relationships in the Eleventh-Century Mediterranean: Reassessing the "Maghribi Traders"', *Past & Present* 216 (2012): 3–40.

Goldstone, Jack A. 'Lessons from the English Price Revolution of the Sixteenth and Seventeenth Centuries', *The American Journal of Sociology* 89 (1984): 1122–60.

Greif, Avner. *Institutions and the Path to the Modern Economy: Lessons from Medieval Trade*. Cambridge: Cambridge University Press, 2006.

Grice-Hutchinson, Marjorie. 'Contributions of the School of Salamanca to Monetary Theory as a Result of the Discovery of the New World'. In *Economic Thought in Spain. Selected Essays*. Ead. 1–22.

———. *Early Economic Thought in Spain 1170–1740*. London: Allen & Unwin, 1978.

———. *Economic Thought in Spain. Selected Essays*. Edited by Laurence S. Moss and Christopher K. Ryan. Aldershot: E. Elgar, 1993.

———. 'Martin de Azpilcuetas "Comentario resolutorio de Cambios"'. In *Vademecum zu zwei Klassikern des Spanischen Wirtschaftsdenkens*. Edited by Bertram Schefold. Düsseldorf: Verlag Wirtschaft und Finanzen, 1998. 49–72.

———. 'The Concept of the School of Salamanca: Its Origins and Development'. In *Economic Thought in Spain. Selected Essays*. Ead. 23–29.

———. *The School of Salamanca. Readings in Spanish Monetary Theory 1544–1605*. Oxford: Clarendon Press, 1952.

Grierson, Philip. *Numismatics*. Oxford: Oxford University Press, 1975.

Grimm, Jacob, and Wilhelm Grimm. *Deutsches Wörterbuch*. 16 vols. Leipzig: S. Hirzel; Munich: Deutscher Taschenbuch Verlag, 1854–1971.

Häberlein, Mark. *The Fuggers of Augsburg: Pursuing Wealth and Honor in Renaissance Germany*. Charlottesville: University of Virginia Press, 2012.

Häbler, Konrad. *Die überseeischen Unternehmungen der Welser*. Leipzig: C. L. Hirschfeld, 1903.

Hahn, Karl. 'Die ältesten Schneeberger Zehntrechnungen', *Neues Archiv für Sächsische Geschichte und Altertumskunde*, 53 (1932): 35–50.

Hall, Hubert. *A History of the Custom-revenue in England: From the Earliest Times to the Year 1827*. London: E. Stock, 1892.

Hamilton, Earl J. *American Treasure and the Price Revolution in Spain, 1501–1650*. New York: Octagon, 1934.

Hann, Chris M., and Keith Hart. *Economic Anthropology: History, Ethnography, Critique*. Cambridge: Polity, 2011.

Harcourt, Bernard. *The Illusion of Free Markets: Punishment and the Myth of Natural Order*. Cambridge, MA: Harvard University Press, 2011.

Hattenhauer, Christian. 'Bürgschaft'. In *Handwörterbuch zur deutschen Rechtsgeschichte*, 2nd ed., 4th delivery, col. 770–74. Edited by Albrecht Cordes et al. Berlin: Schmidt, 2008.

Heckenast, Gusztáv, ed. *Aus der Geschichte der ostmitteleuropäischen Bauernbewegungen im 16. –17. Jahrhundert*. Budapest: Akadémiai Kiadó, 1977.

———. 'Die mitteleuropäische Handels- und Finanzkrise der Jahre 1512/1513 un (sic) der ungarische Bauernkrieg'. In *Aus der Geschichte. id.* ed. 107–12.

Heckscher, Eli F. *Der Merkantilismus*. 2 Vols. Trans. G. Mackenroth. Jena: G. Fischer, 1932.

Herzog, Lisa, and Axel Hometh, eds. *Der Wert des Marktes: Ein ökonomisch-philosophischer Diskurs vom 18. Jahrhundert bis zur Gegenwart*. Berlin: Suhrkamp, 2013.

Hesse, Helmut, and Gerhard Müller, eds. *Über Luthers 'Von Kauffshandlung und Wucher'. Vademecum zu einem frühen Klassiker der Weltliteratur*. Frankfurt: Verlag Wirtschaft und Finanzen, 1987.

Hilferding, Rudolf. *Das Finanzkapital: Eine Studie über die jüngste Entwicklung des Kapitalismus*. Vienna: Brandt, 1910.

Hirschman, Albert O. *Entwicklung, Markt und Moral – Abweichende Betrachtungen*. Munich: Hanser, 1989.

Historische Kommission bei der Bayerischen Akademie der Wissenschaften, eds. *Die Chronik von Clemens Sender, Die Chroniken der schwäbischen Städte, Augsburg*. Vol. 4. Leipzig: S. Hirzel, 1894.

Höffner, Josef. *Wirtschaftsethik und Monopole im fünfzehnten und sechzehnten Jahrhundert*. Jena: G. Fischer, 1941.

Hollaender, A. 'Die vierundzwanzig Artikel gemeiner Landschaft Salzburg 1525', *Mitteilungen der Gesellschaft für Salzburger Landeskunde* 71 (1931): 65–88.

Homer, Sidney, and Richard Sylla. *A History of Interest Rates*. New Brunswick: Rutgers University Press, 1991.

Hoppit, Julian. 'Bounties, the Economy and the State in Britain, 1689–1800'. In *Regulating the British Economy, 1660–1850*. Edited by Perry Gauci. Farnham: Ashgate, 2011): 139–60.

———. 'The Nation, the State, and the First Industrial Revolution'. *The Journal of British Studies* 50, no. 2 (2011): 307–31.

Howell, Martha C. *Commerce before Capitalism in Europe, 1300–1600*. Cambridge: Cambridge University Press, 2010.

Hümmerich, Franz. *Die ersten deutschen Handelsfahrten nach Indien 1505 und 1506*. Munich: Oldenbourg, 1922.

Hutchison, Terence. *Before Adam Smith. The Emergence of Political Economy 1662–1776*. Oxford: Oxford University Press, 1988.

Ingrao, Bruno. 'Free Market'. In *Markets and Organization*. Edited by Richard Arena and Christian Longhi, 61–94. Berlin: Springer, 1998.

Internationales Autorenkollektiv, eds. *Geschichte der ökonomischen Lehrmeinungen*. Berlin, 1965.

Iseli, Andrea. *Gute Policey. Öffentliche Ordnung in der frühen Neuzeit*. Stuttgart: Ulmer, 2009.

Isenmann, Eberhard. *Die Deutsche Stadt im Mittelalter 1150–1550*. Cologne: Böhlau, 2012.

Isenmann, Moritz, ed. *Merkantilismus. Wiederaufnahme einer Debatte*. Stuttgart: Franz Steiner, 2014.

Issing, Otmar, ed. *Geschichte der Nationalökonomie*. 4th ed. Munich: Vahlen, 2002.

James, Harold. *The Creation and Destruction of Value: The Globalization Cycle*. Cambridge, MA: Harvard University Press, 2009.

Jensen, Jørgen Steen, ed. *Coinage and Monetary Circulation in the Baltic Area, c. 1350–c. 1500*. Copenhagen: Nordisk Numismatisk Unions Medlemsblad, Nationalmuseet, 1982.

Jones, David Wayne. *Reforming the Morality of Usury: A Study of Differences that Separated the Protestant Reformers*. Dallas: University Press of America, 2004.

Jones, Eric L. *The European Miracle: Environments, Economies and Geopolitics in the History of Europe and Asia*. 3rd ed. Cambridge: Cambridge University Press, 2003.

Jordan, Stefan. *Theorien und Methoden der Geschichtswissenschaft. Orientierung Geschichte*. Paderborn: Schöningh, 2009.

Junghans, Helmar, ed. *Leben und Werk Martin Luthers von 1526 bis 1546*. Vol. I. Berlin: Evangelische Verlagsanstalt, 1983.

———, ed. *Luthers Ethik: Christliches Leben in ecclesia, oeconomia, politica = Luther's Ethics in the Realms of Church, Household, Politics. Referate und Berichte des Elften Internationalen Kongresses für Lutherforschung, Canoas/RS 21–27 July 2007*. Göttingen: Vandenhoeck & Ruprecht, 2010.

Karant-Nunn, Susan. "'Fast wäre mir ein weibliches Gemüt verblieben": Martin Luthers Männlichkeit'. In *Luther zwischen den Kulturen*. Edited by Hans Medick and Peter Schmidt, 49–65. Göttingen: Vandenhoeck & Ruprecht, 2004.

Kaufmann, E. 'Bürgschaft'. In *Handwörterbuch zur Deutschen Rechtsgeschichte*. Vol. 1, 565–69. Edited by Adalbert Erler and Ekkehard Kaufmann. Berlin: Erich Schmidt Verlag, 1971.

Kaufmann, Thomas. *Geschichte der Reformation*. Frankfurt: Verlag der Weltreligionen, 2009.

Kiessling, Rolf. 'Im Spannungsfeld von Markt und Recht'. In *Ökonomie und Recht – historische Entwicklungen in Bayern*. Edited by Christoph Becker and Hans-Georg Hermann, 73–98. Münster: LIT Verlag, 2009.

———. *Die Stadt und ihr Land. Umlandpolitik, Bürgerbesitz und Wirtschaftsgefüge in Ostschwaben vom 14. bis ins 16. Jahrhundert*. Cologne: Böhlau 1989.

Klueting, Harm. *Das konfessionelle Zeitalter Europa zwischen Mittelalter und Moderne. Kirchengeschichte und allgemeine Geschichte*. Darmstadt: Wissenschaftliche Buchgesellschaft, 2007.

Knape, Rosemarie, ed. *Martin Luther und der Bergbau im Mansfelder Land*. Lutherstadt Eisleben: Stiftung Luthergedenkstätten in Sachsen-Anhalt, 2000.

Koch, Philipp. *Gerechtes Wirtschaften: das Problem der Gerechtigkeit in der Wirtschaft im Lichte lutherischer Ethik*. Göttingen: V & R unipress, 2012.

Kocka, Jürgen. *Geschichte des Kapitalismus*. Munich: C. H. Beck, 2013.

Kolb, Gerhard. *Geschichte der Volkswirtschaftslehre. Dogmenhistorische Positionen des ökonomischen Denkens*. 2nd ed. Munich: Vahlen, 2004.

Koselleck, Reinhart, Wolfgang J. Mommsen and Jörn Rüsen, eds. *Objektivität und Parteilichkeit in der Geschichtswissenschaft*. Munich: Deutscher Taschenbuchverlag, 1977.

Koslowski, Peter. *Prinzipien der ethischen Ökonomie*. Tübingen: J. C. B. Mohr, 1988.

———, ed. *The Theory of Ethical Economy in the Historical School: Wilhelm Roscher, Lorenz von Stein, Gustav Schmoller, Wilhelm Dilthey and Contemporary Theory*. Berlin: Springer, 1995.

Kroker, Werner, and Ekkehard Westermann, eds. *Montanwirtschaft Mitteleuropas vom 12. bis 17. Jahrhundert. Stand, Wege und Aufgaben der Forschung*. Bochum: Vereinigung der Freunde von Kunst und Kultur im Bergbau, 1984.

Krugman, Paul R., Maurice Obstfeld and Marc J. Melitz. *International Economics. Theory and Policy*. 15th ed. Boston: Pearson, forthcoming.

Kula, Witold. *An Economic Theory of the Feudal System: Towards a Model of the Polish Economy 1500–1800*. London: NLB, 1976.

Kurz, Heinz D. *Geschichte des ökonomischen Denkens*. Munich: Beck, 2013.

Lambert, Malcolm. *Medieval Heresy. Popular Movements from the Gregorian Reform to the Reformation*. 2nd ed. Oxford: Blackwell, 1992.

Landes, David S. *The Wealth and Poverty of Nations. Why Some Are So Rich and Others So Poor*. New York: W. W. Norton, 1998.

Landwehr, Achim. *Geburt der Gegenwart: Eine Geschichte der Zeit im 17. Jahrhundert*. Frankfurt: Fischer, 2014.

———. *Policey im Alltag: Die Implementation frühneuzeitlicher Policeyordnungen in Leonberg*. Frankfurt: Klostermann, 2000.

Lane, Frederic C., and Reinhold C. Mueller. *Money and Banking in Medieval and Renaissance Venice, Vol. I: Coins and Moneys of Account*. Baltimore: Johns Hopkins University Press, 1985.

Langholm, Odd Inge. *Economics in the Medieval Schools: Wealth, Exchange, Value, Money and Usury According to the Paris Theological Tradition 1200–1350*. Leiden: Brill, 1992.

———. *The Legacy of Scholasticism in Economic Thought. Antecedents of Choice and Power*. Cambridge: Cambridge University Press, 1998.

———. 'Martin Luther's Doctrine on Trade and Price in Its Literary Context', *History of Political Economy* 41, no. 1 (2009): 89–107.

———. 'Monopoly and Market Irregularities in Medieval Thought', *Journal of the History of Economic Thought* 28 (2006): 395–411.

Laube, Adolf, Annerose Schneider and Sigrid Looss, eds. *Flugschriften der frühen Reformationsbewegung (1518–1524)*. Vol. 1. Berlin [East]: Akademie Verlag, 1983.

———, Max Steinmetz and Günter Vogler. *Illustrierte Geschichte der deutschen frühbürgerlichen Revolution*. Berlin [East]: Dietz, 1974.

Laures, John. *The Political Economy of Juan de Mariana*. New York: Fordham University Press, 1928.

LeGoff, Jacques. *The Birth of Purgatory*. Chicago: University of Chicago Press, 1984.

Lehmann, Helmut T., ed. and E. Theodore Bachmann, gen. ed. *Luther's Works, Vol. 35: Word and Sacrament I*. Philadelphia: Fortress Press, 1960.

Leppin, Volker. *Martin Luther*. Darmstadt: Wissenschaftliche Buchgesellschaft, 2006.

———. *Die Reformation*. Darmstadt: Wissenschaftliche Buchgesellschaft, 2013.

Lopez, Robert S. *The Commercial Revolution of the Middle Ages, 950–1350*. Cambridge: Cambridge University Press, 1995.

Luschin v. Ebengreuth, Arnold. *Allgemeine Münzkunde und Geldgeschichte des Mittelalters und der Neueren Zeit*. 2nd ed. Munich: R. Oldenbourg, 1926.

Lütdke, Alf. *Herrschaft als soziale Praxis: Historische und sozial-anthropologische Studien*. Göttingen: Vandenhoeck & Ruprecht, 1991.

Lütge, Friedrich. *Geschichte der deutschen Agrarverfassung vom frühen Mittelalter bis zum 19. Jahrhundert*. Stuttgart: Ulmer, 1963.

Luther, Martin. *Gesammelte Werke*. 120 vols. Weimar: Böhlau, 1883–2009 [*usually abbreviated WA*].

Martin Luther's Tischreden I, Meyers Volksbücher. Leipzig: Bibliographisches Institut: 1906.

Martin Luther's Tischreden III. Von guten Werken – vom Gebet. Leipzig: Bibliographisches Institut, 1906.

Martin Luther's Tischreden V. Vom Ehestande. Leipzig: Bibliographisches Institut, 1903.

Works of Martin Luther. Vol. 4. Philadelphia, PA: A. J. Holman/Castle Press, 1931.

Schulz, Robert C., and Helmut T. Lehmann. eds. *Luther's Works, Vol. 46, Christian in Society III*. Philadelphia: Fortress, 1967.

Tappert, Theodore G., and Hartmut Lehmann, eds. *Luther's Works, Vol. 54, Table Talk*. Philadelphia: Fortress, 1967.

Lutz, Heinrich. *Conrad Peutinger. Beiträge zu einer politischen Biographie*. Augsburg: Die Brigg, 1958.

MacCulloch, Diarmaid. *The Reformation*. New York: Penguin, 2005.

Macek, Josef. *Die hussitische revolutionäre Bewegung*. Berlin [East]: Deutscher Verlag der Wissenschaften, 1958.

Macfie, A. L. 'The Scottish Tradition in Economic Thought', *Scottish Journal of Political Economy* (June, 1955). Reprinted in *The Scottish Contribution to Modern Economic Thought*. Edited by Douglas Mair, 1–18. Aberdeen: Aberdeen University Press, 1990.

Magalhães, J. Romero, ed. *Historia de Portugal, Vol. 3: No Alvorecer da Modernidade (1480–1620)*. Lisbon: Estampa, 1993.

————. 'A estrutura das trocas'. In *Historia de Portugal, Vol. 3*. Edited by J. Romero Magalhães, 315–53.

Magnusson, Lars. 'Is Mercantilism a Useful Concept Still?' In *Merkantilismus. Wiederaufnahme einer Debatte*. Edited by Moritz Isenmann, 19–38. Stuttgart: Franz Steiner, 2014.

————. *Mercantilism: The Shaping of an Economic Language*. London: Routledge, 1994.

————. *Nation, State and the Industrial Revolution: The Visible Hand*. London: Routledge, 2009.

Mair, Douglas, ed. *The Scottish Contribution to Modern Economic Thought*. Aberdeen: Aberdeen University Press, 1990.

Malanima, Paolo. *Pre-modern European Economy: One Thousand Years (10th–19th Centuries)*. Leiden: Brill, 2009.

Mandeville, Bernard (de). *The Fable of The Bees: or, Private Vices, Public Benefits*. London, 1705.

Marques, Antonio H. de Oliveira. *Geschichte Portugals und des portugiesischen Weltreiches*. Stuttgart: Kröner, 2001.

Marshall, Peter. *The Reformation: A Very Short Introduction*. Oxford: Oxford University Press, 2009.

Mauelshagen, Franz. *Klimageschichte der Neuzeit. 1500–1900*. Darmstadt: Wissenschaftliche Buchgesellschaft, 2010.

Mayer, T., ed. *Die Welt zur Zeit des Konstanzer Konzils*. Konstanz: Thorbecke, 1965.

Mayhew, Nicholas J. 'Money Supply, and the Velocity of Circulation in England, 1300–1700', *Economic History Review*, Second Series, 48 (1995): 238–57.

————. 'Not Sterling: A Reply to Prof. Miskimin', *Economic History Review*, Second Series, 49 (1996): 361.

————. 'Prices in England, 1170–1750', *Past & Present* 219, no. 1 (2013): 3–39.

————. *Sterling. The History of a Currency*. London: Penguin, 1999.

Medick, Hans, and Peter Schmidt, eds. *Luther zwischen den Kulturen*. Göttingen: Vandenhoeck & Ruprecht, 2004.

Meller, Harald, and Landesamt für Denkmalpflege und Archäologie Sachsen-Anhalt, eds. *Fundsache Luther. Archäologen auf den Spuren des Reformators*. Stuttgart: Theiss, 2008.

Mertens, Bernd. *Im Kampf gegen die Monopole. Reichstagsverhandlungen und Monopolprozesse im frühen 16. Jahrhundert*. Tübingen: J. C. B. Mohr, 1996.

Metz, Rainer. *Geld, Währung und Preisentwicklung. Der Niederrheinraum im europäischen Vergleich: 1350–1800*. Frankfurt: F. Knapp, 1990.

Middell, Matthias. 'Marxistische Geschichtswissenschaft'. In *Kompass der Geschichtswissenschaft. Ein Handbuch*. Edited by Joachim Eibach and Günther Lottes, 69–82. Göttingen: Vandenhoeck & Ruprecht, 2002.

Miskimin, Harry A. 'Not Sterling: A Comment on Mayhew's Velocity', *Economic History Review*, Second Series 49 (1996): 358–60.

Mokyr, Joel. *The Enlightened Economy: An Economic History of Britain, 1700–1850*. New Haven, CT: Yale University Press, 2009.

Möllenberg, Walter. *Die Eroberung des Weltmarkts durch das mansfeldische Kupfer*. Gotha: F. A. Perthes, 1911.

————. *Das Mansfelder Bergrecht und seine Geschichte*. Wernigerode: Harzverein für Geschichte u. Altertumskunde, 1914.

Mötsch, Johannes. 'Die Wallfahrt St. Wolfgang bei Hermannsfeld'. In *Religiöse Bewegungen im Mittelalter. Festschrift für Matthias Werner zum 65. Geburtstag*. Edited by Enno Bünz, Stefan Tebruck and Helmut G. Walther, 673–702. Cologne: Böhlau, 2007.

Mück, Walter. *Der Mansfelder Kupferschieferbergbau in seiner rechtsgeschichtlichen Entwicklung, Vol. 2: Urkundenbuch des Mansfelder Bergbaus.* Eisleben: self publ., 1910.

Muldrew, Craig. *The Economy of Obligation: The Culture of Credit and Social Relations in Early Modern England.* New York: St Martin's Press, 1998.

Müller-Armack, Alfred. *Religion und Wirtschaft. Geistesgeschichtliche Hintergründe unserer europäischen Lebensform.* 3rd ed. Berne: Haupt, 1981.

Mulsow, Martin. *Prekäres Wissen: Eine andere Ideengeschichte der Frühen Neuzeit.* Berlin: Suhrkamp, 2012.

Munro, John H. 'Deflation and the Petty Coinage Problem in the Late-Medieval Economy: The Case of Flanders, 1334–1484', *Explorations in Economic History* 25, no. 4 (1988): 387–423.

———. 'The Medieval Origins of the Financial Revolution: Usury, Rentes, and Negotiability', *The International History Review* 25, no. 3 (Sep., 2003): 505–62.

———. 'The Monetary Origins of the "Price Revolution"', In *Global Connections and Monetary History, 1470–1800.* Edited by Dennis O. Flynn, Arturo Giráldez and Richard von Glahn, 1–34. Aldershot: Ashgate, 2003.

———. 'Price Revolution'. In *The New Palgrave Dictionary of Economics.* 2nd ed. Vol. 6. Edited by Steven N. Durlauf and Lawrence E. Blume, 631–34. Basingstoke: Palgrave Macmillan, 2008.

Nehlsen-von Stryck, Karin. 'Das Monopolgutachten des Rechtsgelehrten Humanisten Conrad Peutinger aus dem frühen 16. Jahrhundert. Ein Beitrag zum frühneuzeitlichen Wirtschaftsrecht', *Zeitschrift für Neuere Rechtsgeschichte* 10 (1988): 1–18.

Neuhaus, Helmut. ed. *Die Frühe Neuzeit als Epoche.* Munich: Oldenbourg, 2009.

Nogueira, Carlos A. da Silva. *Elementos de História Económica Portuguesa (da integração na economia euro-atlântica à actualidade).* 2nd ed. Lisbon: Lusolivra, 1997.

North, Douglass C., John Joseph Wallis and Barry R. Weingast. *Violence and Social Orders: A Conceptual Framework for Interpreting Recorded Human History.* Cambridge: Cambridge University Press, 2009.

North, Michael. *Das Geld und seine Geschichte. Vom Mittelalter bis zur Gegenwart.* Munich: Beck, 1994.

———. 'Das Reich als Wirtschaftsraum'. In *Heiliges Römisches Reich Deutscher Nation 962 bis 1806 – Altes Reich und neue Staaten, 1495 bis 1806. Essays.* Edited by Heinz Schilling, 159–70, Dresden, 2006.

———. *Kleine Geschichte des Geldes. Vom Mittelalter bis heute.* Munich: Beck, 2009.

———, ed. *Von Aktie bis Zoll. Ein historisches Lexikon des Geldes.* Munich: Beck, 1995.

Nye, J. V. C. *War, Wine, and Taxes: The Political Economy of Anglo-French Trade, 1689-1900.* Princeton, NJ: Princeton University Press, 2007.

Oberman, Heiko A. *Luther: Mensch zwischen Gott und Teufel.* Berlin: Severin und Siedler, 1981.

Oexle, Otto Gerhard. 'Wirtschaft. III: Mittelalter'. In *Geschichtliche Grundbegriffe. Historisches Lexikon zur politisch-sozialen Sprache in Deutschland, Vol. 7* . Edited by Otto Brunner, Werner Conze and Reinhart Koselleck, 526–50. Stuttgart: Klett-Cotta, 1992.

Ogris, Werner. *Elemente europäischer Rechtskultur.* Vienna: Böhlau, 2003.

Outram, Dorinda. *The Enlightenment.* 3rd ed. Cambridge: Cambridge University Press, 2013.

Paas, Martha White, John Roger Paas and George C. Schofield. *Kipper und Wipper Inflation, 1619–23 – An Economic History with Contemporary German Broadsheets.* Yale: Yale University Press, 2012.

Parthasarathi, Prasannan. *Why Europe Grew Rich and Asia Did Not. Global Economic Divergence, 1600–1850.* Cambridge: Cambridge University Press, 2011.

Pawlas, Andreas. *Die lutherische Berufs- und Wirtschaftsethik: Eine Einführung.* Neukirchen: Neukirchner Verlag, 2000.

Peukert, Helge. 'Martin Luther: A Modern Economist'. In *The Reformation as a Precondition for Capitalism.* Edited by Jürgen G. Backhaus, 13–63. Münster: LIT Verlag, 2010.

Pfister, Christian. 'Climate and Economy in Eighteenth-Century Switzerland', *Journal of Interdisciplinary History* 9, no. 2 (1978): 223–43.

Pfister, Ulrich. 'Consumer Prices and Wages in Germany, 1500–1850', *CQE Working Papers* 1510, Center for Quantitative Economics (CQE), University of Münster, 2010.

————. 'Die Frühe Neuzeit als wirtschaftshistorische Epoche. Fluktuationen relativer Preise 1450–1850'. In *Die Frühe Neuzeit als Epoche*. Edited by Helmut Neuhaus. Munich: Oldenbourg, 409–34, 2009.

————. 'German Economic Growth, 1500–1850, Contribution to the XVth World Economic History Congress, Utrecht, August 3–7, 2009.

————. M. Uebele and H. Albers, 'The Great Moderation of Grain Price Volatility: Market Integration vs. Climatic Change, Germany, Seventeenth to Nineteenth Centuries'. Unpublished working paper, 2011.

Pierenkemper, Toni. *Geschichte des modernen ökonomischen Denkens. Große Ökonomen und ihre Ideen.* Göttingen: Vandenhoeck & Ruprecht, 2012.

Piketty, Thomas. *Capital in the Twenty-first Century*. Cambridge, MA: The Belknap Press of Harvard University Press, 2014.

Pincus, Steven. 'Rethinking Mercantilism: Political Economy, the British Empire, and the Atlantic World in the Seventeenth and Eighteenth Centuries', *The William and Mary Quarterly* 69, no. 1 (January, 2012): 3–34.

Plattner, Stuart, ed. *Economic Anthropology*. Stanford: Stanford University Press, 1989.

Polanyi, Karl. *The Great Transformation*. Boston: Beacon Press, 1944.

Pollard, Sidney. *Marginal Europe: The Contribution of Marginal Lands since the Middle Ages*. Oxford: Clarendon Press; New York: Oxford University Press, 1997.

Prak, Marten R. *The Dutch Republic in the Seventeenth Century: The Golden Age*. Cambridge: Cambridge University Press, 2005.

Pribram, Karl. *Geschichte des ökonomischen Denkens*. Vol. 1. Frankfurt: Suhrkamp, 1994.

Priddat, Birger P. 'Kameralismus als paradoxe Konzeption der gleichzeitigen Stärkung von Markt und Staat. Komplexe Theorielagen im deutschen 18. Jahrhundert', *Berichte zur Wissenschaftsgeschichte* 31 (2008): 249–63.

Prien, Hans-Jürgen. *Luthers Wirtschaftsethik*. Göttingen: Vandenhoeck & Ruprecht, 1992.

Recktenwald, Horst Claus. *Geschichte der Politischen Ökonomie. Eine Einführung in Lebensbildern*. Stuttgart: Kröner, 1971.

Reinert, Erik S., and Arno Daastøl. 'The Other Canon: The History of Renaissance Economics. Its Role as an Immaterial and Production-based Canon in the History of Economic Thought and in the History of Economic Policy'. In *Globalization, Economic Development and Inequality: An Alternative Perspective*. Edited by Erik S. Reinert, 21–70. Cheltenham: Edward Elgar, 2004.

Reinert, Erik S., ed. *Globalization, Economic Development and Inequality: An Alternative Perspective*. Cheltenham: Edward Elgar, 2004.

————. *How Rich Countries Got Rich... And Why Poor Countries Stay Poor*. London: Constable 2007.

———— and Arno Mong Daastøl. 'Production Capitalism vs. Financial Capitalism – Symbiosis and Parasitism. An Evolutionary Perspective and Bibliography', *Technology & Governance Working Papers*, no. 36, 2011.

———— and Francesca Lidia Viano. *Thorstein Veblen. Economics for an Age of* Crises. London: Anthem, 2012.

Reinert, Sophus. *Translating Empire: Emulation and the Origins of Political Economy*. Cambridge, MA: Harvard University Press, 2011.

Riello, Giorgio. *Cotton. The Fabric that Made the Modern World*. Cambridge: Cambridge University Press, 2013.

Rieter, Heinz. 'Justis Theorie der Wirtschaftspolitik'. In *Johann Heinrich Gottlob von Justi, Grundsätze der Policey-Wissenschaft*. Edited by Bertram Schefold, 45–80. Düsseldorf: Verlag Wirtschaft und Finanzen, 1993.

Rieth, Ricardo. *'Habsucht' bei Martin Luther: ökonomisches und theologisches Denken, Tradition und soziale Wirklichkeit in der Reformation*. Weimar: Böhlau, 1996.

————. 'Luthers Antworten auf wirtschaftliche und soziale Herausforderungen seiner Zeit'. In *Luthers Ethik: Christliches Leben in ecclesia, oeconomia, politica = Luther's Ethics in the Realms of Church,*

Household, Politics. Referate und Berichte des Elften Internationalen Kongresses für Lutherforschung, Canoas/ RS 21–27 July 2007. Edited by Helmar Junghans, 137–58. Göttingen: Vandenhoeck & Ruprecht, 2010.

Rittmann, Herbert. *Deutsche Geldgeschichte 1484–1914.* Munich: Battenberg, 1975.

Robinson, J., and K. Wiegandt, eds. *Die Ursprünge der modernen Welt. Geschichte im wissenschaftlichen Vergleich.* Frankfurt: Fischer, 2008.

Rodrigues, Jorge Nascimento. *Portugal. O Pioneiro da Globalização. A Herança das Descobertas.* 2nd ed. Lisbon: Centro Atlantico, 2009.

Rodrik, Dani. *The Globalization Paradox: Democracy and the Future of the World Economy.* New York: W. W. Norton, 2011.

Roncaglia, Alessandro, *The Wealth of Ideas. A History of Economic Thought.* Cambridge: Cambridge University Press, [2005] 2009.

Roover, Raymond de. 'Scholastic Economics: Survival and Lasting Influence from the Sixteenth Century to Adam Smith', *The Quarterly Journal of Economics* 69 (1955): 161–90.

Roper, Lyndal. 'Martin Luther's Body: The "Stout Doctor" and His Biographers', *American Historical Review* (April, 2010): 351–84.

Roscher, Wilhelm. *Geschichte der Nationaloekonomik in Deutschland.* Munich, 1874.

Rosner, Peter. *Die Entwicklung des ökonomischen Denkens. Ein Lernprozess.* Berlin: Duncker & Humblot, 2012.

Rössner, Philipp Robinson. 'Bad Money, Evil Coins? Coin Debasement and Devaluation as Instruments of Monetary Policy on the Eve of the "Price Revolution"'. In *Cities – Coins – Commerce. Essays Presented to Ian Blanchard on the Occasion of his 70th Birthday.* Edited by Philipp Robinson Rössner, 89–120. Stuttgart: Franz Steiner, 2012.

———. 'Das friderizianische Preußen (1740–1786) – eine moderne Ökonomie?', *Vierteljahrschrift für Sozial- und Wirtschaftsgeschichte* 98, no. 2 (2011): 143–72.

———, ed. *Cities – Coins – Commerce. Essays Presented to Ian Blanchard on the Occasion of his 70th Birthday.* Stuttgart: Franz Steiner, 2012.

———. 'Das Friderizianische Wirtschaftsleben – eine moderne Ökonomie?'. In *Friedrich der Große in Europa. Geschichte einer wechselvollen Beziehung*, 2 Vols. Edited by Bernd Sösemann and Gregor Vogt-Spira, 375–90 (Stuttgart: Franz Steiner, 2012).

———. *Deflation – Devaluation – Rebellion. Geld im Zeitalter der Reformation.* Stuttgart: Franz Steiner, 2012.

———, ed., *Economic Growth and the Origins of Modern Political Economy: Economic Reasons of State, 1500–2000.* (Milton Park and New York: Routledge, 2016) (forthcoming).

———. 'Mercantilism as an Effective Resource Management Strategy: Money in the German Empire, c. 1500–1800'. In *Merkantilismus. Wiederaufnahme einer Debatte.* Edited by Moritz Isenmann, 39–64. Stuttgart: Franz Steiner, 2014.

———. 'Monetary Instability, Lack of Integration and the Curse of a Commodity Money Standard. The German Lands, c. 1400–1900 AD', *Capital and Credit Markets* 47, no. 2 (2014): 297–340.

———. 'Money, Banking, Economy'. In *Medieval Culture: A Compendium of Critical Topics.* Edited by Albrecht Classen. Berlin: De Gruyter, forthcoming.

Rothschild, Kurt W. *Ethik und Wirtschaftstheorie.* Tübingen: J. C. B. Mohr, 1992.

Rublack, Ulinka. *Reformation Europe.* Cambridge: Cambridge University Press, 2005.

———. 'Grapho-Relics: Lutheranism and the Materialization of the Word', *Past & Present* 5 (2010) 144–66.

———. 'Matter in the Material Renaissance', *Past & Present*, May 2013, 41–84.

Safley, Thomas Max. 'Bankruptcy: Family and Finance in Early Modern Augsburg', *Journal of European Economic History* 29 (2000): 43–76.

———, ed. *The History of Bankruptcy: Economic, Social and Cultural Implications in Early Modern Europe.* New York: Routledge, 2013.

Sandel, Michael J. *What Money Can't Buy. The Moral Limits of Markets*. New York: Farrar, Straus and Giroux, 2012.

Sandmo, Agnar. *Economics Evolving. A History of Economic Thought*. Princeton, NJ: Princeton University Press, 2011.

Sargent, Thomas J., and François R. Velde. *The Big Problem of Small Change*. Princeton, N. J. : Princeton University Press, 2002.

Schattkowsky, Martina, ed. *Das Erzgebirge im 16. Jahrhundert: Gestaltwandel einer Kulturlandschaft im Reformationszeitalter*. Leipzig: Leipziger Universitätsverlag, 2013.

Schefold, Bertram, ed. *Vademecum zu drei klassischen Schriften frühneuzeitlicher Münzpolitik*. Düsseldorf: Verlag Wirtschaft und Finanzen, 2000.

———, ed. *Vademecum zu einem Klassiker des Kameralismus: Johann Heinrich Gottlob von Justi, Grundsätze der Policey-Wissenschaft*. 5–44. Düsseldorf: Verlag Wirtschaft und Finanzen, 1993.

———, ed. *Vademecum zu zwei Klassikern des Spanischen Wirtschaftsdenkens*. Düsseldorf: Verlag Wirtschaft und Finanzen, 1998.

———. *Wirtschaftsstile: Studien zum Verhältnis von Ökonomie und Kultur*. Vol. 1. Frankfurt-on-the-Main: Fischer, 1994.

———, ed. *Wirtschaftssysteme im historischen Vergleich*. Stuttgart: Franz Steiner, 2004.

———. 'Der Nachklang der historischen Schule in Deutschland zwischen dem Ende des zweiten Weltkriegs und dem Anfang der sechziger Jahre'. In *Erkenntnisgewinne, Erkenntnisverluste. Kontinuitäten und Diskontinuitäten in den Wirtschafts-, Rechts- und Sozialwissenschaften zwischen den 20er und 50er Jahren*. Edited by Karl Acham, Knut Wolfgang Nörr and Bertram Schefold, 31–70, Stuttgart: Franz Steiner, 1998.

———. 'Wirtschaft und Geld im Zeitalter der Reformation'. In *Vademecum zu drei klassischen Schriften frühneuzeitlicher Münzpolitik*, 5–58.

———. 'Edgar Salin and his Concept of "Anschauliche Theorie" ("Intuitive Theory") during the Interwar Period', *Annals of the Society for the History of Economic Thought* 46 (2004), 1–16.

Schilling, Heinz, ed. *Aufbruch und Krise. Deutschland 1517–1648*. First published in 1994; Berlin: Siedler, 1988.

———, ed. *Heiliges Römisches Reich Deutscher Nation 962 bis 1806 – Altes Reich und neue Staaten, 1495 bis 1806. Essays*. Dresden, 2006.

———. *Martin Luther. Rebell in einer Zeit des Umbruchs*. Munich: Beck, 2012.

Schindling, Anton. *Bildung und Wissenschaft in der frühen Neuzeit, 1650–1800*. Munich: Oldenbourg, 1994.

Schirmer, Uwe. 'Teil F 3. 4. Ertragsstrukturen der kursächsischen Ämter 1580 (Map)'. In *Atlas zur Geschichte und Landeskunde von Sachsen*. Edited by Landesvermessungsamt Sachsen. Dresden, 2006.

———. 'Reformation und Staatsfinanzen. Vergleichende Anmerkungen zu Sequestration und Säkularisation im ernestinischen und albertinischen Sachsen'. In *Christlicher Glaube und weltliche Herrschaft. Zum Gedenken an Günther Wartenberg*. Edited by Michael Beyer, Jonas Flöter and Markus Hein, 179–92. Leipzig: Evangelische Verlagsanstalt, 2008.

———. *Das Amt Grimma 1485–1548. Demographische, wirtschaftliche und soziale Verhältnisse in einem kursächsischen Amt am Ende des Mittelalters und zu Beginn der Neuzeit*. Beucha: Sax Verlag, 1996.

———. 'Der Finanzplatz Leipzig vom Ende des 12. bis zur Mitte des 17. Jahrhunderts. Geldwesen – Waren- und Zahlungsverkehr – Rentengeschäfte'. In *Der Finanzplatz Leipzig*. Edited by Markus A. Denzel. Frankfurt-on-the-Main, forthcoming.

———. *Kursächsische Staatsfinanzen (1456–1656). Strukturen – Verfassung – Funktionseliten*. Stuttgart: Franz Steiner in Kommission, 2006.

———. 'Vor- und Frühreformation in thüringischen Städten. Eine Zusammenfassung'. In *Vor- und Frühreformation in Thüringischen Städten* (1470–1525/30). Edited by Joachim Emig, Volker Leppin and Uwe Schirmer, 437–60, Cologne: Böhlau, 2013.

Schmidt, Karl-Heinz. 'Merkantilismus, Kameralismus, Physiokratie'. In *Geschichte der Nationalökonomie*. 4th ed. Edited by Otmar Issing, 37–66. Munich: Vahlen, 2002.

Schmidt-Wiegand, Ruth. 'Bürgen muss man würgen, aber nicht an den Leib reden'. In *Handwörterbuch zur deutschen Rechtsgeschichte, 2nd ed., 4th delivery*. Edited by Albrech Cordes et al., col. 737–38. Berlin: Schmidt, 2008. .

Schmoller, Gustav (von). 'Zur Geschichte der national-ökonomischen Ansichten in Deutschland während der Reformations-Periode', *Zeitschrift für Gesamte Staatswissenschaft* 16 (1860), 461–716.

Schnabel-Schüle, Helga. *Die Reformation 1495–1555*. Stuttgart: Reclam, 2006.

Schremmer, Eckart, ed. *Geld und Währung vom 16. Jahrhundert bis zur Gegenwart*. Stuttgart: Franz Steiner, 1993.

——— and Jochen Streb. 'Revolution oder Evolution? Der Übergang von den feudalen Münzgeldsystemen zu den Papiergeldsystemen des 20. Jahrhunderts', *Vierteljahrschrift für Sozial- und Wirtschaftsgeschichte* 86 (1999), 457–76.

Schrötter, Friedrich Freiherr von. 'Das Münzwesen des Deutschen Reichs von 1500 bis 1566', *Jahrbuch für Gesetzgebung, Verwaltung und Volkswirtschaft* 35 (1911) and 36 (1912). Reprinted in Friedrich von Schrötter, *Aufsätze zur deutschen Münz- und Geldgeschichte des 16. bis 19. Jahrhunderts (1902–1938)*. Edited by Bernd Kluge, 3–76. Leipzig: Reprintverlag Leipzig im Zentralantiquariat, 1991.

Schumpeter, Joseph A. *History of Economic Analysis*. New York: Oxford University Press, 1954.

Schüttenhelm, Joachim. 'Zur Münzprägung und Silberversorgung süddeutscher Münzstätten im frühen 16. Jahrhundert'. In *Montanwirtschaft Mitteleuropas vom 12. bis 17. Jahrhundert. Stand, Wege und Aufgaben der Forschung*. Werner Kroker and Ekkehard Westermann, 159–69. Bochum: Vereinigung der Freunde von Kunst und Kultur im Bergbau, 1984.

———. 'Problems of Quantifying the Volume of Money in Early Modern Times. A Preliminary Survey'. In *Precious Metals, Coinage and the Changes of Monetary Structures in Latin-America, Europe and Asia (Late Middle Ages – Early Modern Times)*. Eddy H. G. Van Cauwenberghe, 83–98. Leuven: Leuven University Press, 1989.

Scott, Tom. 'The Reformation and Modern Political Economy: Luther and Gaismair Compared'. In *Die deutsche Reformation zwischen Spätmittelalter und Früher Neuzeit*. Edited by Thomas A. Brady, 173–202. Munich: Oldenbourg, 2001.

———. 'Economic Landscapes'. In *Germany. A New Social and Economic History 1450–1630*. Edited by Bob Scribner, 1–32. London: Arnold, 1996.

———. *The Early Reformation in Germany: Between Secular Impact and Radical Vision*. Farnham: Ashgate, 2013.

———. 'The Economy'. In *The Short Oxford History of Europe: The Sixteenth Century*. Edited by Euan Cameron, 18–57. Oxford: Oxford University Press, 2006.

Scribner, Bob, ed. *Germany. A New Social and Economic History 1450–1630*. London: Arnold, 1996.

Seabright, Paul. *The Company of Strangers: A Natural History of Economic Life*. Princeton, NJ: Princeton University Press, 2004.

Sedgwick, Peter H. *The Market Economy and Christian Ethics*. Cambridge: Cambridge University Press, 1999.

Sedláček, Tomaš. *Economics of Good and Evil. The Quest for Economic Meaning from Gilgamesh to Wall Street*. Oxford: Oxford University Press, 2011.

Sen, Amartya. *Development as Freedom*. New York: Knopf, 1999.

Sennett, Richard. *The Corrosion of Character: The Personal Consequences of Work in the New Capitalism*. New York: W. W. Norton, 2000.

Serrão, Joaquim Veríssimo. *História de Portugal, Vol. III: O Século de Ouro (1495–1580)*. 2nd ed. Lisbon: Editorial Verbo, 1980.

Simrock, Karl, ed. *Die deutschen Volksbücher, gesammelt und in ihrer ursprünglichen Echtheit wiederhergestellt, Vol. V: Deutsche Sprichwörter*. Frankfurt H. L. Brönner 1846.

Skidelsky, Robert, and Edward Skidelsky. *How Much is Enough? Money and the Good Life*. London: Allan Lane, 2012.

Slotta, R., and S. Müller. 'Zum Bergbau auf Kupferschiefer im Mansfelder Land'. In *Martin Luther und der Bergbau im Mansfelder Land*. Edited by R. Knape, 9–27. Lutherstadt Eisleben: Stiftung Luthergedenkstätten in Sachsen-Anhalt, 2000.

Smith, Adam. *Theory of Moral Sentiments*. [1759] Edited by Knud Haakonssen. Cambridge: Cambride University Press, 2002 .

Smith, Adam. *The Wealth of Nations, Books I–III*. Edited by Andrew S. Skinner. repr. London: Penguin Classics, 1999.

Söllner, Fritz. *Geschichte des ökonomischen Denkens*. Berlin: Springer, 1999.

Sösemann, Bernd, and Gregor Vogt-Spira, eds. *Friedrich der Große in Europa. Geschichte einer wechselvollen Beziehung*. 2 Vols. Stuttgart: Franz Steiner, 2012.

Sprenger, Bernd. *Das Geld der Deutschen. Geldgeschichte Deutschlands von den Anfängen bis zur Gegenwart*. 3rd ed. Paderborn: Schöningh, 2002.

Spufford, Peter. *Money and its Use in Medieval Europe*. Cambridge: Cambridge University Press, 1988.

Stadermann, Hans-Joachim. *Der Streit um gutes Geld in Vergangenheit und Gegenwart. Enthaltend drei Flugschriften über den Münzstreit der sächsischen Albertiner und Ernestiner um 1530 nach der Ausgabe von Walther Lotz*. 1893; repr. Tübingen: Mohr Siebeck, 1999.

Stanziani, Alessandro. *Rules of Exchange. French Capitalism in Comparative Perspective, Eighteenth to Early Twentieth Centuries*. Cambridge: Cambridge University Press, 2012.

Stasavage, David. *States of Credit. Size, Power, and the Development of European Polities*. Princeton, NJ: Princeton University Press, 2011.

Stern, Fritz, ed. *The Varieties of History. From Voltaire to the Present*. New York: Meridian, 1956.

———, and Jürgen Osterhammel, eds. *Moderne Historiker. Klassische Texte von Voltaire bis zur Gegenwart*. Munich: Beck, 2011.

Stern, Philip J., and Carl Wennerlind, eds. *Mercantilism Reimagined: Political Economy in Early Modern Britain and Its Empire*. Oxford: Oxford University Press, 2014.

Straube, Manfred. 'Nahrungsmittelbedarf, Nahrungsmittelproduktion und Nahrungsmittelhandel im Thüringisch-Sächsischen Raum zu Beginn des 16. Jahrhunderts'. In *Festschrift Othmar Pickl zum 60. Geburtstag*. Edited by Herwig Ebner, et al., 579–88. Graz: Leykam, 1987.

———. 'Notwendigkeiten, Umfang und Herkunft von Nahrungsmittellieferungen in das sächsische Erzgebirge zu Beginn des 16. Jahrhunderts'. In *Bergbaureviere als Verbrauchszentren im vorindustriellen Europa. Fallstudien zu Beschaffung und Verbrauch von Lebensmitteln sowie Roh- und Hilfsstoffen (13. –18. Jahrhundert)*. Edited by Ekkehard Westermann, 203–21. Stuttgart: Franz Steiner, 1997.

———. 'Zum überregionalen und regionalen Warenverkehr im thüringisch-sächsischen Raum, vornehmlich in der ersten Hälfte des 16. Jahrhunderts'. Unpublished Diss. Phil. B (=*Habilitationsschrift*). 4 vols, Leipzig, 1981.

Strieder, Jakob, ed. *Die Inventur der Firma Fugger aus dem Jahre 1527*. Tübingen: Lapp'sche Buchhandlung, 1905.

Strohm, Theodor. 'Luthers Wirtschafts- und Sozialethik'. In *Leben und Werk Martin Luthers von 1526 bis 1546*. Vol. 1. Edited by Helmar Junghans, 205–23. Berlin: Evangelische Verlagsanstalt, 1983.

Stromer von Reichenbach, Wolfgang. *Oberdeutsche Hochfinanz 1350–1450*. Wiesbaden: Franz Steiner, 1970.

———, ed. *Venedig und die Weltwirtschaft um 1200*. Stuttgart: Thorbecke, 1999.

Stump, Phillip H. *The Reforms of the Council of Constance (1414–1418)*. Leiden: Brill, 1994.

Suhle, Arthur. *Deutsche Münz- und Geldgeschichte von den Anfängen bis zum 15. Jahrhundert*. 8th ed. Berlin: Deutscher Verlag der Wissenschaften, 1964.

Swedberg, Richard. *Principles of Economic Sociology*. Princeton: Princeton University Press, 2003.

Tawney, R. H. *Religion and the Rise of Capitalism: A Historical Study*. New York: Harcourt, Brace & Co., 1926.

Thirlwall, A. P. *Growth and Development. With Special Reference to Developing Economies.* 7th ed. Houndmills: Macmillan, 2003.

Thompson, Edward P. *Customs in Common.* New York: New Press, 1991.

Tilemann[us], M. *Muentz Spiegel* [...]. Frankfurt, 1592.

Treu, Martin, ed. *Martin Luther und das Geld. Aus Luthers Schriften, Briefen und Tischreden.* Wittenberg: Stiftung Luthergedenkstätten in Sachsen-Anhalt, 2000.

Tribe, Keith. *Strategies of Economic Order. German Economic Discourse, 1750–1950.* Cambridge: Cambridge University Press, 1995.

Vierhaus, Rudolf. 'Rankes Begriff der historischen Objektivität'. In *Objektivität und Parteilichkeit in der Geschichtswissenschaft.* Edited by Reinhart Koselleck, Wolfgang J. Mommsen and Jörn Rüsen, 63–76, Munich: Deutscher Taschenbuchverlag, 1977.

Volckart, Oliver. 'Regeln, Willkür und der gute Ruf: Geldpolitik und Finanzmarkteffizienz in Deutschland, 14. bis 16. Jahrhundert', *Jahrbuch für Wirtschaftsgeschichte* 2 (2009): 101–29.

Vries, Jan de. *European Urbanization, 1500-1800.* Cambridge, MA: Harvard University Press, 1984. .

───── and Ad van der Woude. *The First Modern Economy: Success, Failure, and Perseverance of the Dutch Economy, 1500–1815.* Cambridge: Cambridge University Press, 1997.

─────. *The Industrious Revolution: Consumer Behavior and the Household Economy, 1650 to the Present.* Cambridge: Cambridge University Press, 2008.

Vries, Peer. 'Governing Growth: A Comparative Analysis of the Role of the State in the Rise of the West', *Journal of World History* 13 (2002): 67–193.

Walch, Johann Georg, ed. *D. Martin Luthers Colloquia oder Tischreden.* Halle, 1743.

Wenner, Ulrich. '"Fundgrubner, Berckhauer und Schlacktreiber" – Montanwortschatz bei Martin Luther'. In *Martin Luther und der Bergbau im Mansfelder Land,* edited by Rosemarie Knape, 205–17. Lutherstadt Eisleben: Stiftung Luthergedenkstätten in Sachsen-Anhalt, 2000,

Westermann, Angelika. *Die vorderösterreichischen Montanregionen in der Frühen Neuzeit.* Stuttgart: Franz Steiner, 2009.

Westermann, Ekkehard. *Bergbaureviere als Verbrauchszentren im vorindustriellen Europa. Fallstudien zu Beschaffung und Verbrauch von Lebensmitteln sowie Roh- und Hilfsstoffen (13. –18. Jahrhundert).* Stuttgart: Franz Steiner, 1997.

─────, ed. *Das Eislebener Garkupfer und seine Bedeutung für den europäischen Kupfermarkt, 1460–1560.* Cologne: Böhlau, 1971.

─────. 'Der wirtschaftliche Konzentrationsprozeß im Mansfelder Revier und seine Auswirkungen auf Martin Luther, seine Verwandte und Freunde'. In *Martin Luther und der Bergbau im Mansfelder Land.* Edited by Rosemarie Knape, 63–92. Lutherstadt Eisleben: Stiftung Luthergedenkstätten in Sachsen-Anhalt, 2000.

─────. 'Zur Silber- und Kupferproduktion Mitteleuropas vom 15. bis zum frühen 17. Jahrhundert', *Der Anschnitt* 5–6 (1986): 187–211.

─────. 'Silberproduktion und -handel. Mittel- und oberdeutsche Verflechtungen im 15. /16. Jahrhundert', *Neues Archiv für Sächsische Geschichte* 68 (1997/1998): 47–65.

─────. 'Zur weiteren Erforschung kommerzialisierter Agrargesellschaften Mitteleuropas und ihrer Konflikte im ersten Drittel des 16. Jahrhunderts', *Studia Historiae Oeconomicae,* 15 (1980): 161–78.

Winkler, Hannelore. 'Der Wortbestand von Flugschriften aus den Jahren der Reformation und des Bauernkrieges in seiner Einheitlichkeit und landschaftlichen Differenziertheit', Univ. PhD Diss., Leipzig, 1970.

─────. *Der Wortbestand von Flugschriften aus den Jahren der Reformation und des Bauernkrieges.* Berlin: Akademie Verlag, 1975.

Wong, Roy Bin. *China Transformed: Historical Change and the Limits of European Experience.* Ithaca, NY: Cornell University Press, 1997.

Wood, Diana. *Medieval Economic Thought.* Cambridge: Cambridge University Press, 2002.

Wurm, Johann Peter. *Johannes Eck und der oberdeutsche Zinsstreit 1513–1515*. Münster: Aschendorff, 1997.

Zanden, Jan Luiten van. 'Die mittelalterlichen Ursprünge des "europäischen Wunders". In *Die Ursprünge der modernen Welt. Geschichte im wissenschaftlichen Vergleich*. Edited by James A. Robinson and Klaus Wiegandt, 475–16. Frankfurt: Fischer, 2008.

———. *The Long Road to the Industrial Revolution. The European Economy in a Global Perspective, 1000–1800*. Leiden: Brill, 2009.

———. 'The "Revolt of the Early Modernists" and the "First Modern Economy": An Assessment', *Economic History Review*, Second Series, 55, no. 4 (2002): 619–41.

Ziegler, Bernd. *Geschichte des ökonomischen Denkens. Paradigmenwechsel in der Volkswirtschaftslehre*. 2nd ed. Munich: Oldenbourg, 2008.

Zorn, Günter, ed. *Akten der Kirchen- und Schulvisitationen in Zwickau und Umgebung 1529 bis 1556*. Langenweissbach: Beier & Beran, 2008.

Zuijderduijn, C. Jaco. *Medieval Capital Markets: Markets for renten, State Formation and Private Investment in Holland (1300–1550)*. Leiden: Brill, 2009.

INDEX

Lightning Source UK Ltd.
Milton Keynes UK
UKHW012156150121
377089UK00001B/37